COSMOS

CRUMBLING

COSMOS CRUMBLING

American Reform and the
Religious Imagination

ROBERT H. ABZUG

New York   Oxford
OXFORD UNIVERSITY PRESS
1994

Oxford University Press

Oxford   New York   Toronto
Delhi   Bombay   Calcutta   Madras   Karachi
Kuala Lumpur   Singapore   Hong Kong   Tokyo
Nairobi   Dar es Salaam   Cape Town
Melbourne   Auckland   Madrid

and associated companies in
Berlin   Ibadan

Copyright © 1994 by Oxford University Press, Inc.

Published by Oxford University Press, Inc.,
198 Madison Avenue, New York, New York 10016-4314

First issued as an Oxford University Press paperback, 1994

Oxford is a registered trademark of Oxford University Press

Library of Congress Cataloging-in-Publication Data
Abzug, Robert H.
Cosmos crumbling : American reform and the religious imagination /
Robert H. Abzug.
p.   cm.   Includes bibliographical references and index.
ISBN 0-19-503752-9
ISBN 0-19-504568-8 (Pbk.)
1. Social reformers—United States—History—19th century.
2. Social problems—United States—History—19th century.
3. Church and social problems—United States—History—19th century.
4. United States—Church history—19th century. I. Title.
HN57.A548   1994
303.48'4'0973—dc20   93-4785

9 8 7 6 5 4 3

Printed in the United States of America
on acid-free paper

FOR

Ken Stampp, mentor and friend,

AND

Penne Restad, this book's tireless champion

PREFACE

IN THE FORTY YEARS before the Civil War, Americans developed a peculiar variety of political and social action we have come to call "reform." Abolitionists stormed against the cruelties of slavery. Temperance zealots hounded producers and consumers of strong drink. Sabbatarians fought to make Sunday an officially recognized sacred day. Woman's rights activists proclaimed the case for sexual equality. Others offered programs of physiological and spiritual self-reform: phrenology, vegetarianism, the water-cure, spiritualism, and miscellaneous others. "Even the insect world was to be defended," Emerson mused, "and a society for the protection of ground-worms, slugs, and mosquitoes was to be incorporated without delay."[1]

Cosmos Crumbling: American Reform and the Religious Imagination explores the religious roots of reform and argues for the crucial importance of cosmological thinking to its creation. The choice of religion per se as the central theme of reform history is hardly surprising. Scholars who have chronicled these movements have usually and quite properly noted the "religious" tone or substance of reform, whether in the identification of antebellum movements with revivalism, changes in Calvinist theology, the histories of particular sects, or doctrines of millennial mission. I move beyond these approaches, however, in at least three distinctive ways.

First, I find importance in the cosmologies of reformers, especially those that encompass a wider gyre than formal theology. Second, I analyze the religious aspects of reform ritual, especially in the movements that hoped to reorder the details of everyday life. Third, I am concerned with the relation between sacred and profane elements in reform, treating religious dimensions of social and personal life as equal in importance to those of the so-called secular realm.

This last point is crucial. All too often, scholars have been guided by the assumption that "religion" exists largely as a conscious or unconscious cover for something else: status anxiety, the quest for control of one class by another, personal or collective neuroses, a reaction to the shocks and realities of new social and economic environments, or some other psychological or material concern. Recent socioeconomic and psychological interpretations of reform have mostly given a perfunctory nod to "religion" and then interpreted it for its "real" social, psychological, or political significance. Reform studies have thus shared in the modern trend toward psychological and materialist reductionism.[2]

I do not reject the importance of social, psychological, or political aspects of reform, nor do I underestimate the impact of economic change in nineteenth-century America. Yet we can only understand reformers if we try to comprehend the sacred significance they bestowed upon these worldly arenas. For even as some of today's scholars glean mostly "secular" significance from religion, the antebellum reformer saw mainly transcendent meanings in politics, society, and the economy.[3] We must concentrate on the religious imaginations of reformers in order to grasp the essential nature of reform. As a result, my stress on the originators of reform cosmologies rather than the details of social movements has dictated a certain progression of topics. I have created, in fact, a kind of genealogy of reform cosmology that begins with the American Revolution and ends with "the woman question" and its shattering of reform unity.

Cosmos Crumbling: American Reform and the Religious Imagination addresses by implication certain enduring themes in American culture. Not only are most of the issues reformers grappled with before the Civil War still with us in one form or another; so are various dilemmas concerning the place of religion in a free society and the difficulties of social advocacy where direct political solutions seem unavailable. The role of the reformer itself, though it has evolved in some very interesting ways and even become a significant part of the established social order, remains in many ways a radical religious calling.[4]

Indeed, when viewed as a special kind of religious impulse nurtured within our culture, the reformer's search for sacred connection takes on a significance far more profound than any single advocacy or the particular denominational roots of reform. Antebellum reformers defined a rugged style of modern piety peculiarly suited to the amorphous spiritual crises experienced by individuals in modern pluralistic societies. By the middle of the twentieth century, reformers began to emerge from Jewish, Catholic, and liberal Protestant cultures, in addition to their traditional evangelical sources. Modern varieties of feminism, utopianism, and dietary reform, as well as civil rights, environmental, and anti-war advocacies have all been shaped in important ways by such religious types. By lending sacred significance to the issures of political and social life, antebellum and modern reformers have exerted an influence on politics and society far greater than one might expect from any quantifiable measure of their popularity or resources. They have made what began as a peculiarly Protestant, largely New England, style of social action into one truly American in reach and sensibility.

In the course of writing this book, I received encouragement and aid from numerous organizations, scholars, and friends. I want to recognize their help without implicating them in whatever errors may still be found in the text. First, I wish to thank the National Endowment for the Humanities for a summer grant that freed time to work on this project, and the University of Texas at Austin for support during a crucial semester and summer of writing. Over the years, I have also benefited from the courtesy and expertise of librarians at the University of Texas, the Clements Library of the University of Michigan, Boston Public Library, Widener Library at Harvard, and the National Institutes of Health.

At Oxford University Press, I very much thank my editor, Sheldon Meyer, who, with tolerance, watched this project change shape, turn corners, and drag on and on. He also made key editorial comments on the final manuscript that have made this a better book. I also greatly appreciated the superb editorial work of India Cooper.

Various friends and comrades in scholarship brought to this work their knowledge and critical skills. Kathryn Baker, Ruth Bloch, Jane Bowers, Peg Caffrey, Larry Friedman, Walt Herbert, Peter Jelavich, Richard John, Drew McCoy, and Clarence Walker read various chapters and offered important insights and corrections. Lee Bowman, Dave Bowman, Tom Cole, Bob Crunden, Seth Fein, Dan Horowitz, Howard Miller, and Ken Stampp read most or all of the chapters and made extremely helpful comments. In particular, I wish to thank David Brion Davis and Bert Wyatt-Brown for their encouragement and for searching criticism of significant portions of the manuscript. Most of all, however, I thank my wife, Penne Restad, whose willingness to extend her expert editorial skills and historical wisdom to every page of every chapter in this book was only matched by the patience with which she watched the manuscript grow. As for Ben and Johanna, they have made it all worthwhile without lifting a finger.

CONTENTS

PROLOGUE:
Ultraists, Seekers, and the Soldiery of Dissent   3

Part One: Foundations of the Reform Cosmology   9
I: Benjamin Rush and Revolutionary Christian Reform   11
II: Lyman Beecher and the Cosmic Theater   30
III: War in the West: The Radical Revival   57

Part Two: Evangelical Reform   77
IV: The Temperance Reformation   81
V: Sabbatarianism and Manual Labor   105

Part Three: Radical Transformation   125
VI: William Lloyd Garrison and the Birth of
    Abolitionism   129
VII: The Body Reforms   163
VIII: The Woman Question   183
IX: Woman's Rights and Schism   204

NOTES   231
INDEX   277

COSMOS

CRUMBLING

PROLOGUE

Ultraists, Seekers, and the Soldiery of Dissent

Reformers have held an especially ambiguous place in our
national consciousness. Even sympathetic observers have sometimes felt,
with Ralph Waldo Emerson: "When we see an eager assailant of one of
these wrongs . . . we feel like asking him, What right have you, sir, to
your one virtue?"[1] Yet Americans have been deeply moved by the reformer's dedication, finding in the steadfast will of a William Lloyd Garrison, an Elizabeth Cady Stanton, or a Martin Luther King Jr. the very
essence of heroism. They court our fascination, whether we focus on their
virtues or their odd and often abrasive fervor. Gadflies on the periphery of
society yet deeply rooted in it, reformers remain essential but enigmatic
characters on the American scene.

The ambivalence that antebellum reformers inspired, when not related
directly to the issues they agitated, mostly derived from a trait central to
their character: the tendency to apply religious imagination and passion to
issues that most Americans considered worldly. In accounting for the rise
of antebellum reform, Emerson noted "that the Church, or religious party,
[was] falling from the Church nominal" and reappearing "in temperance
and non-resistance societies; in movements of abolitionists and socialists;
and in very significant assemblies called Sabbath and Bible Conventions;
composed of ultraists, of seekers, of all the soul of the soldiery of dissent,

and meeting to call in question the authority of the Sabbath, of the priest-hood, and of the Church."[2] They were saints in the process of abandoning their own "Church nominal," whose zeal the world found by turns inspir-ing and menacing.

The lives of reformers confirmed Emerson's description of reformers as between church and society. Some, like the abolitionist Theodore Dwight Weld and the phrenologist Orson Squire Fowler, entered early adulthood assuming the ministry would be their fate. Other future reformers became ministers, only to find their spiritual quests moving beyond the limits of the church. The vegetarian Sylvester Graham, the abolitionist Henry C. Wright, and the communitarian John Humphrey Noyes all tried tradi-tional ministries before turning to reform. Sarah Grimké's exclusion from the Quaker ministry epitomized a special frustration with the church that led to forthright advocacy for woman's rights. Others, who had never considered a career in the church, reached revelatory moments concerning their reform vocations in unchurched moments of sacred transcendence. For example, health reformer William Andrus Alcott received his calling on a mountaintop in Connecticut. These anomalous men and women did not abandon the realm of the sacred in championing "social" causes. Rather, they made religious sense of society, economy, race, politics, gender, and physiology.

Such characters defy much of what passes for scientific sociological, psychological, or political analysis, this despite the fact that reformers have deeply affected the conduct of politics and the shape of society. Only Max Weber's term "religious virtuoso" comes close to describing the re-former as a social type. Weber had in mind individuals whose conscious-ness in most cases seemed tuned to heavenly rather than earthly matters, and who in most societies lived as monks, holy men, mystics, and the like. In Protestant societies, however, which focused on the earthly and frowned upon formal holy orders, such types, as one scholar put it, "find their honor and their struggle everywhere on God's earth."[3]

In fact, reformers comprised something of an informal religious order, mostly voluntary orphans from a society whose everyday workings aroused deep misgivings. At odds with the world in its "natural" state and bent upon sacralizing all the world's order in accordance with their vision of God's plan, they made it their business to clarify the ways in which the most personal and most cosmic issues interconnected. Their *mentalité* grew not only from their intimate knowledge of an everyday material world but also as a function of their estrangement from it. A felt commonality of spirit and ultimate purpose transcended the varieties of reform endeavor and the sometimes heated squabbles over strategies and issues.

Reform took its particular American shape as a result of the historical circumstances attendant to its birth, especially the profound spiritual up-heaval caused by three major forces that significantly altered the possibilities of sacred life in the new nation. The first was the Constitution's endorsement of separation of church and state and religious toleration, norms that eventually spread from the federal level to the individual states and created a new social and institutional framework for religion. The second was a battle over the definition of America itself, as nation and as idea, in the years following the Revolution. Finally, the transformation of the economic life of the nation from a pre- or proto-industrial state to that of a maturing commercial-industrial marketplace reset many of the terms of everyday discourse and provided much of the symbolic repertoire for the reformers' envisioned order.

Together these developments created in the minds of many a sense that their era was what, in the twentieth century, the theologian Paul Tillich has called a *kairos*. A *kairos* is a moment in history marked by entry of the Kingdom of God into human affairs. The historian David Brion Davis, applying Tillich's idea of a *kairos* to reform, has described it as a period in which an "eschatological leap" becomes possible, one "that overcomes a 'demonic power' and then transcends the limits of previous political, racial, and economic history."[4] Reformers emerged as technicians of just such an American *kairos*, responding to a religious crisis endemic to the "modern" condition and exacerbated in the United States by disestablishment and religious pluralism. They shaped their agenda from the social, political, and economic turmoil of the day, but within a millennial and sometimes apocalyptic sense of America's role in the cosmic drama.

Reform sects arose largely in New England, a region particularly hard hit by each of these historical forces. Before the Revolution, New England's religious establishments helped spin a web of daily ritual and belief that connected individuals, society, and Heaven into a comprehensible cosmos. Dissenters and heretics there might be, both in organized sects and as practitioners of less formal religious arts; yet they themselves understood their acts as dissent or heresy and often gloried in that fact. Despite the tensions created by wayward religious spirits, the very existence of such dissent reinforced the established view of the cosmos by vivifying the contrast between Truth and Error.

The American Revolution changed all that. It challenged the legitimacy if not always the actual position of religious élites and, more important, made religious toleration and disestablishment social norms. In the first years of the nineteenth century, many New Englanders had the sense that a spiritual free-for-all had replaced cosmic order. All might claim to possess religious Truth under the protection of the Constitution, but such claims concealed a brewing crisis. How could one serve authentic religious needs for Truth and validate religious experiences in Truth when religious freedom had made the world an arena of competing truths? No scholar has yet attempted to gauge comprehensively the profound personal, spiritual, and historical implications of this *nova:* a society with no official religion and with officially protected religious liberty.[5]

The search for sacred connection in such a world produced a variety of responses. The majority of Americans welcomed the right to choose their church, create a new one, or be free of organized religion entirely. They participated in an explosion of religious creativity and conflict: Baptist and Methodist "Dissenters" soon became the dominant American churches. Individual preference in ritual or belief spawned scores of Christian sects. Freethinkers launched attacks on organized religion and "priestcraft." Prophets founded faiths based on new dispensations and discoveries, most notably Joseph Smith's creation of Mormonism.[6]

Even those who benefited most from religious freedom had serious doubts about the doctrine, for they had created or expanded churches as an expression of Truth. However, the new freedom seemed most disturbing to members of the established churches of New England. While they endorsed religious freedom, they harbored uneasy feelings that it had left a void of spiritual order. In other regions, and especially in the states of New York and Pennsylvania, pluralism had been an established fact since the seventeenth century. Thus the revolution only served to emphasize well-established community norms. In New England, where the intermeshing of social, political, and ecclesiastical power remained strong, anxiety so pervaded the social and religious landscape in the first decade of the nineteenth century that it often found bitter expression in the pulpits of Congregational and Presbyterian churches and in the political culture of the Federalist party. This dark strain was no simple expression of lost power and status. It reflected a keen sense of faith dislocated and of a spiritual order destroyed.

The spectacular growth of the nation's economy and territory provided additional sources of real and imagined disorder, and new measures of virtue or vice. Already spiritually shaken, New England was one of the first regions to feel significant tremors from the revolution in manufacturing and commerce. All the ambivalence traditionally associated with pietistic Protestantism's grappling with individual material success became resymbolized for an era in which the marketplace, the factory, the city, and the competition of individuals for wealth and advantage became keynotes of American culture. To reformers as to their Puritan forebears, industriousness meant virtue. However, worldly competition unbridled by a sense of the sacred spelled spiritual doom. Individualism was intrinsic to the Protestant tradition but, unchecked by a sense of community, it foretold disaster.

The post-Revolutionary generation in New England largely embraced the Republic's possibilities, which for most meant accepting pluralism, re-creating church life as an adjunct to a new middle-class existence, and profiting from the new economy. Yet the religious virtuosos among them met the same situation by seeking paths to the sacred built upon new ideals and symbols. Indeed, they revived the covenant tradition of their ancestors, transferring a sense of chosenness from New England to the United States (though sometimes confusing their region for the nation). The Revolutionary image of an America bathed in millennial splendor, one already a self-congratulatory cliché in popular discourse, became for reformers the basis of a self-scrutinizing national piety.[7]

The sweep of such a religious vision was apparent not only in the lives and words of reformers but also in the reactions of their audiences. Consider the case of Mrs. Sturges, who in 1835 heard Theodore Dwight Weld preach against slavery. She returned home deeply agitated, collapsed in a chair, and dreamed a dream. She found herself transported to the far reaches of the universe, her eyes scanning the Earth's wonders and horrors. Finally she fixed upon an America aglow in its riches and freedom, where the humble claimed equality with the wealthy. She gazed in admiration and declared: "It is my country."[8]

At that moment a mysterious presence tapped her shoulder and begged her to look again. She still saw only a happy, industrious people and a land filled with schools, churches, and "emporiums of commerce." The stranger then directed her eyes southward. There, the white population was "thinly scattered and enervated," while black multitudes gleaned a "scanty harvest from the luxuriant soil, and impoverished rather than enriched their oppressors." The slaves themselves labored "beneath a scorching sun—their backs lacerated by the whip—scourged, maimed, loaded with irons—subject to every insult—and exposed to every gust of unbridled passions." Even as groans and lamentations filled her ears, Mrs. Sturges wept in shame to think that the laws of her nation sanctified slavery. She heard a voice from Heaven: "Vengeance is mine I will repay saith the Lord."

The stranger then pointed out the abolitionists, with only Bibles for weapons, hounded and vilified by other citizens, including fellow Christians, simply because they sought freedom for the slave. "It was, as if a viper stung me," she recalled, "—and covering my face with both my hands, and laying my mouth in the dust,—I cried, 'Unclean, unclean! O Church of the living God! come out of thine abominations, and wash their hands of this sin.'" Mrs. Sturges then watched as God removed the slaves' chains and "a mighty army of blacks" rose in bloody rebellion. The shrieks of the dying in her ears, she awoke fearing that what had been a dream might soon become a reality.

Mrs. Sturges's vision demonstrates the ways in which social, economic, and personal issues came alive within the reform cosmology.[9] It constituted a broad sacralization of the world, where sacred and profane were of a piece. Weld preached to her about slavery, but within a sacred drama of American identity. Mrs. Sturges's identification of "emporiums of commerce," schools, and churches reflected values blossoming in an increasingly market-dominated America, as did her identification of slavery as an inefficient and cruel use of labor. But she framed these observations within a literally cosmic setting of divine judgment. Each level of understanding made sense in terms of the other, and both merged in a seamless eschatological script. [10]

That was the essence of reform, the radical joining of Heaven and earth that attracted thousands of passionate adherents and just as surely scandalized many more. Reformers positioned themselves both within the culture and just outside, taking as their mission a kind of alienated engagement in the discourse of society. They sought to sacralize the world in its own language and in spite of itself. Judged by the standard of complete and direct victories, they mostly failed. Abolitionists alone did not free the slaves. Feminists did not immediately win equality for women. Temperance advocates did not end drinking. Grahamites did not convert the nation to vegetarianism. Neither phrenologists nor hydropathists made permanent inroads into the health professions.

Nonetheless, the reformer's influence passed into society-at-large. By reformulating sacred understandings of society in a mixture of three tongues—the common political language of Republicanism, the religious language of Christianity, and the ever more persuasive vocabulary of the natural sciences—reformers did succeed in creating alternative vocabularies for understanding American society. They provided a sacred structure of meaning that, while hardly incorporated as the code of daily life by most Americans, helped redefine the nature and limits of civic virtue.

PART

ONE

*Foundations of the
Reform Cosmology*

I

Benjamin Rush and Revolutionary Christian Reform

Aт exactly nine in the morning on July 4, 1788, as a cloudy but rainless sky hung over Philadelphia, the bells of Christ Church joyously announced the beginning of the Grand Federal Procession. Partisans of the recently ratified Constitution had created an unprecedented public extravaganza to celebrate the fulfillment of the Revolution and the future of the new republic. Representative contingents of farmers, manufacturers, civil and military leaders, clergy, professionals, and tradesmen—five thousand in all—paraded placards and floats in a mile-and-a-half-long file. By afternoon the three-mile route had been marched and the orations made, and seventeen thousand citizens gathered to toast Republicanism with glasses of beer and cider.[1]

Benjamin Rush, signer of the Declaration of Independence and physician to the Continental Army, basked in the warmth of that day. Years of sacrifice during the war; frustrations over the Articles of Confederation; and sober recognition of the many issues that divided the citizens of the land: these melted away in the fervor of the moment. The Procession, he wrote a few days later, had united "the most remarkable transports of the mind which were felt during the war with the great event of the day . . . to produce such a tide of joy as has seldom been felt in any age or country." It had been "the happy means of uniting all our citizens. . . . 'Tis done!" he exclaimed. "We have become a nation."[2]

Rush, in his less enthusiastic moments at least, knew that it would take more than a parade to create a nation. A year before, he had reminded Americans: "There is nothing more common than to confound the terms of *American Revolution* with those of *the late American war*. The American war is over: but this is far from being the case with the American Revolution." Americans had to fashion a united country from thirteen states of varied and often jealously guarded interests, with the knowledge that the greed, factionalism, and corruption of which they accused the British might also be found among themselves. In addition, those who fought as one for independence differed as to how they might fulfill the promise of 1776. From the British surrender at Yorktown through the War of 1812, Americans struggled to define and implement the revolution that "the late American war" had made possible.[3]

In doing so, post-Revolutionary Americans also generated national ideals, conceptions of Republicanism, and techniques for solving the problems of society that became for later generations the bases for defining national character. For antebellum reform, and most especially for the abolitionist movement, the Declaration of Independence's bold assertion that all men were created equal overshadowed virtually all other inheritances from the Revolutionary era. Yet in more complex ways, the shape of reform owed much to the Revolutionary period. Nowhere are these contributions more richly represented than in the life and vision of Benjamin Rush.

Rush's own addition to the ferment of thought about the American future, little studied compared to the epochal contributions of Jefferson, Hamilton, Madison, and Adams, addressed problems relatively untouched by the great Constitution-makers. Rush emphasized the need not only to create a republic but also "to prepare the principles, morals, and manners of our citizens" so that they would honor and defend it. Only if the very fiber of everyday personal and social life were imbued with a common set of Republican values and virtues, he believed, could the great experiment succeed. Toward this end Rush developed a remarkable program for social and personal change: abolition, temperance, elimination of the death penalty, humane treatment of criminals and the insane, educational reform (including provision for female education), and numerous other causes. Unique in their day, the specific concerns and comprehensiveness of his agenda in many ways also prefigured antebellum reform.[4]

Rush's particular approach to nation-building drew from three late eighteenth-century intellectual currents: Republicanism, Scottish Enlightenment philosophical and medical thought, and millennial Christianity. Yet his reform vision did not involve the simple merging of abstract ideas. It can only be understood by tracing the ways in which Rush's religious passion shaped an Enlightenment Christian reform vision of individual, society, and cosmos. We see a man deeply concerned with religious issues, but one whose spiritual questioning led him away from the conventional churchly life and toward a vision that drew upon the human body, the social structure, and basic Christianity for its rituals and symbols. In short, he became an idiosyncratic religious virtuoso.

Rush's religious sensibility was molded by men and women whose own intense enthusiasms flourished in the revivals that touched the American colonies from the late 1730s into the 1740s, which scholars have called the Great Awakening.[5] The Awakening defies easy analysis. While the American tour of English evangelist George Whitefield was the catalyst for many of the Awakening revivals, others seemed to have ignited solely from local conditions. Nor were the results consistent. Sometimes revivals led to the crumbling of religious establishments and the founding of new sects, while at other times they aided established churches.

Nonetheless, some dominant themes emerge. Preachers pitted themselves against what they deemed to be cold and rational religion, urging instead a warm piety made possible by conversion. They preached against the corruptions of worldly wealth and emphasized the equality of all men and women before God. Many saw in the heightened emotions of the revival itself a sign that the Second Coming of Christ, which would inaugurate the Millennium, was imminent. Whether in packed churches or in vast outdoor meetings, ministers brought together thousands of souls from all sects and walks of life who sometimes shared only spiritual frustration and a thirst for salvation. At the same time, these preachers drew heated opposition from clergy and laymen who found their style un-Godly and who saw in their work the destruction of churchly communities. For its adherents, however, amid a cacophony of bitter words between warring factions, the Great Awakening engendered a surge of burning hope for personal conversion and millennial splendor.

The Awakening had already begun to quiet by the time of Rush's birth on Christmas Eve 1745, but the boy grew up surrounded by its living legacy. Benjamin, though also descended from Quakers and Presbyterians, was baptized in his father's Anglican faith. However, the death of John Rush five years later left the boy's religious life in the hands of his mother. Susanna Rush, a partisan of the Awakeners in the Presbyterian church, began taking him to Philadelphia's Second Presbyterian Church. Its minister, Gilbert Tennent, had been among the most effective and controversial itinerant preachers during the Awakening. Tennent had calmed down considerably by the 1750s, but his charismatic appeals still deeply impressed the young boy. Rush especially remembered the minister's egalitarianism. "The Rich, and the Poor, Black and White," he wrote on the occasion of Tennent's death in 1764, "had equally free access to his Person."[6]

Rush was exposed more profoundly to Awakening traditions when in 1754, at age eight, he entered Nottingham, the boarding school run by his uncle, the Reverend Samuel Finley. In a famous sermon, *Christ Triumphing, and Satan Raging* (1741), Finley had argued that the revivals and the opposition they engendered signified nothing less than the prophesied battle between the forces of God and the Devil that would precede the Millennium. In fact, he proclaimed, "the Kingdom of God is come." Finley's strident millennialism had only slightly faded by the time young Rush came to Nottingham; it infused the boy's education with the mood of cosmic combat and added a piquant edge to a curriculum framed in piety.[7]

In 1759, after six years at Nottingham, Rush entered the College of New Jersey (now Princeton) at the age of fourteen. There he had brief but telling contact with the college's new president, the Reverend Samuel Davies. Davies had been, like Tennent and Finley, in the forefront of the Presbyterian Awakening. In the late 1740s and 1750s, Davies rallied dissenters in the fight for religious toleration. During the French and Indian War he stirred many with patriotic sermons that stressed the unity of the colonies even as his religious appeals celebrated the unity of the faithful. Rush knew him for only a year, but that was enough time for Davies to make a major impact. He especially took to heart the president's simple command to Rush's graduating class of September 1760: "Bravely live and die, serving your *generation*—your *own* generation."[8]

At graduation almost fifteen years old and ready to make his mark in the world, Rush found the legacy of his Awakener mentors both rich and troubling. He readily embraced their ideals of piety, religious toleration, millennial hope, and public spirit, as well as their incipient sense of an intercolonial "American" identity. At the same time, this audacious spiritual inheritance posed a difficult question for the young man. Was he worthy of such a trust? An eager student schooled in ideals but too young to understand the limits of human endeavor might find in the challenges of a Tennent, Finley, or Davies a damning indictment of his own shortcomings. This must have been especially so for Rush, who knew little of his own father and was forced to measure himself against distant models rather than the everyday behavior of a father whom he also knew as a real person.

It did not help that Rush the religionist competed with Rush the dashing young gentleman. He might condemn Philadelphia's "vice and profanity" and fear that its young men were "wholly devoted to pleasure and sensuality," but much of that complaint originated in the self-reflection of one whose various transgressions included sleeping with another man's wife. Perhaps for such secret reasons, his spiritual life ebbed. He worried about his soul but moved only imperfectly toward the change of heart that lay at the center of the Awakening experience. The inheritor of a grand religious vision, he nonetheless could not find his own corner of peace within it.[9]

This sense of being in a spiritual shadow surely informed Rush's choice of career. Though many expected him to become a minister, he himself felt unfit for the task. Late in 1760, after consultation with both Davies and Finley, he finally chose medicine and began his apprenticeship with Dr. John Redman. "Now how inglorious must this study appear when set in competition with Divinity," Benjamin confessed to a friend in 1761, "—the one employed in advancing temporal happiness, the other eternal—one applying remedies to a fading, mortal Body, the other employed in healing the sickness of a Soul immortal and everlasting."[10]

Rush's apprenticeship and medical study, however, brought him close to contemplation of eternity. As he helped Redman on his rounds during the city's bouts with influenza, yellow fever, and other diseases, it was inevitable that he grapple with issues of the soul in treating and comforting the sick and dying. By the beginning of 1766, Rush had begun to face his own sinful nature and to thirst after union with God. "The religious impressions that were made upon my mind at this time," he remembered, "were far from issuing in a complete union to God . . . , but they left my mind more tender to sin of every kind, and begat in me constant desires for a new heart."[11]

With this new sensitivity, Rush traveled to Edinburgh in 1766 to continue his medical education. Scotland, home of the most orthodox sort of Presbyterianism, might have provided him a fertile atmosphere for religious fulfillment. He gave his soul every chance, discussing theology with the legendary Whitefield and other ministers. However, in these new surroundings his sense of sin abated, and so did his thirsting after God. He became enamored of medical studies and thrilled at the discussion of what for him was a new way of looking at the world: Republicanism. Fellow students exposed him to the writings of Algernon Sydney, the seventeenth-century advocate of the ideology, and he came to share his classmates' sense that English history had been the story of corrupt decline since Cromwell.

The alternative that Republicanism offered was a country of virtuous individuals who maintained an equally virtuous government through division of authority among various estates and in various governing entities. In the late 1760s, most considered such ideas to be visionary notions. For Rush, however, as for a small but growing number in England and America, the Republican critique was a revelatory set of ideas. Since it challenged the very heart of the monarchical system, it represented at least implicitly a questioning of the bases for all authority. No wonder that Rush later credited the "ferment" in his mind created by discussions of Republicanism with unhinging his confidence in every idea he had once taken for granted.[12]

This we know only from Rush's retrospective reflections, and much evidence exists to show that his conversion to Republicanism took longer than an instant. Still, his choice of *ferment* seems particularly apt to describe the unsettling mix of excitement and anxiety churning in his mind. In England, through his discovery of Republican ideals, Rush had experienced something like a religious change of heart. Even as the future Saint might get a glimmer of the wonder of grace but take years to surrender to the fullness of its power, Rush embraced Republicanism as an understanding of the world attuned to God but only slowly came to endow it with the specifics of its sacred meaning.

Still, it must have had some immediate impact on Rush's political vision. For one thing, Republicanism made sense of events that had already begun to unfold in the American colonies. The year before he came to Scotland, Rush had forthrightly supported protests against the Stamp Act. Then it had been a matter of simple justice and a nascent American pride. The English Republicans' theory of decline, however, fit the Stamp Act Crisis into a broader historical struggle against corrupt monarchy. Rush might have gotten a first glimmer that he would be involved in a struggle as heroic and earthshaking as the Great Awakening, the leaders of which had shaped and shadowed his young life.

New signs of crisis met Rush when he returned in 1769 to a Philadelphia alive with political turbulence. No one yet advocated independence, but activists all over the colonies had begun to speak the language of a separate colonial identity. Proclaiming loyalty to the King, at the same time they saw in most demands from the Crown a violation of their rights as English subjects. Like Rush, they had discovered in Republicanism the vocabulary with which to express the meaning of their political future. Yet it remained an inchoate vision, governed by an implicit clash of English and American identities that few wished to face.

Though clearly sympathetic to colonial resistance, Rush spent the early 1770s building his medical practice and shunning open participation in politics. Slavery finally sparked him to action. His friend Anthony Benezet, the famous Quaker antislavery activist, asked him to aid in efforts to pass a tax bill in the Pennsylvania Assembly that would make importation of slaves highly uneconomical. Rush responded with *An Address to the Inhabitants of the British Settlements in America, upon Slave-Keeping*.[13] The pamphlet advocated an end to the slave trade and the gradual emancipation of those already in bondage (Rush himself owned a manservant). It denied that slavery benefited the slave and that Africans were naturally suited for labor in southern climes. It also ridiculed the idea that the existence of slavery among the Hebrews was a legitimate religious defense of the modern institution.

Rush readily admitted that most of his arguments were old. What was new was his presentation of the antislavery case within a framework of American identity and Godly judgment, within the millennial/apocalyptic vision so common to colonial religious thought during the Awakening.[14]

He asserted that the vaunted English liberties that colonists guarded so jealously could not prosper side by side with slavery, that liberty must be for all or for none. He reminded "ADVOCATES for American Liberty" that the "eyes of all Europe" were upon them, expecting them to preserve "an asylum for freedom in this country" even if it should disappear elsewhere in the world. Furthermore, he argued, slavery was a "Hydra sin," and failure to deal with it would court God's punishment. "Remember that national crimes require national punishments," he warned; ". . . [they] cannot pass with impunity, unless God shall cease to be just or merciful."[15]

Even before the leap to rebellion, then, Rush had fashioned a specific component of America's Republican agenda—abolition of slavery and the slave trade—and had linked America's fate in God's universe to that cause. That Rush should also be first stirred to action not by the grievances of his fellow colonists, but rather by an evil in which colonists were deeply implicated, underlined a self-scrutiny that became a central feature of his commitment to independence. It was a tone built upon high expectations, for by Rush's light America, if it fulfilled its mission, would lead the world to the Second Coming prophesied by the Great Awakening. While numerous ministers and pamphleteers had begun to envision the colonial struggle as part of a Manichean millennial fray between the forces of God (the colonists) and those of the Devil (the King), few as yet had joined Rush and Benezet as critics from within.[16]

There was another significant difference between Rush and most ministers in the construction of the religious meaning of issues abroad in the land. If Rush the religious virtuoso felt obliged to criticize his own society even as he condemned England, he did so outside the domain of theology. He had taken the Awakening spirit of ecumenicism one step further in creating sacred issues whose resolution made no reference to sect or particulars of conversion. Rush had forged a vision of a sacred drama in which human actions concerning society sparked God's reward or punishment. In short, he began to display that peculiar sense of social piety that would become, a half-century later, the hallmark of the antebellum reformer as religious virtuoso.

When the colonists declared independence, Rush devoted himself to the cause with enthusiasm and sacrifice. As a member of Congress and medical advisor to the army, he worked tirelessly to improve the health of the patriot troops. He brought to his labors the same unflinching self-scrutiny that informed his antislavery pamphlet, sometimes appearing to be as hard on his comrades as he was on the British. He sought in the actions of individual Americans a virtue as perfect as his dream of millennial revolution. The corruption of public officials, wavering and often pragmatically changing loyalties, and the exhaustion to be expected in such a struggle: all these mocked Rush's dreams for a republic.

He worried most about military leadership. Perhaps because he imagined the Revolution to be the first battle in a grand millennial fray, Rush
described the Continental Army's needs in terms of the Old Testament.
"We have only passed the Red Sea," he wrote to Patrick Henry in 1778. "A
dreary wilderness is still before us, and unless a Moses or a Joshua are
raised up in our behalf, we must perish before we reach the promised
land." What he found was something quite different: "4 Major Generals—
Greene, Sullivan, Stirling and Stevens. The 1st a sycophant to the general
[Washington], timid, speculative, without enterprise; the 2nd, weak, vain,
without dignity, fond of scribbling, in the field a madman. The 3d, a
proud, vain, lazy, ignorant drunkard. The 4th, a sordid, boasting cow-
ardly sot." Rush even questioned Washington's leadership. So insistent
were his criticisms that he and a few others were accused of plotting
against the Revolutionary leadership.[17]

Military leaders were not the only ones to come under Rush's scrutiny.
He and not a few others worried about lack of virtue in common soldiers,
especially as symbolized in the practice of growing their hair long. To
assertions that this fashion indicated rebellious attitudes and slothfulness,
Rush added his scientific argument that long hair caused colds (it stayed
wet longer after a rain) and gave lice a convenient nesting ground. He also
condemned war profiteering and the generally affluent conditions of the
late 1770s as being destructive of the moral fiber needed to win the war. As
a result, Rush sometimes expressed satisfaction when conditions took a
turn for the worse. For instance, he saw a positive "new era" in American
politics caused by the British capture of Charleston, South Carolina, in
May 1780. "Our republics cannot long exist in prosperity," he wrote to
John Adams on that occasion. "We require adversity and appear to possess
most of the republican spirit when most depressed."[18]

Nonetheless, Rush thrilled to final victory over the British in 1783. After
all, there remained the challenge of building a republic *despite* success and
prosperity. But how would that be done? Most Revolutionary leaders
recognized that the translation of revolutionary zeal into a Republican
reality involved both the creation of new institutions and the preservation
of ideals of Republican virtue among the populace. Many assumed or
hoped that the creation of a Republican political system would encourage
an enduring sense of public virtue. For most of the Revolutionary leadership, politics and the creation of a new political structure became the
field of battle upon which various views of human nature and possibility
were tested.

Rush approached the problem from a very different angle. In the decade
after victory at Yorktown, he developed a reform program to remake
individuals and institutions into perfect reflections of Republican virtue.
He shared the view of many that constitutions and simple freedom would
not eradicate the darker side of human nature. Rather one must start with

programs that from birth to death encouraged virtue and built a true republic from the individual outward to society. In this sense Rush was perhaps more sanguine in his revolutionary hopes than most of his fellows, for transforming human nature was no easy task.

Rush's reform vision covered a great expanse from personal to social activity, but its details can only be understood fully in terms of Rush's underlying assumptions about America, humankind, and cosmic history. As already noted, he shared with many others the belief that the Revolution marked an epochal step toward the millennial day. Some meant by the Millennium the literal return of Christ, and some meant an age of perfect peace in which Christ's spirit would inform every act and thought. Rush never made his own specific metahistorical vision clear. However, he believed that America must lead human efforts to prepare the world for that prophesied era.

Identification of America as the nation to lead the world to millennial splendor was not uncommon and led most often to a simple adoration of the nation in the forms that recent scholars have called "civil religion." Rush the virtuoso, as his earlier pamphlet on slavery indicated, assumed that American leadership in the millennial fray depended upon the nation's ability to maintain its virtue among and above other nations. More specifically, it meant that Americans must fully embrace Republicanism, an ideology that he came close to equating with Christianity.

One might properly ask why Rush the religionist felt it necessary to transmute Christianity into Republicanism. In an overwhelmingly Christian nation, why not simply promote Christian virtue through revivals of religion? The most obvious answer is that Rush, like so many others of his generation, was swept up in the romance of the Revolution and at first tended to fuse his conceptions of sacred and profane history. The political means of the Revolution became sacralized as the human means for helping to fulfill prophecy.

Equally important, Benjamin Rush had grown to manhood not only influenced by the Great Awakening but also within a society that had grappled with the reality of religious pluralism for some time and had more or less made its peace with toleration. Rush's own background in Presbyterianism, Quakerism, and Anglicanism reflected only part of the religious spectrum that had learned to live together within Pennsylvania. Finding a ritual life that would bring Christians together meant drawing upon a cosmic vision outside of the individual sects, yet celebrating the general human virtues associated with each.[19]

Rush found that vision in the Scottish Enlightenment, and more particularly in the scientific doctrine that lay at the core of his medical system: environmentalism. He summarized his basic views on an environmentalist-based reform program in "The Influence of Physical Causes upon the Moral Faculty" (1786); in it one can see the width and breadth of his vision.

He argued that the capacity for choosing between good and evil, although innate, was deeply affected by the climate in which it developed and the condition of the body in which it was housed. Thus clarity of thought and, ultimately, the choice for virtue or vice might be affected by, among other things, climate, diet, choice of drinks, hunger, disease, style of labor, amount of sleep, pain, degree of cleanliness, odors, music, preaching, medicine, forms of punishment, and forms of government.

Rush wished to create a "science of morals" by tracking the environmental origins of virtue and vice. Philosophers, legislators, physicians, parents, schoolmasters, and ministers could consult the findings of such a science and adjust minute environmental influences to produce optimal moral and intellectual performance. In doing so one could eventually "extirpate war, slavery, and capital punishment" from society, make more intelligible the truths of Christianity, and in other ways effect "the reformation and happiness of mankind."[20]

Rush's dynamic sense of environmentalism produced a complex series of rituals and symbols aimed at sustaining a pious Christian Republicanism. It distinguished Rush from a number of other important contemporary adherents of environmental doctrine, including Jefferson and his circle, who saw in it a way of explaining the differences exhibited by various races and groups of humankind. Rush, for his part, saw environmentalism as the basis for a careful reshaping of everyday life. Given the long-term goals as well as the particulars of that reshaping, his reform program amounted to a first step toward perfecting the American Republic through the resacralization of everyday life.

The aim of sacralizing the social environment can be seen most comprehensively in Rush's educational ideas, for he viewed the school as the key social instrument for reform and spent much time working out a multifaceted instructional environment. "Of the Mode of Education Proper in a Republic" (1784) set forth his ideas on the schooling of young Republicans. Rush argued that education had better be done in America rather than abroad, since the prejudice for patriotism took hold most securely in the first twenty-one years of life. He favored a uniform system of education, one that would "render the mass of the people more homogeneous, and thereby fit them more easily for uniform and peaceable government." A common education would counterbalance the varieties of American backgrounds.[21]

Rush placed Christianity at the very foundation of a Republican education. While "every religion that reveals the attributes of the Deity is worth supporting," and while religious toleration was a cardinal value of Republicanism, he nonetheless recommended that the New Testament be a key source of learning. "A Christian cannot fail of being a republican," he noted, and for a variety of reasons. Genesis disproved the divine right of kings; the Gospel inculcated "humility, self-denial, and brotherly kindness" and taught a central Republican value, "that no man 'liveth unto himself.'" And, of course, the Golden Rule was essential to Republican virtue.[22]

He also asserted that the main purpose of education was to train "men, citizens, and Christians" rather than "scholars," that in fact the system should "convert men into republican machines." Unless citizens in a republic "perform[ed] their parts properly, in the great machine of the government of the state," society would soon be spoiled by the reintroduction of monarchy or aristocracy. Each citizen was a part of the Republic and "must be fitted to each other by means of education before they can be made to produce regularity and unison in government." Here, though expressed in enlightened Republican language, lay the catechistic principles that informed contemporary and later evangelical educational enterprises, from Timothy Dwight's to Horace Bushnell's.[23]

More specific recommendations followed. Anticipating the work of Noah Webster, Rush argued that schools should stress the teaching of the "American language with propriety and grace" so as to create pride in the new country. History, chronology, commerce, and chemistry were all important, as were lessons in "all the means of promoting national prosperity and independence, whether they relate to improvements in agriculture, manufactures, or inland navigation." All learning in one way or another prepared young citizens for a productive life, useful to self, family, and state.[24]

Rush's environmentalism naturally led him to a companion program of "physical discipline" that would create Republican bodies as well as Republican minds. Diet should consist of broths, milk, and vegetables. Spirituous liquors should be avoided. The day should proceed in alternating periods of study, manual labor, sleep, and silent solitude; contact with others should be closely watched so that "those great principles in human conduct—sensibility, habit, imitations and association"—could be given "proper direction."[25]

Rush's program had been outlined with men in mind. However, he had not forgotten the preparation of women for what he saw as their proper role in a republic. He advocated instruction not only "in the usual branches of female education" but also in "the principles of liberty and government" and the "obligations of patriotism." No champion of equality, Rush nonetheless saw women as crucial to the creation of that environment necessary to promote Republican values. After all, women were the silent partners of male endeavor. "The opinions and conduct of men are often regulated by the women in the most arduous enterprizes of life," Rush noted, "and their approbation is frequently the principal reward of the hero's dangers, and the patriot's toils." Besides, he observed, "the first impressions upon the minds of children are generally derived from the women. Of how much consequence, therefore, is it in a republic, that

they should think justly upon the great subject of liberty and government!"[26]

Having set forth the basic rationale, curriculum, and conditions for a
Republican education, Rush proceeded in the years that followed to suggest an institutional structure appropriate to his plan. In 1786, he outlined
a system of education for Pennsylvania as a model for other states. He
advocated a pyramid of institutions: one state university, four colleges
located in different regions of the state, and free schools for every town-
ship. "By this plan the whole state will be tied together by one system of
education," he argued, each institution acting in concert with the others to
supply students and teachers with a common culture. "The same systems
of grammar, oratory and philosophy, will be taught in every part of the
state, and the literary features of Pennsylvania will thus designate one
great, and equally enlightened family." Toward this end he helped found
Dickinson College and was instrumental in restructuring the curriculum of
the University of Pennsylvania. Two years later, Rush broadened this
notion of unity through education in his plan for a "Federal University,"
which would be a source of common culture and concerted Republican
efforts in a large and diverse country and would spur "a golden age of the
United States."[27]

Such grand institutional plans were just one part of Rush's environmental approach to education. At the other end of the spectrum were his
tinkerings with every detail of classroom life, a penchant vividly illustrated
in another of his major essays, "The Amusements and Punishments
Which Are Proper for Schools." He rejected common forms of children's
play; they ruined clothing, wasted strength, impaired health, were noisy,
excited the passions, and were "calculated to beget vulgar manners." Instead Rush recommended amusements that would be "most subservient to
their future employments in life." For instance, he approved of a particular
game reportedly played at a Methodist college: "A large lot is divided
between the scholars, and premiums are adjudged to those of them who
produce the most vegetables from their grounds, or who keep them in the
best order." In the winter one might play at mechanical arts. "Where is the
boy who does not delight in the use of a hammer—a chisel—a saw?" Rush
asked. "And who has not enjoyed a high degree of pleasure in his youth, in
constructing a miniature house?" Even if a student were heading for a life
in the professions, such exercises in the agricultural and manual arts would
be a healthy outlet for creative passions.[28]

Amusements also gave students a break from the classroom. Rush worried about the physical, and therefore moral, injury done young scholars
by obliging them "to sit too long in *one place*, or crowding too many of them
together *in one room*." Bodies were literally bent out of shape and exposed
to fevers and "morbid effluvia, produced by the confined breath and per-

spiration of too great a number of children." Strength and relief would come from simply getting these bodies outside and moving.[29]

Among amusements to avoid, Rush took special pains to make a case against hunting, or "gunning" as he put it. It hardened the heart, was no longer necessary to provide food, consumed too much time, led boys into "low, and bad company," and exposed the young hunter to accidents, fever, and long abstinence from food that would lead "to intemperance in eating, which naturally leads to intemperance in drinking." But that was not the half of it. To the argument that young men should learn to wield arms for defense of country, Rush countered that such training fostered "hostile ideas towards their fellow creatures." Instead educators should "instill into their minds sentiments of universal benevolence to men of all nations and colours." Since "wars originate[d] in error and vice," they would cease when education had done its job of eradicating war's causes. In case of attack from less virtuous enemies, Rush was sure, God would protect his chosen people. Enemies would turn their ships around because they would "find nothing in us congenial to their malignant dispositions; for the flames of war can be spread from one nation to another, only by the conducting mediums of vice and error." Given the proper chance, the reform of childhood games might lead the world to the abolition of war.[30]

As for punishments, here too Rush advocated replacing "barbarous" practices with those conceived in reason and love. He noted that civilized society had long ago abandoned corporal punishment for adults, and that only in the schools did such practices survive. Abolition of corporal punishment would be a blow against Satan. "I have sometimes suspected that the Devil who knows how great an enemy knowledge is to his kingdom," Rush mused, "has had the address to make the world believe that *feruling*, *pulling* and *boxing ears*, *cudgelling*, *horsing*, &c. and in boarding schools, a *little starving*, are all absolutely necessary for the government of young people, on purpose that he might make both schools, and school-masters odious, and thereby keep our world in ignorance; for ignorance is the best means the Devil ever contrived, to keep up the number of his subjects in our world."[31]

The alternatives to harsh physical discipline were quiet counseling and admonition, after-school confinement, or silent public disgrace. If none of these worked, the child should be dismissed from school so as to prevent corruption of other children. "It is the business of parents, and not of school-masters," Rush maintained, "to use the last means for eradicating idleness and vice from their children." Such a policy would accomplish two things. First, children would be spared the degradation and physical harm attendant to corporal punishment. Second, the schoolmaster, who had previously earned the hatred and ridicule of the community by his association with "despotism and violence," might take his rightful position as, "next to mothers, the most important member of civil society."[32]

Rush saw other important battlefields in addition to education. The foremost enemy was alcohol. As early as 1772, he had advocated moderation in drinking, arguing that spirits stimulated the body and disturbed natural functions. He thus rejected the common medical wisdom, which endorsed the healthful properties of liquor. Undaunted by criticism and only confirmed in his suspicions by observation of Revolutionary soldiers, he reopened his crusade in 1782 with a newspaper piece entitled "Against Spirituous Liquors." It attacked the time-honored custom of supplying farm laborers with rations of liquor. Instead of refreshing the body, he observed, spirits tended to "relax the stomach, quicken the circulation of the blood, and thus dispose it to putrefaction." In addition, spirits were expensive, unloosed quarrels and "indecent language," and inspired other mischief. Rush suggested four substitutes: "Bonnie-clabber" (sour milk), cider or small beer, Indian corn tea, or, best of all, vinegar and water sweetened with molasses or brown sugar.[33]

Rush published his classic pamphlet on hard drink, *An Enquiry into the Effects of Spirituous Liquors upon the Human Body, and Their Influence upon the Happiness of Society*, in 1784.[34] The *Enquiry* featured an argument similar in its comprehensiveness to his educational theories. Rush began by listing the immediate effects of drinking: talkativeness, good humor expressed in "an insipid simpering," swearing, disclosure of secrets and other forms of immodesty, and combativeness. Some drinkers, he noted, indulged in "singing, hallooing, roaring, imitating the noises of brute animals, jumping, tearing off clothes, dancing naked, breaking glasses and china, and dashing other articles of household furniture upon the ground or floor." The chronic effects were even worse: loss of appetite, "discharge of a frothy and viscid phlegm," obstructions of the liver, jaundice, coughing that often turned into consumption, diabetes, rash-like eruptions known as "rum buds," bad breath, belching, epilepsy, gout, and madness.[35]

The social effects of drink mirrored this destruction of the body. Alcohol preyed upon the family, alienating husband from wife and child from parent. The drinking magistrate inspired fears of corruption and "subversion of public order and happiness." Urban drinkers often bankrupted their entire estates to pay "tavern debts"; farmers ruined their land and animals, while their children cavorted "filthy and half clad, without manners, principles and morals." As for the drunkard minister? Here words failed Rush: "If angels weep—it is at such a sight." Rush concluded, "Thus we see poverty and misery, crimes and infamy, diseases and death are all the natural and usual consequences of the intemperate use of ardent spirits."[36]

Later, Rush wrote pamphlets detailing his plans for female education, prison reform and the abolition of capital punishment, peace, humane treatment of the insane, and temperance in the use of tobacco. All expanded on the basic themes of a unity of health between the individual's body and the body politic. All implicitly or explicitly sought to advance the millennial goals of Republicanism. All were based on an extremely detailed working out of environmentalist assumptions concerning personal habits and institutional settings, and all assumed that each ill was vulnerable to straightforward, scientific solution. Together these plans constituted a blueprint for the detailed construction of society and the ritual conduct of everyday life, all bent on creating a sacralized Christian Republican way of life.

Rush seemed confused on only one issue, the black presence in America. In his *Address to the Inhabitants of the British Settlements . . . on the Slavery of the Negroes* (1773), he had damned slavery and the slave trade. After the Revolution had been won, he continued to campaign against the institution and for the humane treatment of slaves. Not only slavery but the fate of the free black community in white society vexed Rush's sense of Republicanism and Christian benevolence. Few, including Rush, believed that blacks could be made equal and full partners in the new nation. How could one find a place for them in the Republic? Rush had always been able to discover answers to problems in scientific inquiry. He thought he might develop a proper policy toward blacks by joining others who sought to find the reason for their skin color. In a paper read before the American Philosophical Society in 1797, he speculated that it was caused by "a disease in the skin of the leprous kind." Such a finding dictated that blacks be treated "with humanity and justice" and at the same justified "keeping up the existing prejudices against matrimonial connections with them." Thus, according to Rush, Republican America could act in humane and Christian fashion and at the same time isolate blacks as one might isolate others with a serious illness. For Rush, this was no thin veil for conscious malevolence. Indeed, within the notion of their maintaining a largely separate community until cured of their leprosy, he championed free blacks in Philadelphia and kept up his campaign against slavery.[37]

Despite his troubled solution to the question of race, Rush's reform program, so careful in its detail and so cosmic in its ultimate goal of a Republican road to the Millennium, marked a striking break with a pre-Revolutionary world of royal authority and established churches. In place of this crumbling cosmos, Rush envisioned a world in which everyday life would be recast in terms of Christian Republican virtue. Not surprisingly, Rush's immersion in reform radically altered his relationship to Presbyterianism. First signs of trouble appeared in 1785, when he accused John Ewing, pastor of the First Presbyterian Church, of "*lying, drunkenness, and unchristian language.*" Political bickering in the churches irked him as well. Most of all, Rush became increasingly convinced that salvation was possible for all humankind, and that the Calvinist doctrine of limited election was anti-Republican.

He formally severed his ties with the Presbyterians in 1787.[38] In a letter explaining his move, Rush indicated his new view of the relationship between the churches, religion, and American destiny. "I still wish to maintain a friendly connection with them," he wrote Ashbel Green, "and I heartily forgive them for all the injuries I have received from them, and I pray God to deliver them from the influence of bad men and to spare them to compose a part of the Redeemer's new empire in America." "America" as a sacred presence had become Rush's new church, beside which all others were minor sects whose truths were to be judged against the imperatives of American millennial mission. His reform program became the standard against which other views were to be judged. Indeed, it might be said that Republican reform had become the ritual and symbolic content of this new church.[39]

Having broken with Presbyterianism, Rush felt freer to attack its theological essence. For instance, when in 1788 his tract against capital punishment drew fire from a Boston minister, Rush condemned the attack as one based upon "severe Calvinistical principles" and rejected them in no uncertain terms. "It is impossible to advance human happiness," he wrote Jeremy Belknap, "while we believe the Supreme being to possess the passions of weak or wicked men and govern our conduct by such opinions." He then quoted Luke 9:56 to support his reform vision—"The Son of Man came not to destroy men's *lives*, but to *save* them"—and argued that the passage refuted "all the arguments that ever were offered in favor of slavery, war, and capital punishment."[40]

Rush's exasperation with the churches surfaced again in 1791 as he and others helped Philadelphia's blacks to establish their own church. Rush expected little from white congregations. "The clergy and their faithful followers of every denomination," he noted bitterly, "are *too good* to *do good.*" He had already seen the Quakers object to blacks making temporary use of a Friends' schoolhouse for worship because part of the service consisted of singing psalms. Rush slyly predicted that most help would "come from the Deists, swearing captains of vessels, and brokers of our city." Over a year later, reporting on the progress of the black church project to Jeremy Belknap, he noted that "the old and established societies look shy at them." Rush drew a succinct lesson from this and similar encounters: "To feel or to exercise the true Spirit of the Gospel nowadays seems to require a total separation from all sects, for they seem more devoted to their forms or opinions than to the doctrines and precepts of Jesus Christ."[41]

His own Republican vision had crystallized even as he lost faith in formal churches. "Republicanism is a part of the truth of Christianity," he declared in 1791. "It derives its power from its *true* source. It teaches us to view our rulers in their *true* light." A year later he added that the Bible was against all kinds of monarchy, whether kingly or "whether found in the absurd ideas of apostolic succession or in the aristocracy of Presbyterianism." The Republican belief in the universal love of God for all humankind, which Rush saw as prevailing more and more in America, promised both a spiritual and "a temporal kingdom in the Millennium." That hope had become the basis of a "new principle of action prompting a practical godliness." Monarchy, slavery, war, intemperance, ignorance, capital punishment, punishment of any sort whose result was not reformation: all these would "speedily end" as men and women became instruments for good. "In the meanwhile let us not be idle with such prospects before our eyes," he declared to Jeremy Belknap. "Heaven works by instruments, and even supernatural prophecies are fulfilled by natural means." The Millennium was to be made, and neither backward churches nor the Devil could deter those, like Rush, who wished to make it. "It is possible we may not live to witness the approaching regeneration of our world," he continued, "but the more active we are in bringing it about, the more fitted we shall be for that world where justice and benevolence eternally prevail."[42]

Even as Rush brought together the radiant strands of his Christian Republican vision, however, darker signs began to appear. Indeed, if the 1780s had been the moment of millennial dreaming, the 1790s became the time of that dream's undoing. On the national scene, controversies over economic policy and the ratification of Jay's Treaty, and heated battles between the political parties, augured badly for Rush's vision of Republican government. Violent opposition in the form of the Whisky Rebellion further threw the great experiment in doubt, as did news that the once admired French Revolution had turned into a bloodbath. In Rush's own Philadelphia, the year 1793 brought a four-month siege of yellow fever, with recurrences in 1794, 1797, and 1798. Rush devoted every waking hour to the treatment of victims and the search for a cure. Controversy over his approach to the fever, both in theory and practice, led to a protracted libel suit. As early as 1793, Rush began to turn to Jeremiah rather than Revelation for inspiration. "The language of heaven in the wars, famine, and pestilence which now prevail more or less all over the world," he wrote to a friend, "seems to be 'Seekest thou great things? Seek them not, for behold, I bring evil on all flesh.'"[43]

By 1798, Rush had begun to separate the religious from the political visions, which he had merged in Christian Republicanism, and to move toward religious as opposed to political and social solutions. He said as much to Noah Webster, sympathizing with Webster's bleak Federalist assessment of the world but observing that "it seem[ed] to be reserved to Christianity alone to produce universal, moral, political, and physical happiness." Rush predicted "nothing but suffering to the human race" as long as the world embraced "paganism, deism, and atheism." Eight years later he wrote in despair to John Adams: "All systems of political order and happiness seem of later years to have disappointed their founders and advocates. Civilization, science, and commerce have long ago failed in their attempts to improve the condition of mankind, and even liberty itself, from which more was expected than from all other human means, has lately appeared to be insufficient for that purpose."[44]

Rush was not alone in his retreat from Revolutionary millennialism. The 1790s and early 1800s witnessed a similar move among many ministers who had once preached a millennialism focused on the American Revolution and its role in cosmic history. Now they, like Rush, withdrew from politics and turned to a pre-millennial vision in which the woeful events of the period—domestic political strife and the violence of France's revolution—became signs of the darkness that would threaten the Earth before the end of days. What mattered now was faith in God, not the futile political ideas of human beings. Yet unlike Rush, the churches and their ministers transformed this retreat into a plan of victory. Rejecting politics as the road to the Millennium, they now saw the conversion of the world as the instrument of American destiny and began an earnest campaign of Bible distribution as well as foreign and domestic missions to preach the Gospel.[45]

Rush certainly supported the propagation of the faith. In fact, he was instrumental in the founding of Philadelphia's first Sunday school in 1791. In 1808, he helped form a local Bible Society.[46] But his heart was not in such efforts, certainly not compared to his zeal for Republican reform. A political vision had sparked his life's work and his millennial hopes, and no campaign simply to save souls could possibly compare.

During the War of 1812, Rush found new reasons to condemn the nation. His great hopes for marshalling the resources of American society under the banner of Republicanism, with a common language and a common set of values, had disappeared. Party strife, the war itself, and distance from the Revolution had all exacerbated the worst tendencies in the American system. Writing again to Adams, he imagined the nation as a ship "manned by sailors of six different nations. . . . Suppose the ship to be over-taken by a storm," he continued, "and the captain and mates to be able to speak the language of but one class of the sailors. What do you suppose would be the fate of that ship?" His despair drove him back to the Calvinism of his youth, and in particular to Samuel Finley's sermon *On the Madness of Mankind*. "The present times," he lamented, "have added many facts in support of his position."[47]

In March 1813, Rush asked Thomas Jefferson, as a "sincere old friend of 1775," a simple but chastening question: "From the present complexion of affairs in our country, are you not disposed at times to repent of your solicitude and labors and sacrifices during our Revolutionary struggle for liberty and independence?" Five weeks later Rush died. He was buried in the graveyard at Christ Church, whose bells had once proclaimed the Grand Federal Procession but now tolled in mourning for a founder of the Republic.[48]

Rush's retreat from reform, his return to the mood if not the theology of Calvinism, and his bitter sense of the nation's future were more the result of crushed hopes than of disastrous realities. Rush had dreamed an implausible dream, the transformation of a diverse and unsettled people into a unified nation whose hallmark would be personal, social, and political virtue. He compounded that folly by seeking such a goal under the banner of Republicanism, which in its practical constitutional form insured the kind of individual freedom that made his task well-nigh impossible.

Rush's reform ideas, however, were neither simple folly nor mean-spirited attempts at social control. Rather they echoed an enduring theme in American life, the relation of mission to American identity. As early as the seventeenth century, Puritan ministers had begun preaching jeremiads, warning their flocks that God's wrath would be visited upon them should they forsake what historian Perry Miller highlighted as their "errand into the wilderness." Implicit in the warning was a celebration of chosenness, indeed the creation and reinforcement of a very special relationship to God. By expressing what were ultimately religious concerns in terms of social and medical issues, Rush created a language for the jeremiad suited to a post-Revolutionary America that endorsed pluralism and religious toleration. A new American civil religion had found its critic from within, even if in the 1780s and 1790s few were listening.

In 1798, as Rush reflected upon his growing disillusionment, he could find but one source of hope. "New England may escape the storm which impends our globe," he wrote, "but if she does, it will only be by adhering to the religious principles and moral habits of the first settlers of that country."[49] No doubt he had in mind a holding action conducted by a saving remnant of the Republic, yet he had unwittingly identified the region that would give birth to new reform endeavors. Ironies abounded, for New England's nurturing of antebellum reform had much to do with its religious establishment's struggles against pluralism. Reform grew not only from a naive revolutionary zeal but also from the same despair that had poisoned Rush's fondest dreams. Finally, rather than remaining the project of one man, it came to define the work of a significant minority of New Englanders and others who grew up in the forty years prior to the Civil War. Instead of perishing in the anarchy Rush perceived all around him, little more than a decade after his death the dream of a Christian republic reappeared with a holy vengeance.

II

Lyman Beecher and the Cosmic Theater

"[THE EARTH] was designed as a theatre on which to display sovereign mercy in redeeming and preparing *a people for the Lord*," an Orthodox minister assured the Connecticut legislature in 1821. "All the revolutions in the moral world, from creation to the end of time, shall subserve the same great object. *To purchase unto* himself *a peculiar people*, and to set up a kingdom which shall have no end, the eternal son of God *bowed the heavens*, came down, and expired upon the cross."[1] For believing Christians, this cosmic play was a palpable historical drama. God was its author. It began in Eden, developed in the world, and would culminate in a world without end. Its cast encompassed humankind—saints and sinners, men and women, common and chosen peoples—as well as the suprahuman characters of God Himself, His son the Christ, and the sworn enemy—the Antichrist. God knew who would play what role, how long the play would last, and how the unrehearsed finale would unfold. Human beings, bound to play their parts, could only take guesses educated in observation of the world and study of the Bible.

For most Christians in America of 1821, the cosmic drama lent a sacred framework to existence. Life in its profane dimensions predominated, punctuated by ritual reminders of the sacred. Communities marked their weeks with the Sabbath and church meeting, and their years with the few holy days Protestants allowed themselves to celebrate. Rites of passage linked the lives of individual Christians to the cosmic drama: baptism, conversion, communion, marriage, death. Sacred and profane realms were separate but connected, each gaining definition from the other.

For Protestant religious virtuosos of the 1820s, however, the sacred world encompassed the primary drama of life. They divined in objects and events all around them important signs of the times, portents of Godly intervention and of turning points in the procession toward the end of days. Nor were American virtuosos in the early nineteenth century lacking in epochal earthly events to ponder as the new nation approached its fiftieth anniversary. In the past quarter-century alone, the United States had undergone a major and peaceful political revolution, fought a second war against England, doubled its territory, and experienced the first exhilarating and disturbing signs of a vast commercial and industrial revolution that would transform its national life and the individual lives of its citizens. In light of these events and personal revelations, significant numbers of virtuosos created new versions of the cosmic drama and sought to reshape old churches or found new ones.

Of course, men and women had been revising the Christian drama since the crucifixion. But the explosion of cosmological speculation that occurred in the aftermath of the American Revolution was exceptional in more than quantity. Most prior theological experimentation among Christians had taken place under the thumb of or in opposition to ecclesiastical authority, marking those engaged in significant departures of doctrine for severe punishment or even death. In America, beginning during the colonial period and accelerating rapidly in the 1770s and beyond, religious freedom, separation of church and state, and the delegitimation and ultimate disestablishment of official religious authority bred a qualitatively different situation. The free atmosphere for religious speculation and church formation fostered many free consciences and an almost dizzying degree of spiritual indeterminacy. In a society that tolerated almost unlimited versions of religious certainty, all with the right to be preached and none preordained as more truthful than the other, there remained no social anchor of religious Truth.

Spiritual experimenters and dissenters reacted to toleration with a mixture of glee and uneasiness. Their new freedom often indicated to them an ever-quickening millennial march. This was true not only for the Baptists and Methodists, the two dissenting sects to gain most from the unleashing of faith, but also for new sects that the democratic and libertarian strains of the Revolution had fostered. In the hills of New England, Shakers, Freewill Baptists, Unitarians, and Universalists rebelled against Calvinist authority. Throughout New England and across the rest of the colonies, "Christian" movements under the leadership of Elias Smith, James O'Kelley, Barton Stone, and Alexander Campbell revolted against theological authority and asserted the right of common folk to read the Bible for themselves. For many in these sects, the Revolution had literally been the beginning of the end of days. They wrote special roles for themselves that would help bring down the curtain on history and raise it on eternity.[2]

At the same time, few of these beneficiaries of religious freedom were tolerant of others. They usually sought to establish their revelation as *the* revelation. Some in fact had been spurred to the surety of new dispensations by the very experience of spiritual confusion in the world of many faiths. This was certainly the case with Mormon church founder Joseph Smith, who at age fifteen had communed with God in the woods because he could not make sense of the competing claims of churches and evangelists. God told him to seek the true and as yet unrevealed faith, for each of those that existed was "wrong" and an "abomination." The "Christian" John Rogers put it more succinctly when he advised his fellow members in the Church of Christ: "When we speak of other denominations, we place ourselves among them, as one of them. This, however, we can never do, unless we abandon the distinctive ground—the apostolic ground—the anti-sectarian ground, we have taken."[3]

Among guardians of the remaining traditional religious establishments, reaction to colonial pluralism and the Revolution's emphatic endorsement of freedom of religion as a norm was also mixed. In the middle colonies, where early on religious diversity and other social realities forced de facto toleration, any uneasiness caused by a heightened post-Revolutionary spiritual freedom was more than balanced by resignation and even pride in the record of toleration.[4] Many of New England's Presbyterian and Congregationalist ministers reacted quite differently. They had begrudgingly lived with a modicum of religious toleration in the colonial period, certainly so after the Great Awakening.[5] They had, it was also true, been among the earliest to flock to the Revolutionary cause and to prophesy its millennial possibilities.

Yet events in the post-Revolutionary period filled them with foreboding. Political strife, religious heterodoxy, and bloody turns in the French Revolution undercut their faith in political roads to the Millennium. At the same time, religious freedom unhinged what was for them society's one steadfast source for wisdom and hope. To their mind, religious freedom in practice had begun to breed the same rancor afflicting party politics; more important, it placed what once was considered heresy on an equal footing in the world with revelation. It left as an open question the future of religious Truth in a free society.

For a significant party of New England religious virtuosos, securing Truth and the Godly community against the claims of a tolerant society became the central theme of an ongoing and revolutionary rewriting of the human connection to the sacred drama. Antebellum reform, though it dealt with issues we normally conceive of as profane, arose within that project. The vast social, political, ideological, psychological, and economic transformations afoot in the early American republic provided the earthly stage for the birth of reform and in a hundred ways shaped its development. Yet at heart the originators of reform saw human events through a special metahistorical lens, the peculiar refractions of which developed from a crisis in New England Calvinism's cosmic identity.

The roots of this crisis lay in New England's tight intertwining of social, political, and religious orders, which had created a way of life that varied in significant ways from the nation at large. Contemporaries recognized the region's peculiar social organization. Some, like Benjamin Rush, saw New England as a last hope against the "storm" of anarchy they feared as engulfing the world, but only if the region adhered "to the religious principles and moral habits of the first settlers."[6]

The "principles and moral habits" of the Puritan founders inadequately described the reasons for New England's eventual place at the center of antebellum reform. Nor could one simply credit it to an intense New England piety or introspection (as if such qualities did not exist in abundance elsewhere). Rather it was the sacred communal identity forged by the founders and later generations of New Englanders that allowed some to create a broad religious vision conducive to reform.

Any explanation of reform must begin, therefore, with an appreciation of the special place New Englanders made for themselves in cosmic history. They had founded Massachusetts Bay as a "city upon a hill," in covenant with God as His people in the last days of earth. They were spiritual Israel, successors to the Jews of the Old Testament. New England divines interpreted turnings of human affairs as commentaries on the faithfulness of their people to the dictates of their holy bargain: to create a society that cleaved to the laws of God. Ministers preached jeremiads that assumed the chosenness of New England even as they excoriated its people for violating God's trust.[7] The realities of an increasingly complex and heterogeneous colonial society became in this prophetic understanding a source of challenge for God's chosen ones. Orthodoxy's sons and daughters grew up, generation after generation, with some version of this drama spread out before them, and with the promise of a role in its unfolding.

New Englanders embedded a sense of mission and identity into church and town polity and, indeed, into the very structure of daily existence. Challenges abounded, and fallings off of enthusiasm as well. Orthodoxy could not prevent Separatist and Baptist defections or withstand royal support for the Church of England. Despite dissent from within, challenges from without, and a steep decline in the churches' direct power over social, political, and economic life, the Puritan vision of chosenness managed to pervade the sinews of everyday consciousness.[8]

New England thus entered the Revolutionary era as a highly articulated and self-directed culture within the broader and far less formed panorama of American colonial life. At first the Revolution and the immediate post-Revolutionary era seemed to pose no great challenge to the old religious order. Yet New England's divines had not counted on the threats that the rise of a political party system, the institutionalization of religious freedom, and an ever more vigorous agitation for disestablishment would pose to New England's consciously intertwined religious and social order. All combined to darken the clouds over Orthodoxy, creating for some a sense that a massive conspiracy had been planned to destroy Godly order in New England.[9]

In the past, for instance, religious dissenters had shared the general sense of New England community and mission even as they campaigned for their own rights. Religious strife became much more divisive after the Revolution. As the party system gained strength in the late 1790s, dissenters more often than not voted Jeffersonian while Orthodoxy voted Federalist. Disestablishment quickly became a central political issue. In Massachusetts, Unitarians posed a newly revitalized challenge from within, successfully campaigning against strict Calvinists for leadership in churches and at Harvard College. Something unexpected was unfolding in the cosmic drama, and many among the Orthodox began to see the Antichrist in every Deist pronouncement or hint of political intrigue.[10]

The fate of the Federalist Party in the early nineteenth century complicated matters. Its slow death in the wake of Jeffersonian attacks and victories culminated in delegitimation at the Hartford Convention. Yet even before Hartford, Orthodox Calvinists themselves began to lose faith in the Federalists. Young and active members of the party began to emulate the party tactics of the Jeffersonians, and some even courted votes by endorsing disestablishment. The old Orthodox worldview seemed to be cracking from within as well as besieged from without.[11]

With the social and political structures that confirmed their cosmic vision threatened on every side, New England's Orthodox ministers scrambled for solutions on a variety of levels. Politically, most became even more entrenched in their support of traditional Federalist values though often disappointed in individual Federalist politicians. They stiffened their defense of religious establishment. Calvinists also broke from Harvard and other institutions diseased by Unitarianism, creating Andover and other colleges and seminaries as centers of Orthodox education. Congregational and Presbyterian churches combined efforts in 1801 under the Plan of Union to spread their version of the Gospel and to bring multitudes into the churches through revivals. If the Antichrist had arrived in the forms of Deism, Unitarianism, and Jeffersonianism, Orthodoxy's reading of the cosmic drama still told them that God would ultimately be victorious at Armageddon, and that they only need redouble their efforts to play their part.

Yet conducting such a counterattack undermined long-standing assumptions about conversion, church polity, and the relationship between minister, church, and society. Uneasiness haunted the church as it took steps that were controversial in Orthodox circles: promotion of revivals, ever broader church organizations, and lay participation through voluntary societies that sometimes challenged ministerial authority. Various theological positions emerged that continued debates begun during the Great Awakening and before, adding new twists to old questions.[12]

From this donnybrook historians have generally derived the theological sources for reform. Some have especially stressed the emergence of doctrines of human ability, free will, and "disinterested benevolence" as themes in New England Calvinism that freed individuals from the straitjacket of predestination and fostered social movements. Yet even more important, and subsuming such pointed theological exploration, was something a bit more elusive: the emergence of a new understanding of the cosmic drama among New England's Calvinists. A variety of ministers meeting day-to-day circumstances and a handful of religious virtuosos together shaped felt experience into a new and cohesive metahistory.

The seminal figure in this broad reworking of the relation between humankind, America, and millennial history was Timothy Dwight, poet, essayist, minister-theologian, and president of Yale. Dwight was born in western Massachusetts in 1752, great-great-grandson of Solomon Stoddard and grandson of Jonathan Edwards. He entered Yale as an undergraduate in 1765, where he demonstrated not only an interest in theology but also a wide-ranging "musical" sense of the world as expressed in devotion to literature and especially to poetry. He wrote and studied verse, and after he became a tutor at Yale he and some of his fellows informally added belles lettres to the staid curriculum. He presented as his master's thesis in 1772 "A Dissertation on the History, Eloquence, and Poetry of the Bible." He also felt called to politics, and by 1775 he strongly supported the Revolutionary cause. In fact, his educational innovativeness and Revolutionary sympathies caused Yale to fire him.[13]

Dwight left Yale to become chaplain of the First Connecticut Brigade of the Revolutionary army. His father's death forced him to leave the army to support his family in Northampton, Massachusetts, where he began a school and entered politics. He also preached on occasion but resisted calls from churches until the congregation of Greenfield, Connecticut, lured him in 1783. His preaching achieved a wide reputation, and in 1795 Yale asked him to replace Ezra Stiles as the college's president.

By then Dwight had come to believe, with many other ministers, that conspiracies of Deists and infidels threatened the very existence of American society. At Yale he waged war against what he saw as rampant unbelief and dangerous mimicry of the French Enlightenment and Revolution. Whether in fact Yale's students had strayed so far from tradition or responded so enthusiastically to Dwight have been points of historical debate.[14] Yet whatever Dwight's impact on the college community in general, he made a striking impression on a coterie of students that included Lyman Beecher, Asahel Nettleton, and Nathaniel William Taylor. They were taken especially with Dwight's fusion of belief in a powerful Calvinistic God and His immediacy in human affairs with decidedly novel doctrines of sin and free will.

Dwight recognized that the old faith must change to incorporate, in its own way, the activist essence of Enlightenment and Republican humankind. While he never denied original sin, he remained ambiguous about its nature and its complete hold on human character. To be sure, he noted, man was "rebellious, sinful, and odious to his Maker." Yet Dwight also believed that some parts of human nature remained "innocent" or imbued with "natural conscientiousness," and that these traits explained the ability of even "natural" man sometimes to obey God.[15]

He argued further that human beings were "moral agents" possessed of free will to obey or disobey. "I wish it understood," he underlined, "that I intend a real agent, a being whose thoughts, affections, and actions, are his own." Otherwise God might seem a tyrant, and such a characterization hardly seemed acceptable in the wake of a war of independence against a despotic king. Whereas the so-called Old Calvinists posited such absolute sovereignty in God as to make the actions of humans pitiful, Dwight held that free will and God's power were not contradictory. "God's foreknowledge of voluntary actions does in no respect lessen, or affect [man's] freedom," he argued; "although it renders their future existence absolutely certain."[16]

Dwight stressed faith as an active force in an age of action; he respected human will in a nation built upon citizen responsibility. In creating humans as free agents, God had made it so that individuals must be moved and educated to a choice for grace. Using such "means of grace" as a thorough religious education and powerful preaching, the church, its ministers, and laypersons could prepare the unconverted to accept God's grace if He should decide that individual to be worthy.[17] But that was not enough. Parallel to Rush's sense of the responsibilities of Republican citizenry, Dwight saw the purpose of religion as benevolent action as well as faith. "Real religion is ever active," he asserted; "and always inclined to do, as well as to say. The end, for which man was made, and for which he was redeemed, was that he might do good, and actively glorify his Creator."[18]

Dwight's doctrines of benevolence worked within a broad social and metaphysical context, one forged during the Revolutionary and post-Revolutionary eras. He was by turns and sometimes at one and the same time a fervent believer in the American future, a profoundly partisan champion of New England as a model society for the rest of America, and a fearful Manichean who saw the world as an arena for the battle between the forces of Good and Evil that would precede the end of days. In 1787, for instance, he envisioned an America that would be:

> Chain'd to no party; by no system bound;
> Confining merit to no speck of ground;
> Nor Britons, Frenchmen, Germans, Swiss, or Huns,
> Of earth the natives, and of heav'n the sons,
> Regarding, loving, all the great and good,
> Of ev'ry rank, clime, party, sect and blood.[19]

However, in the same work, he condemned the America that was, in which "Ten thousand follies" and the interests of "each jealous state" threatened the Republican experiment.[20]

When posed as a contrast between ideal and real, Dwight's vision of America had much in common with that of Rush. However unlike Rush, whose Enlightenment vision of progress and sole concentration on America per se made his Republican faith extremely vulnerable to disappointment, Dwight placed his view of events in a more durable drama. He saw history as a part of the heightened conflict between God and the Devil, in which grave setbacks would ultimately be turned right. The signs of the time that so disheartened Rush actually goaded Dwight to more enthusiastic battle. Through it all he saw the towns of Connecticut as social ideals that would remain though America itself might temporarily fall prey to Evil.

His disappointments with America as a whole, in fact, caused Dwight to emphasize the Connecticut ideal, making it a specimen of society as close to Eden as fallen humankind could produce. For seven years he worked on the poetic expression of this ideal as found in his own town; *Greenfield Hill* was published in 1794, the year before he came back to Yale as its president. The social fabric of the Connecticut town had replaced generalized republican ideals as the core of Dwight's social faith. In the last section of the work, "The Vision," he proclaimed a vaunted future for America, but only if it became like Greenfield Hill. Dwight was suggesting that, to use Kenneth Silverman's phrase, "America ought to be Connecticutized."[21] To Dwight, those who prevented this transformation—Deists, Illuminati, or infidel Jeffersonians—became soldiers in the Devil's legion.

Dwight's vision of America as harbinger of the Millennium, his Manichean vision of Satan's legions at work, and his idealization of New England society all helped shape Orthodoxy's sense of the world in the late eighteenth and early nineteenth centuries. He was not the only one to formulate the universe in these terms. Yet Dwight's views and his active promotion of revivals of religion to bolster Orthodoxy exerted a formative influence over significant members of the generation of Calvinists who charted the initial course of antebellum reform. In the realm of theology, he inspired the influential work of his student and secretary, the Reverend

Nathaniel William Taylor. Taylor's "New Haven Theology" formalized Dwight's more implicit notion of free agency and functioned as both the basis for and extension of New England revivalism.[22]

Yet no one of Dwight's disciples was more important to the history of reform than Lyman Beecher, easily the most influential preacher of his day and the one most deeply engaged in the day-to-day reform struggle for a Christian society. As opposed to Taylor, who wrote and thought within the relatively traditional bounds of theology, Beecher audaciously reconceived the cosmos. Beecher's ever-shifting sense of the cosmic drama borrowed from virtually every aspect of Dwight's complex and seemingly contradictory formulation of American destiny but in the end created its own new and powerful sense of the role of Christians in American society. Few played as visible and controversial a role in the early days of reform as Beecher, both as an advocate of change to his own generation and as a voice of moderation to the young radicals of the late 1820s. He was truly a religious virtuoso, imbued with a sense of personal mission and constantly at work creating and adjusting his sense of the role of individuals and his own society in the sacred drama.

Lyman Beecher was born in 1775 to David and Esther Lyman Beecher. Unlike Taylor, whose élite Connecticut family and prominent minister-grandfather groomed him for a comfortable entry into the clergy, Beecher rose from common and non-clerical roots. His father was a New Haven blacksmith. His mother died of consumption two days after his birth, and David was unwilling to raise him even after remarrying, so Lyman grew up in the care of his farmer aunt and uncle, the Lot Bentons of neighboring Guilford. Despite his lack of churchly background, Lyman early on displayed an inordinate fascination with God and the sacred aspects of existence. Years later some of his most vivid boyhood memories attested to the power of religion in his life. He remembered a night lit so bright by the northern lights that one could read beneath the sky, and a "blood-red arch" that stretched from "horizon to zenith." As the family stared in awe, Lyman's Uncle Stephen remarked, "Ah! we don't know at what time the day of judgment will come—at midnight or at cock-crowing." Beecher cried in fright that the day had arrived. Only the comforting of his nurse—"she talked with me about my soul"—calmed him down.[23]

The Benton family's religiosity nourished the young man's spiritual hunger. Prayers, Bible-reading, his aunt's conversion when Lyman was ten, and the reproofs of those around him when he "sinned" made piety an everyday affair. Once a neighbor caught him playing on the Sabbath and told him that God would put him in the fire and burn him "forever and ever." "That took hold," he remembered. "I understood what fire was, and what forever was. What emotion I had thinking, No end! no end! It has been a sort of mainspring ever since."[24] Beecher recalled that on one Sabbath he could not resist the urge to hunt rabbits but was so tormented that he returned home and "took the big Bible, and read Susanna, Bel and the Dragon, and Revelations till I was tired." He then amused himself by making some wood boxes but became so "conscience-smitten" that he threw them all in the fire.[25] Yet the lessons of church made no impression: "I never heard Parson Bray preach a sermon I understood."[26]

Beecher's vital sense of religion complemented a nervous, excitable, and questing mind. Ever restless as he plodded through his farm chores, Beecher seemed destined to fail at the steady trades of his family. As his uncle once told him, he "would never be good for anything but to go to college."[27] He went to Yale in 1793, there to be converted and deeply influenced by Dwight. To Beecher, whose sense of religious virtuosity lay in an active and experimental sense of the sacred, the new president became the perfect teacher. Dwight provided the young man with a model of muscular piety and effective preaching and beckoned him into a profession suited to his talents.

Beecher began his first ministry at East Hampton, Long Island in 1799. He moved in 1810 to the more important pulpit at Litchfield, Connecticut, a post that put him at the center of Connecticut's troubled Standing Order (the name given to Connecticut's powerful church establishment). In 1826, he moved to Hanover Street Church, Boston, where he thrust himself into the thick of the Unitarian controversy and the activities of the first national reform societies. Throughout this first part of his career, he reformulated New England's and America's place in cosmic history, one in which reform would play a crucial role.

The year 1799 was a good one for a reform-minded graduate to enter the ministry. The first tangible organizational fruits of Orthodoxy's disenchantment with politics had begun to appear as many ministers and laypersons turned single-mindedly to the spread of the Gospel. They touted domestic and foreign missions as the true road to millennial splendor. The conversion of fellow Americans might bring order to cities and towns they perceived as unhinged by foreign ideas and new freedoms, and to frontier settlements desperately in need of the Bible and religion's civilizing force. The conversion of the world would be America's contribution to hastening the glorious end of days.[28]

This turn to missions, modeled on contemporaneous British efforts but imbued with American meanings, encouraged an evangelical tone in the churches and produced a growing number of organizations to do various kinds of missionary work. There were, of course, the foreign missions. But domestic projects also began to appear in the form of voluntary societies. In 1791, Philadelphians, including Benjamin Rush, founded a citywide Sunday School Society. In 1792, the Connecticut General Association of the Presbyterian Church began coordinating efforts to organize churches for emigrant settlers in New York. Various domestic missionary societies were founded in Massachusetts and Connecticut in the late 1790s and early

1800s. In 1816, Bible distribution societies in the middle states and New England combined to form the American Bible Society. A year earlier, evangelicals of the Presbyterian and Congregational churches had formed the American Education Society, whose goal was to promote the training of ministers in unprecedented numbers to staff global missionary efforts.

Lyman Beecher actively engaged in these efforts but made his special contribution in the campaign for "moral societies" aimed at bringing public life into line with what most devout Calvinists conceived of as the outer signs of sacred order. In addition to promoting organizational efforts, he preached sermons over the years in which he placed various reform efforts within the cosmic drama. In his sermons one can see the extension and modification of Dwight's vision of America and New England's status as "spiritual Israel," follow the shift from a cosmic drama in which a tribalistic New England comprised the elect to one in which Beecher declared open entry to all Americans (and truly all human beings) who would surrender themselves to God, and trace the evolution of the mission of the elect from tending God's world to battling the Devil as the millennial day approached.

This commitment to reform blossomed early in his ministry at East Hampton, where he helped to create a local society and preached a sermon to justify such a novel effort, *The Practicability of Suppressing Vice, by Means of Societies Instituted for That Purpose* (1803).[29] The sermon placed reform efforts within the traditional conception of a Godly community that, even as Beecher spoke, had been under challenge for some years. He began by noting that the battle against vice had been a matter of great importance through the ages; the stickier question was whether societies of citizens formed for such a purpose were "a practicable thing." He argued yes: just as God had provided a remedy for every disease in nature, so in society He had provided for citizens to act in concert against evil.[30]

He defended this seemingly unremarkable proposition by positing a view of original sin learned from Dwight. "The majority," Beecher noted, "are in the beginning moral. They have the power, and if awake, the inclination, to limit the prevalence of vice." Sin grew powerful through its own deceit, the indifference of society, and the passive fear of individuals. Moral societies awakened the individual. They also allowed a citizen to act without fear against sin, since "numbers [were] prepared to uphold him, and back his reproof." As a weight thrown in on the side of virtue in the battle for "public opinion," a reform society could stigmatize as moral crimes behavior that remained legal in a republic with guarantees of personal and religious freedom.[31]

Beecher also demonstrated that such organizations had proven themselves in history. He recounted the success of a late seventeenth-century society that battled sin in a debauched London, and the victories of a similar group in Maryland. More recently, he noted, citizens of Franklin,

Massachusetts, formed a society for the reformation of morals and, in 1798, a Philadelphia committee was created to "aid the civil magistrate in the suppression of vice and immorality."[32] Beecher admitted that such action might cause controversy but argued that controversy was preferable to allowing sin and vice to flourish unchecked. He urged the citizens of East Hampton to look at their own recent success. "It has not indeed made its members perfect," he stated, "or annihilated vice in the community. Did any expect it would? We are not angels, but men."[33]

Beecher anticipated a more serious problem, and also revealed his own characteristically incomplete acceptance of religious toleration, when he discussed the "popular distinction, craftily made between immorality and irreligion." Some in the community might agree to attack immorality, especially actions that threatened "the security both of life and property," but not irreligion, which injured "no one but the subject." He rejected such an easy distinction, asserting that irreligion was the "most fruitful cause" of immorality and quoting George Washington to the effect that a "national morality [could not] prevail in exclusion of religious principles."[34]

When Beecher listed his targets, he revealed that at the heart of the matter was the preservation of a sacred order in communal life. "The name of God is blasphemed," he began; "the bible is denounced; the sabbath is profaned; the public worship of God is neglected; intemperance hath destroyed its thousands, and is preparing the destruction of thousands more; while luxury, with its diversified evils, with a rapidity unparalleled, is spreading in every direction, and through every class."[35] The crucial sins, then, were public violations of the sacred—breaking the Sabbath, taking the Lord's name in vain, neglecting worship—or those private vices that destroyed sacred sensibility. All had to do with defiance of a Godly order. Beecher feared that liberty would be destroyed by sin, but he made it clear that he was referring not so much to the liberty gained through the Revolution as to the Godly and organic liberty of civic life in New England.[36]

Having looked at the community, Beecher placed reform in a broader historical and cosmic setting. He noted that the founders of New England had built their system on religion. They "taught it to their children, they taught it in their schools, and made provision to have it taught on their sabbath. . . . Religion is the corner stone; remove it, and the building falls."[37] Now that their society had become part of a republic, he argued, the role of religion was crucial: "In proportion as the fear of God is effaced, crimes will abound." Such blasphemy would end in tyranny.[38] Beecher saw the local congregation and New England as the key guardians of national well-being: "let every town reform, and the reformation will be national."[39] Beecher gave his parishioners a choice: preserve the virtue and glory of the past or meet disaster at the hands of God. This last point was, in fact, the essential message that would thread its way through all his sermons, even as new causes evolved.

Less than three years later, Beecher delivered *The Remedy for Duelling*, a sermon of far more urgent tone that typified the increasing gloom settling over Orthodox New England.[40] On July 11, 1804, Aaron Burr had killed Alexander Hamilton in a duel. For many in the land, the event became an electrifying symbol of the decline of the same public order that Orthodoxy had proclaimed as essential to the preservation of liberty.[41] *The Remedy for Duelling* articulated that fear but couched both problem and solution in important new ways. It personalized sin and its consequences and proposed a political solution that pointed toward evangelical rather than peculiarly Federalist unity.

Beecher took Isaiah 59:14–15 as his text: "And judgment is turned away backward and justice standeth afar off; for truth is fallen in the streets, and equity cannot enter." From the first page he evoked the mood of the jeremiad. The "profligate example" of the Israelites' rulers, the ruin of their society, and most especially the apathy of the common people stood as a warning. As yet no equally dire condition afflicted New England. However, many of America's leaders already posed as men of honor while despising the "laws of their country and their God" and "adjust[ing] with weapons of death their own private quarrels." As among the Jews, those who might have stopped such a cardinal evil as duelling remained "indolent spectators of the wide-wasting evil."[42]

Officeholding duellists, Beecher argued, had created an aristocracy of sinners who showed only contempt for the common man. The highly touted code of honor, he chided, existed as "the guardian of honorable men only. . . . It is for the interest of this noble portion of the human race that honor legislates. But for you, the common people, the ignoble vulgar, it has no concern."[43] He might be "a gambler, a prodigal, a fornicator, an adulterer, a drunkard, a murderer, and not violate the laws of honor."[44] Yet a perverted system of honor and the cachet of upper-class privilege and education that came with it protected the duellist from realizing his sin.[45]

Those who have characterized the social vision of Beecher as élitist have, in fact, not grappled with his sermon on duelling. It attacked special privilege and defended a cohesive society of common values and virtues. The enemy was the caprice of individual privilege that defied common law and morality. Duelling was a "system of absolute despotism, tending directly and powerfully to the destruction of civil liberty."[46] By breaking the law and forcing others to do so without regard for consequences, it struck at the heart of the republican social compact.[47] It openly mocked the equal enforcement of and "sacred regard to law" that were essential to a republic. Moreover, it restrained "liberty of speech and of the press," for "who will publish, when the duellist stands before him with pistol at the breast?"

Indeed, who would choose to enter public life if he wished to avoid the duel?[48]

Beecher decried the evils of duelling in ways that prefigured later reform rhetoric. The duellist became the first in a line of social sinners—later would come the drunkard, the slaveholder, and others—who were largely to be feared rather than pitied, their dire effect on society far outweighing the implicit pathos of their own condition. He painted the consequences of sin in a colorful, personalized rhetoric that became routine in abolitionist, temperance, and body reform advocacy: "Ah, it is done!—the blood streams.—The victim welters on the ground. And see, the victor savage running from the field."[49] No longer vice in general, but rather a particular, hydra-headed act laden with symbolic and real implication, threatened the nation.

Beecher proposed his remedy. The public should express their outrage by voting duellists out of office.[50] Apathy would only bring disaster. He feared that duelling would become "as common, as irremediable, and as little thought of, as assassination is in Spain, in Italy, and South-America."[51] Yet the people of these societies, without the benefits of true republican government, were less responsible for their situation than Americans would be. Like the Israelites, Americans had it within their power to reform; they could quickly snuff out duelling at the ballot box. If they did not, they became "partakers in the sin" and "accountable for all the evils which will ensue, and which you may now, so easily prevent."[52] Indeed, by the end of the sermon the threat seemed imminent. "Duelling is a great national sin," Beecher declared. "With the exception of a small section of the union [New England], the whole land is defiled with blood."[53] God watched, "his quiver full of arrows, his sword impatient of confinement. Ten thousand plagues stand ready to execute his wrath."[54]

Beecher delivered *The Remedy for Duelling* at a time when the Federalist party had begun to suffer mightily at the hands of the Jeffersonians. Yet he pointedly spoke of duelling as a domain of the privileged, not of one or another political persuasion. "The crime we oppose is peculiar to no party," he stressed; "it is common to all."[55] Nor was this a cynical ruse. Certainly Beecher voted Federalist, but he also had been disillusioned by the political system in general and driven toward a course above party politics marked out by essentially conservative Christian principles. Nor should a partisan subtext be assumed simply on the basis of the Burr-Hamilton duel. Rather, Beecher gave his sermon in an era marked by incidents of political violence in which some of the most publicized cases were instigated by Federalists.[56]

Beecher's real vision was not Federalist but Manichean, one that polarized the world into those who defended Godly order in society and those who attacked it. In the short run, the Federalists might seem friendliest to his cause. However, all political parties had one primary and corrupting goal: to win elections. Beecher played for sacred stakes, God's approbation of America. In fact, the duelling sermon contained his boldest assertion yet of the role of the believing Christian in the social and political world. "If only the members of christian churches become decided in their opposition to duelling," he declared, "it will produce a sensation through the state. . . . But ten persons, in every congregation in the state, would constitute a weight of influence, ultimately decisive."[57]

The sermon on duelling thus envisioned a third force in politics, at once beyond the reach of partisanship and informed by a sacred vision of America. Yet the "nation" he referred to seemed most often to be New England rather than the United States. Furthermore, Beecher's cosmic drama still promised "only" a morally healthy society. Reform's truly national and millennial metaplay had not yet been conceived.

The decade following this sermon, however, brought challenges to New England and to Orthodoxy that spurred a profound change in Beecher's thought. A coalition of Jeffersonians, non-Orthodox religionists, and renegade Federalists pressed for disestablishment of the church in Connecticut, while in Massachusetts disestablishment efforts and a Unitarian insurgency compounded Orthodoxy's woes. On the national scene, Jefferson's disastrous Embargo Act of 1807, an attempt to prevent British seizure of American ships and impressment of American sailors by declaring economic neutrality in the Napoleonic Wars, left New England's ports desolated. By 1812, the United States was at war with Britain.

To Beecher and others in Orthodoxy's ranks, these events smacked of the end of days. After all, the Baptists, Methodists, Episcopalians, and an assortment of fringe sects who attacked the established churches also supported those in power who were fast making irreligion the watchword of American society. They also had brought on a war in which America aided infidel France against an England that had spearheaded the drive for Christian missions around the world. Many of New England's Orthodox ministers saw in these events nothing less than the coming together of the armies of the Antichrist before Armageddon.[58]

This stance resulted in a double focus. Looking outward, ministers forthrightly criticized the Jeffersonian government, the war, and various other sins of the opposition. Looking inward, they excoriated the chosen people of New England for being lax in their holiness. Beecher, in his published sermons, concentrated on the latter theme and, in the tradition of the region's sermonizing, spelled out sources for renewal.[59]

A Reformation of Morals Practicable and Indispensable, preached in New Haven on October 27, 1812, was a burning jeremiad.[60] Beecher's literal message resembled that of *The Practicability of Suppressing Vice* (1803) and paraphrased or quoted verbatim large portions of the earlier piece.[61] Yet its tone reflected the desperation of New England in 1812. Ezekiel 33:10 was

Beecher's watchword: "Therefore, Thou, O son of man, speak unto the house of Israel, thus ye speak, saying, if our transgressions and our sins be upon us and we pine away in them, how should we then live?" The consequences of the embargo and war were bad enough. Yet New England had forged a covenant with God, and the punishment awaiting an unrepentant breaker of covenants would be worse still. "If the Most High should stand aloof, and cast not a single ingredient into our cup of trembling," Beecher declared, "it would seem to be full of superlative woe. But he will not stand aloof. As we shall have begun an open controversy with him, he will contend openly with us."[62]

America's Israel must choose, figuratively and literally, between life or death. Beecher made it clear that he meant New England, indicating little sense of a broader American identity. He even implied that the American Revolution had led to his own region's undoing, compromising its unique "institutions and habits." "Divested of these," Beecher warned, "like Samson shorn of his locks, she will become as weak and contemptible as any other land."[63] He vivified the fast-deteriorating state of affairs and its ultimate meaning: "Drunkards reel through the streets. . . . Profane swearing is heard, and even by magistrates, as though they heard it not. . . . The Sabbath is trodden down by a host of men, whom shame alone, in better days, would have deterred entirely from the sin." The everyday habits that had held New England society together were being destroyed at the foundation: "The mass is changing. We are becoming another people."[64]

Beecher preached a return to the spirit of pre-Revolutionary New England. New Englanders had "listened to the syren song of vain philosophy and floated listlessly down the stream" till very close to the precipice: "Shall we despair to row back, when danger inspires courage, and calls aloud for a common effort?"[65] He reminded his audience: "Our fathers were not fools; as far from it were they as modern philosophers from wisdom." They understood the wickedness of man and the need for "moral restraint," parental authority, and the "coertion of law." With such wisdom they had "established, and for a great while preserved, the most perfect state of society, probably, that has ever existed in this fallen world."[66]

Beecher called for a mighty effort to reconstruct the sacred order of the fathers. Voluntary societies, rather than being simply instruments for moral enlightenment, should act as "a sort of disciplined moral militia." Beecher insisted on the thorough and vigorous enforcement of existing laws against Sabbath-breaking, intemperance, and other "immorality." In addition, he recommended that "a more extended concert could be formed of wise and good men, to devise ways and means of suppressing vice and guarding the public morals."[67]

Finally, he underlined the importance of preserving "indissoluble the connexion between sin and shame." The modern tendency had been to muddy the distinction between right and wrong by avoiding public censure of those engaged in vice. "If we would reform the land," he affirmed, "we must return therefore, to the stern virtue of our ancestors, and lay the whole tax of shame upon the dissolute and immoral."[68]

For Beecher and those like him, at stake was spiritual Israel and the Godly way of life it had perfected. "Another New-England, nor we, nor our children shall ever see," he cried, "if this be destroyed." The fact that New England was "becoming another people" assumed cosmic historical meaning. For it was not simply a strict code of laws that made New England what it was, but rather the Providential nature of its mission and its American setting. "No where could they have succeeded," he emphasized, "but in a wilderness, where they gave the precepts and set the example, and made, and executed the laws."[69]

Beecher's concerns were not with sacred issues as opposed to democratization, disestablishment, economic policy, the Federalist demise, the war with England, or even the fate of the Republic. Rather he saw developments in what we call the secular sphere as shadows of the cosmic drama, as the sinews of human action and fortune that tied society's history to God's metahistorical calendar. They were signs of the time through which to read unfolding developments in that drama. "The day of vengeance is in his heart, the day of judgment has come," he admonished his flock; "the great earthquake which sinks Babylon is shaking the nations, and the waves of the mighty commotion are dashing upon every shore."[70]

To Beecher the signs of God's "strange work of national desolation" were everywhere apparent in the United States. The economy had slumped. The party system had "shaken our institutions to their foundations, debased our morals, and awakened animosities" that threatened "dismemberment and civil war." From the coast came "the alarms and the plagues of war." From the frontier came "too the trumpet of war, mingling with the warhoop of the savage, and the cries and dying groans of murdered families." In a clear reference to slavery, Beecher warned that "in the south, a volcano, whose raging fires and murmuring thunders have long been suppressed, [was] now with loud admonition threatening an eruption."[71]

However, in true jeremiadical counterpoint, he assured his audience that all was not lost. In New England, the laws, customs, and God-fearing people necessary to a reformation were sufficient to the task. His people need only repent and reform. "He has promised to help them," Beecher declared, for they were God's chosen ones. "The God in whose help we confide," he reminded his listeners, "is also our fathers' God, who remembers mercy to the thousandth generation of them that fear him and keep his commandments. Within the broad circumference of this covenant we stand."[72]

Beecher saw the workings of God in revivals of religion, in new efforts at missionary work within the nation, and in the creation of societies to combat moral crime. "The last vial of the wrath of God is running," he noted with millennial glee. "The angel having the everlasting gospel to preach to men has begun his flight." New England must act: "On the confines of such a day shall we despair? While its blessed light is beginning to shine, shall we give up our laws and institutions and sink down to the darkness and torments of the bottomless pit?"[73]

By concentrating on the apocalyptic implications of the war period, Beecher and numerous other ministers in New England avoided a calamity that might have come crashing down upon them when the war finally ended. While the Hartford Convention dealt a death to the Federalist party, and advocates of disestablishment gained ground in both Massachusetts and Connecticut, these events clarified Beecher's vision of the cosmic drama instead of destroying it. Indeed, Beecher and his compatriots soon offered their own compelling contribution to the swelling of nationalist pride and identity that followed the war.[74]

At the heart of this transformation lay the emergence of a new way to look at New England, America, and the millennial future. Beecher led, and many others eventually followed, in transferring New England's identity as spiritual Israel to America as a whole, and in widening the almost tribalistic sense of chosenness from New Englanders to the regenerate of America and the world. In doing so, Beecher and others moved the ministerial tradition they represented from the narrowness of the New England drama toward one no less Manichean but infinitely more dynamic.[75]

The change was not sudden, and the first steps seemed quite in line with older defenses of tradition. In the war and post-war period, Beecher and other ministers across Connecticut and Massachusetts were seeking to curb vice in the form of Sabbath-breaking, intemperance, and law enforcement. Following the example of British missionary organizations, they also were consolidating efforts to spread the message of revealed Christianity throughout the world. Benevolent and missionary societies that had begun piecemeal in the late 1790s and early 1800s now accelerated their work as part of a program of renewal in dark and prophetic times.[76]

Beecher was at virtually every turning. He took the lead in organizing the clergy of his state for regular evangelical itineraries, helped found in 1813 the Connecticut Society for the Suppression of Vice and Promotion of Good Morals, and, in the decade following 1815, helped create from state and local groups a variety of national Bible and missionary societies. These efforts formed the organizational background and immediate antecedents of radical reform.

The reform and benevolent societies of this period looked both backward and forward, and the tension of contradiction surfaced almost as soon as they were created. For example, Beecher's Connecticut Moral Society, which had initially seen itself as "a sort of disciplined moral militia" to aid and pressure civil authorities in the enforcement of blasphemy, Sabbatarian, and intemperance laws, soon found that this produced little in the way of results.[77]

Success was possible only for a reform vision geographically more inclusive and non-denominational in its outlook. Beecher's sermons, as reflections of both a visionary and an activist, are particularly useful in tracking this transformation. He came to speak of America in place of New England when it came to millennial destiny, and he turned more optimistic about its prospects. Increasingly he also took a position of evangelical ecumenicism in defining proper recruits for the elect in the great struggle against Evil. In doing so, he questioned the wisdom of his clerical forebears on the crucial point of membership, and on that basis he rewrote New England's metahistory. These developments brought him to spiritual maturity and confidence and contributed to the creation of a cosmic landscape that became the natural backdrop of radical reform.

One can see the process of change beginning as early as his 1814 sermon *The Building of Waste Places*, an elegy to a once holy Connecticut landscape scarred by spiritual division and loss.[78] "Not a few societies have ceased to hear those doctrines of the Gospel," Beecher lamented, "by the instrumentality of which the Spirit of God awakens, converts, and sanctifies men. A number of churches have become feeble, and, by hard struggling, prolong from year to year the enjoyment of divine institutions; while some have long since fallen, and are now lying in utter desolation."[79] Beecher sought to account for this tragic decline in the heartland of spiritual Israel and to suggest means of restoring Christian virtue and unity.

He thus recast sacred history by stressing the mistakes of the spiritual ancestors he had previously held up as ideals of Christian wisdom. Firm in his evangelical commitments and sure that the world divided most easily into the regenerate and the unregenerate, he saw the roots of future divisions among New England's Christians in the compromises of his forebears concerning church membership. Especially deplorable to Beecher was the so-called Half-way Covenant, which he charged had allowed those "destitute of piety" to become church members and have their children baptized. The purpose had been to bolster church membership, but the result was that "owning the covenant . . . became a common, thoughtless ceremony."[80]

Beecher argued that the Half-way Covenant began a process that eventually led to the "convulsions" of the Great Awakening. "The opposition which was made to this work of God by the unconverted, the formal and the timid," Beecher noted, excited "intemperate zeal" and prejudice against "a learned ministry and the congregational order." It "rent many churches, and laid the foundation for that diversity of religious opinion and worship" that lay at the root of Connecticut's problems.[81] Meanwhile, infidel philosophies and party strife had polluted the spiritual stream, while church battled church over minor points and competed for members. All these forces contributed to the rising power of those who wished to disestablish the Orthodox church and in fact end any kind of state support for religion.[82]

What could be done? According to Beecher, ministers from strong congregations should preach to congregations without ministers; evangelists should comb the state and renew interest in religion; Sabbath schools should be created across the state to provide for the coming generation. All these efforts could be funded and supervised by church associations. If the churches made such efforts, God might then "build the old wastes among us by a high hand, and an outstretched arm."[83]

Beecher's critique of the fathers in *Building of Waste Places* helped etch for himself a distinctive place among New England divines. His evangelical program, especially in its almost singular devotion to revivals as the key to conversion, moved well beyond Timothy Dwight's vision.[84] In his 1817 sermon at the ordination of Dwight's son Sereno, preached just eight months after the death of the senior minister, Beecher made clear the separation from his spiritual father.[85] As opposed to virtually every one of his prior published sermons, *The Bible a Code of Laws* made no reference to New England tradition per se. It asserted the centrality of the Bible and the absolute necessity of conversion to the proper comprehension of God's laws. The variation of the cosmic drama it recounted pitted regenerate against unregenerate rather than New England against the Antichrist. Beecher's enemies were now Unitarians, Episcopalians, and freethinkers, or any who scoffed at the Bible as a divine gift or who saw little difference between human beings in their natural and converted spiritual states.

Against these assorted enemies, Beecher celebrated the global democracy of conversion rather than Yankee tribal claims. Defending the veracity of witnesses who attested to their change of heart, he embraced all of humankind. Women, children, men young and old, rich and poor, reformed sinners, Europeans, Americans, and Hottentots had all declared "that with them, old things had passed away, and all things become new."[86]

Beecher's restructuring of the cosmic drama became even more evident after a coalition of Orthodoxy's enemies finally secured disestablishment in Connecticut in 1818. At first depressed by this apparent victory for infidelity, Beecher came to see it as a blessing in disguise. He recounted this change of mind as a revelation in the overblown prose of the famous "Toleration Dream."[87] Yet his positive assessment of the disestablished church also drew upon a new reading of religious history, one he set forth in *The Design, Rights, and Duties of Local Churches*.[88] In essence, he asked: How did we come to this place? The historical frame widened from New England to the entire history of humankind.

Beecher began at the beginning. The first Church of God, "commencing its operations soon after the fall," was a patriarchy run by a priest, the one common ancestor of the various peoples of the earth. The patriarch's longevity, Beecher recounted, "extending in the first ages to nearly a thousand years," rendered a Bible unnecessary "and gave to his precepts and example, authority for the maintenance of truth and the instituted worship of God."[89] The next stage of church history came as society progressed from the pastoral to the agricultural and commercial states, and from one kin group to amalgamated tribes and constituted nations. These changes, the reduction in longevity to about "one hundred and twenty years," and the scattering of families destroyed traditional patriarchy. Humankind traded "the knowledge and worship of the true God, for the fictions and impurities of idolatry."[90]

The Jews reacted by organizing a church based on associations of families, "each of which was made responsible to the community for its fidelity in upholding the instituted worship, and for the fidelity of each, the whole community [was] made responsible to God."[91] God gave to the Jews a written revelation and a temporary dispensation, so that true religion might be preserved until the "desire of nations had come" and Christianity was born. Christians began the tradition of deeming those who came together to maintain God's ordinances as a church, "a society incorporated by the God of heaven with specific chartered privileges." This was the origin of the local church, he noted, and such churches would someday embrace all the world.[92]

Beecher sought this new spiritual lineage because events of the past decade had delegitimated prior understandings. Much as new sects often traced their practices to the primitive church, so Beecher felt the necessity to establish anew the bona fides of his own faith. He knew that God's covenant with the Puritan churches made no sense in a pluralistic world where state and church had been separated, and in which the field of action was America and not New England.

Having placed the local church in a broad (humanity since the beginning) rather than narrow (New England) cosmic history, Beecher listed its functions: to prepare believers for Heaven; to protect the purity of the Gospel; to maintain holy order in society, including the protection of the Sabbath and maintenance of public worship of God; to educate the young and the non-believer in true religion; to raise up teachers and ministers of the Gospel; and to aid in the spread of the Gospel by missionaries throughout the country and the world.[93]

Most important, however, membership in a church must be limited to those who stood in "personal holiness in the sight of God, and a credible profession of holiness before men." In justifying such a requirement, he again looked beyond New England to all of history, beginning with God's rejection of Cain's offering and acceptance of Abel's "by faith." He noted that God also welcomed Abraham, Isaac, and Jacob, while shunning the faithless Ishmael and Esau. The Jews earned their right to be the chosen of God by faith but lost it forever "by crucifying the Lord of glory." In the Christian era, true membership in the church could only come by the experience and profession of faith.[94]

As a result, Beecher endorsed a broad but specifically defined ecumenicism. He called upon denominations that required demonstrations of personal holiness for membership, "though differing in their forms of worship and modes of administration, and to some extent, in their views of doctrine," to regard each other with "christian affection," to refrain from "all acts of mutual aggression," and to cooperate in the common interests of "the Redeemer's kingdom." The new battle lines of a holy war were taking shape. Those who supported the standard of a change of heart battled against Popery, freethinking, Unitarianism, Episcopalianism, and other unregenerate philosophies or faiths. Revivals of religion across the land and the world became the basic strategy of ultimate millennial victory.[95]

Therein lay a contradiction, for in Beecher's vision religious toleration remained an unassimilated idea. In a strategic sense he might greet disestablishment as a great challenge, but what was one to do about the progress of religious error in the world and its deleterious effects on individuals, society, and the coming of the millennial day? It might not be enough to rebuild the waste places. Beecher continued to reconstruct the terms of the drama; old characters played augmented roles, and the grand finale—the millennial day—began to take on new and more vivid shape. A holy war made possible by religious liberty still had the ultimate goal of wiping out heresy.

In 1823, Beecher delivered the definitive battle cry against the unregenerate, *The Faith Once Delivered to the Saints.*[96] Broaching the central issue in no uncertain terms, he named the articles of true Christian faith. Religious Truth, he asserted, made it clear that men were free agents; that divine law required love of God and love of man; that man's ancestors had violated the law of their own free will (original sin), and that this apostasy, repeated by all men, could only be atoned through faith in Jesus Christ. Only God through the Holy Spirit could save men, but ordinarily saving grace would not be withheld from one who honestly opened himself to faith; while the faithful would receive salvation, the sinner would be punished forever. Beecher concluded with two essential points. God expressed on earth a providential government and history "known and approved of by him from the beginning." Finally, God revealed Himself "as existing in three persons, the Father, the Son, and the Holy Ghost; possessing distinct and equal attributes, and, in some unrevealed manner, so united, as to constitute one God."[97]

Beecher called these truths "the Evangelical System," while those who opposed them were advocates of "the Liberal System." Unitarianism and historical Biblical scholarship, as well as all other forms of overt and covert infidelity, were offenders against the faith.[98] In order to protect religious Truth against pollution in a pluralistic society, he advocated a system of literary institutions guided by the tenets of evangelicalism. Members of the evangelical churches, Beecher declared, should in fact "withhold her sons from those literary institutions which are hostile to the doctrines of grace" and guided by a "perverted literature."[99]

Beecher underlined the church's responsibility to tell the truth about the wages of sin and misbelief even in a society tolerant of error, because sins that are not crimes by society's definition would still be punished in eternity. "The character, law, gospel, and providence of God, are realities," he noted, "as unmodified by human opinion, as the laws of the natural world." Whether criminal or not, behavior against "the true character and government of God" would bring on personal and social calamity.[100] Beecher thus reasserted the need to preach the wages of sin and error, whoever might take offense. "The Scribes and the Pharisees would not have been offended at Christ, but would have admired his catholic spirit," he noted, "if to his doctrine he had subjoined; 'These are my opinions;—but those who differ from me, are doubtless honest and sincere, and will be mercifully accepted by our heavenly Father.'"[101] If one did not preach the horrid truth, one was condemning one's audience to eternal Hell.

Such doctrines became extremely important to the development of reform. They encouraged the invocation of higher-law doctrine by abolitionists and others involved in controversial reforms. When applied in a nondenominational social setting, they implicitly demanded a fleshing out of symbols, rituals, and doctrines of sin and atonement. Reform was nothing if not a system of moral law created to augment and at times supersede the law of the state.

Also relevant to reform was Beecher's post-disestablishment disillusion with politics. He recognized that members of local or regional churches were now part of a national and pluralistic state, one that could not promote local preferences in religion. Beecher argued, in fact, that only on occasion did it seem proper for Christians to speak as one on great national questions: in the debate over a declaration of war or, "as in England, the abolition of the slave trade." He reminded his audience that "the injudicious association of religion with politics, in the time of Cromwell, brought upon evangelical doctrine and piety, in England, an odium which has not ceased to this day."[102] As a result, he now totally rejected a close alliance of church and political party. "It annihilates spirituality of mind," he declared, "prevents a spirit of prayer, and efforts for revivals of religion; and renders christians the mere dupes and tools of unprincipled, ambitious men." Nor was an established church to be desired. Once it had served the purpose of foundation-building, but now it could only cause denominational strife.[103]

Meanwhile, signs of the time in the mid-1820s brought new portents of progress and danger to Beecher and other New England evangelicals increasingly prone to millennial Manicheism. On the side of the Lord, American commercial growth, progress in education, and territorial expansion signalled the rising fortune of God's nation. Continued reports of revivals in New England and the West, the formation of national Bible and tract societies, and increased American participation in foreign mission work gave confidence to evangelicals that American power would be arrayed in the ranks of Christianity. In the world beyond America, the advance of British missions also buoyed hopes. The victories of Bolívar in South America symbolized the growth of democracy and the demise of the papist empires in the Western hemisphere.

At the same time, the Devil continued to wreak havoc in Europe and threaten the United States. Turkey and Greece were enmeshed in bloody struggle, while in Russia and France tyranny, intrigue, and revolt left the masses of people ignorant and in chains. At home, the Missouri Compromise of 1820 had again displayed the power of the same Southern slaveholders who had instigated the War of 1812, while the near election of Jackson in 1824—Jackson the warrior, drinker, and owner of slaves—gave politics an air of dark foreboding.[104] Indeed, no party existed to uphold the evangelical view, and as most states expanded their electorates by dropping or reducing landholding requirements for white males, the coming danger seemed even more ominous.

As if to underline his concern for this crescendo of portent, Beecher accepted a call from the Hanover Street Church in Boston, where he moved in 1826. The move was in keeping with his changing vision of the evangelical struggle, for by moving to one of evangelicalism's major capitals he committed himself to the international struggle more than to the well-being of a single congregation. That commitment received vivid expression in his sermon before the American Board of Missions, *Resources of the Adversary and Means of their Destruction* (1827).[105] He announced that the great millennial conflict was nigh, one in which the Gospel of the heart would become "the predominant spring of action, and its morality the governing rule of all mankind."[106] God's enemies would be many: idolaters; imposters such as Moslems and Jews; the Pope and his church; despotic governments and the societies they controlled; crime, by which Beecher meant Sabbath-breaking, theatergoing, intemperance, breaking the Golden Rule in commercial enterprise, and partaking of false codes of honor; liberal religion; and the false prophets of impure revivals.[107]

Beecher asserted that such opposition had in fact created the "great commotions and distress of nations" prophesied as prelude to the universal reign of Christ on earth.[108] "Great voices will be heard in heaven, saying, The kingdoms of this world are become the kingdoms of our Lord and of his Christ: as the voice of many waters, and of mighty thunderings, saying, Alleluia for the Lord God omnipotent reigneth."[109] The Christian's role in this grand finale lay in the promotion of revivals. "All other means," Beecher declared, "—science, legislation, philosophy, eloquence, and argument—have been relied on in vain." No longer could the righteous be defensive; their watchword must be "March."[110]

Beecher's other watchword was "More." Christians needed more faith in the church of God, more intense love of Jesus, more decided action, more courage, more vigorous effort to increase the number of evangelical churches, more evangelical education for the young, more charitable effort, and more joint action across denominational lines. "Like the tribes of Israel," he declared, "we may all encamp about the tabernacle of God— each under his own standard—and when the ark advances, may all move onward, terrible only to the powers of darkness."[111]

In December 1827, at Plymouth, Massachusetts, Beecher sketched out further dimensions of his metahistorical vision in a sermon appropriately entitled *The Memory of Our Fathers*.[112] Having experienced disestablishment and struggled through a period in which he reformulated the proper relation of church to society and cosmic history, he had come to Plymouth to resacralize the American nation. In doing so, he extended his label of "spiritual Israel" now not only to Christians but to the Christian nation of the United States of America. It had become the model for what all nations must become before the millennial day arrived.

At first he defined America's greatness by measuring its light implicitly against the world's darkness, expanding his sense of the causes of ignorance and poverty to include economic deprivation. "The monopoly of the soil," he asserted, "must be abolished." It had left man in ignorance and sin. The majority of humankind had been degraded as slaves or tenants too long, working for a small minority who had crushed them "beneath the weight, and have lived on the borders of starvation; the sickness of a week, and often of a single day, rendering them paupers." Yet Beecher worried also about workers, the urban poor, and the rootless among the military. The holding of land among the few, he noted, had more recently "sent another large class of the community into manufacturing establishments, to wear out their days in ignorance and hopeless poverty; and another to the camp and navy, where honor and wealth await the few, and ignorance, and an early grave, the many." He called for radical action to redirect the energies of those previously "tortured by their oppressions" to states of "ignorance, improvidence, reckless indifference, turbulence, and crime. . . . Man must be unshackled and stimulated. But to accomplish this, the earth must be owned by those who till it."[113]

"To effect the moral renovation of the world," Beecher asserted, certain corollary changes must also be made. Despotic governments must be turned into democratic republics: "The mass of mankind must be enlightened and qualified for self government, and must yield obedience to delegated power." Humankind's "rights of conscience" must also be restored. All must be given the skills and rights to discern religious truths without official churches and religious intolerance. "It has been contended, that christianity cannot exist in this world without the aid of religious establishments," Beecher noted rhetorically. "But, with more truth it might be said, that, from the beginning to this day, it has existed in spite of them."[114]

Strange enough to hear these words from a minister who had once defended Connecticut's Standing Order, it was stranger still to hear them in a sermon glorifying the memory of the Puritan fathers. Yet Beecher's reconciliation of old and new even rejuvenated the Puritan idea of a "city on a hill." God needed an example, he said, to guide the world in its search for new institutions: "Some nation, itself free, was needed, to blow the trumpet and hold up the light." No such bastions of liberty and faith existed in Africa, Asia, or continental Europe. England came closest, but it was overburdened with monopolies of land and power. Only the history of the United States bore the hallmarks of God's grand plan.[115]

Of course, Beecher noted, America itself had evolved. With independence and the growth of the nation, religious pluralism and liberty made impossible the old institutions of moral discipline. Then "God began to pour out his Spirit upon the churches; and voluntary associations of christians were raised up to apply and extend that influence, which the law could no longer apply." These were the "providential substitutes for those legal provisions of our Fathers" that had become obsolete.[116] God's blessing on the institutions of the United States had made it a new spiritual Israel and explained its triumphs. The miracle of America's survival, Beecher declared, "the enemy beheld with wonder, and our Fathers with thanksgiving and praise."[117]

With this crown of chosenness, America would enter the millennial fray. America's example had already inspired revolutions in France, Spain, Naples, and Greece. Although such uprisings had been unsuccessful, Beecher maintained, similar attempts to gain freedom would someday succeed: "[Tyrants] can no more hold the heaving mass, than the chains of Xerxes could hold the Hellespont vexed with storms."[118] Closer to home, westward emigration posed the greatest challenge. Voluntary societies must take the Gospel beyond the Mississippi, beyond even the Rockies, and "pour their waters of life into the ocean beyond; and from the north to the south, they must bear salvation on their waves." At home and abroad, the battle raged and Christians responded. "Such an array of moral influence as is now comprehended in the great plan of charitable operations," Beecher trumpeted, "was never before brought to bear upon the nation. It moves onward, attended by fervent supplications, and followed by glorious and unceasing effusions of the Holy Spirit."[119]

By 1827, then, Beecher had restructured the vision of his sacred world. Having begun his career as a defender of hierarchy and New England's special chosenness, he now shouted the battle cry of liberty and consecrated the American nation as a new Israel to lead the nations to a millennial and democratic renovation of human existence. "It shall bring down the mountains, and exalt the valleys," he declared; "it shall send liberty and equality to all the dwellings of men. . . . Nor will the change be transient; it is the last dispensation of heaven for the relief of this miserable world, and shall bring glory to God in the highest, and upon earth peace, and good will to men."[120]

Lyman Beecher had come a long way in twenty years. He now offered defensive, class-ridden, tribalistic New England a new and militant millennial faith. Beecher envisioned the cosmic drama as one of universal struggle between the children of light and the children of darkness, led by an American nation in covenant with God. Ironically, such a development had only been possible because of the special sense of New England mission and its two-hundred-year-old tradition of intertwined earthly polity and Godly covenant. That irony would remain as, in the middle and late 1820s, radical New England religious virtuosos moved beyond Beecher in their work of universal emancipation.

III

War in the West: The Radical Revival

As signs of battle between God and the Devil heightened evangelical anticipation, New England's evangelicals responded with stronger measures. No longer would they battle sin simply town by town. New organizations such as the tract, Bible, and missionary societies, originally founded to bolster the old order, came closer to defining a new one. Yet even as they applauded their advances and united against common enemies, an unsettling air of doubt and stress tinctured their spiritual world. At least some among them felt contradictions between old and new ways, while others felt lost in the whirl of change. Like a complicated and powerful chemical reaction, such visions, tendencies, hopes, and fears combined to produce a radical and angry explosion of revival energy. That explosion in turn helped trigger radical reform.[1]

The first eruption occurred on New England's western frontier, where eyewitnesses to an evangelical revival sweeping that region reported as much rancor as harmony, a showering of grace that thundered sacred disorder on a scale that called to mind the legendary Awakening of the 1740s. The villains were not Baptists or Methodists nor some fringe sect but rather Presbyterian ministers and youthful converts who shared the millennial visions of New Divinity ministers like Lyman Beecher. How was it that revivals among New Englanders, so calm and harmonious in Connecticut, could take on the tenor of war in New York?

The answer was complex. Presbyterian and Congregational churches in New York's "burned-over district," first of all, found themselves in the more open atmosphere of what just had recently been frontier. They felt more strongly the pressures of rival churches and of discontent within their own congregations. New England transplants had attempted to reconstruct some of the corporate sense of town life that they had left behind, but in the freer environment of the West such efforts failed.

First, the towns and cities in western New York that came of age in post-Revolutionary America lacked the ruling structures and traditions of New England's establishment. Dissenters from old New England—Baptists, Methodists, Unitarians, and Universalists, as well as freethinkers—all proselytized, worshiped, and criticized each other openly, although they might sometimes unite around the watchword of "priestcraft" against the older establishments. At the same time, under the terms of the Plan of Union of 1801, innovators from within the old churches faced ecclesiastical oversight not from New England but rather from the conservative Philadelphia Presbyterian General Assembly.

Second, the rapid development of commercial and industrial economies in key cities such as Rochester, Troy, and Utica, among others, attracted all varieties of working people. This heterogeneity and the ever-expanding geography of these cities made problematic any organic sense of community. Economic expansion thus brought with it a palpable instability that defied any easy communal definition.[2] A fluid social structure combined with doctrines of individual liberty inherent in the revolutionary tradition and its structural counterpart, the party system, made replication of anything resembling the corporate traditions of Massachusetts or Connecticut out of the question. The changing realities of the new American nation far outpaced the ability of the old New England order to reproduce itself.

For many New England emigrants to the West, this presented no problem. Some had come precisely to escape the traditional limits put on religious dissent and creativity in their old towns, and they engaged in an intense, freewheeling promotion of their versions of religious Truth. Groups such as the Shakers and Campbellites found the tabula rasa of sparsely settled New York State an open field for experimentation. Baptists and Methodists vigorously recruited members and publicly debated theological points with Presbyterians and others. Striking new religions such as Mormonism took root in this free soil, taking advantage of its possibilities and reacting to the spiritual anarchy it seemed to proclaim.[3]

Even the once established churches could not help but be affected by such freedom, for if in New England dissent and rebellion grew up in the shadow of Orthodoxy, in New York Orthodoxy's experience was shaped by the boundlessness of experimentation. The "fit" of social standing, public respect, and good works no longer automatically insured that one possessed religious Truth, that the cosmos was in order. In fact, there were few socially instituted signs that one could any longer use as a yardstick for holiness. The flattening of hierarchies and the relativization of religious truths led to spiritual confusion. Furthermore, the temptations for consumption and display in a galloping economy eroded the New Englander's tradition of associating holiness and simplicity, especially in the boom towns. Change and temptation had beclouded those outer signs that gave Christians a sense of living within a sacred society. A writer for the Utica *Christian Repository* captured the mood perfectly:

> A covetous spirit—want of brotherly love—disregard of the sabbath— an alarming neglect of parents rightly to educate their children—an aversion to the exercise of discipline, on the alleged ground that it is repugnant to brotherly love and charity—a prevailing disposition to excuse, if not justify, and even imitate, the fashionable indulgences and vices of the present day—an unusual thirst for novelty, even in the things of religion—and a fondness for show and parade, especially in dress and equipage.

He went on to complain: "In looking over a promiscuous assembly, a stranger would be at a loss to distinguish Christians either by the simplicity of their dress, or their humble deportment."[4]

In this atmosphere of creeping indeterminacy, civil war broke out within the Presbyterian church, a war between those who wished to gird up the old lines of denominational and theological distinction and those, predominantly young men and women, who felt betrayed by the old church. From within this environment emerged two ministers—Charles Grandison Finney and Nathan S. S. Beman—who did most to shape the rebellion. Unlike Lyman Beecher, these rebel ministers had but weak ties with tradition. Finney had angrily festered in a painful daze when Orthodox paths to the sacred reached dead ends. Neither they nor their enemies displayed the finesse of a Beecher, nor his care for the delicacy of the social order. The rebels in the West burned with a yearning to renew the covenant amidst millennial hope and apocalyptic fear, but they acted with the fury of those who lacked secure moorings in the world.

Beman and Finney, the first a rebellious member of the regular ministry and the second a self-defined, self-made Christian itinerant whose church credentials were marginal, illustrated in their lives and influence the ways religious virtuosos could at crucial moments reformulate the sacred even in the most tradition-bound of sects. They deeply affected the religious life of the West, reform, and ultimately American religion in general. Beman, after facing various trials before Presbyterian bodies for heresy and bad temper, eventually became the acknowledged leader of New School Presbyterianism and an outspoken abolitionist. Finney was perhaps the most influential evangelist of the nineteenth century.

As opposed to Lyman Beecher, who grew up and trained in the heartland of New England Congregationalism, Nathan S. S. Beman was a product of its peripheries. Born in New Lebanon, New York, in 1785, Beman moved five years later with his family to a farm on the border of New York and Vermont. In many ways his youth was that of a farm boy, except that early on he demonstrated a propensity for religious matters. Beman received a typically incomplete education in his hometown and thirsted for something better. In 1803, he attended Williams College for some months. Lack of money forced him to return home, yet on the strength of a bit of education and some personal influence, he secured the position of local schoolmaster. In 1804, he began attending Middlebury College, which recently had been established by Orthodoxy to train ministers. There he experienced a religious revival. There too he came under the sway of Middlebury's president, Jeremiah Atwater, who had been a protégé of Timothy Dwight at Yale and apparently passed on to the young man Dwight's sense of the world. Beman graduated as valedictorian in 1807.[5]

He then moved to Newcastle, Massachusetts, as a schoolteacher and boarded with the local Congregational minister. Soon Beman was studying theology and searching his soul. In May of 1808, he gained membership in the Congregational church. Licensed to preach, he was called in 1810 to the Third Congregational Church of Portland, Maine, just as the Madison administration was moving toward war with England.

Signs of the embargo abounded in Portland: the unemployed wandered its streets, and empty wharves gave their silent testimony to economic catastrophe. When New England's churches protested the inevitable declaration of war, Beman contributed a scathing sermon. Like many ministers, he heaped scorn upon those who had made the war and pointed his finger at the specific religious failings of the President and his community. "In the city of Washington," he noted, "the Sabbath day is hardly known; and the Chief Magistrate of this Christian land rarely, if ever, graces a church with his presence. Surely the people of New England—the descendants of the pious pilgrims—ought to set a better example."[6]

Young Beman cut the figure of a typical New England minister wedded to the Orthodox worldview and its sense of New England's chosenness. However, ill health and the recommendation of a warmer climate for recuperation changed his life, sending him to Georgia for the next ten years. There he prospered as a minister and educator and was seriously courted for the presidency of the University of Georgia. After the death of his first wife, he married in 1821 a young widow, Caroline Bird Yancey, and by so doing became the owner of three slaves (whom he sold a year later) and a member of the local aristocracy.[7]

Such good fortune seemed only to bring out the Yankee in Beman. He had never lost touch with his native region and even traveled north to preach at various times during his southern residency. "Being uncommonly gifted in oratory," noted an 1816 account of his sermonizing during a trip to Connecticut, "he drew together a multitude of hearers from all quarters. The Holy Spirit attended his preaching, and he was peculiarly faithful to his Master, and the souls of his hearers. He was evidently made an instrument in the hand of God."[8]

That was in Connecticut. In Georgia he must have felt himself truly a stranger in a strange land, and no more so than when in 1821 he took over the editorship of *The Missionary*, an evangelical weekly he had helped found in 1819. Beman railed against intemperance, the theater, duelling, gambling, leisurely Sabbaths, and other regular features of southern life that rankled his pietistic mind. He urged the formation of moral reform societies and endorsed the American Colonization Society (though he condemned more straightforward emancipation plans as "wild and destructive"). Beman's editorials seemed mostly to court lively opposition. No doubt many Georgians agreed with John Taylor of Kentucky, who in his *Thoughts on Missions* (1820) claimed to smell in such activities "the New England Rat."[9] Not surprisingly, then, he accepted a call from the First Presbyterian Church in Troy, New York, and by the spring of 1823 had moved his family to that city.

In Troy, Beman's confidence and creativity blossomed, and by the mid-1820s he had articulated a distinctive theology that brought both praise and controversy. Beman's vision was less detailed and less wedded to the tradition of the local church than Beecher's, and more specifically concerned with the sacralization of America. He could imagine America in ways that Beecher could not, and could more easily create an all-embracing symbolic meaning for the nation. Beman's whole history had been of a man on the move, with less formal theological training and more varied geographical experience.

Beman revealed his metahistorical vision as it concerned the relation of religion to intellectual achievement in delivering an alumni address at Middlebury in 1825. Refuting the rationalist charge that religion hampered intellectual pursuits, Beman used the occasion to reconceive the cosmic drama and place America centrally within its millennial finale. Especially for a Calvinist, Beman's arguments seemed peculiarly unhampered by doubt about human ability. He saw religion and intellect as intertwined and prone to perversity if separated one from the other. Despite Adam's fall, he declared, men were "capable of attainments which [were], in their character, diversified and sublime." Indeed, though he assured his audience that religion and intellect could not "restore man to the participation of the Tree of Life, yet they can and do conduct him back, at least, to the confines of that Paradise which he has lost."[10]

Against the common but "utterly false" assertion that Christianity hampered intellectual pursuit, he argued that knowledge and religion were "associated in the same scenes; they exert[ed] their energies upon the same theatre." Throughout history pagan nations had produced "ignorance, puerility, and vice." Even Socrates, Plato, and Aristotle had to reject their society's religion in order to release their genius. "They had seen," Beman asserted, "though with a dim eye and at an immeasurable distance, that lamp which was lighted up on the summit of Mount Zion."[11]

What, then, of the claims that Christianity repressed intellectual inquiry? These, Beman noted, were all the fault of a Roman church that, "though it wears a christian name, and is covered by a christian mantle, was generated in the foulest principles of the human heart."[12] Not so Protestantism, which by returning to the Bible and true faith furnished the building blocks of "mental and moral philosophy." He declared: "Wherever religion and letters have established their empire, there the throne of despotism must crumble."[13] The American Revolution, in its overthrow of despotism and establishment of the individual's right to inquiry and conscience, became a model for the world.

But what of slavery in the Protestant United States? Beman unflinchingly condemned slavery as a curse to master, slave, and the unborn children of each. He declared that in slave societies not intellect, nor virtue, nor independence could prosper. In no country was slavery a greater menace or contradiction than in the United States. Yet without specifying course of action, he assured his audience that a people of such piety, intelligence, and national spirit would find a "magnanimous and liberal" method of ending its reign.[14]

Beman then concerned himself with the inevitable contrasts between America and Europe, especially the disparaging remarks of Europeans. They insisted that "every thing here was constructed upon a small scale." The great thunderstorms, hurricanes, volcanic eruptions, and earthquakes, they argued, had caused "degeneracy" in all living things. "Men have been frightened into intellectual dwarfs," so the argument ran, "and the beasts of the forest have not attained more than half their ordinary growth!"[15] Beman retorted with a litany of American success from victory in the Revolution to gains in commerce. As for "deeds of zeal and valour" in religion: "Let our missionaries in the bosom of our own forest, in the distant regions of the East, and on the islands of the great Pacifick, answer the question." Only in intellectual pursuits did the young nation lag, but he was sure that intellect too would soon bloom as the nation matured.[16] Meanwhile, America had become the beacon light of nations. It had been a model for South American revolutions. Now its song of freedom had returned to Europe, "sung by the Grecian bard and emulated by the Grecian hero," and would soon spread to other peoples. "When I reflect upon the part which this country is probably to act in the renovation of the world," Beman concluded, "I bless God, that I am a citizen of this great Republick."[17]

Beman's was not only an uncompromisingly national, as opposed to New England, vision; it also made no distinctions among Protestants at all. For instance, when listing the great minds produced by Protestant understandings of the world, he included Alexander Campbell, leader of the radical Campbellites. God had commissioned America to undertake a "holy enterprise" to spread its "moral power . . . to the very limits of the earth" precisely because by and large its people followed versions of the true faith, while the infidels, tyrants, and papists who opposed them resided largely in Europe and across the rest of the non-American world.[18]

Beman had worked out the related theological basis for this vision of Protestant America united in holy war many months before, then published his views in January 1825 as *Four Sermons on the Doctrine of the Atonement*.[19] He basically argued that all human beings could seek and be hopeful of salvation, not simply an elect few. Beman stressed a doctrine that not only was totally democratic, but also placed active responsibility on the free will of every soul. No one was assured of salvation; it came only to those who surrendered themselves to God. Beman argued that Christ had died to atone for the sins of all humankind, but only some would choose to partake of saving grace. "Some deny the Lord that bought them," he asserted, "and bring on themselves swift destruction." Still others "behold and wonder, and perish."[20]

This was hardly unusual doctrine. Certainly the popular denominations offered the possibility of universal election and the responsibility of human choice. Yet for Presbyterians, and especially for the Presbyterian churches of western New York, which were influenced by the conservative Philadelphia presbytery, Beman's views were nothing less than heretical. To reject the doctrine of limited election was to repudiate explicitly a key element of the Westminster Confession and therefore the very heart of Presbyterianism.

Still, many ministers had come to underemphasize limited election. Beman's own confidence in propounding his views indicated that, at least as concerned this particular doctrine, there might exist a kind of unspoken rejection. Such a contrast between what was written and what was believed indicated the existence of important differences between formal, traditional doctrine and that which made everyday sense in the new republic. Election not only grated hard against democratic values but also seemed at odds with the spirit of toleration and religious liberty. These dissonances resounded louder still in the West, whose very identity was shaped by democracy, fluidity, and toleration. Beman's was a logical re-

working of the doctrine of atonement in light of American evangelical
practice, but it was unlikely to gain favor among the conservative Presbyterians who wielded power in upstate New York.

For years, Presbyterians had been used to debating Baptists, freethinkers, and others about the social implications of theology and sacred
rites.[21] Now from Beman's Presbyterian pulpit came doctrines more suitable to the Baptists and Methodists. Beman had only propounded the position Beecher was moving toward, an evangelical ecumenicism flavored by
the covenantal social vision of the Presbyterian and Congregational traditions. Yet for a minister to reject doctrine in such an explicit manner
involved rebellion of the most profound sort, powered by pent-up rage and
the promise of blissful transformation, and filled with fears of real and
imagined enemies. Old School Presbyterians in Beman's congregation did
not disappoint. They accused him of heresy and promoted already current
rumors about his stormy marriage. Talk circulated about a trial before the
local presbytery.

Meanwhile, Beman had heard of extraordinary awakenings in Oneida
County, where a Presbyterian revivalist named Charles Grandison Finney
had brought hundreds into the churches with doctrines much like his own.
Beman tried his hand at promoting a revival in that spirit but met with
only mixed results. He wrote to Finney for help. "There is great excitement in the church and out of the church," Beman explained in August
1826. "Some of the professors are awake—that is a few, but the great mass
hang back and some opposed with great bitterness. Sinners are fighting
with all their might."[22]

Finney shared with Beman a heady, democratic sense of salvation and a
deep-seated contempt for complacent Orthodoxy. At the same time, his
personal history had formed a very different if complementary ally for
Beman in the revival wars. Born in 1792 in Warren, Connecticut, Finney
was two when his entire family moved to Oneida County, New York, and
settled in the town of Hanover. His early education included exposure to
music; Finney took up the violin and bass viol. He distinguished himself as
an athlete as well, and he showed enough bookish proficiency for the Lake
Ontario town of Henderson, where the family moved in 1808, to employ
him as a schoolmaster.[23]

He thus displayed some of the same energy and musicality as Beman.
However, Finney never managed to channel his prodigious spiritual energies in traditional ways. Unlike Beman's, his exposure to the church had
been tantalizing but slight. Neither of his parents professed religion, and,
if we are to rely on his *Memoirs*, the badly phrased "absurdities" he and the
townsfolk heard from itinerant ministers served more as butts of jokes than
as paths to salvation.[24] Nor did he share the New England clergy's opposition to the War of 1812. Whereas Beecher and the young Beman ser-
monized against the conflict, Finney tried to enlist in the naval militia. Yet

he did befriend the Congregational Church's choirmaster in Hanover, perhaps hinting at his very musical sense of the sacred.

Late in 1812, Finney returned to Warren, Connecticut, in order to continue his education and prepare for college. There he was able to attend church services regularly for the first time in his life. Years later he stressed the shock of realizing that the church's beloved minister, Peter Starr, had a gestureless, "monotonous, humdrum way of reading what he had probably written many years before."[25] How must Finney have felt? His *Memoirs* recorded the incident as one of a series of encounters with muddled ministers, the better to herald Finney's own inspired appearance on the religious scene. Yet one also gets some sense of the anger and frustration that Finney's famished heart must have carried for a minister and a church that gave him no spiritual nourishment.

Finney's worldly adventures paralleled his spiritual wanderings and disappointments. Bright, energetic, but already over twenty years old, he lacked direction. He joined Warren's Masonic Lodge in hopes that fellow Masons might aid in his search for a proper calling. He also thought college might help, but he was discouraged in this plan by a teacher who pushed him to seek his fortune in the world. Finney left Connecticut in 1814, spent the next four years teaching in New Jersey, and then returned to Henderson to help his family through a period of his mother's declining health.

Finally, in the adjoining town of Adams, he began a legal apprenticeship and what seemed to be a life's profession. Meanwhile, his spiritual cravings increased, and a deep sense of his own sinfulness surfaced. He attended the local Presbyterian church and soon was directing its choir. He also sought instruction in religion from its new minister, George W. Gale. Gale and Finney clearly had a close but troubled relationship, one that in many ways mirrored more Finney's frustrated faith than Gale's shortcomings. The minister sought to aid the troubled young man despite Finney's hostility.

Yet according to Finney, Gale only hindered his search. In fact, he claimed that his legal study piqued his hope for salvation. The biblical references found in his law books made him buy his first Bible, while Blackstone's discussion of the question of free will enlightened his own inner searchings pertaining to sin and salvation.[26] In 1821, he attended an inquiry meeting. Finney's memory of the event contrasted his own nervous readiness for conversion—"my very seat shook under me"—with Gale's stultifying instruction. However, as with the Reverend Starr, this account from his *Memoirs* was shaped to fit a carefully constructed drama. Gale himself remembered a different Finney at that meeting, one who asked him solemnly whether he ever might become a Christian. "I told him he might be converted," Gale remembered, "but if he were it would be something very similar to God's exercising miraculous power. . . . It was not teaching that he needed. It was compliance with what he knew already."[27]

In early October 1821, Finney fell for several days into a deeply troubled spiritual state and, in the end, experienced a dramatic conversion. He described the final moments in which the Holy Spirit embraced him:

> I could feel the impression like a wave of electricity, going through and through me. Indeed it seemed to come in waves and waves of liquid love; for I could not express it in any other way. It seemed like the very breath of God. I can recollect distinctly that it seemed to fan me, like immense wings. . . . I wept aloud with joy and love. . . . These came over me, and over me, one after the other, until I recollect I cried out, "I shall die if these waves continue to pass over me."[28]

Finney's troubled road to pure rapture deeply informed his later ministry, one based more on the power of the individual than on the efficacy of the formal church. Blackstone's exposition of the full accountability of individuals before the law had opened the door that ministers and formal theology had shut. Finney would recall that "Gospel salvation seemed to me to be an offer of something to be accepted; and that it was full and complete; and that all that was necessary on my part, was to get my own consent to give up my sins, and accept Christ."[29]

Nonetheless, Finney sought religious education and a cachet from the presbytery and Gale himself. In fact, he wished to become a licensed preacher. Gale, apparently somewhat disturbed by the mystical tendencies of Finney's conversion and other irregularities in the lawyer's beliefs but also appreciative of his magnetic talent, unsuccessfully appealed to Princeton, Andover, and Auburn seminaries to fund an education for Finney. The minister then took the convert under his wing and began to teach him the fine points of theology, though not without much wrangling.[30]

For six months Finney studied. When George Gale fell ill and needed a replacement, he had the presbytery examine his student for a preaching license six months early. The ministers passed him, but the people of Adams would not have the young man for a pastor. Gale found him a post as a preacher for the Female Missionary Society "to labor in the Northern parts of the County of Jefferson and such other destitute places in that vicinity as his discretion shall dictate."[31]

Finney now had the opportunity to be on his own, without ministers hovering over him. He preached first in the spring of 1824, at Evans Mills, where he made little headway and his only notable success was the conversion of the local tavern keeper. More important, he met "Father" Daniel Nash, an experienced and somewhat mystical older preacher who joined Finney in his labors. Nash, literate but also used to the unorthodox ways of the frontier, had over the years gained a wide reputation as a backwoods holy man. He heard Finney, renewed his sense of commitment to God, and traveled with Finney for a time. Nash, according to George Gale, specialized in prayer. Sometimes his prayers were silent, sometimes he prayed aloud, and often he experienced demonstrable agony, what he called "spiritual travail," over the state of those in need. He kept lists of people for whom he should pray, at times singling out individual prospects for conversion in a spoken "prayer of faith."[32]

Together Finney and Nash set revival fires in Jefferson County and began to get a reputation in New York State. On July 1, 1824, the Presbytery of St. Lawrence ordained him a minister. We know little about these early meetings except that they must have been a bit more emotionally demonstrative than most other Presbyterian revivals. At DeKalb, New York, Finney specifically endorsed Methodist revival techniques in the face of local Presbyterian objections to instances of spiritual fainting at a Methodist meeting. When Finney himself preached there, he moved several Presbyterians to emotional collapse. In the end, he brought the town's churches together under the sway of his more freewheeling methods.[33]

Fate then brought Finney to Oneida County, where the religious community had for some time been discussing such issues as the wisdom and efficacy of revivals, the nature of the Millennium, and general spiritual problems facing the population. Unlike Finney's frontier audiences, starved for spiritual satisfaction and excitement and with much toleration for innovation, those in Rome and Utica were more expert in their faith. In fact, they had fought over a variety of issues within the Presbyterian and Congregational churches themselves and debated still others with local Universalists, Methodists, and Baptists. In all, local religionists found danger on all sides, within and without, but had little sense of a solution that would unite all parties.

Increasing numbers, however, were finding that "degeneracy" within their own churches might be the root cause of the problem. They had allowed their members, some said, to partake of the world with the abandon of unbelievers. Six months before Finney commenced his revival, a writer in the revivalist-oriented *Christian Repository* prophesied the angry cleansing that was to come. "The great body of professing christians in this country, even in our orthodox churches," he wrote, "instead of emulating the apostles and primitive disciples of our blessed Lord, has entered the lists with the ungodly for a worldly prize. . . . They engage in all the money-making schemes of the present day, are partners with ungodly men, in their ungodly gain, and select their calling or business with as little regard to the glory of God as the wicked themselves."[34] To recall the complaint of 1823, "a stranger would be at a loss to distinguish Christians."[35]

This was not the complaint of all Presbyterians but rather of those insurgents of Beman's stripe who, as laypersons and ministers, sought a more militant church and eventually took control of the Oneida Presbytery. The Reverend John Frost of Whitesborough typified this new spirit; in recounting the history of his congregation, he implicitly emphasized his own use of new means and thus his contribution to its well-being. He had taken over a feeble congregation in 1813 and within four years had added 83 members. In the revivals of 1819 and 1821, he added 111 members. He broke a three-year fallow period between 1821 and 1824 by directly confronting sinners with their acts and encouraging public vows of personal holiness. Others fostered similar growth in towns across the county.[36]

The atmosphere was ripe for revivals and controversy. From August 1825 through the spring of 1827, revivals spread from town to town through the county. They began before Finney's arrival and appeared in places where he never preached. Yet at the center of the whirlwind was his powerful presence. Finney came to the town of Western late in September 1825. After listening to the elders of the church there bemoan the fact that God did not answer their prayers, he scolded them for blaming God and not looking to their own failings. He was so effective that the elders, though at first angered, broke down in tearful confessions and prayers of forgiveness. That began a campaign in which the evangelist preached every weekday evening and three times on the Sabbath, in addition to visiting prospective converts in their homes. In the end, he claimed 140 converts. Finney's fame spread and invitations to preach poured in from churches throughout Oneida County.[37]

In late December, he entered the Erie Canal city of Rome, where, according to one source, a revival had begun simply on the basis of the news from Western. "Worldly business was to a great extent suspended," he reported. "Religion was the principal subject of conversation in our streets, stores, and even taverns." The town seemed transformed. Drinking dropped sharply, public fights diminished, and the populace voluntarily engaged in strict observance of the Sabbath.[38]

A revival began in Utica, the largest city in the county, on New Year's Day 1826. Sparked by reports from Rome and by home visits of ministers and church elders, Presbyterians began a period of "heart-searching" and watchful waiting that burst into enthusiasm when Finney arrived on February 1. The preacher scolded his audiences for "their departures from God, their backsliding in heart, their lukewarmness, their love of the world and conformity to it," and he emphasized the necessity for them to approach God with a "broken spirit, of deep and thorough repentance" before He would save them. Soon hundreds thronged to hear Finney berate them but offer hope for salvation; by November 1826, converts numbered about five hundred.[39]

In Western, in Rome, and now in Utica, Finney had achieved almost instant fame and recognition, and that encouraged him to embolden attacks on sinners. He and his converts spread out into the surrounding towns, inflaming the entire presbytery. However, his so-called new measures, in reality mostly adaptations of common Methodist and Baptist revival practices, clashed in Oneida County with a more literate and tradition-oriented clergy and laity. Where Finney and his supporters saw light, many others saw fanaticism. Finney and his helpers not only preached at church and held inquiry meetings but also followed individuals on the street, into stores, and to their homes in order to confront them with their sinfulness and push them toward surrender to God. Prayer meetings mixed men and women and were addressed by both sexes. Echoes of the emotionalism of the popular sects came through Father Nash's presence and the promotion of an atmosphere that allowed the vocal expression of emotion in groans, sighs, faintness, and other manifestations. Those who felt uncomfortable with such methods were damned in public as "cold Christians" or worse.

Young men and, especially, young women in the Utica area seemed most affected by the revival, and this in itself produced an excited situation. The youth of Oneida County in the 1820s were, according to Mary Ryan, "buffeted most violently" by the changing economy and social structure and a sense of uncertainty about the future. Older Presbyterians feared the "restless and wandering activity of youth." The rhetoric of generational tension informed various theological debates; as far back as 1812, the Reverend Elijah Norton had revealed his deepest fears when he argued that the Baptist and Methodist practice of adult baptism had "a direct tendency to kill and murder fathers and mothers." By the 1820s, youthful rebellion seemed to be gnawing at the Presbyterian patriarchy from within.[40]

Nor was that perception unfounded. The young, and especially women, felt betrayed by the church of the elders as they faced an uncertain future within a social and religious structure that seemed incapable of offering them assurance of salvation. Hundreds of youths embraced Finney's penetrating logic and uncompromising reproaches to "cold hearts" and "sinners." Many found salvation, and some also a calling. In an almost unprecedented manner for Presbyterians, they even joined Finney's revival efforts as a "holy band," a kind of militia to organize prayer meetings and to confront sinners in streets, stores, and their own homes. Most famous among them was Theodore Dwight Weld, who at first mocked Finney and then fell under his sway. Others, especially ministerial students from Auburn Seminary, participated as well.

Such students represented a generation beyond that of Beman and Finney, New England religious virtuosos two generations removed from the smaller, more personal, and structured world of ministerial apprenticeship. They trained in an age in which the evangelical spirit dominated, and in which educational institutions emphasized more an abstract mission than a day-to-day apprenticeship with real ministers. In all, it led them to an extraordinary concentration on the cosmic drama as painted in missionary goals, and to an extraordinary insecurity concerning their future roles. It also made them hungry for assertive leadership that might lead them from their betwixt-and-between position. They found it in Finney, Beman, Frost, and other revival protagonists.[41]

These youths sometimes voiced denunciations that expressed deep-seated generational anger. Indeed, the ministers of the Oneida Association charged them with shouting: "'You old, grey headed sinner, you deserved to have been in hell long ago'—'this old hypocrite'—'that old apostate'—'that old grey headed sinner, who is leading souls to hell'—'that old veteran servant of the devil,' and the like."[42]

The militancy of these youths, Finney's own rhetorical style, and the mystical presence of Father Nash pushed the atmosphere of events in Oneida County far beyond the level of decorum associated with Presbyterianism. This turbulent state attracted, and in turn was made more excitable by, the participation of Baptists and Methodists. As a result, the revival and its methods were attacked by liberal Unitarians, freethinkers, and conservative Presbyterians. A pamphlet war broke out, Unitarian Ephraim Perkins firing the first shot and inspiring the Finneyite Oneida Presbytery to publish their *Narrative* in self-defense. Others joined in on Perkins's side, including the Reverend William Weeks and his group of Presbyterians.[43]

The clash of views on the revival revealed a culture in turmoil. Finneyites burned with a sense of religious Truth and fears of the Devil's legions on all sides and sought to reform the churches in millennial expectation. Unitarians and freethinkers feared the reassertion of Orthodox community power and angrily contested the vicious attacks of the revivalists. Conservative Presbyterians resented accusations of cold-heartedness or irreligion simply because they felt uncomfortable with Finney's tactics, and they feared the revival would tar "proper" evangelicalism. Yet to emphasize any one incident or motive would be to miss the central reason for the intensity of controversy surrounding the revival: that is, Finney and his followers were implicitly acting out a new and different vision of sacred order, one that borrowed details from other primitivist movements but was itself of a unique totality. Each side talked—or raged—past the other because the premises of each concerning the holy life and its relation to God and society differed.

Not that the differences were always readily apparent. The Finneyites were driven by a vision in some ways quite close to that which Beecher had developed in the 1820s. They shared his evangelical and Manichean vision of an approaching showdown between the forces of the Lord and those of the Devil, and so they damned in no uncertain terms Deists, Catholics, Unitarians, Universalists, and Episcopalians. Unlike Beecher, however, they felt no compunction about similarly treating those in the Orthodox churches they considered to be unregenerate. This readiness to condemn those of their own church reflected, as much as anything else, the frustrating experience Finney and many of his converts had with Presbyterianism.

They also placed little faith in study or reflection but rather wagered all on the dramatic choice between salvation and damnation. Finney telescoped the lengthy process of conversion, so revered in the Puritan experience but already condensed in Beecher's evangelicalism, into a day's or an evening's change of heart. The old conversion experience stressed self-reflection and study as well as an extended struggle with inner emotions. It also led to an individual's integration into an ongoing congregation that in turn stood at the center of a structured and heterogeneous community. The Finneyite conversion experience, much like those in Baptist and Methodist meetings, paralleled but greatly compressed these essential stages, and in doing so suggested a vastly altered sense of community. Rather than a congregation arranged in hierarchies and statuses, one's church became the invisible church of Saints, egalitarian and undifferentiated as to age and sex. One's earthly community became that of Finney's evangelical army.

The full implications of conversion in the revival only reverberated in the lives of a minority of his converts. Most simply found the revival an avenue of hope for salvation, joined the church of their choice, remained unalienated from their families, and settled back into a normal social existence. They took what they needed. However, those who emerged from the Finney revival to become reformers were in truth rebels against the narrowness of denomination and geography, fully ready to accept and expand upon the logic of millennial evangelical militancy. They truly posed a threat to order—not so much to the physical order of society as to the sacred order that linked more conservative religionists to the cosmos. The Finneyites sought to reorder the sacred as it revealed itself in society in anticipation of the imminent millennial day.

Finney's opponents, no less pious, envisioned the church's role quite differently. They believed in Christian eschatology, but the imminence of the Millennium seemed less real to them. Unlike Finney and many of his converts, those who looked askance at the revival's demeanor felt more integrated into the everyday life of human society and saw the role of religion in light of that integration. The church had been placed on earth to maintain the word of God and to bring individuals, in due time, to the wonders of salvation. Social peace, learning, tranquility, Christian humility, and respect for the sex and age hierarchies of a God-given natural order: these were the watchwords of conservative Presbyterians as they criticized the revival.

Presbyterian detractors objected specifically to the revival's offenses against the institution of patriarchy, both in relation to respect for one's elders and to the place of women. They intoned the Fifth Commandment and Jesus's instruction to Timothy: "Rebuke not an elder, but entreat him as a father, and the younger men as brethren; the elder women as mothers; the young as sisters, with all purity."[44] Further, they reasoned that young converts had little experience in judging religious feeling and no doubt thought "vastly more highly of themselves" than was warranted. "Under such circumstances," William Weeks declared, "to put them forward, to make much of them, to tell how well they appear, and to make comparisons between them and old Christians to the disadvantage of the latter, can scarce fail of doing them great injury."[45] It was a violation of sacred order as set forth by God at Sinai and by Jesus to his disciples, and it was a violation of common sense.

The same was true of women leading prayer meetings at which men were present. Women, Weeks argued, had an important role to play in the sphere in which God had placed them, and that included leading prayer at strictly female prayer meetings or in the family and school, if no male was available. In mixed meetings they should be silent. The consequences of violating the sphere were staggering: "Were the female members of our churches to be pressed out of the sphere which God has assigned them, we fear, that although some good might be the accidental result in some instances, it would so diminish their power of doing good in general, as to prove a great calamity to the church, and a great hindrance to the prosperity of religion in the world."[46]

The revival's critics also rejected the Finneyite approach to conversion. "The practice of hurrying awakened sinners from meeting to meeting," they charged, "and of talking to them at every opportunity, without giving them time for retirement, and self examination, and study of the scriptures, we think is full of danger." That danger was false conversion and the abuses to which it led: "The strength of a church does not consist in its numbers, but in its graces. The filling it up with false converts is the way to destroy it."[47]

Hasty conversion was symptomatic of a general lack of sacred decorum in the revival's proceedings—"loud groaning, speaking out, or falling down, in time of public or social worship"—and a tendency to let feeling control judgment. The Finneyites saw these as authentic signs of struggle and described them in spiritual terms. "Many have been in deep distress," one revival partisan wrote, "and felt what it was to travail in birth for souls. With this burden pressing upon their hearts, they have cried to God for help, feeling they could not let him go without a blessing."[48] Yet how such struggles could be viewed can be seen clearly in one critic's description of Father Nash's "prayer of faith":

He was indeed wonderful for praying, and perhaps exceeded all others in the frequent repetition of "O, God Almighty—Come, God Almighty—come down—break in upon them." After continuing these strains, sometimes for a whole hour, alternately upon his knees, but more frequently sitting back upon his heels—and writhing as in an agony, throwing himself as far back as he could, and recover; and then bringing his head forward into his chair, rising and bringing the weight of his fists to bear upon it, and give emphasis to his expressions; after continuing thus *agonized* in prayer, as he called it, for a whole hour, he would sometimes pitch forward into his chair, sometimes throw himself backwards—sometimes rise and walk as though hurried with a resistless impetus and cry "O! God! O! God! O! God!"[49]

Unitarian critics made their own case against the Finneyites, one that at its strongest protested the mean-spirited criticism applied to legitimate religions in a land of religious toleration. "Sometimes by directly naming and sometimes by well understood allusion to most other religious sects and opinions than their own," one noted, "Deists, Infidels, Universalists, Socinians, and Unitarians and sometimes Episcopalians, have been all classed together and swept away with the same besom."[50] One witness testified that during the revival at Trenton the Unitarian church was denounced as the "seat of the Devil, the Synagogue of Satan, a nest of vipers, a nest of serpents; and on one occasion adders and rattlesnakes."[51]

Thus when Finney answered Beman's call in the summer of 1826, he had already stirred up a storm. Not surprisingly, the joint efforts of Finney and Beman in the promotion of a Troy revival only multiplied the possibilities for controversy, especially since Troy's eminence as an economic and educational center and its position in the eastern part of upstate New York, closer to New England, guaranteed that shots fired there would be heard in Massachusetts and Connecticut.

The Troy revival was marked as much by vituperation as by grace. The charges leveled at the Finney forces in Oneida County surfaced again in Troy, but this time they were made against Beman as well as Finney and his band of followers. According to one critic, revival converts invaded stores and houses, singled out a person, and cried, "You are going to hell," or, "Have you an interest in Christ," or, "Are you a Christian?" Beman's own sermons took on an accusatory tone. He scolded and threatened members of his church; he called them sinners and urged them to repent. He introduced the "prayer of faith," used inquiry meetings and the "anxious bench," and in general borrowed the militant spirit of the Finney camp.[52]

Finney himself attracted scores of people curious to see the sensation of Oneida County. It was after this, presumably heartened by the arrival of his colleague, that Beman supposedly hounded a Mrs. Weatherby in her own home. He accused her of avoiding him, excoriated her religious practices, and urged her to adopt the "prayer of faith" for herself and her family. Beman was angry that she had taken offense at his last sermon, in which he pointed out several parishioners and told them that they were "ten times more the children of hell than before." He had added, "I could call you by name, but I will not; but God Almighty will call you by name."[53]

At a later date, Finney and Beman together pursued Mrs. Weatherby into the house of her sister-in-law and there browbeat both women. Mrs. Weatherby told her husband what had happened, and he went to see Beman about it. As soon as Weatherby raised the question of his wife, Beman repeated several times: "Capt. Weatherby, you will go to hell; God will send you to hell." The exasperated captain threw Beman on the floor several times, held him there, and only released him in response to his wife's pleading. Later, two of Beman's young helpers came to the Weatherbys' house, verbally abused the "ungodly" husband, and accused the wife of lying about Beman's behavior.[54]

The critics noted other instances of deplorable behavior, as when Beman called one of the aged members of the Presbyterian church "an old hypocrite and an old liar." Or when he insisted that women should pray publicly "with great agony and tears." Or when, at an anxious inquiry meeting, he told one young man: "I advise you to go home and bespeak your coffin, and get your winding sheet ready, for I see death in your countenance."[55]

The accusations were endless, and no doubt many were substantively true. Beman had caught the angry invective of the Oneida revival and had been helped along by Finney and his enthusiastic band. Influential members of his church brought formal charges against him before the presbytery. At this and succeeding trials, Beman never denied the nature of his attacks, only whether the accusers had presented exact quotations or other evidence that could be totally corroborated. The tactic won him acquittals every time, and the "success" of the revival brought him accolades from a sympathetic New School majority of Presbyterians in Troy.[56]

A very different sort of confrontation unfolded simultaneously with Beman's trials in Troy. Although Beman and Finney shared a basic commitment to the evangelical crusade with others in New England, the rumors of excesses greatly disturbed Beecher and others whose evangelical vision was tempered with a more conciliatory relationship to their own communities. They felt uncomfortable with some of the "new measures" and, in addition, greatly feared that perceived excesses would supply ammunition to Unitarian, infidel, and Episcopal enemies. Especially offended was Asahel Nettleton, whose own calmer revival techniques had met with much success in old New England.

Initial steps aimed at reconciling the two groups failed, and finally Beecher, Finney, Nettleton, and others on each side agreed to meet at New Lebanon, New York, in July 1827. There they hoped to clear up misunderstandings and find common ground. Beecher and Nettleton thought they would intimidate and best these amateurs from the West, but instead the New School ministers of the West ably defended their innovations and fought the easterners to a draw. Though Beecher remembered warning Finney not to enter New England proper, the fact was that they agreed on the important issues, and a firm reconciliation was prevented only by Asahel Nettleton's injured pride. Another meeting two years later in Philadelphia brought Finney and Beecher together.[57]

Even as Finney and Beecher moved closer together, an eerie and largely unrecorded story of the Finney revival enacted itself as the old structures were blown apart by the angry thirst for salvation. The new measures and prayers of faith did not always work, even on those most willing to submit to the revival's message. An unsuccessful plunge into the revival might leave an unsuspecting soul stripped of the old securities yet unconvinced of personal grace, in a spiritual void from which there appeared to be no escape.

A case in point is Theodore Erastus Clark, Theodore Weld's cousin and the son of an important family in Utica. Burning with anger and filled with hope for salvation, Clark greeted Finney enthusiastically. Yet from 1827, when he first surfaces in the sources, to 1831, when he disappears, little but frustration dominated his spiritual life. In December 1827, he confessed that neither faith nor calling had come to him, and that he awaited a *"fearful awakening."*[58] By the following spring, even as he volunteered for revival work, he noted his own spiritual despair: "My life has been a succession of dreams, most of them unpleasant, and if any have not been so, their end has been disappointment. My heart is so cold that I can feel its chill within me."[59] After another year: *"I am no Christian."*[60] A year and a half later, during a revival at Troy: "I am more than 5000 degrees behind the spirit of the time here. I feel absolutely like a lump of ice."[61] And in May 1831: "I have as little life as an oyster. As someone expressed it, 'I want a volcano in my breast' to break up the rocky state of unbelief and stupidity." In the family it was rumored that he eventually succumbed to the primitive appeal of the Campbellites.[62]

Having spun out of the orbit of tradition and into the vortex of the revival, Clark and others were not guaranteed salvation or calling. For some the revival was an end to spiritual worry; for others it was the beginning of an unending search for sacred connection.

PART

TWO

Evangelical Reform

EVEN AS the revival in the West pushed evangelicals in the East further from their origins and speeded up an inevitable open conflict in the churches, another phenomenon surfaced: ministers and laypersons began to agitate questions concerning the social and educational order from the perspective of militant evangelicalism. The causes they chose—temperance, Sabbatarianism, and manual labor—mostly had at least modest histories and seemed in one sense on a continuum from the past. Yet the functions these causes served and the style in which they were promoted served to underline what was new about them.

One can describe this growth in a number of ways, but for our purposes a single major theme will suffice. The first moral societies and even the first temperance societies were largely seen as adjuncts to a social order, playing important roles by articulating the duties of Christians in their covenantal relationship to God. Their existence was certainly linked to actual social circumstances, but they functioned more as reminders of a sacred order than as organizations expecting to change behavior in a radical way. After all, society and church were only a check on the faulty, fallen will of human beings facing the temptations of sin.

Evangelicals had a different view. Their rise to social and religious consciousness in a world fast abandoning outer orders or undercutting them with relativistic judgments on their validity left them at once with great freedom and deep fear, one symptom of which was their Manichean vision of the world. For example, Nathan S. S. Beman, in asserting the optimistic view that man could achieve paradise on earth by progress in the spirit of God, implicitly hinted that the individual could also quickly descend to Hell and society could crumble if positive, muscular, willed obedience to the word of God did not come quickly. The evangelical order was based on the individual's commitment to holiness, not simply to social order as communicated by a sacred social structure.

But what would the tests be of this individual sacred order beyond the first, quickly achieved step of conversion? How would one live, by what signposts, in a world that supplied an ever-changing and evanescent offering of wants and needs? By what rituals and symbols would such order be preserved? Reform began to answer such questions. In the late 1820s, the three most important reform causes were temperance, Sabbatarianism, and manual labor. The histories of these movements illustrate important aspects of reform development that eventually led to the full flowering of such causes as abolitionism, feminism, and the whole range of mature antebellum reform activity. Sabbatarians sought to reinstate strict Sabbath observance in a society that was fast losing its corporate sense of Sunday as a sacred day. Manual labor reform represented a different sort of phenomenon. Young zealots took what had been a simple reform of seminary curriculum and forged a new system of holiness and radical identity based on the body. Temperance sought to curtail or eliminate the drinking of alcohol.

The new militancy concerning each issue, and the almost simultaneous appearance of all three, point to less obvious unities. Most important, Sabbatarianism, temperance, and manual labor each broached questions of ritual and symbolic order in society and the individual. They provide a fascinating contrast of strategies for restoring that order and thereby reestablishing the sacred essence of society. Their programs looked both backward and forward as they emphasized what for Protestants were radically new sources for sacralizing the self and society.

IV

The Temperance Reformation

"THE WORLD has turned over since we were born," Huntington Lyman reminded Theodore Dwight Weld on Weld's eighty-eighth birthday in 1891. Lyman recalled helping his father, a minister, prepare for a meeting of local Congregational clergy. He took a wheelbarrow to the store "to get the essentials" for the "holy men," which included generous amounts of beer. "After shaking to see the head and tasting to get the flavor," Lyman wheeled home a full load. At the meeting the ministers discussed the "many failures of effectual grace" and decided to "preach against extravagant use of rum." Lyman remembered at other times greeting ministers at the door who "had been overtaken in afault (got drunk)" and wished his father to represent them before the Association. Yet a marked change had occurred, he mused, with now "not so many church records recording that 'Bro Zephas Hooker had again been overtaken with the same fault and wanted again to be forgiven.'"[1]

The world had indeed turned over on the issue of alcohol, especially for activists like Huntington Lyman and Theodore Dwight Weld, who cut their eyeteeth in reform by preaching the gospel of temperance. To their converted minds, the distinction between ministers enjoying a few rounds of beer after their deliberations and the "extravagant use of rum" smacked of hypocrisy. Yet hypocrisy had little to do with the old view, for it was only in about 1826 that a sea change occurred in American attitudes toward alcoholic beverages. In that year, evangelical clergy and interested laypersons formed the American Temperance Society, which began an enormously influential campaign against drinking that ultimately led millions to question their prior attitudes and prompted significant numbers of legislatures to consider serious legal restrictions against alcoholic consumption.

In the years before 1826, Americans consumed alcoholic beverages with little or no sense that they were violating any moral or physiological laws. Drinking was part of the workday and leisure time of most adult Americans and some children. Rituals of drink bound individuals together in the worlds of elections, funerals, weddings, meals, work breaks, and, it would seem, just about any other social moment. In addition, most considered alcohol to be more healthful than the water generally available for drinking.[2] One student of alcohol consumption has estimated that in 1825 on average each American fifteen years of age or older consumed about seven gallons of alcohol each year (the alcoholic content of close to forty gallons of beverages containing the substance). The country, he concluded, was indulging in "a spectacular binge."[3]

Yet over the twenty-five years that followed, consumption of alcoholic beverages took a precipitous downturn. By 1850, per capita alcohol consumption for Americans over fifteen had fallen to about 1.8 gallons a year.[4] Many forces contributed to this striking change. Better drinking water became available in many locales; the nature of industrial work and the logic of the marketplace encouraged values of industriousness and sobriety that changed the place of alcohol in daily life; and an emerging middle class began to make temperance an emblem of virtue. Most of all, however, evangelical visionaries in the American Temperance Society formulated a powerful argument against drink that forged these tendencies to an almost revolutionary consciousness. Millions took the pledge; temperance lecturers criss-crossed the country making new converts; and old distinctions between temperate and intemperate drinking, as well as between weak and ardent spirits, disappeared for many as the enemy became alcoholic beverages in any strength or form.

Most of the early leaders of the antebellum temperance movement came from New England. Indeed, early on New England's founders had endowed intemperance with a more pointedly social meaning than it had in other colonies. Increase Mather, bewailing the perceived decline of New England in 1673, had cried "Wo to Drunkards" and labeled drunkenness a sin. Yet Mather still considered liquor to be a creation of God and both healthful and pleasing if used in moderation. He thus compared, in the jeremiad tradition, the habits of the fathers and the sons. "When as our Fathers were *Patterns of Sobriety*," he noted, "they would not drink a cup of wine nor strong drink, more than should suffice nature, and conduce to their health." Later generations, Mather complained, "could transact business, nor hardly ingage in any discourses, but it must be over a pint of wine or a pot of beer."[5] His son Cotton expressed similar sentiments a half-century later, though his emphasis on drunkenness as destroyer of social and Godly order was more pronounced than his father's.[6]

The distinction between moderate drinking and intemperance retained its power through the end of the eighteenth century and into the nineteenth. Benjamin Rush, whose pamphlets detailing the deleterious effects of liquor were conceived within his plan for the creation of Republican virtue, still allowed for some drinking, and he strongly differentiated between distilled spirits and beer or cider. The former were "*Antifederal*" and enslaving drinks, while the latter were "invaluable FEDERAL liquors." He gained some support among post-Revolutionary notables and could thrill to the scene at the end of the Grand Federal Procession, when all gathered for a virtuous beer-and-cider bash.[7] Still, the influence of Rush's views spread slowly. He was ignored by the general populace in his own day, as indeed was his entire reform program. In fact, Rush had his greatest influence fifteen to twenty years after his death when his "medical model" that "scientifically" described the impact of drink on individual bodies and the body politic proved useful to the evangelical temperance campaign.[8]

The growth of the evangelical vision of alcohol paralleled closely the development of the evangelical cosmic drama. Thus drink, along with Sabbath-breaking and blasphemy, became an important symbol of sin against Godly order during the Jeffersonian ascendency. However, Orthodox New England's concerns about social and Godly order came more and more to focus on abuse of alcohol after 1811. The Federalist decline was just one factor. The embargo and the War of 1812 added severe economic and social strains to the region, making conditions ripe for drink's temptations and producing more visible signs of intemperance's ravages.[9] Thus the moral societies that Beecher and others created in the period of the War of 1812 made strong pleas for governmental enforcement of moral order.[10]

That the clergy should so specifically emphasize drink as a threat to moral order had much to do not only with the general fear that pervaded New England at this time but also with the fact that highly visible acts of public drunkenness, bad omens in and of themselves, also directly flouted the rule of law. The legal codes of most New England states carried statutes limiting patronage, hours, and sales of alcoholic beverages at "groceries" and taverns, especially for local inhabitants. Yet by the beginning of the nineteenth century such laws went largely unenforced. Thus Lyman Beecher, in his sermons on moral decline, emphasized that all that need be done was to enforce the law. Unenforced laws tended to delegitimize all laws.[11]

Such a threat also inspired the Congregational Association to create the Massachusetts Society for the Suppression of Intemperance (MSSI) in

1813. Although 25 percent of the members were Orthodox clergy, its rolls also included both Unitarians and Episcopalians. All had a shared interest in maintaining public order during the hard times before and during the War of 1812, and all three groups represented different segments of those élites who felt responsible for the cohesion of society. Their program was not very radical. It stressed the dual themes of drinking as a disruption of public order and, implicitly, the free violation of laws as a threat to the structure of society. In the main, they proposed enforcement of the laws prohibiting selling liquor on the Sabbath or to known drunkards, gambling in taverns, and rowdiness near taverns.[12]

Despite the proliferation of forty local branches, the Society failed in its mission and suspended operations in 1823. It had excluded Methodist and Baptist dissenters who might well have supported the cause. In addition, the virulence of Orthodoxy's new evangelical attacks on the Unitarians and Episcopalians effectively destroyed the possibility of alliances among these élites. The MSSI, like the religious establishment and its assumption that a sacred moral order must be imposed on society as a whole rather than created through individuals, reflected a dying order rather than the evangelical revolution to come.[13]

Even before the crisis of 1811–12 had spurred Connecticut and Massachusetts ministers to action against alcohol and its deleterious effects on the Godly order, a portent of future events was being enacted on the New England frontier. In 1808, Dr. Billy J. Clark of Moreau, New York, read Rush's treatise on alcohol, feared for the future, and urged the local minister to help him form a temperance society. Forty-three local citizens pledged to abstain from distilled liquors unless required for medicinal purposes and from wine unless as part of religious or public ceremony. They agreed to pay fines of twenty-five to fifty cents for violations, though no one could be assessed more than two dollars in any one year.[14]

Unlike the MSSI, Moreau's society seemed keenly attuned to the democratic, non-clerical sensibility of the age. This was apparent from the Reverend Lebbeus Armstrong's opening address at the first meeting. "In this enlightened age, and in this free country," he declared, "where every man is at full liberty to adopt that system for the regulation of his own conduct which he deems most congenial with his feeling and interest," few would agree to any course of action without having been thoroughly convinced of its correctness.[15]

To counter those who saw the idea of temperance as a "deprivation of the liberties peculiar to the appetite, and as an infringement on the natural rights of man," Armstrong asserted that a survey of the evils that befell humankind would reveal "the greatest part of them originating from an intemperate use of spirituous liquors." The choice might be to lose a little liberty and gain a society free from most evil. The physiological workings of alcohol, he noted, were well known. The personal effects—"melancholy instances of the ruinous and destructive effects of spirituous liquors, in the loss of character, of property, of happiness, and, finally, the loss of life itself"—were visible everywhere. "How many of the human race," he asked, "who were once temperate and industrious; whose fair estates have been earned by the sweat of their brow, have fallen victims to poverty, shame, disgrace, and to death, by abandoning the principles of temperance, and by giving themselves over to the brutal force of ungovernable appetite!?"[16]

This inexorable downward spiral often began innocently in an occasional drink, which soon led to the taking of a daily morning dram. Thus the man of virtue might unknowingly be dragged into intemperance and soon sacrifice his character to intemperance. Next he lost his reputation and his property, endangering his own and his family's very subsistence and his own life. As for the unfortunate's fate after death, "let *Divine Inspiration* declare, and it will inform us that drunkards are denounced among the black catalogue of the enemies of holiness, who shall not inherit the kingdom of God."[17] The social consequences were equally serious. Intemperance caused public brawls, vicious physical attacks, and even murder. Such cases overburdened the court system and cost much in taxes.[18]

How would the Moreau temperance society act against the evils of intemperance? It would educate citizens as to the consequences of drinking alcoholic spirits, propose substitutes, and encourage members to abstain by taking a pledge. The money saved from dues and fines would pay for useful books to be disseminated to the public. Soon young and old alike would be reading instead of drinking, set straight by "useful, instructive, and religious books" rather than diverted by the "confused company at the tavern or grog-shop." All of this could be accomplished if society members strictly adhered to the temperance pledge and encouraged others to stop drinking.

Armstrong attacked some common arguments against abstinence. He warned that those who protested that they were moderate drinkers might already be on the road to intemperance. Membership in the temperance society afforded such an individual a mechanism for ending his fatal courtship with alcohol. Going it alone, one would be "liable to the failings and frailties of human nature." Indeed, Armstrong speculated, "none knows but what God, in His providence, has devised and superintended the *erection of this institution, to save some of US from unforeseen danger and impending* RUIN!"[19]

The Moreau society prefigured the temperance movement of 1826 in several ways. It focused on the individual and self-reform rather than on society, and it employed laymen as leaders. In its view, temperance was a matter for all to ponder, as all were equally prone to destruction by intemperance. It created a scenario in which alcohol attacked the relatively innocent person, rather than one in which the sinner found in alcohol another mode of expression for his sinfulness.

Yet it is the dissimilarities that by contrast highlight the most extraordinary features of the later movement. The Moreau society expected relatively modest results in its community rather than on a regional or national scale. Nor did it expect either perfection or total abstinence from all alcoholic beverages. It emphasized ritualized abstinence from ardent spirits and imposed fines only for breaking one's oath; evangelical temperance would move toward social ostracism and churchly excommunication. Unlike the mature temperance movement, the Moreau society had no women members. Finally, its argument against alcohol was made almost entirely from moral logic and personal illustrations. It lacked a broad social and metahistorical millennial vision.

Progress toward wedding a democratic, individualistic vision of temperance to the dramatic evangelical view of cosmic history proceeded over the next two decades. The very process of founding the Massachusetts Society for the Suppression of Intemperance and the Connecticut Moral Society highlighted the dangers of drink and gave reformers experience in the field, even if it did not produce a viable campaign. Developments in missionary realms, especially in the founding of the tract and Bible societies, contributed other tools that would be harnessed by the new temperance society.

Yet above all, temperance advocates needed a new metahistory within which to place the use of alcohol. The power that the evangelical vision added to the social and cosmic sense of drink's horrors can be seen plainly in Lyman Beecher's series of six sermons on temperance, which he delivered late in 1825 and published in 1827.[20] Intemperance was, according to Beecher, "the sin of our land, . . . that river of fire, which is rolling through the land, destroying the vital air, and extending around an atmosphere of death" that might "defeat the hopes of the world."[21] Beecher's labeling of intemperance not only as sin but as "the sin of our land" marked a major departure from his views of 1811–12. He had seen threats from a host of sins, each of which reflected the unregenerate nature of man. His singling out of intemperance suggested that strictures on acceptable drinking must be drawn ever tighter. Even "occasional exhilaration of the spirits by intoxicating liquors, as produces levity and foolish jesting, and the loud laugh" was intemperance. "The cheerfulness of health, and excitement of industry, and social intercourse," proclaimed Beecher, "is all which nature demands, or health or purity permits."[22]

Beecher, turning to Rush, gave a minute description of the workings of the stomach, "the silver cord of life, and the golden bowl at the fountain, and the wheel at the cistern," lest anyone doubt the danger even the smallest drop of alcohol might pose to the unsuspecting drinker. Alcohol artificially exercised the stomach, distended its muscles, and made it dependent on habitual drinking to bring it to life, till it demanded gratification with "irresistible" force. The stomach needed progressively more alcohol to excite itself, and soon it wore out. The spiritual costs were worse than physical suffering. "It is an immortal being who sins, and suffers," he declared; "and as his earthly house dissolves, he is approaching the judgment seat, in anticipation of a miserable eternity." Drink transformed "all that was once lovely and of good report" and left its victim "a ruined animal."[23]

Beecher therefore found it important to unmask the early signs of intemperance so that dangers to self and others could be nipped in the bud. An individual, he noted, usually began by drinking only on special occasions. Soon, however, he created his own special occasions and even started drinking at a regular time every day. Then he concealed his habit. Meanwhile, physical signs betrayed the condition: reddened eyes, flushed complexion, trembling hand, or irritability. Personality changes also spoke of the sin. "He is not the same husband, or father, or brother, or friend," Beecher noted. As for the spirit, "his religious affections are dead when he is sober, and rise only to emotion and loquacity and tears when he is drunk." Alcohol so insidiously gained ascendency that though many talked of the prudent use of ardent spirits, they "might as well speak of the prudent use of the plague." Thus Beecher scoffed at those who advocated "a gradual discontinuance," for few were equal to the task. "There is no remedy for intemperance," he declared, "but the cessation of it."[24]

Beecher moved from the personal to outline the threat of intemperance to the nation. He noted the importance of physical health to the nation and pointed out that intemperance sapped this very life blood of America. "Even now," he asserted, "no small proportion of the deaths which annually make up our national bills of mortality, are cases of those who have been brought to an untimely end, and who have directly or indirectly, fallen victims to the deleterious influence of ardent spirits." Intemperance destroyed the national intellect, crippled the military power of the nation, and destroyed the substance of patriotism: "A nation of drunkards would constitute a hell."[25]

He reinforced these points by creating what amounted to a taxonomy of intemperance's influence. In discussing the question of alcohol's effects on national industry, he described a moral mathematical relationship that might stump even the modern statistical model-maker. National losses incurred from intemperance—"the labor prevented by indolence, by debility, by sickness, by quarrels and litigation, by gambling and idleness, by mistakes and misdirected effort, by improvidence and wastefulness, and by the shortened date of human life and activity"—would soon send the nation into bankruptcy. Every town's poor tax was increasing, channeling useful capital to care for a mostly alcohol-driven impoverished class. "Add the loss sustained by the subtraction of labor," Beecher declared, "and the shortened date of life, to the expense of sustaining the poor, created by intemperance; and the nation is now taxed annually more than the expense which would be requisite for the maintenance of government, and for the support of all our schools and colleges, and all the religious instruction of the nation."[26]

Beecher also announced a theme that would soon appear in his sermon *Memory of the Fathers*: the dangers inherent in a drunken underclass. Conditions for revolution bore a direct relation to the proportion of those in the population who had "no right in the soil, and no capital at stake, and no moral principle." The intemperate constituted a growing "corps of irreligious and desperate men, who have something to hope, and nothing to fear, from revolution and blood." Beecher placed the issue squarely before his audience:

> We boast of our liberties, and rejoice in our prospective instrumentality in disenthralling the world. But our own foundations rest on the heaving sides of a burning mountain, through which, in thousands of places, the fire has burst out, and is blazing around us. If they cannot be extinguished, we are undone. Our sun is fast setting, and the darkness of an endless night is closing in upon us.[27]

He was preaching, in other words, a jeremiad about alcohol: those whom God had chosen to bring the world to Christ were fast destroying themselves with drink.

As in any jeremiad, there existed solutions. Beecher used the remaining three sermons to set forth his program. "Intemperance is a national sin," he repeated, "carrying destruction from the centre to every extremity of the empire, and calling upon the nation to array itself, *en masse*, against it." Furthermore, he noted, its growing dimensions dictated drastic efforts. Voluntary abstinence or public pressure on consumers, producers, and sellers of ardent spirits would not suffice. Nor could laws limiting sales and consumption succeed, since magistrates could not and would not enforce such laws when the public wanted to drink. Voluntary associations could not be expected to provide enough aid to make enforcement possible. In short, Beecher concluded, the solution "must be made universal, operating permanently, at all times, and in all places." Anything else was a "temporary expedient."[28]

The solution was simple: "IT IS THE BANISHMENT OF ARDENT SPIRITS FROM THE LIST OF LAWFUL ARTICLES OF COMMERCE, BY A CORRECT AND EFFICIENT PUBLIC SENTIMENT; SUCH AS HAS TURNED SLAVERY OUT OF HALF OUR LAND, AND WILL YET EXPEL IT FROM THE WORLD." Mere moral suasion would not work if drinking and the selling of ardent spirits had the implicit moral endorsement of the law. "Like slavery," he declared, "it must be regarded as sinful, impolitic, and dishonorable."[29]

The abolition of the slave trade and the institution itself in the northern states provided Beecher with a meaningful precedent, for it was a rare example of a society outlawing on moral grounds practices or institutions that brought it wealth. More important, Beecher argued that, as in the case of the slave trade, "the amount of suffering and mortality inseparable from the commerce in ardent spirits, renders it an unlawful article of trade." He made the comparison directly:

> We have heard of the horrors of the middle passage—the transportation of slaves—the chains—the darkness—the stench—the mortality and living madness of wo—and it is dreadful. But bring together the victims of intemperance, and crowd them into one vast lazar-house, and sights of wo quite as appalling would meet your eyes.
>
> Yes, in this nation there is a middle passage of slavery, and darkness, and chains, and disease, and death. But it is a middle passage, not from Africa to America, but from time to eternity, and not of slaves whom death will release from suffering, but of those whose sufferings at death do but just begin. Could all the sighs of these captives be wafted on one breeze, it would be loud as thunder.[30]

If prohibition seemed the only solution, the fact remained that the public hardly shared Beecher's sense of the problem. How could one dramatize the effects of such a deceptive evil? Certainly Beecher had not abandoned pungent prose, but he also suggested that it was "high time to enter upon the business of collecting facts" and publishing the "statistics of temperance." It was the only way for the public to understand "the height, and depth, and length, and breadth of this mighty evil."[31]

Beecher outlined a practical program to bring public sentiment around to prohibition. Ministers and newspapers should be flooded with the awful statistics. The American Tract Society should volunteer its presses to aid in this effort. A special association ought to be created to devote itself strictly to temperance agitation. Employers ought to offer substitutes for the use of ardent spirits "as an auxiliary to labor." All Christians should band together to stop intemperance and, in the not too distant future, to exclude from church membership all who drank or traded in ardent spirits. All believers in temperance should avoid commerce with grocers who also sold liquor. Once these efforts began to have a salutary effect, temperance advocates could petition legislatures with some hope of success.[32]

Overarching the problem of temperance was Beecher's version of the cosmic drama and America's participation in it. "Every thing needful to a perfect state of society can exist without [commerce in ardent spirits]," Beecher affirmed; "and with it, such a state of society can never be attained. It retards the accomplishment of that prophecy of scripture which foretells the time, when the knowledge of the Lord shall cover the earth, and violence and fraud shall cease."[33]

The American Society for the Promotion of Temperance, usually referred to as the American Temperance Society (ATS), was founded only months after Beecher gave his sermons. Its purpose was to spearhead efforts to work on the agenda he and others had set forth. On February 13, 1826, sixteen board members ended their organizational meeting with a pledge of personal abstinence and an appeal to all in the broader evangelical community to follow their lead. The ATS in time came as close as any organization to meeting its founders' millennial expectations. After only three years, the organization had one thousand chapters and approximately a hundred thousand members. By 1835, five thousand chapters had been formed and a million persons had joined. The Society did its work through tracts, lecturers, and the local societies. Members pledged to abstain from alcohol and to encourage others to join them.[34]

Although Beecher had helped in its creation, the central figure at the ATS was the Reverend Justin Edwards. By tracing the development of his particular interest and approach to temperance reform, we can see yet another genius of the sacred at work. Edwards was twelve years younger than Beecher, a graduate of Williams College (1810) and Andover Theological Seminary (1811), and part of Nathan Beman's generation of New England ministers. Edwards had stayed in the orbit of New England power and in fact became something of a younger Beecher. Whereas Beecher led an older generation out of the eighteenth century, Edwards grasped the genius of the new era and channeled his charismatic presence through it.[35]

Edwards was chosen to be minister of the Congregational church in Andover, Massachusetts, in 1812. He apparently excelled at his tasks, gaining the confidence of his congregation as a personal embodiment of *"Bible truth."* According to a minister who knew him in those early years, young and old alike placed their souls in his care. "The aged felt it safe to confide in one who, though young in years, had so enriched his mind with heavenly wisdom," the colleague remembered.[36] Another minister described his presence: "His deep-toned voice, often tremulous from the swelling emotions of his heart; his tender beaming eye; the whole expression of his countenance and demeanor, [was] as if he lived in sight of the holiness and bliss of heaven."[37] His religious virtuosity was marked by the quiet knowing of God.

Edwards's deep sense of communion served his parishioners well in an age of evangelical revolution, but it also turned his sights beyond the congregation. Edwards founded the Andover Moral Society in 1814. He also helped found the New England Tract Society in that year, and by 1821 he was its corresponding secretary; indeed, its headquarters was in

Andover until 1825. In short, he was of that generation of ministers in New England proper that saw the enormous possibilities of preaching the Gospel through means and to numbers unheard of before the new century. He helped organize Sabbath schools, Bible classes for adults, and concerts of prayer for foreign missions. He was driven by his holy sensibility and goaded by the apocalyptic spirit that enveloped New England in the years surrounding the War of 1812. In 1815, for example, he promoted a monthly concert of prayer for revivals of "pure and undefiled religion [as] the only thing which can possibly save our sinking country."[38]

His contribution to the temperance cause must be understood within this vision of the evangelical battle. He first broached the subject of drink in two sermons on April 4, 1816 (the state fast day), criticizing the custom of drinking at funerals but elaborating as well on the broad significance of drink for the Christian community. He pronounced not only a new principle of action but also a vision of millennial consequences should temperance become the watchword of society. The sermons linked personal, social, and cosmic implications of drink, ones that far exceeded the more commonly held justifications for temperance enforcement that looked simply to the maintenance of Godly order. In the morning, he detailed the travails of the intemperate not only on earth but also after death: "Earthly woes pass away, but another cometh quickly—they lose *the soul*. They go away into everlasting burnings."[39]

In the afternoon, Edwards confronted the social implications of intemperance. He described the destruction wrought in society by liquor and posed a simple question: "Shall this enemy be continued among us, or shall we declare a war of extermination, and root it out?" The war he declared was not on the drunkard but on those who countenanced the practice of moderate drinking and who engaged in the production and distribution of strong drink. To the objection that moderation brought much pleasure and little harm, he noted that moderate drinking was the door through which the drunkard entered the prison of his habit. Enunciating the central theme of temperance reform as it came to be a decade later, he asked: *"Shall temperate men continue the temperate use of strong drink, and thus keep open the door to intemperance, idleness, dissipation, drunkenness, poverty, wretchedness, and death; or shall they forbear, and thus shut the door against those evils forever?"*[40]

Such an argument was similar to that of the Moreau society. The real departure came with Edwards's vision of what would happen to those who were incurable drunkards. Here we see his quiet holiness transformed into the calm gaze of a revolutionary as he assayed the millennial future. "Let temperate men give up the use of strong drink," he declared, "and the evil will very soon be done away, for all who are now intemperate will die soon, and when they die there will be none to fill their places." The intemperate may "distress us for the present," he added, and may do their mischief "while here." But God had decreed that soon they would "go to their own place, and the earth be relieved of her burden."[41]

Edwards came close to proposing, in fact, a gradualist Armageddon in which righteous Americans would fight a war of attrition against Evil in the form of the drunkard. To enter the lists on the side of the Lord, the temperate citizen need only sever his ties with drink, and God would do the rest. In 1816, Edwards did not claim that all social evil came from alcohol, and thus did not maintain that temperance would usher in the Second Coming. As we shall see, however, later temperance advocates moved much closer to such an assertion.

By the mid-1820s, Edwards had turned to the temperance cause in earnest. Shocked by two deaths in Andover caused by excessive drinking, he reasserted his doctrines in 1824 in two new and widely circulated sermons. By this time, his novel doctrine had become an obsession and trademark. The Reverend William A. Hallock remembered "that the report of [the lectures] filled the region around; and that the main idea was seized by all, and passed from mouth to mouth, 'Keep the temperate people temperate; the drunkards will soon die, and the land be free.'"[42] Edwards followed these sermons with the publication in 1825 of *The Well-Conducted Farm*, a temperance tract that continued the logic of his earlier sermons.[43]

Supposedly inspired by the experiment of S. V. S. Wilder of Bolton, Massachusetts (later a board member of the ATS), *The Well-Conducted Farm* recounted the story of a farmer who encouraged and then required his farmhands to stop drinking on the job. Soon he only hired those who had given up all strong drink both on and off the job. Despite the cynicism of his neighbors, the temperate farmer succeeded beyond all expectations and far exceeded the production of rival farms. The message was clear. Personal temperance aided one's own and society's cause so much that one ought to use economic and other pressures to force others to the same position. Those who became temperate would grow in grace and fortune, while the others would go bankrupt and die. *The Well-Conducted Farm* represented the most specific application yet of Edwards's doctrine of promoting temperance and letting the drunkard or the recalcitrant reap the whirlwind.

Not surprisingly, Edwards became a key force behind temperance agitation and helped preside over the founding of the American Temperance Society in 1826. A few days before the official founding of the ATS, he repeated in new form the philosophy and intended reach of the new society. "We are at present fast hold of a project for making all people in this country, and in all countries, temperate," he wrote; "or rather, a plan to induce *those that are now temperate to continue so*. Then, as all who are *intemperate* will soon be dead, the earth will be eased of an amazing evil."[44] Here was a temperance version of the conversion of the world and the end of days. It was a concrete program sure to have great appeal to a public already turning more and more to the bracing call of evangelicalism.

Still, the placement of temperance within the broader evangelical campaign does not begin to explain why it should have had such striking success, for it caught the public's imagination with far greater success than any other cause. Surely one factor was the visibility of evils caused by liquor. In addition, the practical advantages of sobriety in an industrial and commercial age, whether at home, at work, or in relation to one's superiors, were surely also clear.[45] Yet three other reasons seem quite as compelling, especially when one considers the large numbers of temperance adherents whose possible economic and social motivations were quite varied or nonexistent (at least in the direct sense), yet whose religious thirsts were in many ways quite similar. First, temperance agitators, through vivid use of statistics and a combination of millennial and patriotic logic, were able to create a compelling picture of society that wedded the fate of the nation to the evangelical crusade, and did so through social "facts" rather than simple moral appeals. Second, at a moment in the religious life of the nation when the traditional systems of ritual and symbolic life for all sects, and especially for Presbyterians and Congregationalists, were being challenged by religious freedom and disestablishment, temperance provided an attractive version of ritual identity for Christians. Finally, while temperance advocates did not promise salvation for taking the pledge, this simple act did bring to new recruits significant credit and sense of sacred invocation.

Most striking was the temperance movement's use of statistics. Statistics provided an unprecedented, portentous, and detailed picture of both American society and the problem of drink for a public unused to the sophisticated use of numbers. The power of numbers lay largely in the ability to define as a specifically ascertainable historical trend a situation previously referred to only as a moral state. Numbers also carried with them an indefinable but powerful magic, something akin to the equations used by millennial prophets to figure out the moment of the apocalypse or of Christ's arrival. Placed within the evangelical metaplay, statistics made the hazy notion of an American nation sliding to perdition, and, for that matter, an awakened public flocking to the temperance banner, palpable prophetic realities.

The use of statistics by temperance advocates comprised but one chapter in a much larger story of the invention of statistical thinking around the end of the eighteenth century. Before 1800, there had been only rudimentary attempts to conceive of social reality as a set of populations, activities, geographical areas, and trends expressed in detailed and related sets of numbers. The world of the complex census burst on the scene in America in the early nineteenth century and added a social dimension to the five senses. A society previously comprehended strictly from personal experience, supplemented by pictures, maps, and literary description, now took on new and powerful shape when expressed in numbers.[46]

The American romance with numbers had grown steadily in the eighteenth century as a direct influence from England but became a particular hallmark of Republicanism in late eighteenth-century plans for the ideal Republican curriculum. This in turn was complemented by a growth in the popularity of statistical descriptions in gazetteers and histories, whose American authors sometimes claimed "a minuteness of facts, and circumstances, not common in European productions."[47]

The creation of this picture complemented more pointedly Republican uses of statistics. As early as the 1790s, the "facts" came to be seen as an antidote for the plague of parties and factions. If only all sides knew the true dimensions of society, the argument ran, there would be little debate as to what ought to be done to secure the Republic. In addition, statistical portraits of the obviously heterogeneous country gave it a psycho-aesthetic unity, making of its parts a synthetic whole comprised of various parts outlined by statistical attributes. These factors and arguments for the usefulness of statistics to the state inspired a movement (albeit unsuccessful) in the 1790s for a census to be taken in 1800 that would be far more elaborate than the one produced in 1790.[48]

Significantly, Timothy Dwight joined James Madison and Thomas Jefferson in being a principal advocate of the detailed census. He thought it would aid Americans in visualizing the prospects of the nation and would also help policy-makers to serve the public good.[49] Indeed, Dwight pioneered the use of census statistics in his survey of the northeastern states published posthumously in 1821–23 as *Travels in New England and New York*. They were incorporated as a novel part of the panorama, adding a skeleton of hard fact to detailed descriptions of the landscape and impressionistic evaluations of various cultures that established a social reality and predicted a future.[50]

Although Dwight and others of his generation normally used statistics to measure the glory of the new nation, such data also revealed the darker sides of society. In fact, early temperance reformers saw their worst fears confirmed by what the numbers told them. The 1816 report of the MSSI featured devastating "facts and calculations" to underpin its claim that alcohol was destroying the social order. The report claimed that Americans spent $33 million annually on alcohol and that seven-eighths of those in the poorhouse drank to excess. These were claims made without attribution, but they marked the beginning of a trend toward ever-increasing use of the most sophisticated and wide-ranging statistics to prove the destructive capacity of liquor.[51]

By combining statistics with Rush's pamphlet and new research on the physiology of drinking, temperance advocates could create a "scientific" picture of the problem that took the drinking process from the mouth of the drinker, through his stomach to the rest of his body, to the inevitable physiological and mental results, to their impact on self and family, and then to the body of society. The powerful combination of statistical and medical evidence alone, when read as moral "facts," energized a new surge of temperance support. But when one put such facts within the developing evangelical view of metahistory, they created the most frightening of prospects: a society suffering from a "factually" provable slide into sin that was destroying its millennial hopes and would soon rend the social fabric itself.[52] Statistics made the nation visible, and therefore imaginable, as an entity that must be reformed or die.

Take, for instance, Heman Humphrey's widely distributed tract *A Parallel Between Intemperance and the Slave Trade* (1828).[53] Using an example of misery well known to Americans and universally condemned, the African slave trade, Humphrey underscored the horror of intemperance by making statistical comparisons between the two. Two pages of seemingly precise calculations later, Humphrey concluded:

> Shipment of slaves, say in 1786, from *twenty-five to thirty thousand.* Brought into a worse bondage, by intemperance, in 1828, *thirty-six thousand.* Deaths by the slave-trade, from *ten* to *fifteen thousand*—by ardent spirits, *thirty-six thousand!* Thus, where the slave trade opened *one* grave, hard drinking opens *three.*[54]

Having shown that intemperance produced three times as many victims as the slave trade, Humphrey turned to the personal effects of each. He described the tortures of the slave ship but asserted that intemperance was worse because it was self-inflicted and therefore involved the destruction of soul as well as body. He then widened the argument to a social and economic plane, graphically surveying almshouses and insane hospitals and labeling the inmates in each as primarily victims of intemperance. And he indulged in a bit of moral mathematics: since each had a family, intemperance made miserable "the hearts of *four-hundred thousand* families (and this probably a moderate estimate)"; what, he wondered, "must be the mighty aggregate, of misery which sends up its ceaseless groans to heaven from every part of the land!"[55] Compared to intemperance, the slave trade seemed a modest calamity.

Intemperance more than even slavery, according to Humphrey, also endangered Republican institutions. If some thought the "quiet servitude of two millions of people [was] a sleeping volcano," then what of the "*two hundred thousand*" active members of the army of intemperance? They voted, they served as public officials, they joined the churches of God. They would destroy the nation. The logic of his comparison showed Humphrey that if intemperance were a greater evil than the slave trade, then Congress, which had wisely ended the trade in slaves, must also end the trade in alcohol, and local communities must end licensing the sale of ardent spirits. The temperate of society must unite "to drive the monster from our land." Humphrey concluded, "If intemperance is worse than the slave-trade, let every *Christian*, every *patriot*, every *philanthropist*, gird himself up to the great work of reform, and never cease from it till it shall be accomplished."[56]

On the stump, temperance orators used similar arguments to visualize the stakes of reform and to magnify the images of hell. Theodore Dwight Weld, who joined the temperance campaign in the late 1820s after his conversion at the hands of Finney, used a combination of statistics and particularly colorful imagery to bring home the tragedy of drinking. He declared that alcohol "killed more bodies and damned more souls, than any other [cause] which could be named." Statistics pulled from his pocket showed that there were over 300,000 drunkards (in a country whose total population was about 12,900,000) and that 30,000 died annually from their drinking; that of the 200,000 paupers in the country, half had reached that state through alcohol; that of the 20,000 criminals annually committed to institutions, 80 percent were led to crime through intemperance; that of the 3,000 insane persons committed annually, half had been driven mad by drink; and that if any one took "an inventory of all the murders committed in the land for a single year," he would find that "99-100th of them were committed by intoxicated men." Weld noted that these calculations were startling but true, and that they had been reached by extrapolating from the statistics for a single county.[57]

Weld saw himself as appealing to the reason rather than the passion of his audience, but he believed that part of such an argument was to hold up "to their view facts in all their blood." So he dramatized them. He imagined the 150,000 paupers passing "along in all their rags." If that did not impress the audience, he asked them to imagine "if your last bed was going under the hammer, and your wives and children were already on their way to join this motley group." Then came the 1,500 insane—"now behold that maniac laugh"—and 16,000 criminals "dungeoned by the use of intoxicating drink." The parade ended with a finale of 300,000 drunkards—"see them spewing and hear their dreadful oaths." And soon after "pile up 30,000 bodies of dead men, in all their blood." That was the cost of intemperance.[58]

While Weld blamed the drunkard for choosing to drink, he indicated that a "universal insecurity of life and property which quivered all the land over" had driven many to make that choice. But the choice had been made, and it had been wrong and unpatriotic. "Suppose we could knock on the coffin-lid of the patriots of '76," Weld asked, "and those venerable forms should start into life, and each with his contribution should pass around this house, and say to each one of you, 'What will you give to save your country? All your country requires is, that you stop drinking ardent spirit.'" And he asked questions of his own: "Didn't Jesus die on the cross? Can't you stop drinking?"[59]

In succeeding lectures, Weld responded to objections. Many dealt with the naturalness of alcohol as a food. Was it not God's creation? Did it not give a person energy? To all he answered no, and he recommended cold water as a natural, God-given substitute. When one questioner declared that he drank moderately, could take care of himself, and wondered why he ought to take a temperance pledge or join a temperance society, Weld noted that "sippers" inevitably became heavy drinkers and joined the rest in drunkards' graves.[60]

Weld revealed broader implicit understandings of the movement in his answers to other questions. To the man who feared that taking the pledge would limit his liberties, Weld answered that "the very texture of society was interwoven with pledges—and that it could not exist without them." To those who feared the movement's real aim was a return to religious establishment, he noted that all types had taken the pledge, including Unitarians, Roman Catholics, infidels, Jackson men, Wirt men, and Clay men. To the man who declared, "I can take care of number one. It is not my business to go Don Quixoting around the world," Weld asked whether he would withhold aid from a sick neighbor. The facts cried out for a concerted effort to save the nation.[61]

Both the quantified perception of intemperance and the quantifiable response to save the nation also tended to create the mood and terms of a prophetic, numerological vision. For centuries Christians had sought in the numbers and important dates of the Bible some clue as to the precise moment at which the Millennium would arrive. Often such numerological evidence appeared in temperance tracts to predict doom from the increasing count of alcohol-related crimes reported or to project a millennial happiness from new membership figures for temperance societies. In the very first issue of the New York State Temperance Society's *Temperance Recorder*, just preceding almost three pages of mostly glowing reports of growing membership roles for temperance societies within the state, in the country, and abroad, the editors published a piece entitled "The Temperance Reformation a Harbinger of the Millenium."[62]

While the article argued rather mundanely that talent and money lost to the churches and to the missionary cause would be regained as fewer souls were lost to intemperance, it also contained a curious and grand description of the world without drunkards. "Take out of the world all the misery of which intemperance is either directly or indirectly the cause," it declared, "and the change would be so great that for a moment you would almost forget that the earth was still in any degree laboring under the original curse. Take away all the vice and the crime with which intemperance is identified or connected, and it would almost seem as if the 'holy Jerusalem had descended out of heaven: to dwell with men.'" Who would then need the exertions of missionaries and churches? The article only implied such a question but posed another. Imagining temperance's work so well done, it asked, "say whether its *direct* influence in bringing forward the millenium does not far exceed your most vivid conceptions?"[63]

The perhaps unintended challenge to the churches in such a global reading of the eventual effects of the temperance campaign underlined a central feature of the movement in the 1830s. Temperance reformers, following the logic of their argument, in fact challenged the traditional conception of the church on both a ritual and substantive level. Seeing the state of the world and religion through the lens of abstinence, the pledge, and millennial possibility, the most radical of temperance men and women sought to purify the church and the movement through three principal steps: requiring of all members a pledge that they would drink *no* alcoholic beverages, including wine, beer, and cider; banning the use of fermented wine in communion rites; and excluding from church membership all who drank. As a result, some accused radical temperance reformers of creating a new religion. These critics were not far wrong.

All three measures reflected an evangelical creed loosed from denomination and creating its own rituals. Significantly, the original exclusion of Unitarians and other enemies of Protestant evangelicalism was dropped; membership and even leadership, though still largely evangelical, soon included not only Unitarians but also Episcopalians, Roman Catholics, and freethinkers. What brought them together was a common pledge not to drink. The nature of that pledge evolved over the first decade of the existence of the American Temperance Society, which itself had not adopted a formal pledge of total abstinence even from ardent spirits until 1831.[64]

A number of factors influenced the rise in popularity of a stricter pledge, one that covered not only distilled liquors but also cider, beer, and wine.[65] First, the temperance argument as it developed in the 1820s, replete with scientific evidence concerning the evils of alcohol in all its forms, as good as said that all would be better off limiting their beverages to cold water. The question of avoiding distilled liquor versus teetotal abstinence had been in part a political one, based on an assessment of what one might expect to accomplish in the real world. It was also a religious one, since wine was used for communion. In addition, an increasingly younger membership in the temperance societies of the 1830s, a group relatively unattached to tradition and more convinced than even their elders of the singular efficacy of the pledge, pressed for total abstinence. In 1836, the American Temperance Society, meeting at Saratoga Springs, New York, accepted the new pledge as its own.[66]

The significance of the teetotal pledge reached far beyond the simple exclusion of a few varieties of alcoholic beverages. It institutionalized in extreme form what had been a basic notion of temperance for some time:

that it was the key to social and moral perfection. A new Manicheism, based not on evangelical versus Unitarian but on pledge-taker against non-pledge-taker, grew into a kind of religion of its own. Calvin Colton, once a great supporter of evangelical revivals, noted this development with disdain when he wrote of temperance and the reform spirit in general as *Protestant Jesuitism*. Another writer protested that "temperance turned into a religion with its revivals, its conversions, it hymns, its new measures."[67]

Such a complaint indicated more than hyperbole, especially considering the careful discussion of some critics. "If a man finds that a private vow, or social pledge, animates his virtue," wrote the Reverend Leonard Withington, "he is undoubtedly at liberty to make them; provided always he does not confound the secondary with the original obligation, and substitute for the law of God the commands of men."[68] Withington argued that temperance societies had made the pledge "a permanent obligation" that stood in their mind "rank and file with the everlasting ordinances of God." It therefore acted as a pharisaical "bar in the way of our duty," which like a smoking lamp "obscures the clear beams of the sun of truth." He feared that for every social evil there might be a pledge, and that soon the Ten Commandments itself would be "surrounded with human pledges." Commandments would no longer be kept because of love of God but rather because of fear of man. "Such pledges are like the very stimulating drink they oppose," he declared; "they quicken the mind for a time, and then leave it flagging and dead."[69] They and reform had become substitutes for the church itself:

> Some ardent minds, charmed with this new discovery, actually supposed they had found a new secret for reforming the world. The wonderful Elixir was at last discovered; the philosopher's stone of the moral world was found. So far was this carried, that it was much more important for a man to sign a pledge than to join a church.[70]

In doing so, temperance reformers had reshaped further the relationship of church, individual, and cosmos in an ever-unfolding drama. They had put the pledge above the church, and tested the virtue of the churches by their willingness to exclude from membership manufacturers, sellers, or drinkers of ardent spirits. Strong condemnation would not do. The General Assembly of the Presbyterian Church had tried that in 1830, only to be criticized by the American Temperance Society for not going all the way.[71] Indeed, the Society had even posed the following question for its first essay competition: "Is it consistent with a profession of the Christian religion, for persons to use, as an article of luxury or of living, distilled liquors; or to traffic in them? And is it consistent with duty, for the churches of Christ to admit those as members, who continue to do this?"

Moses Stuart, Andover's professor of Sacred Literature, answered no to both and carried off the prize.[72] Stuart's argument, which firmly equated intoxication with the most heinous of sins and advocated excluding such sinners from church membership, revealed a developing tension over the status of wine among temperance advocates that underlined their alienation from the churches. It also was emblematic of a continuing search among the pious for the proper terms of chosenness. Stuart began by limiting his inquiry to distilled liquors. He then produced a series of citations to prove that intoxication met with condemnation in the Bible.[73] Yet, he said, many had argued that one could use distilled liquors without becoming intoxicated. Returning to the Bible for wisdom on this subject, he confronted the problem of what alcoholic drinks Scripture allowed, in what amounts and at what times. How did such beverages compare in nature to those that Americans drank? He concluded:

> The temperate use of wine in its natural state, was common among the Hebrews, and was not prohibited, except in certain cases. . . . The drinking of pure wine to such excess as to produce intoxication in any degree, all banqueting, revelling, etc., was strictly and every where prohibited, under penalties of the most awful nature. The use of intoxicating liquors, i.e. medicated wines and strong drink (shekhar), is every where spoken of with discouragement and disapprobation.

This last ban applied especially to kings, princes, and Nazarites, or devotees, which Stuart further defined as those who have separated themselves "from the follies, fashions, and unlawful pursuits of the world, and consecrated [themselves] in a peculiar manner to the service of God."[74] For the true Christian, this was the standard by which to be judged. "If the time do ever come," Stuart remarked, "when the great body of Christians shall seriously consider that they are *Nazarites to God*, 'a chosen generation, a royal priesthood, a holy nation, a peculiar people' (1 *Peter* 2:9), then, I trust, they will take into serious consideration the statutes which regulated the priesthood and the Nazarites of old, with regard to the use of intoxicating drinks."[75] Moses had, in short, brought the question of chosenness full circle. In thirty short years a line of New England evangelicals had moved from New England tribalism to American nationalism to evangelical Christian universalism back to temperance tribalism.

A problem existed, however, for if neither the Nazarites nor the priests could imbibe, what of the use of wine in communion? The answer lay, according to Stuart, in a close historical look at the Bible. The simple wines of Palestine were fermented and purified, but in alcohol level they came nowhere near qualifying for the label "intoxicating liquor."[76] The wines of Stuart's day, however, were by no means weak and unadulterated. Drawing upon a pioneering study of alcohol content that made its way through temperance circles in the 1820s, Stuart pointed out that what

Americans commonly called "wine" contained from 8.79 percent to 22.96 percent alcohol, with brandies, ports, and Madeira having significantly more. The "grape-liquor" of the Bible no doubt contained at most half the alcohol of the weakest modern wines.[77]

Biblical injunctions, Stuart concluded, clearly prohibited distilled spirits and "mixed wine" drinks such as brandy, and they also most certainly prohibited the use of most of what passed for "wine" in the modern age as a "usual beverage" or a "luxury."[78] While he did not recommend church discipline for a member who mistakenly used a little wine for medicinal purposes or on special occasions and without breaking moral injunctions to be sober, he thought the secular uses of wine should be classified along with distilled spirits and other intoxicating beverages.[79]

At this point Stuart turned a corner. To Scripture, he added the proof-text of the mind and body of man. "Jehovah is the God of *nature*, as well as of *revelation*." God asserted and revealed His commandments in relation to alcohol through our physiology, the effect of alcohol on health and usefulness, and the "evils which such liquors lead the intemperate to inflict on others." The body having been sacralized as a means of revelation, Stuart brought forth the arguments of Rush and others concerning the poisonous physical and moral qualities of alcohol.[80] He argued that those who traded in such poisons and those who used them were partners in crimes against themselves, society, and Christ and should be barred from church membership as long as they could not sincerely take a pledge of total abstinence.[81]

At no point did Stuart question the legitimacy of using wine in the communion. However, with increasingly militant temperance reformers raging against every drop of alcohol, even this small area of toleration evaporated as they made an ever more attenuated scriptural argument concerning the nature of Palestine wine. They rejected Stuart's interpretation of biblical wine as a lightly fermented, weak alcoholic drink, insisting instead that it was unfermented grape juice.[82] On this issue many in the churches drew the line. While pious Christians might accept Stuart's argument from a theoretical point of view, especially since he allowed for ceremony and attacked habitual drunkards whose chosen spirit happened to have been fermented rather than distilled, the ultra-teetotal position of the late 1830s and 1840s seemed much more an attack on the heart of Christianity than a useful step toward reforming the world's drinking habits.[83]

In a replay of the Finney revival, more moderate religious souls began to see temperance as well as other voluntary reform societies as causes of dissension rather than Christian good. The wine issue emboldened them to a degree not possible before. W. L. Breckenridge asserted forthrightly that "the wine of the scriptures possessed an intoxicating quality, and that fact did not render their moderate use injurious to man or offensive to

God."[84] The Reverend Leonard Withington accused the temperance and other reform societies of destroying the possibility of Christian unity. "They are the pernicious suckers," he declared, "growing around the old village oak, exhausting its strength, withering its leaves, and marring all its beauty."[85]

Withington showered his contempt on the American Temperance Society especially for its abandonment of moral suasion in favor of prohibitionist legislation in the late 1830s and 1840s. Yet in reality the shift had been one of degree. From the beginning, Beecher and others explicitly called for legal prohibition once public opinion could be marshalled behind such a move. Edwards's original vision of a temperate society emerging as the intemperate died never excluded the possibility of legislation to enforce temperance. The early explosion of pledge-taking and membership augured well for fulfillment of Edwards's dream by voluntary means, so few pressed for legislation. By the late 1830s, however, as opposition appeared even in the churches, and as the statistically impressive list of pledges did not bring an appreciable reduction in the visible problems connected with drink, legislation became an appealing shortcut to the Millennium.

Most of all, the centrality of the pledge and moves toward legislation got a major boost from a rude awakening among middle-class evangelicals to the fact that a growing number of workers and others lived in a lower social world, which seemed to foster intemperateness and was immune to the genteel pleas of the temperance society. Edwards and other early temperance reformers had always conceived of a class of intractables, one whose existence was doomed by God. However, they had not imagined it to be explicitly congruent with the lower social and economic classes. As commercial and industrial growth accelerated in the 1840s, transiency, unemployment, and the growth of working-class districts across the North created a more class-fixed image of an intemperate lower culture. In some ways, the existence of such a culture was reassuring to middle-class evangelicals, who could now measure their own virtue by invidious comparison. At the same time, the expected disappearance of drunkards had not occurred, raising doubts as to the efficacy of Edwards's novel formulation and making anti-liquor legislation more appealing as a way of safeguarding the peace of society from otherwise uncontrollable "others." Those who had pledged to abstain voluntarily now seemed to be crowning themselves as a new establishment, one that should legislate and enforce a moral order much as the churchly establishment had done.

If the existence of a more permanent intemperate class inspired confusion and sparked campaigns for legislation, even more confusing was the explosion of temperance activity among working-class men and women in the 1840s—the Washingtonian movement—that challenged both anti-temperance and old temperance conceptions of society and the cosmos.

The Washingtonians, according to legend, began when in the spring of 1840 six drinkers in Baltimore decided to give up their habit and encourage others to do so, by forming the Washington Temperance Society. The Washingtonians recruited mostly among artisans, unskilled workers, and even those in the netherworld of poverty. Rather than organize only the temperate, they explicitly sought to reform the seemingly incurable drunkard. After significant successes in Baltimore, they fanned out over the North and then beyond. By 1841 they claimed two hundred thousand adherents, and by 1843 they set the number in the millions. No doubt the real numbers were far lower, but also without doubt the Washingtonians created a following for temperance unprecedented in the history of the movement.[86]

They did so in a simple but controversial way. They emphasized two things only: taking the pledge to stop drinking, and creating a society of the reformed to aid the drunkard's quest for sobriety. The temperance movement in general had certainly been moving toward the pledge as its central ritual, but never outside a more general context of church or profession of religious faith. To the Washingtonians, religion and church seemed a distraction. Most important was giving up drink and supporting those brave enough to take the step.

The explanation for such obliviousness to the churches lay in the Washingtonians' membership. As working-class drunkards, most Washingtonians had no structured relationship to any church and had been despised by many of those in the mainstream denominations. Through the pledge, they had found their own way out of desolation and had embraced a new life. Many joined churches as a result of their new beginning, but they credited their reform to God and to their fellow Washingtonians.

In fact, the Washingtonian movement may be profitably viewed in comparison to the Finney revival and the societies themselves as imitations of the primitive church. Society officials made it a point to bring hope to the despised of the earth, those whom others had written off as hopeless or, worse, as members of the Devil's legions. They worked among those whom Edwards and his temperate legions thought would disappear from the earth.

As in religious conversion, the Washingtonians sought to bring the drunkard to immediate comprehension of his wasted state and immediate declaration of his new intentions. Washingtonians offered hope in what were known as "experience meetings," in its temperance uses a borrowing from recent English working-class anti-liquor campaigns but also in spirit a direct descendant of the Finney revival. Instead of traditional temperance meetings at which basically sober citizens took the pledge as an example for others, Washingtonian meetings featured reformed drunkards attesting to their experiences before and after living by the pledge. In sometimes highly emotional fashion and often in the informal language of the streets, they emphasized the rocky road to sobriety, the wonders of their changed world, and the possibility for any drunkard to change.

These roughs of the reform world, confounding their social betters and in some cases scandalizing them, held a multiplicity of meanings for middle-class temperance reformers. Critics of the temperance movement ridiculed what they saw as this logical outcome of teetotalism: questionably cured and often odd-looking drunkards preaching like ministers to a motley congregation of the recently sober and the hopeful but still degenerate. Most in the temperance movement welcomed the Washingtonians but remained skittish about their departure from tradition. They were sometimes shocked by the working-class atmosphere of Washingtonian meetings, worried about the absence of prayer at the gatherings of many of the individual societies, and afraid that what originally had seemed an outgrowth of their own movement had become too independent.[87]

These specific criticisms may also have been reinforced by less easily articulated feelings. For one thing, the traditional temperance societies had long taken a Manichean view of the sober and intemperate at war with each other, with the drunkard unwilling and unable to be saved. In this argument, physiological and moral arguments combined to form a cardinal principle of temperance: that habitual drunkenness was an incurable enslavement and a sure road to Hell. The phenomenon of thousands of admitted drunkards giving up the bottle under the auspices of a new and strange organization must have disturbed some of the deepest senses traditional temperance reformers had about the world.

Yet in one important aspect the Washingtonians were a logical outcome of the reform process itself. The movement from old Calvinism to evangelicalism, and then from evangelicalism to temperance reform, involved at all points a reworking of the cosmic drama, including the ritual and symbolic terms of that drama for both individuals and society. The very reworking involved the demystification of tradition as well as the search for a new sacred order in keeping with the language and vision of a particular society. That working-class people felt the freedom to create a new ritual and symbolic life around the conversion from drunkenness to sobriety only indicated the continued elaboration of the reform process: the unfolding search for new roads to the sacred in a world whose means of sacralization had become increasingly splintered by the solvent powers of pluralism and freedom.

V

Sabbatarianism and Manual Labor

ABOUT A YEAR and a half after Justin Edwards and his fellows boldly launched the American Temperance Society, Edwards found himself in New Lebanon, New York, aiding in efforts to reign in revival practices among the Finneyites of western New York. Indeed, Edwards took the lead by condemning "invidious comparisons" between "the temporary success of uneducated and ardent young men" with that of "settled pastors"; by declaring that at "social meetings, of men and women, for religious worship, females are not to pray"; and by warning against the "hasty admission of converts" to full communion.[1] Edwards spoke in general about the dangers inherent when evangelists and settled pastors did not operate in harmony, a situation "calculated, or at least liable, to destroy the institution of a settled ministry, and fill the churches with confusion and disorder."[2]

Edwards, of course, could not know that his own project of temperance reform would have just such corrosive effects as it came to maturity in the late 1830s and 1840s. Nor did he understand the full implications of enthusiasm for temperance and evangelicalism even in the late 1820s. Nonetheless, in Finney's realm and also in the heart of Manhattan, new evangelical insurgencies on the part of students, radical ministers, and laypersons were moving toward a vision of evangelical imperatives that soon set them at odds with even such reform-inclined members of the regular clergy as Beecher and Edwards. Those who were comrades-in-arms in 1827 in many cases became enemies by 1834. Though the final straw was abolition, the split in evangelical ranks could already be seen in two other principal reforms of the late 1820s—Sabbatarianism and manual labor.[3]

These causes may not at first glance seem to offer major grounds for disagreement. Maintaining reverence for the Sabbath was an old issue for American Protestants, and one whose history stretched back to biblical times. The manual labor movement, which sought to combine physical labor with traditional seminary curriculum, had its immediate roots in the concern felt by Calvinists of all persuasions about the health of seminarians and the demands to be put on them in an age of heightened ministerial expectation. Yet it was less the causes themselves than the styles and tactics employed by various elements in each movement that caused friction. The points at issue broached major substantive questions: Would reform be subsumed within the general framework of ecclesiastical authority, bending at times to the interests of the church in society? Or would reform follow its own logic of sacralization, connected to but independent of church authority and structure?

Especially important to the developing split in Sabbatarian and manual labor advocacies was the fact that in both movements individuals who had previously played only supportive roles in church life—businessmen and students—took primary leadership roles. They were religious virtuosos whose spiritual impulses remained undomesticated by the education, socialization, and vows of the church. They were evangelical free-lances who, in the widened atmosphere of religious freedom and democratization, felt little trepidation in entering the sacred realm.

Furthermore, to the world of reform at least, they brought distinct advantages. If Edwards, Beecher, and other evangelical ministers had prepared the way by reformulating the cosmic drama in ways conducive to reform, it did not mean that they were best suited for sustained reform action in society. It would take religious virtuosos more familiar with the everyday world of America in the 1820s to shape and extend evangelical ideas into a new piety rooted in the terms of that world.

Not surprisingly, business proved an important locus of creative religious virtuosity. Commerce and industry in the 1820s were among the most innovative and revolutionary arenas of American society, ones where aspiring businessmen employed new technologies and strategies for trade in the cause of profit, and often with the sense that they were leading America to the forefront of progressive forces in the world. Among the founders, it is true, Jeffersonians and Federalists worried each in their own way about the moral implications of the marketplace. However, even they had understood the need of America to be economically self-sufficient. Debates over political economy involved a balancing act between the possible corrupting influence of entry into the marketplace and the need to ensure a prosperity sufficient to preserve the Republican experiment.[4]

Protestantism itself had always evinced an ambiguous attitude toward business and the attainment of riches. Success in the world of one's calling, including business, might be a sign of salvation. The progress of a nation's commerce, as we have seen in Beman's alumni address, might denote national greatness. Yet ever present lay the danger of material indulgence and worse. "Filthy lucre" and its temptations—pride, personal material excess, un-Christian exercise of power—became increasingly relevant topics of sermonizing as the growth spiral of the early republic began to reward investors, manufacturers, and merchants with sums of money beyond their wildest dreams.

Generally speaking, these businessmen were uncritical observers of the economy and society that had brought them riches. However, in notable cases where the experimental piety of the religious virtuoso and the daring of the successful businessman had merged in one mind and body, religious commitment and worldly creativity combined to produce powerful actors in the cause of reform. No better examples of this type existed than Arthur and Lewis Tappan. The Tappans were more than simply pious Christians engaged in business. Both were virtuosos bent on sacralizing all of their own business practices and the world in which they traded. In 1828, they joined forces and sought new ways of making the world conform to Christianity as they understood it. The Tappans acted from their office in New York, that cauldron of the commercial world, where the mission of sacralization met mighty challenges and encouraged innovation. Their verve and bold experimentation remade evangelical reform in ways novel for religion and but appropriate for the age.[5]

The Tappans grew up in Northampton, Massachusetts, in a household of modest means but high religious purpose. Arthur Tappan was born in 1786, his brother Lewis in 1788. Their religious upbringing was dominated by Sarah Tappan, whose own pietistic style was bathed by New Light warmth and circumspection. She believed in an informed religion of the heart and worked with a mother's power to keep piety central to her children's lives. Arthur and Lewis, though they found their calling in the rough-and-tumble world of commerce, made their primary mission a search for the Christian life and the creation of a Christian society. By the mid-1820s Arthur had built a commercial kingdom around the importation of silk. From his office in the Pearl Street store, where he crouched over his crowded desk, he presided over a busy babble of customers, clerks, and order forms, all the time assessing future demands and changes in the market like a seasoned captain on a rough sea. Modest in dress, sometimes feasting on a cracker and cold water for lunch, Tappan cut the figure of a tired saint amid the ebullient excess of his adopted city.

Most important, Arthur Tappan's ship of commerce was also a church, each employee sacralizing work and life in and out of the store. The clerks Tappan hired had to live in approved Christian boardinghouses and lead Christian lives. He also expected them to go to church once a week. Tappan even transformed an upper-story room in his building into a "Bethel," the Hebrew for "House of God," in which employees and employer read morning prayers and performed other devotionals. Tappan extended his pietistic sensibility to business practices as well. Defying the easy credit practices and price-haggling that defined the business style of the age, he ran a cash-only operation and charged fixed though low prices for his goods. At least until the great panic of 1837, such practices ensured Tappan a modicum of stability in an economy filled with small booms and busts. Indeed, Bertram Wyatt-Brown has estimated that Arthur Tappan sometimes grossed over a million dollars a year and probably netted a personal income of between twenty-five and thirty thousand dollars.[6]

Unlike most businessmen of the age, he donated a significant part of that fortune to missionary and reform organizations. Between 1825 and the Panic of 1837, Arthur Tappan was probably the largest contributor to evangelical causes in the land. He was the financial mainstay for the more radical reforms of the 1830s. He helped found and fund the American Tract Society, presided over the American Education Society, helped manage the American Bible Society, and actively worked in the Home Missionary Society and the American Seaman's Friend Society, as well as the American Temperance Society. "This [was] *enjoying* riches in a high degree," Lewis once wrote about his brother's Christian philanthropy, "and is making one live after his death in the good he achieves while living."[7]

Yet Arthur Tappan was not practicing that conservative, traditional charity that had passively supported missionary efforts in the spirit of noblesse oblige. He dispensed his new wealth not to defend an existing social order but to create a new one based upon the imperatives of evangelical Christianity. This became especially evident when Lewis joined the firm in the fall of 1827. Lewis Tappan brought to Pearl Street a business sense and religious virtuosity more experimental than Arthur's, and his muscular energy made him better suited to changing the world than his shy older brother. He would take the Tappan spirit of philanthropy and help fashion from it an engine of radical reform.

Even before he joined with Arthur, Lewis's youthful experiences in the spiritual and business worlds had been marked by speculation and daring rather than steady application. Though he entered the marketplace as a commercial agent and merchant in Boston, by the 1820s he was investing in the riskier business of manufacturing. Some of his investments in textile production were successful; others were not. Yet before and after his move from Boston to New York, his manner in business and reform inclined him to take a chance and to move boldly when he felt instinctively that he was right.

Lewis had demonstrated this same plucky attitude in matters of the spirit. In 1817, he abandoned his mother's Orthodox persuasion to embrace William Ellery Channing's Unitarianism. Yet he did so with the commitment of a religious virtuoso rather than with the relaxed sensibility sometimes attributed to Unitarians.[8] Only one so committed could have engaged in a sometimes angry spiritual debate with his aging mother, who found out about his heresy in 1819 and continually harassed him about it until her death in 1826. Nor was he easy on his fellow Unitarians. When Lewis engaged in a futile battle to found a separate Unitarian denomination, he scolded his own minister for not being "an ultra Unitarian."[9] Lewis himself was clearly an "ultra," seeing a simple connection between belief and action and finding the politics of the world an impediment to grace.

After 1825, as open warfare broke out between Orthodoxy and Unitarianism and each revealed itself in new ways, Tappan began to reconsider his commitments. Could a group that refused to identify itself openly as a sect, for instance, be truly committed to the Christian faith in all its dimensions? He consulted with Lyman Beecher, who reaffirmed the biblical basis for the Trinity. He helped in a surprising conversion of his handyman, one that attested to the power of evangelical religion of the heart. His own financial woes made him wonder about God's judgment on his spiritual course. When Lewis lost his mother, a mire of spiritual guilt further put in question his Unitarianism.

The turning point came when he visited Arthur in 1827 to discuss joining forces in the silk business. Lewis got much more than he bargained for as Arthur led him through the activist world of evangelical piety in New York. When Arthur expressed concern over Lewis's Unitarian views, the younger brother revealed that he had been reconsidering his abandonment of Orthodoxy. Then one day in the fall, after he had returned to Boston, Lewis found himself unable to finish a letter to his father concerning his Unitarian beliefs. He closeted himself in the library, fell on his knees, and instinctively prayed to God "in three persons" and then to Jesus. After this timeless moment of transcendence, he returned to his letter and declared his return to Orthodoxy.[10]

It was, however, a return with a difference. Lewis's peculiar road back to the family faith invigorated his sense of spiritual individuality as well as his commitment. In a manner typical of disappointed believers, he now lashed out against Unitarianism. Having brooked no compromise in his heart on matters of the sacred, he had less patience than ever with religion that compromised with the world. What seemed most important to him was not theological and ecclesiastical quibbling but confronting the spiritual confusion of the world with a bold revamping of human existence. It was the vision of a lay religious virtuoso, whose everyday life was set in the commercial lifeblood of secular society and whose mission was to reconceive that everyday existence in sacred terms.

The first issue with which Lewis grappled was, in fact, his need to make the church more responsive to the sacred senses of the laity. In this he joined with many New England emigrants to New York who had been used to the independence of Congregational churches. The ecclesiastical power that the Presbyterian church exerted on them in New York as a result of the Plan of Union of 1801 seemed stifling. Lewis and other members of Arthur's informal circle of pious laymen, the Association of Gentlemen, tried to create a group of rival Congregational or "Pilgrim" churches. Opposition came from within and without the New England community. Lyman Beecher urged caution. Beecher had been soliciting support from Presbyterians of all stripes in the aftermath of the confrontation with Finney at New Lebanon, and he feared a fissure in the New York City community. Beecher's influence and resistance from the New York Presbyterians stymied the Association's specific plan but not the determination of those involved, for the Tappans and their allies saw the future of Christian effort at stake. "The Dutch & other interests here have paralized even N England men," he wrote in his diary, "and they feel the benumbing influence of timidity, & a compromising spirit, and a fear of man."[11]

Thus they began to work on an even bolder plan, one that would go well beyond the needs of transplanted New Englanders. They sought to bring evangelical light to those social groups previously ignored by well-to-do Presbyterians. As opposed to Beecher, who worried about the deleterious influence of the landless poor but relied upon evangelicalism in general to ameliorate their situation, members of the Association began a campaign to establish an independent group of Free Churches, so-called because they did not charge pew fees. By the early 1830s, the Tappans had helped to establish churches in the worst parts of New York, housed in warehouses or theaters and catering to the physical as well as the spiritual wants of the poor. They and their allies had managed a revolution, and they enlisted Charles Grandison Finney to spearhead the movement.[12]

Even before Lewis's arrival, Arthur had begun experimenting in the sacralization of the world outside his store by bankrolling the *Journal of Commerce* in 1827. He envisioned it as a Christian alternative to the daily newspapers then available, one that in all ways would avoid pandering to the vices and temptations of society. After a rocky first year, he asked Lewis to reorganize it and proclaimed its goal as the creation of a "first rate COMMERCIAL paper" that would provide the latest and most accurate market information available.[13]

It would do this and at the same time strictly observe the Sabbath in all its operations, Lewis proclaimed, even if that meant creating independent news-gathering services to compete with those that worked on Sundays. In addition, by refusing advertisements for the sale of liquors and announcements of theater or circus events, it would "avoid all participation in the gain of those fashionable vices which sap the foundations of morality and religion." However, its agenda would be simple and non-sectarian. "We profess to be friends of Christianity," he declared; "not enthusiasts nor sectarians—and by a liberal and firm support of the moral and religious institutions of the country, we shall hope to merit the patronage of all good citizens."[14] In announcing such an intent, Tappan's market-informed ecumenicism extended far beyond even Beecher's broad evangelical appeal.

The Tappans and other laypersons who were devoted to the sacred restructuring of everyday life turned to areas already broached by Beecher and other evangelicals, but they did so in new ways. One key issue was the Sabbath. The Tappans were not satisfied with their personal adherence to Sabbath rest in business but wished their own efforts to be examples of a new order for all to follow. They supported and were partially responsible for the new energy and creativity exhibited by Sabbatarians in the late 1820s.

SABBATARIANISM

Sabbatarianism, at least in goals, appearances, and self-perception, was clearly the most restorationist of the reform movements of the late 1820s, one that sought the palpable calendrical order of small-town life now passing from the scene. That the Sabbath should become the object of such concern is not entirely surprising. For decades, Beecher and many other ministers saw in Sabbath-breaking one of the key engenderers of disorder in public life. Strict Sabbath-keeping had strong advocates not only in New England but also in Pennsylvania and, indeed, all over the country, especially where Presbyterians and Baptists predominated. Yet by the mid-1820s, at least for virtuosos like Beecher and others who promoted the movement, it had taken on even greater importance. "The Sabbath is the great organ of the divine administration," Beecher declared in 1827, "the only means provided by God to give ubiquity and power to his moral government." If a "stream of pleasure and of worldly cares" distracted the majority of Americans from the sacred devotions of the Sabbath day, he argued, "irreligion w[ould] prevail, and immorality and dissoluteness, to an extent utterly inconsistent with the permanence of republican institutions."[15]

The equation of Sabbath-breaking and the downfall of the Republic may seem farfetched. Yet the idea of the Sabbath and its crucial role in the rhythms of the holy life reached back thousands of years into history; those traditions powerfully informed religious virtuosos of the early nineteenth century as, at least in their minds, the holy day receded in importance.[16]

This was especially true for New Englanders, since their identification
with historical Israel connected them to the biblical originators of the day.

The ancient Israelites had created a day of repose to parallel that day on
which God rested during the creation, the last day of the week. References
to such a day abound in Genesis, Exodus, and Deuteronomy, in which
certain kinds of work are prohibited and time off for servants and animals
is required.[17] Nor was it simply a day of rest. Over the years the Hebrew
tribes enriched Sabbath celebration, for it was a joyous day, and in the
troubled times just before and during the Exile the prophets began to place
extreme importance upon its observance. In Exodus 31:17, God marked it
as "a sign between me and the children of Israel for ever." In times of stress
the renewal of that bond became especially important and even fateful
when put in the language of prophecy. Thus Jeremiah warned that if the
Sabbath was not observed, God would "kindle a fire in the gates thereof
[Jerusalem], and it shall devour the palaces of Jerusalem, and it shall not be
quenched."[18]

For Christians in general, Sabbath observance at first had far less significance as a touchstone of sacred identity. In fact, Jesus himself followed few
of the Sabbath regulations despite criticism from other Jews. Later Christians marked an alternative day, Sunday, as the day of worship, since
tradition had it that the resurrection occurred on the first day of the week.
Puritans and other reformed Protestants, however, in their quest for biblical purity and to distinguish their faith from either Roman Catholicism or
Anglicanism, combined the two sacred days. They worshiped on Sunday
but appropriated much of historical Israel's symbolic view of the day in
their identity as spiritual Israel. Thus the Sabbath in early America was
extremely important, and in New England it became the central ritual
enactment of God's covenant with the Saints and their Godly communities. Breaking the Sabbath became tantamount to breaking the covenant.[19]

In fact, all the colonies passed laws punishing Sabbath-breaking. A
Virginia article of 1610, what one author has called America's first Sunday
law, set loss of provisions, whipping, and, on the third offense, death as
punishment for those who did not attend church on the Sabbath.[20] In
Maryland, working on the Sabbath might lead to fines assessed in tobacco,
whipping, or a three-hour turn in the stocks.[21] The stocks were also used
to punish Sabbath-breaking in Pennsylvania, New York, and Georgia.[22]
The New England colonies passed even more detailed statutes, with similar punishments and a few novel provisions, such as Connecticut's five-
shilling fine for leaving one's residence except to go to church or to do
"some other work necessary then to be done."[23]

The laws themselves functioned as symbolic invocations to Godliness
(as did the occasional Sabbath-breakers hanging in the public stocks) and
molders of the weekly calendar toward sacred ends. Sabbath-breaking also

became an example of wickedness against which the would-be Christian might measure behavior and the Godly community test its virtue. The young Lyman Beecher's bouts with Sunday temptations were but poignant examples of learning through temptation, sin, reflection, and expiation.

It is not at all clear how rigidly the laws were enforced. Not surprisingly, strict Sabbath enforcement was most common in the seventeenth century. Many colonies had graduated scales of punishments, and the laws seem to be aimed at strangers to the community or at those frequenting taverns, hard-to-control locals, or religious dissenters who protested the establishment through objections to Sabbath enforcement.[24] Opposition to a public Sabbath, mostly on grounds of religious interpretation and freedom, developed almost from the beginning. Sometimes it was from within the establishments, as in the case of Roger Williams.[25] For the most part, however, dissenters such as the Quakers and Seventh-Day Baptists, as well as more liberal Protestants, led the way in their conscientious refusal to worship and observe by the rules of the establishment. The increasingly pluralistic reality of the colonies thus led to a mixed and changing status for Sunday observance.

The Revolutionary and post-Revolutionary eras further corroded a commitment to legally enforced Sabbath observance. Constitutional guarantees of religious freedom and separation of church and state put the legality of Sabbath enforcement in doubt; even where laws continued to exist, their enforcement became spottier and in many places a nullity. At the same time, in the cauldron of fear created by the Jeffersonians' perceived neglect of religion and their insistence on disestablishment, Orthodoxy began to see profanation of the Sabbath as an enormous threat. As did Jeremiah, they magnified the significance of Sabbath-keeping and Sabbath-breaking. They envisioned one as preserving the covenant, the other destroying the sacred connection.

The reasons for such a development were numerous. It was convenient to compress the issue of sacred connection onto such a highly visible and simple communal ritual observance. Thus when Congress passed the law establishing the U.S. Post Office and requiring local postmasters "on every day of the week, to deliver, on demand, any letter, paper, or packet, to the person entitled to or authorized to receive the same," those who feared the passing of the sacred in Jeffersonian America found a focus for their very real but more general fears and frustrations.[26] As early as 1811, Sabbatarians began circulating petitions urging the federal government to amend the law so that it would "prohibit mail stages and post riders from traveling, and post-offices being kept open, on Sunday." In another petition of 1811, advocates of the Sabbath worried that the federal government's requirement of mails on Sunday would tend "to justify every species of breach of the laws made for the strict observance of the first day of the week, as set apart by the command of God for his more immediate service."[27]

In addition, as the marketplace advanced in influence, its rationality implicitly challenged the setting aside of a day on which no business could be transacted. Sabbath-keeping became a rallying point for those worried about the corrosive effect of the marketplace and its substitution of acquis-itiveness for Christian values. As Lyman Beecher put it in 1827:

> The secular interests of men are so indissolubly connected, that the stream of business, put in motion by the wicked on the Sabbath day, not only pains the eye of the virtuous, but, as it deepens, and roars, and rolls onward its turbid waters, it draws into itself by the associations of business, a large, and still larger portion of the community; until it spreads unresisted over the land, obliterates the government of God, and substitutes covetousness and pleasure and dissoluteness, instead of godliness and the morality of the Gospel.[28]

A Sabbatarian campaign based on the new evangelical militancy repre-sented by Beecher began in May 1828 with the creation of the General Union for Promoting the Observance of the Christian Sabbath.[29] Broadly committed to the renewal of Sabbath observance as a key to reviving the specifically Christian structure of social life, the group achieved greatest notoriety in their agitation against the 1810 federal law requiring postmas-ters to handle mail on Sunday if it happened to be delivered to the post office on that day. They sought to repeal the law, prohibit Sunday mails, and thus begin to restore Godly order to a fallen community. There was, however, the question of means. No longer could a Standing Order of ministers in an established church dictate Sabbath observance. Rather the new Sabbatarians used the most advanced tools of the new republic's political life: petition campaigns, pressure groups, and congregation-by-congregation agitation of the question at hand. The Sabbatarian campaign thus met the evangelicals' own self-conception, that they fought for the sacred truth by persuading a degenerate society to return voluntarily to Sabbath observance.[30]

Theoretically such an approach should have brought harmony within the movement. However, moderate and radical evangelicals split over just how, and how vigorously, to pursue the cause. The General Union had been founded by Lyman Beecher and a group of moderate evangelicals who sought influence through the sermon, relatively limited public action, and persuasion of important people. Beecher had already criticized the Finney revival for flouting accepted standards of decorum and inflaming rather than informing. He hoped that the Sabbatarian cause could remain free of such excess. Yet the two most influential chapters of the national organization were soon in the hands of influential businessmen highly sympathetic to the Finneyites: Lewis Tappan in New York and Josiah

Bissell of Rochester, New York. While Beecher found it prudent to concentrate on repeal of the postal law, Tappan and Bissell organized campaigns for Sunday closing of bakeries, abattoirs, stores, taverns, theaters, and offices. They also urged an end to commercial transport on the Sabbath.[31]

At the forefront of this radical campaign were young men and women converted in the Finney revival. Here was a cause, they were sure, that would transform the structure of daily life among Americans in the cause of the Second Coming. Toward that end, radical Sabbatarians engaged in campaigns of what many called coercion. In New York and Rochester, cities that lived on commerce, industry, and transport and worked a seven-day week, the radicals attempted to force businessmen to shut down their Sunday operations. Rochester evangelicals openly advocated economic boycott to discipline both transit companies and their Sabbath-breaking passengers. Their tactic was "to act on the owners of steamboats, stages, canal boats, and livery stables; and through the medium of their pockets, to prevent them from furnishing conveyances on the Sabbath, for that large mass of the community who neither fear God nor obey man."[32]

These plans were masterminded by Josiah Bissell of Rochester, who as a businessman also sought to give pious souls a chance to patronize alternative institutions that honored the Sabbath. The most famous of these Sabbatarian enterprises, the Pioneer Line, set up a six-day stagecoach service. As the Tappans had done with their *Journal of Commerce*, Bissell acted the role of the religious virtuoso as a businessman who sought to sacralize his own world of the marketplace rather than to escape from it. The Tappans, for their part, supported the Pioneer stage line despite the advice of some around them. Beecher, who had no quarrel with the basic tactic, warned Lewis Tappan that Bissell needed to trim his sails. "I am a little afraid that our good brother Bissell may need some caution on the subject," Beecher advised. "Having been obliged to raise the steam so high to get under way—it may not occur to him that the Pressure may be too great for necessity or prudence in the remainder of the voyage."[33]

The Tappans also helped initiate massive petition campaigns in New York, ones that were supported by other merchants, artisans, and shop-keepers. Indeed, they transformed the traditionally conservative petition strategy into one that cut across classes and unearthed broad support not only for Sabbatarianism but also for temperance and a general "cleaning up" of public culture in the city.[34] In this sense they literally took Beecher at his word when he warned of the dangers of an exploited and unconverted lower class. The Tappans and allies in the crafts brought the Sabbatarian and evangelical campaigns to working people in New York.

The radical Sabbatarian campaign, however, ended in seeming disaster. Pressure on local businesses was greeted with outrage. Despite the most enthusiastic promotion, the Pioneer Line failed miserably.[35] Petitions to

Congress quickly found their way to the appropriate committee's permanent files.[36] Sabbatarians convinced many evangelicals but alienated many in the general public by their tactics. Opponents from virtually every level of society and every religious persuasion attacked their strong-arm methods as against the spirit of the Republic's free economy, free institutions, and freedom of religion. In terms of public opinion, the Sabbatarian campaign intensified public anti-clericalism.

The failure of Sabbatarianism in the 1820s, then, had much to do with its direct assault on pluralism in public life. Sabbatarians hoped to enforce the Sabbath as publicly sacred despite the wishes of most citizens, and without being able to prove to the skeptical majority that Sabbath-breaking would precipitate major social catastrophe. Radical reformers, meanwhile, had learned their first lesson in the difficulties of transforming society-at-large. The kind of revival enthusiasm and attacks on Sabbath-breaking that might win over a church or even a small town had little chance in pluralistic cities or political assemblies that represented the broad cross-section of Jacksonian Americans. At first, it was a cause whose music only virtuosos could appreciate. Yet the raising of the question may also have won hidden victories, especially in setting the stage for later Sabbatarian movements of a decidedly different nature. Indeed, if one considers the later success of Sunday-closing and day-off legislation, a product of unlikely alliances between labor and the churches, it would not be far from the truth to suggest that radical Sabbatarians lost their own battles but helped to win someone else's war.

MANUAL LABOR

The manual labor movement represented a very different sort of reform. It was a cause that, as opposed to Sabbatarianism, sought a reordering from within the church and the very bodies of its ministers rather than in society as a whole. Its advocates fought for the incorporation of physical labor into the curricula of theological seminaries and other educational institutions. At schools that adopted manual labor, daily schedules mixed routines of milking cows, cutting wood, and other physical chores with the normal demands of academic classes and study time.

Most manual laborites saw increased body stamina and mental quickness as the main benefits, but some extended the virtues of the system to social, economic, and even spiritual spheres. For a brief but crucial moment in the history of American Presbyterianism—between about 1825 and 1834—influential individuals and institutions within the church and among the laity thought that in manual labor they had found solutions to the most pressing problems facing Christianity as it adapted itself to the new world of the young republic. Radical manual laborites created from their work a self-identity and group cohesion that resembled nothing less than what today might be called a revolutionary cadre, one based on self-scrutiny and collective regeneration. Furthermore, the tendency of supporters of the manual labor reform to equate physical health with spiritual health prefigured in the 1820s what would become highly significant in the 1830s and 1840s: popular health reform systems, such as Grahamism, that provided an everyday personal ritual life for reformers even as they went forth to do battle against slavery, liquor, and inequality of the sexes.

Although questions concerning the relation of mind, body, and spirit had been pondered at least since the days of ancient Greece, the particular exposition of educational philosophy cleaved to by manual labor advocates was developed by Philip Emanuel von Fellenberg, a Swiss educator active in the late eighteenth and early nineteenth centuries. Fellenberg founded the Hofwyl school near Bern to demonstrate the moral and physical utility of integrating intellectual and manual labor. Favorable eyewitness accounts of the school began to appear in America around 1820.[37]

The connection between manual labor and the pursuit of the millennial day began, like so many antebellum reforms, in the efforts of Presbyterian and Congregational churches to meet the challenges presented by religious toleration, the rise of the popular Baptist and Methodist churches, and the peopling of the western frontier as it existed in the first two decades of the nineteenth century. The Orthodox churches had founded new theological seminaries to train ministers in greater numbers than ever before in order to meet the new demands of an expanded missionary role. Only then might they hold back the tide of popular religion and insure their own proper place in the vanguard at Armageddon.

Especially among New School ministers like Lyman Beecher and Nathan Beman, the sharpening of millennial mission pointed to a new personal ideal for the ministry. Lyman Beecher spoke for many when in 1827 he detected the *"great commotions and distress of nations* [that] will exist, antecedent to the spiritual, universal reign of Christ on earth."[38] These signs of the time begged for church action. Converting the world through missions, and building a powerful ministry to shepherd America toward what Jonathan Edwards and others had predicted to be its rendezvous with millennial destiny, became the tasks for Christians who shared Beecher's sense of anticipation.

But what sort of ministers and missionaries would be ideal for the momentous tasks ahead? Learned they must be, for that was a key element of traditional Presbyterian and Congregational self-conceptions. Pride in a well-educated clergy became especially important when differentiating themselves from the increasingly popular Baptists and Methodists. But was learning enough? Could that standard, which had sufficed for the town ministry, be the only significant standard for those who would endure the added difficulties of evangelical ministries on what seemed to be the borders of civilization? "No!" declared Garrit P. Judd from his seaside

Christian outpost at Honolulu, and he spoke for many in the missionary community. "We want lion-like men, giant-hearted, who can undertake great things," he continued, "who can bear all things, and endure all things, for the kingdom of Christ's sake."[39] Finneyite John Frost of the Oneida Presbytery echoed Judd when he quoted the late missionary Jeremiah Evarts: "We can get money, and we can get missionaries; but what we want for the triumphant prosecution of this work [are] men of firm constitution, who can endure hardship."[40] Judd, Frost, and Evarts captured in words what was coming to be in the mid-1820s a growing feeling even among more conservative elements that the churches needed a muscular as well as a learned ministry to do battle for the Lord.[41]

This consciousness of the importance of physical strength as part of a ministerial ideal led many in the church to perceive a tragedy unnoticed before: it appeared that the heavy intellectual demands of theological seminary life were turning potentially fine ministers into effeminate, sickly souls hardly capable of hobbling away from the graduation rostrum. Or so it seemed to the American Education Society, whose task it had been to support young seminarians of small means. One of the Society's reports noted with special horror: "The early graves of *thirty* young men, once under the patronage of the American Education Society, who fell the victims of disease before their preparatory studies were completed, and the failure of nearly as many more to enter the ministry in consequence of a loss of health, afford melancholy proof that something should be done to render studious habits less injurious."[42] In an article setting forth his ideal for the ministry, the distinguished southern Presbyterian John H. Rice made a more specific condemnation of the typical seminary experience. "Thoroughly trained scholars," he wrote, "need not be feeble, broken down men, just prepared to go home from their places of education—*and die*. They need not be *consumptive*, or *dyspeptic* or *hypochondriacal*."[43]

The appalling living conditions at Andover, Auburn, and other seminaries were common knowledge and have been documented by scholars. Yet the highlighting of concern about them in the 1820s must in large part be attributed to the new sense of ministerial role and the importance given to an increasingly muscular ministry. Just as many in the church had, in the first decades of the nineteenth century, rejected the traditionally liberal drinking habits of the clergy in favor of at least a certain degree of temperance, so now they had come to replace a lack of concern about ministerial fortitude with a distinct preference for the robust.

Widespread interest in manual labor programs began in the early 1820s. The first major breakthrough came in 1826 when Andover allowed "a few individuals in and out of the Seminary" to engage in light industry "for the purpose of invigorating and preserving health."[44] Soon the trustees widened the program, spending over four thousand dollars to construct a large workshop with a capacity of seventy-five students. At the workbenches, students crafted various kinds of boxes and also practiced traditional cabinetmaking. The program was voluntary; students who elected to participate worked about an hour and a half per day as a group, with free time available to work on individual projects.[45]

Every report agreed that Andover's Mechanical Association was a splendid success. Manual labor seemed capable of working miracles on the bodies of young theologians readying themselves to do battle at Armageddon, or at the very least Samoa or Cincinnati. No wonder, then, that significant programs of either light mechanical and industrial labor or traditional farm work were instituted at a number of important seminaries: Southern and Western Theological Seminary in Maryville, East Tennessee; Theological Seminary in Danville, Kentucky; Manual Labor Academy in Germantown, Pennsylvania; and Oneida Institute in Whitestown, New York. Auburn Theological Seminary, though it had no formal program, provided opportunity for exercise.[46]

A closer look at personal experiences at Andover can give us some insight into just how powerful an influence the labor program might be. Edwards Amasa Park, who would later become one of Andover's most famous theologians, had faced an uncertain future as a student in 1828. After a year of bad health, he had been "reduced to a state of great pectoral weakness and general debility" that "totally disqualified" him from pursuing his studies. Then he joined the Mechanical Association. "Now my natural strength and vigor of body are restored," he assured the readers of the Education Society *Quarterly*; "all unusual symptoms of disease are removed; and I have become habituated to a regular system of physical exercise."[47]

The phrase "a regular system" referred to the argument used by manual laborites that would later become a staple of physiological reform in the 1830s and 1840s. Systematic exercise, they pointed out, not simply physical exertion, provided mental and physical relief, and even a sense of sacred connection. The case of Beriah Green, who later became an important abolitionist, showed how manual labor as systematic exercise also functioned as spiritual exercise.[48] Green had attended Andover before the school had instituted manual labor. As an overworked student at the seminary with additional responsibilities as a teacher at Phillips Academy, he had sunk into ill health and depression. At one point he saw persistent, almost hallucinatory spots before his eyes. Green sought medical advice and was given the current treatments—"leeches, blisters, and the blue pill."

Such treatment afforded him no cure, and his condition worsened when he became "oppressed with the anxieties and fatigues" brought on by an agency for the Board of Foreign Missions. Green was now "spitting blood." "My friends," he remembered, "regarded me as probably near the end of my race." Dismissed from work, Green recovered slightly while resting. At length he found that he could begin to regain some capacity for work by alternating short periods of reading with short stretches of manual labor. Eventually he recovered from his ailments by carefully constructing a system of daily work periods interspersed with periods of mental endeavor. Green's physical efforts became more than simple cures; at least as important, they became ritual invocations and communications with nature. "I keep both ears open to the voice of nature," he remarked at one point. "I have heard her cry, till the voice becomes a shriek, '*To the woodpile! To the wood-pile! To the wood-pile* NOW!' And when I have seized the saw or axe, a thrill of pleasure has seemed to run through every vein, and touch every nerve." Or: "When of a morning I have plunged my face in the water, I have felt the inward promptings of the kind monitor, bidding me bless God for the free use of cold water. How often have I seemed to feel the touch of an invisible hand, setting me free from the lassitude and fatigue, which was crippling and oppressing me!" Freedom and spiritual communion had come as much from putting his life in ritual order as they had from exercise alone.

At Andover, as at most institutions that adopted them, physical programs were voluntary. They were adjuncts to normal curricula, and their advantages were seen as limited: better student health and, in some cases, opportunities for poorer students to work their way through school. Rarely did exercise come to have a greater significance at these seminaries. Especially at Andover, exercise functioned in an academic setting marked by traditional faculties and student bodies. While manual labor clearly mattered, it remained an auxiliary feature of the seminary.

Such was not the case at the Finneyite Oneida Institute, founded directly as a result of the enthusiasms engendered by the 1826 revival. Manual labor itself became the organizing principle upon which the school ran. Exercise and work were woven tightly into the school day. Through manual labor the students of Oneida created a ritual life and sense of camaraderie that translated the heady, iconoclastic, and rambunctiously antihierarchical spirit of the Finney revival into a new and democratic model for living, learning, and working for the Millennium. Manual labor seemed particularly suited to galvanize a group of committed students. On a physical level alone, it coincided well with their youthful vigor. One had to be young to survive the gruelling labor of Oneida's curriculum. Work at Oneida also stressed cooperation, binding committed souls to everyday sharing of routine work.

Oneida Institute, as a product of the Finney revival, also reflected an egalitarian spirit in its structure. From the day of its opening in May of 1827, Oneida's students and their leaders shared authority with the school's formal administration to a degree unprecedented in the world of seminaries and American education in general. This was possible in part because the students had built the institution with their own hands, and in part because students and administrators alike saw it as a bold adventure.

Even the student body symbolized a new turning. Compared to Andover's heavy emphasis on recruitment of decorous and well-connected students, Oneida boasted what one ex-student fondly called "a motley company." Sons of rich families labored side by side with farm boys, and whites with mulatto outcasts saved by the fires of the revival. Even Kunkapot, an American Indian, studied at Oneida for a time.[49]

The students largely dictated and supervised their own schedules. They lived a routine consumed in work and study. The first labor groups began at four in the morning; for the rest of the day, students alternated work with classes and study. Throughout the day, in the fields and at simple meals of bread, pudding, and potatoes, at informal get-togethers and formal meetings, the students talked of millennial mission. They took action. They founded colonization, temperance, Sabbatarian, and missionary inquiry societies.

No wonder, then, that when in 1831 Finney described Oneida to Lewis Tappan and recommended it as the appropriate school for his sons, Tappan jumped at the opportunity. "I was delighted to see young men," he wrote after visiting his sons, "who a few hours previously were reaping, milking, etc come onto the platform before a large assembly and deliver their compositions in Latin and English—orations, poems, colloquys etc with ease and dignity."[50] Tappan and Theodore Dwight Weld, the boys' "Monitor-General" and spiritual guide, became fast friends. Inspired by Weld's magnetism and enthusiasm for manual labor, Tappan funded the new Society for the Promotion of Manual Labor in Literary Institutions and made Weld its general agent.[51]

Oneida's radical atmosphere, however, did not entirely soothe that edge of discontent and experimentation bred in the revival. Indeed, it encouraged the free expression of impatience or disdain when it came to traditional authority and even to the seemingly revolutionary curriculum. Charles Stuart Renshaw, an Oneidan who eventually became involved in antislavery and missionary work, best summed up a pervasive questioning of the traditional course work that was offered as part of the manual labor program. "The desideratum is what course of studies to pursue," he wrote to Finney. "I cannot see what good it will be to study *Latin and Greek*—if I were the best linguist in the universe, it would not aid me in telling a heathen sinner the way to go to the saviour's feet."[52]

This rebelliousness expressed itself in extracurricular areas, sometimes in ways even the most sympathetic outsiders could not understand. For instance, the Oneidans dressed with an almost studied slovenliness. They even offended Finney, their spiritual leader and one who himself had broken ministerial fashion by preaching in a business suit. "When a man appears in good company," he warned them, "let him see that his boots and clothing are clean so as not to create disgust by his inattention to *what they* will insist upon discussing."[53]

Finney misread the Oneidans' coarse appearance as the result of "inattention." Rather these students had created a symbolic costume and badges of honor, displaying a kinship to each other in the style of primitive Christians. But the Oneidans' rough attire not only functioned as a sign of group commitment. It imitated the dress of the common laborer, as well as of John the Baptist, and attested to their wish to transcend a socially exclusive past and to merge into the growing democratic spirit of the age— albeit as radical evangelicals.

Their dress was the outward sign of membership in an amazingly cohesive group of students. Theodore Weld stood at the center of this band, surrounded by the likes of future abolitionists Henry B. Stanton, Sereno W. Streeter, and John Alvord. Distrustful of authority and proud of their youthful vigor, they openly paraded themselves as rivals to the school administration. As Charles Beecher said of the Oneidans, they constituted "a kind of *imperium in imperio*."[54] These worker-students had created a radical sect within the community of Finney converts, one whose members had experienced a second conversion, a fervent but less well recognized physiological regeneration. In terms almost parallel to a traditional religious conversion, all of these students had in one way or another passed from what they conceived of as slavery to physical disorder and disease to the freedom of systematic exercise and spiritual revelation. To them manual labor had been no gimmick, nor even simply a way to avoid ill health and promote missions; it had been the key to a new understanding of right living and harmony with each other and nature's order. In this sense, their experience had been much like Park's at Andover and Green's personal working out of ritualized labor.

At Oneida, however, it became the kind of commitment that transformed manual labor, in the mind of its radical advocates, from a system for improving the ministry to one of broad religious and social implications. In 1831, the Reverend George W. Gale, now head of Oneida, declared to his protégé Finney that its curriculum provided an educational model that would "introduce the Millennium." He promised, "If you and I live twenty years longer, or half that, we shall see it."[55]

Theodore Weld extended this millennial thinking specifically to the social realm, arguing that manual labor provided a cure for class conflict. Even as the Tappans created the Free Churches to bring Christ to the impoverished of New York City, Weld recommended his curriculum as useful to all classes in curing social antagonism. "The chasm between rich and poor," Weld reminded his readers, "already yawns deep and broad; and if it be not speedily bridged, by bringing education within the reach of the poor, it will widen into an impassable gulf." If manual labor might give the poor a boost upward, it also allowed the more comfortable classes to step downward so they might familiarize themselves with the lives of those who toiled with their hands. This would help end class antagonism by familiarizing each class with the honorable labor of the other. "Instead of being driven asunder by jealousies, and smothered animosities," Weld continued, "they [would] approach each other with looks of kindness, and form a compact, based upon republican equality, and the interchange of mutual offices of courtesy and kindness."[56]

Edward Beecher, the zealous son of Lyman and first president of Illinois College, a manual labor school founded in 1830, put the case more formally and completely. As a Republican nation, he argued, America needed an educational system that would meet the wants of the entire community and bind it in mutual respect. In recommending manual labor, he noted its "tendency to elevate the whole community, to prevent the needless alienation of the different orders of society from each other, and to secure an elevated national character, based on the full and harmonious development of all the powers of man, corporeal and social, intellectual and moral."[57]

The visions of Beecher and Weld, naive as they were, nonetheless reflected the evangelical sense of brotherhood in Christ and the importance of reinvigorating a social solidarity perceived lost in the clamor for wealth. They hoped to temper economic conflict with familiarity and mutual respect. Manual laborites took such doctrines and made of them a daringly romantic rebellion.

With such goals and expectations, no wonder the most committed among them might find signs of backsliding and exhaustion even in their own vanguard institution. "Oneida has lost the spirit which she once possessed," Sereno W. Streeter complained in 1832; "her soul is gone." He condemned "an injudicious admission of students, [those] who care[d] for little except the gratification of self." He also found fault with the faculty, complaining that Mr. Grant, a popular language instructor, utterly failed as an exemplar of manual labor virtue. He "lay abed late in the morning," Streeter griped, "drank tea and coffee stoutly and his manual labor consisted in journeying from his room to the backhouse."[58]

Luckily, Lewis Tappan gave Streeter's comrade Weld the task of choosing the site for a beacon-light National Manual Labor Institution, and in 1832 he chose Cincinnati's Lane Seminary. Here, according to one Oneidan, they could "train the soldiers of the Cross within sight of the enemies camp," since the Ohio Valley was "to be the great battlefield between the powers of light and darkness."[59] The Tappans paid the moving and school expenses for Weld's band of manual laborites, who entered Lane Seminary geared for a fight. Committed to defending Lane, which they referred to as their "ship," from the kinds of compromises that drove them from Oneida, the Oneidans flaunted their power and prestige, and at least one of them nicknamed their group the "Illuminati."[60]

Camaraderie ran high, but so did fear. They worried that powerful anti–manual labor men would "crush us by their caresses when they find they can't ever shin us by their kicks," and that the "barkings" of such "dogs" would catch the ears of the trustees.[61] They greeted with a mixture of pride and suspicion the rumors that some trustees, indeed, already "were of the opinion that the Oneida boys had conspired to overthrow Lane Seminary."[62] As twenty-four of an entering class of forty, inseparable and militant, the Oneidans presented an extraordinary challenge to any school administration. They had achieved autonomy from outside authority and an inner solidarity powerful enough to contemplate even more radical stances and actions. The Oneidans had created for themselves a system of values and symbols that shared the ultimate millennial goals of other evangelicals, but in the spirit more of the experimental Tappans than of the world-watching Beecher.

Such a contrast of evangelical style would soon became manifest, in fact, since the Tappans chose not only most of the students, but also the new president of Lane: Lyman Beecher. At first, Beecher and the Oneidans emphasized a common vision of Armageddon and Millennium in the Ohio Valley.[63] However, when student attention turned toward the issue of slavery, Beecher voiced only tepid sympathy. As with Sabbatarianism, the question of how to confront perceived social evil became central and divisive. However, unlike disputes among Sabbatarians, differences over the advocacy of immediate emancipation for America's black slaves could not so easily be swept under the rug. For by attacking slavery in no uncertain terms, the Oneidans, the Tappans, and a new group of reformers under the leadership of William Lloyd Garrison had struck at the heart of the American social and economic system.

PART

THREE

Radical Transformation

TEMPERANCE, Sabbatarianism, and manual labor, while sometimes moving to controversial ground, fit comfortably within the traditional concerns of New England's evangelical establishment. Not so abolitionism, feminism, phrenology, vegetarianism, spiritualism, and the various communitarian experiments that dotted the mid-century landscape of the North. These later movements emerged from profound frustrations experienced by some reformers as they pressed the limits of evangelicalism's cosmic and social visions. They represented a set of radical heresies, a continuation of the ever-widening gyre of spiritual experimentation of which New England evangelicalism had itself once been a part.

Alienated from the web of social and church order, radical reformers sought to make American society holy by broadening and sacralizing the meaning of equality, by making sacred the details of everyday life, and by reimagining the basic structure of society on earth and spiritual being after death. These reformers challenged some of the most basic American assumptions concerning the individual, society, and cosmos: white racial superiority, sexual hierarchy, marriage, prevailing dietary and medical practice, individualistic values of the marketplace, the centrality of the church to religious life, and the nature of death.

The radical transformation of reform began in the late 1820s. At first it proceeded along two fronts, and many individual reformers became involved in both. Abolitionists attacked slavery and racism, garnering angry opposition in all sections of the country and helping to destroy what had seemed to be an impregnable evangelical united front. About the same time, and mostly hidden beneath the din of the slave controversy, several virtuosos created systems of bodily and domestic reform that aimed at sacralizing the details of daily life and health. Soon after, women whose lives had been affected by evangelicalism, abolition, and the reform of everyday life applied lessons they had learned in these causes to protest the unequal status of the sexes. All were stops along the path of an endlessly unfolding spiritual odyssey.

VI

William Lloyd Garrison and the Birth of Abolitionism

IN DECEMBER 1826, nine months after Lyman Beecher had come to Boston, a talented young journalist named William Lloyd Garrison arrived in the same city looking for work. He was searching for spiritual guidance as well. Sunday after Sunday he auditioned the city's famous preachers. He soon decided that Beecher had "no equal," that his sermons proclaimed "Truth—TRUTH—delivered in a childlike simplicity and affection."[1] Garrison embraced Beecher's vision of evangelical reform and by the beginning of 1828 was editing a major temperance newspaper. Only three years later he founded the *Liberator*, which argued for racial equality and labeled as sinners and hypocrites all who claimed to be Christian but opposed the immediate emancipation of the slave.

Garrison's new advocacy set him apart from Beecher and most evangelicals, as well as the vast majority of white Americans. Nonetheless, his plea for the slave galvanized a small but extraordinary group of restless young virtuosos whose yearning for a sacred society had not been satisfied by evangelicalism. Though always a controversial minority, they helped shape a sectional conflict that resulted in civil war and black freedom. In 1865, Abraham Lincoln pointed to their importance when, after being hailed as emancipator of the slaves, the President corrected his flatterer and instead credited emancipation to the army and "the logic and moral power of Garrison, and the anti-slavery people of the country."[2]

Lincoln surely was on to something when he highlighted Garrison's "logic and moral power," for the abolitionist's arguments touched or angered more citizens in the mainstream of American society than any pleas made on behalf of the slave since the Revolution. Yet the source of this power and why Garrison's appeal had such impact have remained unclear. He did not originate the idea of immediate emancipation, nor was he the first to speak out or work intensely against slavery. Rather, he reached beyond prior campaigns of equal moral urgency by emphasizing the imperative of racial equality along with the sin of slavery, and by casting his appeal in the language of militant New England evangelical reform. He rewrote America's cosmic drama in ways that made abolition and racial equality central to its eschatology and gave major roles to blacks and abolitionists. In short, Garrisonian abolitionism gained its power to enlist fervent support or generate fearful outrage from being a radical evangelical heresy.

The special nature of Garrison's vision can be measured against the backdrop of antislavery's short history. For millennia, societies the world over had countenanced slavery as a beneficial institution. Isolated individuals or marginal sects had on occasion protested its destruction of body and soul, but only in the middle of the eighteenth century and only in Europe and its colonies did changes in intellectual and religious consciousness and economic order make a sustained assault on the institution possible. Enlightenment notions of individual freedom and of society as a voluntary compact made slavery seem an unnatural anachronism. A new emphasis on individual virtue, expressed in achievement as well as in moral sensibility, also pointed toward freedom for the slaves and sympathy from those who viewed their degraded state. So too did the implicit values of capitalism and the marketplace, which placed a high value on freely entered contractual relations and especially favored the notion of a free labor market.[3]

These developments in consciousness for the most part provided an environment congenial to the *possibility* of antislavery arguments. However, even when they bred emancipationist ideas, other notions intrinsic to the Enlightenment and capitalism tempered the promotion of immediate action against slavery. Behind most Enlightenment thinking lay a belief that sudden change might upset the harmony of society, and that in any case the forces of progress in history would gradually do away with evil. As for the influence of marketplace values, most often capitalists placed a higher value on the profits gleaned from crops harvested by slaves than on philosophical arguments concerning contracts and free labor.[4]

Especially in England and its colonies, in fact, it took religious zeal to make active antislavery sense out of this new secular environment. The first great push came from English and American Quakers when, as part of a deep self-searching after the Seven Years War, a minority successfully agitated within the sect for a ban on slave trading and slaveholding. Quaker antislavery arguments spilled over into a mainstream made receptive by secular trends and religious revivalism, and they found converts among pious Anglicans in England and evangelicals in both the northern and southern American colonies. Especially during and immediately after the American Revolution, the rhetoric of liberty gave Quaker, evangelical, and natural rights arguments against bondage a powerful if temporary influence. The American Congress joined England in banning the African slave trade, and the states of the North passed gradual emancipation bills.[5]

It would be a mistake to construe such acts and the ideological strains that produced them as being outside of time, place, and situation, or as the beginning of some inexorable march that ended at Appomattox courthouse. Antislavery sentiment always functioned within broader social, political, psychological, ideological, and theological dramas. Expression of opposition or even moral repugnance to slavery meant different things and engendered different actions depending on the context. While Quakers and some revolutionary evangelicals like Benjamin Rush sought in abolition a humane self-cleansing that included consideration of the fate of blacks, many more in the Revolutionary period used the slavery issue within an ingenious rendering of history that bolstered the colonial cause. The British had burdened Americans with slavery's evil, so the argument ran, making colonial slaveholders as haplessly victimized as the slaves. Southerners especially viewed themselves as wedded to a system that had been forced upon them, but unable to act against it because of the dangers inherent in freeing hundreds of thousands of blacks unsuited to freedom and almost certainly filled with vengeful feelings toward whites.

Once Revolutionary idealism concerning slavery had played itself out in the successful banning of the slave trade and gradual emancipations in the North, the nation concerned itself with the practical matters of forging a strong economy, creating a viable economic system, and getting down to the everyday businesses of society, government, and commerce. Moreover, by the 1820s slavery had become too integral a part of the southern economy for a significant number of persons to work for its abolition. Americans increasingly viewed the South's "peculiar" labor system as a seemingly essential, if regrettable, part of the social and economic life of the nation.

The decline of Revolutionary idealism and the incorporation of slavery into American society had their effects on religious arguments against slavery as well. The major churches, many of which had strongly endorsed an end to slavery during and after the Revolution, either backed away from their stands or admitted that nothing could be done about slavery in the United States that would not disrupt church and society.

The Presbyterians, who had passed several antislavery declarations during and after the Revolution, reached their zenith in 1818, when the General Assembly unanimously endorsed a declaration calling slavery a "gross violation of the most precious and sacred rights of nature" and "utterly inconsistent with the law of God." Yet this same declaration condemned "harsh censures, and uncharitable reflection on their brethren" and for the present advised against "emancipating them in such a manner as they will be likely to destroy themselves and others." God would someday show the way.[6]

The Methodists and Baptists similarly moderated their antislavery positions as Revolutionary enthusiasm cooled and the problems of the church in the world took precedence. Methodism had historically opposed slavery thanks to John Wesley's intense hatred of the institution. Early Methodists in America carried on that tradition, and Thomas Coke and Francis Asbury led a successful fight to ban slaveholding among members of the newly created Methodist Episcopal Church of America in 1784, but protests from slaveholders and their ministers forced the church to suspend the rule a year later. Although antislavery Methodists continued to make their appeals, the issue had largely disappeared from view by the 1820s.[7]

The Baptists produced little antislavery commitment in the North but encouraged significant ferment in the South during the Revolutionary era. However, the strong Baptist commitment to freedom of individual conscience, which tolerated antislavery appeals, also allowed the vast majority of congregations and communicants to ignore them. By the 1820s, the Baptists had settled by and large for condemning slavery in theory but treating its existence in America as a political matter separate from the sphere of the church.[8]

The majority of southern and, to a great extent, American clergy, individually and through institutional action and statement, worked out what to them was a meaningful compromise. Accepting the inferiority of blacks and the need for a master if the two races lived side by side, they came to see slavery as "not a beautiful thing, a thing to be espoused and idolized, but the best attainable thing, in this country, for the negro." They worked not for abolition but for the Christian treatment of slaves and for their conversion. "We must leave it [slavery] for God to remove, when his time comes," declared a writer in the *Southern Presbyterian Review*. "It is ours to do the duties of intelligent, decided, fearless, conscientious Christian Masters."[9]

At the core of this ambivalence lay the black presence in America. Uneasy Americans defended the practical need for slavery as a means of controlling blacks. A condemnation of slavery sometimes indicated a discomfort with or fear of the slaves themselves. To advocate cleansing the nation of slavery often carried with it the wish that thereby one might rid the nation of blacks. No wonder that the prospect of black freedom during

the Revolution and after caused Americans to produce a significant literature investigating and accentuating the differences between the races and
the superiority of the white man.

Thus even when abolitionists secured legislation freeing slaves, as
they did in the northern states during the Revolutionary and post-
Revolutionary eras, intense legislative battles and the realities of white
racial attitudes often produced mixed results. Northern slaveholders sold
many blacks to southern slave traders in anticipation of emancipation.
Those freed in the North found their ability to participate in the economy,
politics, and society severely restricted. Only a small number of free blacks
achieved a comfortable material life. The rest were forced to live as pariahs
on the margins of society. During the Missouri debates, through the twenties, and beyond, in fact, antislavery sentiment in the border states and
territories was often inspired by fear that slavery would introduce blacks
into potentially all-white territory. Indeed, laws preventing entry of
blacks—free or slave—were contemplated or passed in nearly every "free"
state.[10]

Not surprisingly, colonization emerged after the War of 1812 as the most
popular and logical reform solution both to slavery and the race question.
The American Society for Colonizing the Free People of Color of the
United States assumed that slavery and free blacks were dangerous anoma-
lies best removed from the American body politic. Founded in 1817, the
Society advocated the transport of "the free people of color" of the United
States to Africa or some other appropriate location. Colonizationists believed that differences in color, talent, and condition, and the fiercely held
prejudice of whites against blacks, would forever make impossible the rise
of black Americans to equality. For blacks, that meant never being able to
fulfill one's promise as an individual or a race. For whites, it meant the
continued presence and growth of a population, in the words of one white
supporter, already "for the most part idle and useless, and too often vicious
and mischievous."[11]

The Society offered something to everyone. It promised free blacks
their own land, where they could prosper without the burden of an advanced and prejudiced surrounding population. To evangelicals it offered
the hope of a Christian assault on the paganism of Africa, with black
emigré-missionaries leading the way. For non-slaveholders north and
south, colonization held open the prospect of cities and towns freed of a
troublesome population. Slaveholders could look to the colonizationists to
remove free blacks who might stir up unrest or outright rebellion among
their slaves. Colonization, the Society declared, would "render the slave
who remains in America more obedient, more faithful, more honest, and,
consequently, more useful to his master."[12] It also provided a safe way for
conscience-stricken slaveholders to emancipate individual slaves.[13]

Colonization garnered ringing endorsements from noted ministers and laypersons but encountered unanticipated resistance from the two groups that were essential to its success: free blacks and slaveholders. The Society had some reason to think that free blacks would find the plan appealing. Numerous free black emigration efforts in the decades prior to its founding convinced them that blacks understood their situation much in the way the Society did.[14] Yet such free black notables as James Forten and Richard Allen, reflecting broader currents in the black community, protested that colonizationists seemed more interested in riveting the chains of the slave population ever more tightly and removing from the country persons they thought of as inferior and troublesome. Though some signed up for resettlement, by the late 1820s unfortunate experiences in Africa and the Caribbean led to disenchantment even among blacks who had once endorsed colonization schemes.[15] For their part, slaveholders remained suspicious of a society mildly antagonistic to slavery, one which counted among its members those known to have emancipationist tendencies. Most important, few slaveholders wished to free slaves whose labor brought them handsome profits.

Despite its impotence, or perhaps because of it, colonization received wide lip service. It offered a position on slavery and blacks that could be defended as being at once a Christian and sensible solution to racial fears on both sides of the color line. Most of all, however, its provision of a weak safety valve for a nation paralyzed on the question of race and slavery revealed just how much the potential mainstream sources of antislavery action had accommodated themselves to the institution's continuing presence.

Exceptional voices, of course, were heard in the teens and twenties. The Reverend George Bourne, an English Presbyterian minister resident in Virginia, published *The Book and Slavery Irreconcilable*, which labeled slavery as "manstealing" and called for "immediate emancipation," in 1816. He publicly condemned slaveholding ministers and refused communion to slaveholders. As a result of his actions, the local presbytery deposed him, a step later endorsed by the General Assembly.[16] Other ministers who took strong antislavery stands eventually left the South, though a handful survived there through the 1820s. The Missouri debates inspired other emancipationists who rejected colonization. Individuals like Thomas Hedges Genin urged that emancipated slaves "be enlightened and formed for good citizens" and pointed to the richness of the slaves' African past. However, they were mostly ignored and forgotten.[17]

More visible was Benjamin Lundy, a Quaker who made the battle against slavery his life's work and who was the most important immediate predecessor to Garrison. Lundy's antislavery position centered on his characterization of the institution as a cruel affront to God and man. He hoped that gradually the nation would come to accept blacks as citizens and to see the injustice of slavery. He published the *Genius of Universal*

Emancipation to effect such a change. At the same time, Lundy supported colonization efforts in the faith that they might aid individual blacks who could not wait for conditions to change, while easing the fears of whites concerning slavery and the free black population. Lundy's greatest strength was perhaps also his weakness. He displayed a singular devotion to emancipation in the style of a Quaker pietist but also shared the tendency of his sect to be satisfied in the role of quiet witness rather than aggressive crusader.[18]

In the early 1820s, Lundy promoted a complete plan of gradual emancipation, one that began with abolition in the territories and the District of Columbia and continued with states sending representatives to a national fact-finding convention. The convention would draw up plans for gradual emancipation and make provisions to ensure equal rights for free blacks in the North and South, including the right to emigrate.[19]

His grand scheme, however, depended upon the responsiveness of a political system that since the Missouri debates was becoming more and more committed to burying the slave issue in the cause of sectional peace. Even as the prospects for political agitation of antislavery diminished, southern whites were beginning to stiffen their opposition to emancipation agitation. By the mid-1820s, Lundy had to reconsider his blueprint. A reading of *Immediate, Not Gradual Abolition*, a pamphlet by the British Quaker Elizabeth Heyrick that expressed frustrations among abolitionists in England similar to those he was experiencing in America, led Lundy to profound doubts about political means and compromise programs.[20] Although he remained sure that God would effect, in the long run, a "gradual spread of reason and the consequent elimination of racial prejudice, which taken together would serve to end slavery," he lost a clear sense of how such a transformation might come about.[21]

Lundy and others who felt the need for more decisive measures supported colonization as a halfway measure, but they were fully aware of its contradictions. If slavery were as sinful and its reality as horrid as emancipationists represented them, only drastic action seemed appropriate. Yet neither Lundy nor other antislavery advocates seemed capable of reframing the slavery issue in this light. The palpable realities of racism, indifference, and a prosperous slave South mocked their faith and led to growing despair.

It was this mood of desperation that William Lloyd Garrison pierced with a bracing new vision of race and slavery in the national and cosmic drama. He took Bourne and Heyrick's doctrine of "immediate emancipation" and Bourne's blunt definition of slavery as "manstealing" and placed them within the terms of New England's evangelical reform cosmology. He revived the Revolutionary generation's notion of slavery as a national sin but turned it into *the* national sin, substituting slavery for intemperance as the bellwether of America's fidelity to its covenant with God. As important, he forthrightly embraced blacks as equal citizens, thus recasting the assumptions inherent in most prior antislavery positions. In all, Garrison created and forcefully argued a revolutionary approach to slavery and race that made its case (initially, at least) in the widely accepted and compelling language of evangelical reform.

That the revolutionary spokesperson for antislavery hailed from New England must have come as something of a surprise to contemporaries, for in the 1820s New Englanders among all Americans had shown the least amount of interest in antislavery or colonization activities.[22] New England's patriot politicians and ministers certainly had been in the forefront of antislavery activities of the Revolutionary era, and Massachusetts led the North in abolishing slavery. However, with the waning of revolutionary ardor, New England's blacks received no better treatment there than anywhere else. They comprised only a small percentage of the region's population and figured little in its well-crafted self-image of chosenness. Even the Revolutionary epics of Timothy Dwight treated slavery in passing and with strange ambivalence.[23]

Garrison began life in this post-Revolutionary New England world. His parents, Abijah and Fanny Garrison, were ill matched, a dour religionist rubbing like flint against a hedonistic (by her standards) sailor. Married in depression-ridden Canada, the couple moved to Newburyport, Massachusetts, in the spring of 1805 to take advantage of New England's newly found prosperity as a neutral trader after the renewal of war between France and England. The Garrisons did modestly well and had William Lloyd, their third child, on December 10, 1805. But the Embargo of 1807 hit Newburyport and the Garrisons hard. Federalist New England, turned to resistance, and Abijah Garrison to rum. Increasingly stern confrontations led Abijah to abandon his wife and children in 1808. For four years Fanny struggled to hold the family together. Brought up in social and economic security, she became a domestic nurse while her children stayed with neighbors, hawked candy in the streets, and collected handouts of food from the rich.[24]

In 1812, Fanny and her oldest son, James, went to Lynn for better work, leaving William in Newburyport with a poor neighbor. Three years later the little boy joined his mother and brother in Lynn and took up shoemaking. The entire family then moved to Baltimore to work at a new shoe factory, but James, who had begun to drink like his father, left the family. William, who yearned to finish school and find a career, returned to Massachusetts soon after.

Shortly before his thirteenth birthday, Garrison finally found a suitable apprenticeship at the Newburyport *Herald*. Journalism provided him security, an education in the world, and a genuine calling. He hungrily pored over the files of the arch-Federalist paper, imbibing the noble, aristocratic, and gloomy worldview of Timothy Pickering and Fisher Ames and making it his own. He joined the local debating society and liked nothing better than to spend his evenings discussing morals, literature, and society with a coterie of like-minded friends. However, the most striking change in Garrison at the *Herald* was his outward appearance. Tired of poverty and enamored of his new status, he began to dress neatly and elegantly. He was, as one of his acquaintances of the time recalled, "unusually dignified in his bearing for so young a man."[25]

The figure Garrison cut reflected more than common pretense and Federalist dogma lightly learned. His penchant for the formal and the orthodox helped him escape a troubled and marginal past. His worship of the titans of Federalism also involved more than simply an aping of aristocracy. No matter that to many Pickering, Ames, and Harrison Gray Otis seemed outlandishly pompous and élitist. They were heroes from his own life, the bravest and most eloquent voices against the embargo and "Mr. Madison's War," the events that destroyed his family. Their arch-Federalism cast the tragedy of the Garrisons in a heroic light.

If Federalist rhetoric illuminated the young apprentice's sense of his own past, it reflected but the earthly dimension of Garrison's avid religious life. He was more than Fanny Garrison's son. He was Fanny's "good" son, whose behavior balanced that of his wayward older brother James in the calculus of family life. As a boy he had delighted in church worship and singing in the choir.[26] He and his mother corresponded in the language of faith, and during his apprenticeships in Newburyport he continued as a choir member and regular worshiper at the Baptist church. He also strictly observed the Sabbath and (less like a Baptist) supported clerical influence in society.[27] He lived the religious life of a young virtuoso, but without any signs of the rebelliousness that would later dominate his stance toward religious establishments.

Indeed, one could detect little rebellion in any quarter of his life. At the *Herald*, Garrison sometimes contributed anonymous pieces, as well as encomiums to Pickering and Otis. He engaged in patriotic flourishes without a second thought about the nation's support of the slave system.[28] The publisher of the *Herald* appreciated his talents and in 1825 helped set Garrison up as publisher and editor of the Essex *Free Press*.

Garrison spent only six months at the *Free Press*, but there he first felt the power of independence and of exposure to new and important influences. He attended a lecture by William Ladd, the pioneering peace reformer, and became a convert to non-resistance. Garrison also published the young poet John Greenleaf Whittier, whose Quaker spirituality suggested to the editor a new realm for his hungry religious imagination.

Only after Garrison sold the foundering *Free Press* in late 1826 and moved to Boston, however, did his vision of the world and reform's sacred promise begin to take shape. For a year he worked at various printer's jobs but mostly delighted in exploring the city. He particularly reveled in the preaching he heard in its various churches. Though still a Baptist, he had not yet undergone the conversion that would prepare him for full communion. He searched for spiritual truth as he listened to Unitarians William Ellery Channing and John Pierpoint.

He thought he had finally found religious wisdom in Lyman Beecher's animated vision of evangelical struggle. Under his influence, Garrison transformed himself in 1827 from a public Federalist and private pietist to an enlistee in the evangelical campaign to resacralize American life. The results were apparent on every page of the *National Philanthropist*, whose editorship he took over in January 1828. The Reverend William Collier, a Baptist city missionary, had founded the *Philanthropist* in 1826 as a temperance paper (one of the first in the nation), "devoted to the suppression of intemperance and its kindred vices, and to the promotion of industry, education, and morality." Garrison met Collier and moved in as a boarder at his house, where he roomed with the paper's printer, Nathaniel H. White. It was not long before White and Collier, impressed by their friend's energy and intelligence, entrusted their paper to him.[29]

Under Garrison's direction, virtually all of the causes that Beecher had championed over the previous twenty-five years found a place in the *Philanthropist*'s columns. The main points of Beecher's sermons on intemperance dominated every issue. So too did lists of crimes and disasters caused by drink. Echoes of the sermon on duelling sounded as Garrison urged voters to judge political candidates by their support of temperance and other moral causes. Garrison fought mail delivery and public transit on the Sabbath. He also declared war on infidelity, endorsing a letter to the paper that suggested suppression of irreligion as "the surest method to suppress intemperance and its kindred vices."[30]

Yet it would be a mistake to see the young editor as a blindly loyal soldier in Lyman Beecher's army. Garrison devoted himself to evangelical causes as part of a personal search for spiritual order, not out of loyalty to church institutions or even reform organizations. His upbringing in the Baptist tradition of dissent and suspicion of clerical order restrained him from uncritical embrace. While he wholeheartedly championed evangelical reform, he felt free to test the consistency of its leaders and extend its logic in ways that advanced his search for the wellsprings of the religious life.

Garrison finally broke from evangelicalism over slavery, but the initial push did not come from New England sources. Slavery figured in his political and religious environment, but in ways that ended more than opened contemplation of its abolition. Among Federalists, slavery had come to play a symbolic role in the struggle with the Jeffersonians. The fact that Jefferson and many in the leadership of his party were slaveholders gave Federalists a repertoire of images and issues whose net effect was to question the commitment of the Jeffersonians to liberty and to characterize them personally as hypocritical tyrants. As early as 1798, the New-buryport *Herald* summed up the two favorite charges. "The planters are generally extremely ignorant, excessively idle, and addicted to all the low vices of drinking, gambling etc.," it declared. "Supported entirely by the labour of his slaves, under the direction of an overseer, the planter reclines at his ease and can live in luxury without any personal exertion." Jefferson himself was a favorite target for his slaveholding and his un-Christian view of the slave.[31] In all, slavery's moral destruction of Virginia functioned as a foil, rendering slave-free New England virtuous by comparison.

Garrison's early editorial career mostly reflected New England's self-satisfied stance on slavery. In the *Free Press* of March 29, 1826, for example, he printed without comment a part of Edward Everett's address to Congress in which Everett vowed that he would be among the first to take up arms against a slave rebellion. However, less than two months later he recommended to his readers a recently published poem, "Africa," which read in part:

> Is it a dream?
> Or do I hear a voice of dreadful import,
> The wild and mingling groans of writhing millions,
> Calling for vengeance on my guilty land?
> "Oh that my head were waters, and mine eyes
> A fount of tears!—Columbia! in *thy* bosom
> Can slavery dwell?—Then is thy fame a lie!

And on July 4, 1826, he celebrated the fiftieth anniversary of the Declaration of Independence earnestly but with a warning: "There is one theme which should be dwelt upon, till our whole country is free from the curse—it is SLAVERY."[32]

Yet joining Beecher's evangelical crusade did not guarantee that Garrison would magnify his interest in slavery. New England evangelicals, who had transformed their tribal visions to the national setting, found the slave question a vexing block to national unity. They mostly ignored it or relegated it to the status of a tragedy for all that would someday be remedied by God. For instance, when Beecher declared that, for the Millennium to come, "man must be unshackled and stimulated" and *"the earth must be owned by those who till it,"* he referred exclusively to the oppressed of Europe.[33] In 1825, the more radical Nathan S. S. Beman condemned American slavery as a blot on the nation but failed to suggest a plan for its abolition. Instead he expressed supreme confidence that some way would be found, most likely by God, to remove the institution.[34] Slavery and the slave trade, when they were considered at all, were conceived of as horrors marginal to the American experience or used to bolster causes evangelicals found more compelling. Thus Beecher's *Six Sermons on Intemperance* and Heman Humphrey's *A Parallel Between Intemperance and the Slave Trade* used both slavery and the slave trade to underline the greater evil of intemperance. When evangelicals did focus on slavery, it was through the Colonization Society.

It took the patient but persistent hand of Benjamin Lundy to make slavery an obsession for Garrison. He received Lundy's *Genius of Universal Emancipation* as an exchange paper at the *National Philanthropist*. Garrison read it avidly and became convinced of the importance of emancipation to American destiny. Lundy came to Boston in March of 1828 and boarded with William Collier, and Lundy and Garrison became fast friends discussing the slave issue. Garrison attended a meeting at which Lundy urged a number of Boston's prominent clergymen to support the antislavery cause.[35] The ministers endorsed Lundy's newspaper but refused to organize an antislavery society or otherwise actively pursue an end to the institution. Only Garrison and a few others stood by the Quaker. "He might as well have urged the stones in the street to cry out in behalf of the perishing captives," he recalled ten years later. "Every soul in the room was heartily opposed to slavery," he continued, "but—it would terribly alarm and enrage the south to know that an anti-slavery society existed in Boston! But—it would do harm rather than good, openly to agitate the subject! But—we had nothing to do with the question, and the less we meddled with it, the better!"[36] Whether because of his disgust with the spinelessness of the clergy, his growing commitment to antislavery, or both, Garrison resigned from the *National Philanthropist* on July 4, 1828.

Lundy returned to Boston in August to address a crowded public meeting at the Federal Street Baptist Church. He argued that emancipationists must move beyond the inadequate if commendable efforts of colonization societies if they wished to rid the land of slavery. Lundy reported on the efforts of 140 emancipation societies, most of them in the South, but pointed out that New Englanders must do their part as well. By the Constitution they were bound to protect slaveholders in case of insurrection. They had a stake in abolition and should form societies of their own to enlighten the public and petition Congress to end slavery in the District of Columbia.[37]

Apparently the Reverend Howard Malcolm, pastor of the church, had not expected even a moderate antislavery appeal. He rose immediately after Lundy's speech to counsel inaction. Malcolm assured the audience that labor demands in the lower South would soon empty the upper South of its slaves. He noted that "God often overrules events in themselves evil, for the promotion of ultimate good," and that in this case the slave trade was the key. In time, he argued, the benevolence of history would allow slavery to die a natural death. These remarks caused an angry stir in the audience, but Malcolm abruptly ended the meeting before other views could be heard.[38]

Garrison's reaction demonstrated his own developing position. In letters to the Boston *Courier*, he endorsed Lundy and savaged Malcolm's remarks. He objected to any endorsement of slave trading and argued that demand in the lower South would beget slave breeding. "The Virginian is as careful to have the prolification of his female slaves unobstructed," he claimed, "as he is anxious to improve the condition of his horses for the next race, or his cocks for the next fight. He places his negroes upon the same footing with his cattle, pigs, and poultry, and the propagation of each is encouraged in proportion to the value of their productions." Garrison pointed out that selling slaves from one region to another did not "relieve the country of its Atlantean burden" and in fact only "consolidate[d] oppression and render[ed] the liability of insurrections still more formidable."[39]

Garrison, however, felt optimistic about antislavery's future and embraced Lundy's strategy as his own. Antislavery societies, he argued, must "unite the moral strength of the country" and "warn, advise, and remonstrate, till the shackles of the oppressed [were] broken by the will, not by the wealth, of the people." He recognized that the task required "much patience, immense exertion, and a strong faith in its ultimate accomplishment." Yet Garrison also seemed to share Lundy's belief that "a majority of the southern people, and even of the slave-holders" wanted slavery abolished, and that those in favor of the institution constituted a small if powerful minority. Slavery might gradually be dismantled if only public opinion could be mobilized against it.[40]

Soon after the Lundy meeting, Garrison helped form a committee of "high-minded, spirited, and philanthropic men" to direct a Massachusetts petition campaign in favor of abolishing slavery in the District of Columbia.[41] In October 1828, supporters of John Quincy Adams asked Garrison to edit the *Journal of the Times* in Bennington, Vermont, and gave him full editorial freedom. Though he acquitted himself well for Adams, Garrison admitted that his true passion lay in promoting reform causes. Every issue touted developments in the temperance cause. Garrison also spent time sparring with Unitarian John Pierpont on the issue of the Sabbath and espousing the peace views of William Ladd.[42] Most strikingly, Garrison promoted "the gradual emancipation of every slave in the republic."[43] In the *Journal*'s first issue he urged the founding of antislavery societies in Vermont.

In November, Garrison penned a petition to end slavery in the District of Columbia. "We are ashamed," it declared to Congress, "when we know that the manacled slave is driven to market by the doors of our Capitol, and sold like a beast in the very place where are assembled the representatives of a free and Christian people."[44] Congress's disheartening response surprised no one. The House voted an inquiry into the slave trade and slavery in the District of Columbia. However, the report of the Committee on the District condemned all agitation for ending slavery and the slave trade as inflammatory and potentially encouraging rebellion among slaves "who would otherwise remain *comparatively* happy and contented." The committee, like the Reverend Howard Malcolm, argued that the slave trade would rid the District of slavery. It also put a rosy construction on the personal effects of the trade: "Although violence might sometimes be done to their feelings in the separation of families, yet it should be some consolation to those whose feelings were interested in their behalf, to know that their condition was more frequently bettered, and their minds [made] happier by the exchange."[45]

"The most refined cruelty," Garrison dubbed the report, "the worst apology for the most relentless tyranny." His anger was colored with despair, for he knew that, with Andrew Jackson about to be inaugurated President, the political system had been effectively closed to antislavery action. However, as with Beecher in an earlier period, disillusion with politics clarified rather than destroyed Garrison's commitments. The fight simply had to proceed in another realm.

Meanwhile, Benjamin Lundy continued to push Garrison toward total devotion to antislavery. In the *Genius* he wrote an open letter to Garrison in which he applauded his loyalty to the slave and hoped that he would "remain *true to the cause*." Having seen other antislavery advocates give up when confronted by unyielding opposition, Lundy recommended to him the example of the Apostle Paul, another reformer whose situation the "lukewarm reformer" might have found hopeless.[46] Garrison replied with a simple vow: "Before God and our country, we give our pledge that the liberation of the enslaved Africans shall always be uppermost in our pursuits."[47] Lundy was convinced. In an extraordinary pilgrimage, he walked from Baltimore to Bennington to propose a partnership: Garrison would edit the *Genius* while Lundy embarked on a speaking and fund-raising tour. Garrison accepted.[48] He published his last issue of the *Journal of the Times* on March 27, 1829, and his first number of the *Genius* on September 2 of the same year.

In the months between editorships, Garrison experienced a great spiritual ferment in which he began to formulate a distinct approach to slavery, one that differed from Lundy's and went far beyond the conservative position of Beecher and most other evangelicals. He fleshed it out for the first time in a Fourth of July oration at Park Street Church, ironically at a meeting in support of the Colonization Society. A week before delivering the address, he made his own assessment of its tone: "Its complexion is sombre, and its animadversions severe."[49] Indeed, Garrison delivered an American jeremiad that avoided easy answers and left few parties unscathed.

From the beginning Garrison merged the typical evangelical warning that America stood on a great precipice, ready to plunge into darkness, with a central focus on slavery as the root of its dilemma. Compare, he asked, the July Fourth "which established the liberties of a brave people" and "gave an impulse to the heart of the world" with the profligacy of 1829. He quickly sketched a scene of American promise weighed down by infidelity, Sabbath-breaking, intemperance, and a political system (Jackson had just been inaugurated) rotten to the core. However, he now emphasized slavery as the cardinal American sin— "a gangrene preying upon our vitals—an earthquake rumbling under our feet—a mine accumulating materials for a national catastrophe."[50]

Appropriate for the day but unusual in evangelical discourse on slavery, he forthrightly declared that the slaves and their condition must be approached on the basis of racial equality.[51] Garrison assumed his audience was familiar with the cruelties of slavery but had thought less about its anomalous existence in a land whose watchwords were "'all men are born equal,'" and that guaranteed as inalienable rights "'life, liberty, and the pursuit of happiness.'" He therefore dispensed with "authentic recitals of savage cruelty" and wished instead to define the duty of Americans by establishing certain propositions. Most basic, he asserted, was not only that slaves had the right to the "prayers, and sympathies, and charities" of Americans but also that the slaves' "claims for redress [were] as strong as those of any Americans could be in a similar situation."[52]

Garrison then attacked his own evangelical comrades for their neglect of duty to the slave. Christianity, he argued, had done "comparatively nothing" for the slave. While the church "explored the isles of the ocean for objects of commiseration," she "gaze[d] without emotion on a multitude of miserable beings at home, large enough to constitute a nation of freemen, whom tyranny has heathenized by law." He fired a summary volley at the churches and their auxiliaries: "The blood of souls is upon her garments, yet she heeds not the stain. The clankings of the prisoner's chains strike upon her ear, but they cannot penetrate her heart."[53]

Turning to the racial assumptions that underlay that neglect and dictated colonization, Garrison again took the ground of equality. Most slaves were entitled to all the privileges of citizenship, he emphasized. "This is their country by birth, not by adoption. Their children possess the same inherent and unalienable rights as ours, and it is a crime of the blackest dye to load them with fetters." Garrison compared the Declaration of Independence's "pitiful detail of grievances" with those of the slave. They were "the stings of a wasp contrasted with the tortures of the Inquisition," and they made American celebration of the unalienable rights of man into "hypocritical cant." He confessed, "I am ashamed of my country. I am sick of our unmeaning declamation in praise of liberty and equality."[54]

Garrison also enlarged upon Lundy's case for northern interest in the abolition of slavery, but he wrapped the practical argument that the North had pledged itself through the Constitution to defend the South against slave insurrection into a very un-Lundy-like drama of impending doom. "I assert the right of the free States to demand a gradual abolition of slavery," he argued, "because, by its continuance, they participate in the guilt thereof, and are threatened with ultimate destruction." Later in the address, he implicated the North more directly:

> We are all alike guilty. Slavery is strictly a national sin. New-England money has been expended in buying human flesh; New-England ships have been freighted with sable victims; New-England men have assisted in forging the fetters of those who groan in bondage.[55]

While Garrison did not endorse coercive measures to end slavery, he claimed for the North the right to use "fair persuasion." Otherwise the Constitution and the Union were expendable. "If we must share in the guilt and danger of destroying the bodies and souls of men, *as the price of our Union;* if the slave States will haughtily spurn our assistance, and refuse to consult the general welfare," he proclaimed, "then the fault is not ours if a separation eventually take place." Nor did he believe that constitutional arguments against antislavery advocacy were honest. What if the slaves miraculously became white, he asked. No one then would talk of constitutional limitations. "No; your voice would peal in the ears of the taskmasters like deep thunder; you would carry the Constitution by force, if it could not be taken by treaty; patriotic assemblies would congregate at the corners of every street."[56]

Garrison, in short, re-created the evangelical drama of American society's sin, declension, and possibility for renewal, and he reset its terms. The troublesome black population, slave and free, which the Colonization Society wished to remove, here shared the rights of all Americans and were the most aggrieved citizens in the land. The evangelical church, which in Beecher's scenario led the children of light against those of darkness, in this version was as lost in darkness on slavery as any group of Americans. The Constitution and American unity, which in the evangelical drama constituted a divine presence to be protected and nurtured, in Garrison's view hypocritically shackled the slave ever tighter.

As a result of this revamping, Garrison envisaged a dramatically different finale to the cosmic drama should America not rid itself of slavery. Beecher and other evangelicals saw the abolition of slavery as a task meant for God in God's time, and they viewed human intervention as threatening a national unity essential to evangelical victory. Garrison saw human inaction as the prime ingredient for disaster. His view of the slave's equality made bloody rebellion, the central fear of slaveholders, a moral certainty in God's universe. They would rise up to claim their God-given rights as the colonists had in 1776. "If we cannot conquer the monster [slavery] in his infancy, while his cartilages are tender and his limbs powerless," he asked, "how shall we escape his wrath when he goes forth a gigantic cannibal, seeking whom he may devour? If we cannot safely unloose two millions of slaves now, how shall we bind upwards of TWENTY MILLIONS at the close of the present century?" Using the imagery slaveholders reserved for slave insurrection to describe slavery itself, Garrison foresaw insurrection as the wages of sin. "Blood will flow like water," he predicted, "—the blood of guilty men, and of innocent women and children. Then will be heard lamentations and weeping, such as will blot out the remembrance of the horrors of St. Domingo."[57]

Despite such a prospect, Garrison specifically ruled out instant abolition, fearing that "the emancipation of all the slaves of this generation" could not be accomplished without possibly "burying the nation in its ruins." Instead he counseled church leadership in a campaign for a gradual emancipation; promotion of African missions; founding of women's benevolent societies to aid degraded black women; support of Congressional colonization efforts and the founding of auxiliary societies "in every State, county, and town"; agitation of the slave issue by newspapers across the land as a means of converting public opinion; and abolition of slavery in the District of Columbia.[58]

It was, then, a vision built upon a fatal contradiction. Garrison, the renegade evangelical who castigated his church and his country, embraced the slave as an equal, and predicted doom in the form of catastrophic race war, still recommended gradual emancipation and standard agencies of change, and he almost reflexively returned to the glow of evangelical hope: "But there is no cause for despair." Christians had already seen how that "horrid gorgon, Intemperance," had been checked. If they campaigned as vigorously and uncompromisingly against slavery, the future was assured.[59]

Not long after his address, though, Garrison moved forever beyond the accepted wisdom of gradualism. By the time he reached Baltimore to edit the *Genius*, he was ready to declare himself for immediate emancipation. Lundy could not go that far but agreed that each editor could say his piece and sign his own articles. Garrison made clear his stand in his opening editorial of September 2, 1829. "Mature reflection," he said, had led him to declare "that the slaves are entitled to immediate and complete emancipation: consequently, to hold them longer in bondage is both tyrannical and unnecessary." It was not for the tyrant to decide when his subject might be free. Expediency for whites also dictated immediatism, because it would be much easier to free and educate two million slaves in 1829 than many more millions years later. "Give them liberation," he declared, "and every inducement to revolt is removed." With jobs, education, and religious instruction, "they w[ould] make peaceable citizens."[60]

The force of logic alone had not brought Garrison to this moment. He had closely followed antislavery's progress in England, reporting on it in the *Journal of the Times* and later in the *Genius*. In 1823, English abolitionists had gained a general commitment from the government to proceed toward gradual emancipation in the British empire. That same year Thomas Fowell Buxton took control of the abolitionist cause in Parliament, and under his leadership a vigorous antislavery campaign began. In addition, a new organization—the Society for the Mitigation and Gradual Abolition of Slavery—replaced the old abolition society. As symbolized by the publication of Elizabeth Heyrick's *Immediate, Not Gradual Abolition* in 1824, the abolition society's modest name masked an increasingly radical strain in the movement. It waged war against slavery across party lines, with efficient petition campaigns, prodigious distribution of periodicals and pamphlets, and highly effective local pressure groups. Although progress was slow in Parliament, antislavery made enormous gains in the broader public.[61]

Garrison was well aware of the different type of struggle he faced in the United States, where slaves and free blacks actually lived in great numbers, where slaveholders wielded mighty power in Congress, and where racism rallied whites in both sections together against an emancipation on American soil. Nonetheless, he was inspired by the fact that America's parent nation and one of the world's great powers could produce such daunting opposition to slavery. Correspondents supplied the *Genius* with speeches, pamphlets, and debate transcriptions from England, many of which the editors published. Garrison viewed each new pamphlet advocating immediate emancipation and each debate in Parliament as a sign that a showdown on slavery was near.[62]

If England provided an example of antislavery renewal, residence in Baltimore enabled Garrison to confront some of slavery's grim realities at first hand and to understand personally what had been abstract concepts but months before. Soon after arriving in Baltimore, he had heard the screams of a slave being whipped in a house near his office, and he noted in the *Genius* that this was "nothing uncommon." A slave who had just been beaten once visited Garrison and Lundy. The editors counted thirty-five gashes, from neck to hips, on his bleeding back.[63] In Baltimore, he also met and worked with free blacks on a regular basis. Indeed, they and Lundy's fellow Quakers made up virtually his entire social world. The debate over colonization thus took a personal turn as Garrison published arguments against colonization written by his own black friends. At stake were the rights of people he knew and respected. In general, Garrison's months in Baltimore humanized and deepened his loyalty to the black community and to the cause of the slave.[64]

His experience at the *Genius* and life in Baltimore tapped a part of Garrison's personality rarely evident during his editorial stints in New England, where the young would-be Federalist with airs of fine dress and sophistication masked his other self. That other Garrison, the marginal and struggling son of a drunkard from an impoverished home, had a reservoir of empathy to help him feel at home among others shunned by society. Blacks repaid him with a trust based on the fact that he was one of the few whites to stress, in theory and practice, the basic humanity and equality of all human beings.

Such an attitude reflected itself in Garrison's response to *David Walker's Appeal . . . to the Colored Citizens of the World, but in particular, and very expressly, to those of the United States of America,* which appeared in late 1829 and stirred great controversy in the South.[65] Walker, a free black from Boston, penned his protest in trenchant fury, publishing a four-article pamphlet that raged against slavery, the seeming willingness of blacks to remain enslaved, their ignorance, and the hypocrisy of white Christianity and its colonization plans for blacks. The first edition predicted that God would soon "tear up the very face of the earth" over slavery. "I tell you Americans ! that unless you speedily alter your course, *you* and your *Country are gone!!!!,*" he prophesied. A third edition, published in March 1830, appended language specifically encouraging slaves to rebel when "you see your way clear" and assuring them that God would be with them as they triumphed.[66]

The pamphlet's appearance engendered widespread fear across a South still in the shadow of Denmark Vesey's abortive slave revolt of 1822 and embroiled in a tariff debate tinctured by the slave question.[67] The proprietor of a used-clothes shop frequented by sailors making runs up and down the eastern seaboard, Walker had apparently sewn copies of the work into the clothes bought by sailors going South. He hoped that those clothes would in turn be bartered in the South, and that copies of the *Appeal* would fall into the hands of free blacks and slaves.[68] By this strategy or some other, the *Appeal* began to appear in the South. Sixty copies of the pamphlet were found in Savannah alone. The governors of Virginia and Georgia called their legislatures into secret session to consider a response to the panic created by Walker. As a result, Georgia prohibited entry of free blacks into the state's ports. It also made "the circulation of pamphlets of evil tendency among our domestics" punishable by death and outlawed teaching free blacks or slaves how to read or write. Louisiana and North Carolina passed similar laws, while Virginia seriously contemplated the same.[69]

Garrison's reaction to Walker was complicated but deeply respectful. "We have had this pamphlet on our table for some time past," he wrote by way of introducing excerpted reports of southern reactions, "and are not surprised at its effect upon our sensitive Southern brethren." His firm allegiance to non- resistance caused him to "deprecate its circulation," but he could not help but admire Walker's "bravery and intelligence" and the "most impassioned and determined spirit" of his prose. In February, he called the *Appeal* "a most injudicious publication, yet warranted by the creed of an independent people."[70]

In many ways Walker had constructed precisely the same version of cosmic history as Garrison had in his Fourth of July address. Both saw bloody race war as the God-ordained punishment for slavery's continuance and counseled repentance in the form of abolition and black uplift. Both appealed to the egalitarian rhetoric of the American Revolution and decried the hypocrisy that celebrated freedom for whites alone. Garrison asked his white listeners to imagine themselves enslaved and despised in order to grasp the simmering anger of blacks. David Walker made that anger palpable and confirmed Garrison's vision of impending apocalypse.

They differed, of course, in important ways. Walker celebrated race war as an awakening of the dormant strength of the blacks. While he assured whites that quick action to abolish slavery and other injustices would bring peace and forgiveness, his prose reflected no real belief in that possibility. Garrison saw insurrection as a tragic punishment brought on by white inaction, and he concentrated mostly on rousing whites before it was too late. Still possessed of an evangelical optimism that white society could be saved, he worried that the *Appeal*'s distribution might thwart efforts toward that end. However, despite his discomfort with Walker as the prophet of a race war he hoped to avoid, Garrison credited the humanity of his advocacy and the accuracy of his vision. Indeed, Garrison's struggle with Walker's *Appeal* made more profound his own egalitarian commitment to blacks.

Just how radical Garrison's reaction to Walker was can be seen by comparing it to that of other northern whites. These were perhaps best personified in the response of Mayor Harrison Grey Otis of Boston to an appeal by the mayor of Savannah to punish Walker. Otis sympathized with the Georgian as to the "bad and inflammatory tendency of the publication" but ridiculed Walker as a lowly old-clothes dealer, emphasizing the "insignificance of the writer, the extravagance of his sanguinary fanaticism," and the small circulation of the pamphlet. He noted that the writer of the *Appeal* had broken no laws and therefore could not be arrested. However, he promised to warn sea captains and others traveling to the South against carrying the *Appeal* or other provocative writings, mostly so that they could avoid prosecution.[71]

Garrison's understanding of Walker far outreached even that of Benjamin Lundy, who responded to the *Appeal* in the April 1830 issue of the *Genius*. Lundy could "do no less than set the broadest seal of condemnation upon it," fearing the injury it might bring to "our cause." He characterized Walker as indulging "in the wildest strain of reckless fanaticism" and purporting to surround his argument in religious terminology when "religion ha[d] nothing at all to do with it." Lundy saw no bravery or intelligence, nor the "impassioned and determined spirit" Garrison had found. "It is a labored attempt to rouse the worst passions of human nature," Lundy concluded, "and inflame the minds of those to whom it is addressed."[72]

Other whites expended few words on Walker. They simply wanted him killed. Rumors ran wild that southerners had offered a thousand dollars or more to have him assassinated and perhaps ten thousand to have him delivered to the South alive. On June 28, 1830, he was found dead near his shop, apparently the victim of poison. No solid evidence was ever discovered, but never had circumstances made murder seem more likely.

Violence and intimidation threatened antislavery advocates as well. In 1826, Lundy himself had been nearly beaten to death by one of the wealthiest and most brutal slave traders, Austin Woolfolk, when Woolfolk took exception to Lundy's characterization of him as a "monster in human shape." Charged with assault and found guilty, Woolfolk was fined one dollar and court costs.[73] When Garrison referred to Woolfolk's brutality in a column attacking the Baltimore *American and Gazette* for taking slave auction advertisements, the slave trader, who assumed the column had been written by Lundy, threatened his old enemy again. Garrison replied that he had written the piece, and that if Woolfolk wished to discuss slavery or slander with him, he ought to meet him at his boardinghouse. There, Garrison promised, he would convince him of the wickedness of the slave trade or, if he failed, apologize for any unwarranted insults. "Let me assure him, however, that I am not to be intimidated by the utterance of any threats," Garrison asserted, "or the perpetration of any acts of violence."[74] Garrison heard no more from Woolfolk.

He was not so lucky in the case of shipowner Francis Todd. Todd came in for Garrison's scorn when the editor discovered that this New Englander from his own town was engaged in the coastal slave trade. In the *Genius* for November 20, 1829, he recommended that he and his captain be "SENTENCED TO SOLITARY CONFINEMENT FOR LIFE" as "enemies of their own species—highway robbers and murderers." Todd and Captain Brown instituted a suit against Garrison and Lundy, and by February the Grand Jury had indicted the editors for "gross and malicious libel." The ensuing trial hinged more on a debate over slavery than it did on the technical matters of libel law, and the jury took fifteen minutes to declare Garrison (as the writer of the libel) guilty as charged. Garrison's sentence: a fine of fifty dollars and court costs, or six months in prison. Having no money with which to pay the fine, Garrison entered the Baltimore jail.[75]

Garrison's prison experience ranks in importance with the historic incarcerations of Henry David Thoreau in Concord and Martin Luther King Jr. in Birmingham, and it perhaps exceeds them in its extraordinary details. Garrison walked among the prisoners and jail keepers alike as something of a saint. He often dined with the warden's family, was more or less free to visit other inmates, and often aided them in drafting petitions or appeals for their release. For instance, he helped gain a pardon for a highway robber serving a life sentence who had been an exemplary prisoner for years. He lent comfort to captured runaway slaves and debated masters and slave traders who came to get them. He confounded one master by asking him what right he had to his slave, which led to a lengthy discussion of the biblical view of slavery, the fitness of a black to be President, and whether Garrison would allow his daughter to marry a black man.[76]

In short, though homesick for "New England—that paradise of our fallen world!" and "heartily sick" of living in a slave society, Garrison thrived. "Between the labors of my brain, the conversation of my friends, and the ever changing curiosities of this huge menagerie," he wrote to a friend, "time flies away astonishingly swiftly." He penned caustic notes to the judge, the prosecutor, and Francis Todd. He composed Byronic verse on the wall of his cell. He also drafted and published the eight-page pamphlet *A Brief Sketch of the Trial of William Lloyd Garrison, for an Alleged Libel on Francis Todd, of Massachusetts.* "Certainly the fact would astonish all Europe," it concluded, "if it were trumpeted in that quarter, that an American citizen lies incarcerated in prison, for having denounced slavery, and its abettors, in his own country!"[77]

The pamphlet caused a minor stir across the nation, especially among fearful journalists and reformers. Some of his friends sought to have him released. John Greenleaf Whittier asked Henry Clay for assistance, but by the time Clay acted Garrison had been freed by a fateful intercession. Arthur Tappan, having been shocked by the *Sketch*, wrote to Benjamin Lundy that he would pay Garrison's fine and, in addition, refinance the now defunct *Genius of Universal Emancipation*. Garrison was released on the fifth of June.[78]

Some historians have noted Garrison's use of his jail experience as one more demonstration of an egomaniacal "martyr complex" among abolitionists and other reformers, but his own reflections at the time belie such an interpretation. Little more than a month after gaining his freedom, he recalled how one night in jail he lay on his bed and compared his fate to that the slave. He eschewed whatever inclinations he might have had to romanticize his imprisonment and narrowed the similarity to one: they both were confined to captivity in a limited space. "Farther all parallels fail," he wrote. Compared to the slave's lifelong endurance of poor food, clothing, and shelter and, most of all, work for another's gain without even the freedom to read of another world, Garrison dubbed his prison "a palace." "If the public sympathy is so strongly excited in my behalf," he asked, "because justice has been denied me in a single instance, how ought it to flame for two millions of as valuable and immortal souls, who are crushed beneath the iron car of despotism?"[79]

Prison quickened Garrison's radicalization immeasurably. Heading north soon after his release to garner support and to thank the Tappans in person, he was aglow with determination. Lewis Tappan remembered

Garrison's "manly form, buoyant spirit, and countenance beaming with conscious rectitude." In making the cause of the slave truly his own, he had found a holy calling and a firm sense of inner peace.[80]

It was, however, a sorely tested peace. The indifference and even hostility of New Yorkers and New Englanders to his views shocked Garrison. "Their prejudices were invincible—stronger, if possible, than those of the slaveholders," he wrote of his post-release trip north. "Objections were started on every hand; apologies for the abominable system constantly saluted my ears; obstacles were industriously piled up in my path." His best friends urged him not to return to Baltimore, not to pursue his "visionary—fanatical—unattainable" cause. Why should he make himself an exile, "among enemies whose hearts were dead to every noble sentiment?—&c. &c. &c.," he remembered them arguing. "I repeat—all were against my return."[81]

Garrison visited Baltimore only briefly, to stand trial again in a civil procedure brought by Todd and Brown. He and Lundy had already decided not to renew their partnership at the *Genius*. When the trial was put off until the fall, Garrison decided to return to the North. In early August 1830, he circulated a prospectus for a new antislavery newspaper, the *Public Liberator*, to be published in Washington and devoted to immediate emancipation and uplift of the black population. He also announced his intention to promote peace and temperance in his paper, but by now these had become secondary. Garrison sent the proposal to Arthur Tappan and almost instantly received an endorsement and a check.[82]

From August 1830 through January 1, 1831, Garrison toured the northern states to stir up support for the new publication and for the founding of a national society devoted to immediate emancipation. Crucial to garnering a following for the *Liberator* and for the soon-to-be-born American Anti-Slavery Society, this period also marked an extraordinary turning point in Garrison's relationship to evangelical Calvinism. Garrison's disappointment at the clergy's lukewarm reception of Lundy in 1828, and his own very cordial relationship with heretical Quakers in Baltimore, had begun to lay the foundation for a questioning of his own commitments to the Calvinist church and its evangelical campaign. Yet he presented himself as a committed evangelical in most outward ways and had not yet questioned that identity himself.

In 1830 and 1831, however, as he tested his new antislavery views in public, Garrison's religious vision was seriously shaken. To be sure, evangelical influences were still important. A reading of the evangelical Presbyterian radical George Bourne's *The Book and Slavery Irreconcilable* vastly enriched Garrison's speeches and the first issues of the *Liberator*.[83] "Next to the Bible," Garrison wrote of Bourne's pamphlet in 1832, "we are indebted to this work for our views of the system of slavery."[84] For his part, Arthur Tappan kept Garrison within the orbit of evangelical reform, though Tappan himself had for some time argued a more radical line than Beecher.

Despite its evangelical tone, Garrison's appeal courted evangelical hostility but won the open support of those whose religious views he once condemned as irreligious. Throughout his entire lecture tour, he was virtually shunned by mainstream white evangelicals. In Philadelphia, home of the Presbyterian synod, only the Franklin Institute opened its doors to him. His audience consisted almost entirely of Quakers and free blacks, among them James and Lucretia Mott and several others who became lifelong abolitionists.[85]

New England's welcome was mixed but again underlined evangelical hostility and at the same time a new constituency of blacks, Quakers, and Unitarians. In New Haven, sponsored by the Reverend Simeon S. Jocelyn, white pastor of the black Presbyterian church, Garrison spoke to racially integrated audiences. He lectured as well at a black church in Hartford. In both places, Garrison remembered making black and white converts but especially winning the "hearty approval" of blacks. He also privately debated the Reverend Leonard Bacon, one of colonization's great champions.

He met real opposition in Massachusetts. In Newburyport, his hometown but also that of Francis Todd, the trustees of the Presbyterian church refused him a hall. He proceeded to neighboring Amesbury, where he lectured at the Lyceum to so large an audience that his succeeding lectures were moved to a bigger room. Garrison then returned to Newburyport. After a first lecture at the Second Congregational Church, the trustees closed its doors to him. Leaving his native town for Boston, he declared of those who conspired against his appearance: "Let them answer to God and posterity for their conduct; for even this communication shall be read by future generations, and shall identify the ashes of these enemies of their species."[86]

Garrison's luck did not improve in Boston. For two weeks he searched in vain for a free church or hall to speak. He approached Beecher but got little satisfaction. According to one source, Beecher at first excused himself from antislavery activity because he was too busy. "Then," Garrison replied, "you had better let all your irons burn than neglect your duty to the slave." To which Beecher responded: "Your zeal is commendable, but you are misguided. If you will give up your fanatical notions and be guided by us (the clergy), we will make you the Wilberforce of America." It was one more shock to Garrison's naive sense that he was promoting a cause that would find support among the evangelicals.[87]

Finally Garrison placed an advertisement in the *Courier*, requesting a meeting place and declaring that otherwise he would address Bostonians on the Common. Not one church offered its facilities. His only reply came from Abner Kneeland, who offered to sponsor him at Julien Hall under the auspices of the Society of Free Enquirers. Kneeland had been a Baptist and then a Universalist minister, but in 1829 he renounced Christianity in any form to pursue anti-clerical causes. Thus it was with some chagrin that Garrison accepted; he spent a few minutes of his first lecture thanking Kneeland and excoriating the Christian churches who had been surpassed in open-mindedness and generosity by a freethinker, but he nonetheless insisted that only the power of the Gospel could end slavery.[88]

This lecture of October 15, 1830, Garrison's first public address in Boston since July 4, 1829, repeated the themes of earlier lectures on the tour. He denounced colonization as a sham and detailed the crimes of slavery. He spoke of New England's complicity and the calamitous dangers of inaction. His audience was an extraordinary one. Lyman Beecher and other ministers attended, as did a group of young Bostonians that included Samuel E. Sewall, Amos Bronson Alcott, and the Unitarian minister Samuel J. May. Beecher seemed unmoved, but the younger men were transformed. Garrison's denunciations of colonization and advocacy of immediate emancipation and equality for blacks marked a turning point in their lives.

Equality seems to have been the essential revelation. Years later May called Garrison's Julien Hall lecture one that "he only, I believe, at that time, could have written." May continued, "He only had his eyes so anointed that he could see that outrages perpetrated upon Africans were wrongs done to our common humanity; he only, I believe, had his ears so completely unstopped of 'prejudice against color' that the cries of enslaved black men and black women sounded to him as if they came from brothers and sisters."[89]

For May, hearing Garrison was a religious experience. After the address, he turned to his friends and called the speaker "a prophet." Alcott and Seward agreed, and at Alcott's home they sat with Garrison until midnight, until all had been converted to the doctrine that "immediate, unconditional emancipation, without expatriation, was the right of every slave, and could not be withheld by his master an hour without sin." May concluded, "That night my soul was baptized in his spirit, and ever since I have been a disciple and fellow-laborer of William Lloyd Garrison."[90]

May's experience exemplified how closely becoming an abolitionist resembled the experience that lay at the core of religious conversion. Immediate emancipation for Garrison did not refer to a plan but rather to a total change of mind about the equal rights of slaves. He spoke of immediate emancipation without colonization as the "right of every slave," whatever whites thought or did. It was a doctrine that accomplished nothing and everything. No slave became free as a result of its pronouncement. At the same time, the proper and full acceptance of its implications on the part of a white person revolutionized his or her attitude toward blacks. Black and white, it meant, shared the same human, God-given rights. No person, race, or nation bestowed those rights on another, nor could anyone withhold them without sinning and courting devastating consequences. This revelation might engender new tactics for ending slavery, but its deepest impact on whites was the challenge to racist assumptions.

Garrison's power over Samuel J. May and the small but extraordinary band of white New Englanders who converted to abolitionism—what made him a "prophet" among them—was that he led them to a revelation. Racial inequality was so endemic to the structure of everyday life in America that even uneasy religionists like May, Alcott, and Sewall literally could not conceive of race relations differently. Once spoken by Garrison, equality seemed the light that clarified all contradictions. It took a newspaperman from poorest Newburyport, steeped in the language of the culture but by upbringing something of an outsider, to reconceive the cosmos for them in terms of equality.

Still, the number of converts was small. Most of New England remained implacably opposed to or ignorant of Garrison's plans. When he finally started publishing the *Liberator* in Boston on January 1, 1831, his resources were meager. He and Isaac Knapp, its publisher, lived in the spare editorial offices. They could hardly afford type and paper, and sometimes even these necessities were refused them because of the nature of the *Liberator*'s reputation. The venture survived only because James Forten, the black activist and businessman from Philadelphia, Ellis Gray Loring, and Samuel Sewall made a steady supply of small "loans" available to Garrison.[91]

Why had he decided to publish in Boston rather than in the District of Columbia even though, as it turned out, free black subscribers in Washington and Baltimore outnumbered all subscribers in Boston? In public Garrison explained that Lundy had moved the *Genius of Universal Emancipation* to Washington, leaving little need for a second antislavery journal in that city. Yet the conversions Garrison made in Boston, despite all opposition, must have convinced him that his natural battleground was New England. His love of the region and his evangelical sensibility told him that it was most important to convert God's chosen ones, those who would lead the nation once they had seen the light. It was not to avoid slavery but to make abolitionists of the Saints that Garrison stayed in New England.

"To the Public," Garrison's inaugural declaration in the first issue of the *Liberator*, marked him as a regional prophet. He began with an assault not on slavery but rather on those who opposed antislavery in the North *"and particularly in New England."* He declared, "I found contempt more bitter, opposition more active, detraction more relentless, prejudice more stubborn, and apathy more frozen, than among slave-owners themselves."[92] "To the Public" also rang out in the tones of an evangelical jeremiad even as it set forth the revolutionary egalitarian terms of abolitionism. Compare, for instance, the prophetic style of Garrison's defense of the "severity" of his language to Lyman Beecher's justification for advocating total abstinence. Admonishing his readers to forego moderation when it came to slavery, he wrote:

> On this subject, I do not wish to think, or speak, or write, with moderation. No! no! Tell a man whose house is on fire to give a moderate alarm; tell him to moderately rescue his wife from the hands of the ravisher; tell the mother to gradually extricate her babe from the fire into which it has fallen;—but urge me not to use moderation in a cause like the present.

Beecher had similarly attacked prudent drinking:

> I know that much is said about the prudent use of ardent spirits; but we might as well speak of the prudent use of the plague—of fire handed prudently around among powder—of poison taken prudently every day—or of vipers and serpents introduced prudently into our dwellings, to glide about as a matter of courtesy to visitors, and of amusement to children.[93]

Garrison, however, had moved beyond the traditional evangelical formula of encouraging individual commitment to virtue in order to restore a Christian social order. He merged religious concerns for the soul of every individual within Christian society with a radical extension to blacks of the egalitarian principles of the Revolution. He unfurled "the standard of emancipation in the eyes of the nation, *within sight of Bunker Hill and in the birthplace of liberty.*" He thus consecrated Boston as America's city on a hill for true freedom.

Although always an important theme since his antislavery awakening in 1829, and in some sense a restatement of Federalist attacks on Jeffersonian Virginia, the hypocrisy of slavery in a land of freedom became one of Garrison's central motifs in the *Liberator*. Take his "Truisms" of the second issue. "He who calls American slaveholders [tyrants], is a fool, a fanatic, or a madman," he noted; "but if he apologise for monarchical governments, or an hereditary aristocracy, set me down as a tory, and a traitor to his country." Or: "A white man who kills a tyrant, is a hero, and deserves a monument. If a slave kills a master, he is a murderer, and deserves to be burnt." Or: "To doubt the religious vitality of a church which is composed of slaveholders, is the worst species of infidelity."[94]

Garrison made the hypocrisy of American freedom a permanent, literally visible fixture by designing a new masthead for the April 23, 1831 issue. In a woodcut at the center and above THE LIBERATOR appeared a scene from the nation's capital. On the left, with the Capitol in the background, a banner marked LIBERTY floated next to a slave being whipped at a post. At the center and right stood a HORSE MARKET sign and an auctioneer behind a podium labeled "Slaves Horses & other cattle to be

sold at 12 o'c.," with prospective customers in fine suits inspecting a ragged
family of slaves. Outraged editorials appeared condemning the masthead,
and friends counseled the return to a plain design, but Garrison insisted
that it remain. It stayed until 1865.[95]

His was not simply a scornful voice. Especially when in the company of
free blacks, he predicted sweeping changes and made his egalitarian vision
more specific than ever. In an 1831 "Address Before Free People of Color,"
he assured free blacks that they "and the trampled slaves w[ould] all be
free. . . . Each shall sit under your own vine and fig-tree, and none shall
molest or make you afraid." He envisioned a future of "educated men of
color, the Websters, and Clays, and Hamiltons, and Dwights, and Ed-
wardses of the day," as judges, congressmen, and "Rulers of the people—
the whole people."[96]

To white Americans, however, he reiterated his prophecies of race war
as God's punishment for slavery. He let no month in 1831 go by without
repeating his warnings. On January 8, for instance, Garrison began a
series of articles and communications on Walker's *Appeal*. He again denied
endorsing the pamphlet—"We do not preach rebellion"—and assured his
readers that the "possibility of a bloody insurrection at the South" filled
him with "dismay." It was a denial with a difference, for Garrison declared
that "if any people were ever justified in throwing off the yoke of their
tyrants, the slaves are that people." Thus every celebration Americans
made of foreign peoples rising up against tyranny, and every Fourth of
July celebration, "put arguments into the mouths, and swords into the
hands of the slaves."[97]

He bolstered these warnings with reports of actual slave resistance. As
opposed to Lundy, who went out of his way to characterize rumors and
reports of slave revolt as mostly the product of "guilt-burdened minds" or
"imaginary fear," Garrison saw them as fulfillments of prophecy.[98] On
January 15, he prefaced an article concerning rumors of revolt in North
Carolina: "Such is slavery—a war of extermination on either side."[99] In
February, under the title "Revolutionary Symptoms," he asked members
of "our no-danger-from-the-continuance-of slavery party" to heed "several
hints at a dark plot which spread some terror throughout parts of Louisiana."[100]

In April, he printed the dream of a northerner that imagined a nation-
wide race war started by a southern slave revolt. In the dream, masses of
northern militia moved south to aid in crushing the insurrection, leaving
the North unprotected and "subjected to all that the vengeance of infuri-
ated slaves could inflict. . . . Three savages rushed into my house, and
killed my wife and child before my face. Oh! the unutterable barbarities of
that moment!" He awoke "in an agony of horror. Unspeakable was the
relief of finding that all these things were but a dream."[101]

Not all who wrote in the *Liberator* referred to the prospect of revolt in

such gloomy terms. "V.," a frequent contributor to the *Liberator*, imagined
a hymn of insurrection to be sung by the slaves which began:

> See, tyrants, see; your empire shakes;
>   Your flaming roofs the wild winds fan;
> Stung to the soul, the negro wakes;
>   He slept, a brute—he wakes, a man!
>   His shackles fall;
>   Erect and tall,
> He glories in his new found might,
> And wins with bloody hand his right.[102]

Writing about Walker's *Appeal*, "V." reminded Americans of the revolution in Haiti and assured them that its example was "before the eyes of our slaves" and would soon be staged in the United States. "The actors are studying their parts," he noted, "and there will be more such prompters as Walker. At present, they only want a manager."[103] "A Colored Philadelphian" predicted in August that soon the call "'Fight for liberty, or die in the attempt,' w[ould] be sounded in every African ear throughout the world."[104]

Then, on August 31, 1831, came Nat Turner's revolt. On that day and in the days that followed, Turner's small band of slaves killed at least fifty-five whites and courted a bloody reprisal that saw seventeen slaves hanged and many more murdered indiscriminately as militia and vigilante groups searched for rebels and vented their fear and rage. Slaveholders across the South rose up as one against antislavery groups, whom they blamed for the uprising, and moved in many states toward increasingly repressive measures against slaves and any who advocated their freedom.

The bloodiness of the Turner revolt shook Garrison, but the combination of his pacifism and unswerving commitment to treating blacks as equal human beings lent a fullness to his reaction absent in most other quarters. He was appalled by the slaughter, and now that such "scenes at which the heart sickens" were realities he harshly condemned new reports of Walker's *Appeal* being circulated in the South.[105] However, as opposed to Lundy, who again counseled against the "many extravagant exaggerations and even totally *unfounded* rumors" that surfaced in the wake of the Turner revolt, Garrison saw it as tragic confirmation of his own prophecies. "The first drops of blood," he declared, "which are but the prelude to a deluge from the gathering clouds, have fallen." In the first issue of the *Liberator* he had published a poetic vision of a brutal slave insurrection. "What was poetry—imagination—in January," he noted sadly, "is now a bloody reality. . . . Is it not true?"[106]

To the many northern and southern critics who charged Garrison himself with instigating the rebellion through the *Liberator*, he retorted that the cause of rebellion was to be found in the slaves' "stripes—in their emaciated bodies—in their ceaseless toil," and that "invitations to resistance" came in every celebration of American freedom and foreign uprising against tyranny.[107] Only one remedy existed, he argued, and that was immediate emancipation: "So much for oppression! so much for gradual emancipation! so much for the happiness of the slaves! . . . MEN MUST BE FREE."[108]

The Turner revolt also excited Garrison's evangelical sense of stormy battle ahead. "Henceforth there is to be no peace on the earth," he predicted on January 7, 1832, in a New Year's editorial, "no cessation of revolutionary movements . . . until unjust rule be at an end." The chains Americans had placed on two million were "as galling and heavy" as any in the world. The question that remained was simple: "Shall those chains be broken by physical or moral power?"[109]

Meanwhile, Garrison labored on a definitive pamphlet exposing colonization's support of slavery and racism. It was a crucial work, he thought, since even such friends of the *Liberator* as Samuel J. May had taken strong exception to the tone Garrison used when excoriating colonizationists. Garrison combed the Society's journal, the *African Repository*, for evidence of its activities and intentions. In October 1831, he received and immediately published the English abolitionist Charles Stuart's *Letter on the American Colonization Society*, which argued many of the points Garrison had made in speeches and fugitive pieces since late 1829. Material from Stuart found its way as well into the new work.[110]

Garrison published *Thoughts on African Colonization* on June 2, 1832. This 238-page broadside, whose title-page motto read "Out of thine own mouth will I condemn thee" and "Prove all things; hold fast that which is good," overwhelmed May and other doubters with evidence from colonizationists themselves. *Thoughts* argued that the Society was an apologist for slavery; that it recognized slaves as property; that colonization efforts actually increased the value of slaves; that the Society opposed immediate emancipation; that it relied for support on "an irrepressible and agonizing fear of the influence of the free people of color over the slave population"; that it worked to deny the possibility for blacks to improve their lot in the United States; and that free blacks, who considered themselves American citizens with the rights of citizens, were almost unanimously opposed to its efforts.[111]

"There shall be no neutrals," Garrison predicted in his address to free blacks in 1831; "men shall either like me or dislike me." If most Americans came to see Garrison, in his own words, as "a madman, a fanatic, a disturber of the peace, a promoter of rebellion," the prophetic whirlwind of the *Liberator*'s appearance, the bloodbath of the Turner revolt, and the colonization pamphlet drew around him a small but enthusiastic following. Not only free blacks and those whites like Samuel J. May who heard him in Boston, but also a network of New England evangelicals in New York and the West, caught the contagion of Garrison's vision.[112]

In Boston his original converts Samuel J. May and Samuel Sewall gathered others to the cause, including Arnold Buffum, George W. Benson, Oliver Johnson, Maria Weston Chapman, Ellis Loring, and Francis Jackson. Many of Garrison's followers in Boston were Unitarians or Hicksite Quakers, while other early New England abolitionists included the Methodists La Roy Sunderland and Orange Scott. All were of a culture imbued with New England's sense of chosenness.[113]

In New York, Arthur Tappan, who had been a strong supporter of the American Colonization Society but by 1830 had severed his ties over the issue of rum in Liberia, came to appreciate Garrison's breakthrough. Tappan joined Garrison and Simeon Jocelyn in June 1831 to attend the First Annual Convention of People of Color, there to present a plan for a black college in New Haven. It was Tappan's first real contact with blacks, and he soon felt deeply connected to their fate. By August 1831, Arthur's allegiance to Garrison and his sympathy with the egalitarian strains of Garrison's writings had become so strong that his brother Charles complained to R. R. Gurley of the Colonization Society: "I wish Arthur Tappan had let him lay in Baltimore jail."[114] Garrison returned Tappan's interest and admiration. "It may be safely affirmed," he wrote in October 1831, "that no man in the nation is doing so much for the temporal and eternal happiness of his fellow men as Arthur Tappan."[115]

Garrison also won supporters on the farthest reaches of the New England frontier. The Methodist minister Charles B. Storrs, president of Western Reserve College in Hudson, Ohio, and faculty members Elizur Wright Jr. and Beriah Green, all actively involved in various reforms and supporters of colonization, converted to immediate emancipation as a result of reading the *Liberator* and *Thoughts on African Colonization* in 1832. "The more I was troubled with [Garrison's] great fundamental principles," Wright confided in December 1832, "—the more sick I was of that flexible, convenient expediency on which I say my own cause was based. In short, I burnt up my Colonization."[116]

Theodore Dwight Weld, who was lecturing on temperance in Hudson, Ohio, late in 1832, came under the sway of Wright, Storrs, and Green. Just before the trip to Hudson, Weld had given lukewarm endorsement to James G. Birney's colonization work—since "light breaks *in from no other quarter.*" Discussions with the newly minted Hudson Garrisonians brought him to the cause of immediate emancipation. Arthur Tappan wrote as much to Garrison on December 12, and on January 10, 1833, Weld himself revealed to Wright: "Since I saw you my soul has been in travail upon [slavery]. I hardly know how to contain myself."[117]

Weld carried Garrisonian immediatism back to Lane Seminary in Ohio, where he promptly began to organize a series of discussions of colonization and slavery that became known as the Lane Debates. It seemed an unpropitious place. Most of Lane's professors, administration, and trustees were colonizationists at best, and Cincinnati lay across the Ohio River from slavery. Beecher advised Weld against it but would not stand in his way when he set February 1834 as the time for eighteen days of presentations. At the end, enough students had been converted to found a Lane Anti-Slavery Society devoted to immediate emancipation. Moreover, a number of Lane students fanned out in Cincinnati's "Little Africa" to teach reading, writing, arithmetic, and other subjects and to set up Sabbath schools. Weld virtually joined the black community. "If I ate in the City it was at *their* tables," he recalled. "If I attended parties, it was *theirs—weddings—Funerals—theirs—Religious—meetings—theirs*—Sabbath schools—Bible classes—theirs. During the eighteen months that I spent at Lane Seminary I *did not attend Dr. Beecher's Church once.*"[118]

Beecher may have noticed. He sought to defuse and control the students. He wanted them to end their socializing with blacks and to calm their advocacy of immediate emancipation. They would have none of it. Meanwhile, supportive communications from outside poured in. The Tappans, who had just lived through a vicious riot directed against their antislavery activities, urged Weld and his comrades not to "desert" the antislavery fight.[119] "Our hearts are wonderfully knit together," Elizur Wright Jr. wrote from New York after the riots. "And there is a determination henceforth to stick to our holy principles and our glorious leader more closely than ever."[120]

While Beecher was in the East in the summer of 1834, the Board of Trustees at Lane cracked down. They recommended measures that would have snuffed out student rights to organize for any but strictly educational purposes. As in the Sabbatarian cause, Beecher saw himself as the wise man caught between extremes. He wanted compromise and went to the Tappans' store to complain that the students had flouted public sentiment and now were paying for their defiance. Tappan remained unmoved and blasted Beecher for not being an abolitionist. In the end, Beecher signed his name to a Declaration of the Faculty that endorsed the new regulations and, as it turned out, caused the Oneidans and many of their converts to leave Lane rather than be muzzled.[121]

For Lyman Beecher and his dream of evangelical unity, it was the beginning of the end. Lane Seminary, at which Beecher hoped to train an army of ministers to do battle at Armageddon, never recovered from the mass exodus of students. Beecher then watched Presbyterianism fall into schism as Old School factions pressed the church to rid itself of New School adherents, their theological deviations and benevolent societies.[122] Finally, in 1837, the Old School General Assembly abrogated the Plan of

Union, thereby removing the New England strongholds of the New School from the church.[123]

As for abolitionism, the early 1830s marked the high point of unity. Quakers, Garrisonians, and the Tappans and their comrades worked side by side with free blacks amid verbal abuse from all quarters and physical mangling by mobs. Abolitionist activists created local and state antislavery societies across the North and, in December 1833, united to form the American Anti-Slavery Society. Newspapers proliferated, pamphlets were distributed by the thousands, and orators blanketed the farthest reaches of small-town America to spread the gospel of abolition. The numerology of new societies and new members, of circulation statistics for newspapers and pamphlets, seemed to prove a massive conversion of the American body politic to emancipation. The passage of the West India Emancipation Act of 1833 in Great Britain, and the peaceful emancipation that followed in 1834, augured well for precipitous change in the United States.

By the mid-1830s, however, resistance to the abolitionists, economic depression, and inevitable doctrinal disputes pushed antislavery itself into schism. From that time to the outbreak of the Civil War, various antislavery factions followed their own roads. Garrison led his contingent to place abolitionism within a broader radical platform that included non-resistance, woman's rights, and disassociation from government and church. The Tappans continued in a more traditional evangelical framework and in concert with church-oriented agitation. Still others revived political antislavery by launching the Liberty party and helping to shape the Republican party. Free blacks found places within all groups but also raised their voices independently when faced with condescension or discrimination from white abolitionists. While cooperation did occur, more often each faction fought its own war against slavery in isolation and not without a modicum of feuding and backbiting.

Indeed, some historians have argued that the abolitionists, and certainly the Garrisonians, had the least direct role in the events that hurtled the Union toward secession and war. Yet neither the splintering of antislavery nor the fact that Garrison's faithful became perhaps the smallest of its factions should obscure the great turning point of 1831. Garrison had so infused the principle of equality into the antislavery argument that no amount of backsliding in theory or practice could remove it. He had framed the battle against slavery so forcefully within the evangelical drama of imminent Godly vengeance that its power remained even after evangelical unity crumbled and many abolitionists left the churches.

And when the war came and dragged on, no vision but Garrison's seemed quite equal to the task of invigorating the war effort and justifying the losses incurred. When Lincoln issued his Emancipation Proclamation and allowed black soldiers to fight, he did so partly in the spirit of Garrisonian equality. When Julia Ward Howe wrote the "Battle Hymn of the Republic" and soldiers marched to their deaths "to make men free," they did so within Garrison's apocalyptic vision of slavery's end. In 1865, the toll of dead and wounded and landscapes made desolate by war might well have convinced Americans of the cosmic dimensions of their struggle.

VII

The Body Reforms

EVEN AS militant abolitionists and temperance advocates mounted challenges to political, religious, and social norms with new definitions of what it meant to be a Christian nation, a new set of reformers in the early 1830s attempted to create a comprehensive sacred vision of personal life. Sylvester Graham introduced a plan of living based on a vegetarian diet, routinized exercise, and a moderated sexual life; William Andrus Alcott formulated a similar but even more broad-ranging moral physiology; and Orson Squire Fowler adapted Gall and Spurzheim's phrenological science to America's democratic and Christian environment. They based their systems on available scientific research and theories but shaped them into sacralizing codes that promised physical and spiritual well-being and social regeneration. What one contemporary said of Graham's system applied to all the body reforms: "What is now called Grahamism . . . is in fact Bibleism."[1]

The physiological reformers distinguished themselves from Sabbatarians, abolitionists, temperance crusaders, and other activists of the era by concentrating on the private rather than public sphere. Though ultimately the programs of Fowler, Graham, and Alcott promised almost Edenic social consequences, their realm of action lay largely in the sacralization of personal life. They called for nothing less than a radical change in the conception of individual holiness. Without denying some power to evangelical conversion experiences, the body reformers preached a more thorough and permanent change of heart effected through the adoption of sexual, dietary, and other habits that constituted a system of everyday piety and sacred invocation.

Consideration of the sacred significance of the body, of course, had not been absent from reform in the 1820s. Temperance and manual labor advocates in many ways prefigured and encouraged the more comprehensive concerns of later physiological reformers by seeing bodily fitness as a key to social health and a powerful resource of the church militant. However, not until the early 1830s did physiological reform take on a life of its own. Using the body as prooftext, it provided a ritual and symbolic life for a Protestant community traditionally opposed to such sacred rites.

Indeed, as we shall see, the sacralizing claims of Graham, Alcott, and especially Fowler made numerous clergymen take exception to these reforms. Yet the physiological reformers created a set of rules that in many ways resembled ritual systems in most of the world's religions. Buddhism and Hinduism in the East as well as Judaism and Roman Catholicism in the West offered detailed codes of personal behavior that were intimately connected with the maintenance of sacred realms and the Godly life. These systems were most strictly maintained by religious virtuosos in various guises and strata of society. In this regard as well, Graham, Alcott, and Fowler fit the broader pattern of world religion, and on some grounds they must be counted as among the most radical religious virtuosos of the period.[2]

The body reformers, in fact, had much in common with activists who concentrated on the public sphere. All emerged from the same social, theological, and psychological environment and were of the same generation of young New Englanders. All struggled with palpably spiritual issues but found that neither the church nor a career in the ministry satisfied their cravings. And all rescued their sense of sacred order by sacralizing realms of life usually perceived as profane. Furthermore, many of the public reformers confirmed this kinship by adopting Grahamism, phrenology, and Alcott's moral physiology as ritual systems even as their faith in the traditional churches eroded. In all, the body reformers offered one more version of sacred reordering in the face of pluralism's challenge to faith and, more particularly, to New England's sense of chosenness.

Sylvester Graham was the first major physiological reformer to emerge on the scene. Graham was born in 1794 in the town of West Suffield, Connecticut. His father and grandfather were Calvinist ministers, and both had fervently supported the Great Awakening as it swept through the Connecticut River Valley. His father died when he was two, leaving the family without a will and his mother with children to raise. His mother suffered greatly under the strain and could only survive by allowing her children to be raised by others. At age three Sylvester was sent to live with a neighbor, at five with a local tavern keeper, and a year after that with a neighboring farmer. Meanwhile, his mother became completely disabled, sinking into what a local court called "a deranged state of mind." Such a childhood, as Stephen Nissenbaum has noted, might well have inspired in him an apocalyptic sense of expectation and a deep craving for order.[3]

Graham's teenage years and those of his twenties, ones in which he alternated a taste for parties and frolic with guilt and doubt, ended with Graham entering into public debates on the side of temperate drinking. In 1823, he enrolled at Amherst Academy in order to become a minister; there, personal and school pressures pushed him to mental collapse. In 1826, after recuperation and marriage, Graham was licensed to preach. He lectured on temperance but never settled into a church of his own. Finally abandoning hope for a congregation, in 1830 he became an agent for the Pennsylvania Temperance Society.[4]

The years from 1828 to 1831 marked a turning point in Graham's life. Visions of social decay filled his mind. As in the case of William Lloyd Garrison, whose fears of race war overwhelmed his adherence to colonization, Graham worried that the bleak prospect he saw for the world could hardly be righted by temperance or any other single reform. These tensions bristled in *Thy Kingdom Come*, a discourse delivered at Crown Street Church in Philadelphia on December 13, 1829, that ostensibly argued in favor of infant and Sunday schools as the only hope left to win the battle against Evil. Yet Graham's juxtaposition of the beauties of the Millennium and the distance to be traversed left little doubt that the situation called for something more than education and temperance. If the Republican experiment were to succeed, he argued, something must be done about future generations growing up without a moral sense. Borrowing the statistical style from temperance, he asked his audience to contemplate the effects of "millions of children, which are now unseen and unfelt in our Country, with the thousands that are daily gushing into life" raised without religious education. They would "soon unite in one dark and mighty confluence of ignorance and immorality and crime, which will overflow the wholesome restraints of society, and sweep away the barriers of civil law, and sap the foundations of our Republican Institutions; and demolish and desolate all, that as patriots, we love!"[5]

It was in part this portent of social apocalypse that led Graham to study the physiological wellsprings of human action, from which he might gain a complete solution to the problem of moral decline. Lecturing and living in and around Philadelphia, a city still greatly influenced by the medical theories of Benjamin Rush, Graham read widely in Rush's works and in a new book from France, François J. V. Broussais's *Treatise on Physiology Applied to Pathology*, which appeared in Philadelphia in 1826 and which

Graham purchased in 1829. Rush had held that body and mind were debilitated by too much stimulation, whether through diet, bad thoughts, or mental fatigue. Broussais proposed that bodily health depended on balancing the need for nutrition with the inevitable unhealthy stimulation caused by food. Through Broussais, Graham also became familiar with the theories of Xavier Bichat. Bichat insisted that existence itself was a life-and-death struggle between body vitality and inorganic forces (chemical and physical) threatening from without.[6]

Graham fashioned from these ideas an explanation not only of a single body's fate but of a momentous drama being played out in the American Republic. As he read more widely and scanned the sources of worst abuse, he formulated a system of diet and daily living that might regenerate not only individual bodies but also the body politic. By May of 1831, Graham had forsaken temperance preaching in order to lecture on "the Science of Human Life."

The cornerstone of Graham's "Science" was a vegetarian diet (for meat was a deranging stimulant) built around the staple of bread made from unbolted (or Graham) flour. He advocated abstinence from such stimulants as alcohol, tea, or coffee and prescribed systematic exercise to tame the body and to build its defenses against outside invasion. Sex, that most tempting of all stimulations, must be routinized and limited as well. Graham's physiological theory, following Bichat's insights, emphasized that the reduction of irritation to the body would lead to healthy stasis and virtue.

The main sources of problems were two. First, irritating and stimulating food overexercised the body and depleted it of its natural energy and tone. One had to eat, however, so the least stimulating foods were best and were even better in small quantities. Second, sexual desire—"those LAS-CIVIOUS DAY-DREAMS, and *amorous reveries*"—and orgasm itself overstimulated and debilitated the entire set of bodily organs. "The brain, stomach, heart, lungs, liver, skin, and the other organs," he noted, "feel it sweeping over them with the tremendous violence of a tornado." Sex had its place, however, for the Bible commanded human beings to "be fruitful and multiply." Graham's scientific formula for a moderation that served both body and God yielded the recommendation that a healthy, mature male might safely have sex once every month.[7] Only through this comprehensive attack on the roots of human overstimulation could the future of the nation and humankind be assured.[8]

While Sylvester Graham focused on diet, sexuality, and exercise as the keys to individual health, republican virtue, and progress toward the Millennium, Orson Squire Fowler turned to the skull for wisdom. The future giant of American phrenology was born in 1809, son of a pioneer family that had moved from Connecticut to the wilds of upstate New York three years before his birth. He grew up in a Calvinist household and seemed headed for the ministry. As a teenager he studied with a local minister, and by age twenty he had matriculated at Amherst College to prepare further for the clergy.[9]

At Amherst, however, Fowler's spiritual concerns took a new direction as he became familiar with physiological aspects of reform. The Reverend Heman Humphrey, president of the college and a renowned temperance advocate, took him under his wing. Fowler enrolled in the classes of Edward Hitchcock, a professor of chemistry and natural history who had written an early contribution to antebellum moral physiology, advocating in piecemeal form the use of diet and exercise to calm the body.[10] At some point in 1832, Fowler discovered phrenology; as his first hesitant "readings" of skulls seemed to confirm the theory, he became an enthusiast. Fowler even delivered a short course on the subject in the room of his fellow student and friend Henry Ward Beecher, to the good-hearted jeers and objections of Beecher and some others. However, the son of Lyman Beecher changed his mind after being asked to take the negative side in a debate with another student on the topic "Is phrenology entitled to the name of science?" Beecher's preparatory reading for the debate paradoxically converted him to the cause.[11]

Both men had been convinced by an elegant and palpably demonstrable system that promised revolutionary insight into moral and mental character and the possibility of effecting lasting change in individual lives. Simply stated, phrenology held that there was a direct relationship between anatomical detail and mental function. Further, it posited that the brain was divided into thirty-seven physical faculties, each determining particular intellectual and emotional capacities and features of personality and character. Two scientists in Vienna, John Gaspar Spurzheim and Franz Joseph Gall, had created the science. Gall "discovered" the faculties in the 1790s and devoted himself to developing a system by which they could be measured from the external skull. Spurzheim, who was better trained in dissection and anatomy, added another dimension by comparing brain matter in accordance with Gall's ideas. They made extensive visual observations of men and women from all walks of life in order to correlate the location and measurement of faculties with apparent personality traits. Controversy raged in Europe and England wherever Gall and Spurzheim presented their findings, but phrenology attracted a zealous if small following.[12]

The new science made its first important appearance in America in the 1820s as book dealers imported European imprints on phrenology and as American scientists became familiar with it while traveling in Europe. Dr. Charles Caldwell, who had heard Spurzheim lecture in 1821, became America's first major apostle of phrenology. He taught courses on the subject in Transylvania University's medical department and lectured in Boston, Baltimore, Washington, and Cincinnati, founding phrenological societies in some of these cities and earning the title of "the American Spurzheim."[13]

The great turning point in enthusiasm came with the American tour of Spurzheim himself in the summer of 1832. For six weeks he tirelessly canvassed New York and New England, lecturing to doctors, university faculty and students, and the lay public. It was all too much for the scientist, who fell ill and died in Boston in November 1832. Spurzheim's death as well as his wisdom brought new and wide attention to the science, which in turn was given another boost by the 1838 tour of Scots phrenologist George Combe. Soon phrenology was the talk of lay and scientific circles in the Northeast. "Heads of chalk, inscribed with mystic numbers, disfigured every mantelpiece," one newspaper quipped in 1834. "Converts multiplied on all sides, some converts of the Covenant, and some proselytes of the gate."[14] Close to fifty separate phrenological societies bloomed in cities large and small.[15]

Orson Squire Fowler and his brother Lorenzo Niles Fowler, while by no means scientists, transformed this burgeoning presence of phrenological theory by making it accessible to vast numbers of the American public. At Amherst, Fowler, along with Beecher, read the heads of fellow students for a small charge. Beecher, though afterwards a lifelong believer in phrenology, continued his ministerial education. Fowler, who had planned to follow Beecher to Lane Seminary, decided instead to devote his life to "practical" phrenology, which meant essentially the propagation of the faith by all means available in 1830s America: lectures, inexpensive phrenological readings, publication of books, and sale of paraphernalia such as busts and charts. When preaching phrenology, Fowler and his agents solicited members of the audience for a reading of heads. They opened the "phrenological cabinet," a museum of plaster skulls that confirmed the virtue and vice of famous individuals in phrenological terminology and in turn reaffirmed the truth of the science. And they inspired imitators by the score who traveled the countryside in search of heads to read.[16]

Fowler's phrenology aimed at a proper understanding of physical and moral tendencies within the individual. The system was based on ideal sizes for the thirty-seven faculties, which included, among others, Amativeness (sexual love); Alimentiveness (appetite, hunger); Spirituality (intuition, revery); Agreeableness (pleasantness); Cautiousness (prudence); and Approbativeness (ambition, display). "The principle is this," stated Fowler. "Every faculty has its own appropriate aliment and stimulant, by the presentation of which it is excited, and its organ thereby enlarged, and by removal of which its action is diminished, and its size thereby reduced." The reading of a head, then, would isolate areas for change in behavior as well as explanations for personal traits, which in turn could lead the client toward a significantly better life.[17]

If Fowler isolated areas of needed change, William Andrus Alcott told individuals precisely what to do. Even more than Graham, Alcott applied what he saw as the laws of nature to every nook and cranny of daily life. Born in 1798 in Wolcott, Connecticut, he was raised in the milieu of small town New England. Yet unlike Fowler and Graham, he never wished to become a minister. The common folk who surrounded him, he remembered, believed that ministers possessed a certain "native imbecility" and that those who "took to learning" were "weak in the attic." In his autobiography he mentioned nothing about the frustrated youthful yearnings for God and salvation that clouded the lives of so many New England youths, including Graham and Fowler.[18]

Alcott described his problems in more mundane terms. Sickness nagged at him from early childhood on and was all the more disturbing because of the youth's intense desire to "do good," an ambition reinforced by careful readings of Benjamin Franklin's *Autobiography*. This precocious farmer's son dreamed that he might someday be a printer and of use to the public.[19] However, at eighteen he began a six-year stint as a schoolmaster. Illness compromised his ambitions. Long hours of teaching and worries about his effectiveness in the classroom weakened his already delicate health. Gradually he became addicted to patent remedies. He completed a medical education in New Haven in a vain attempt to cure himself, but the demands of the curriculum further weakened him. When he returned to teaching, a new bout of consumption forced him to stop work. "I had as much as I could do," he remembered, "in attempting to keep up a successful war with cough, night sweats, purulent expectorations and hectic fever."[20]

Alcott fell back on the old remedies—Huxham's tincture, quassia, ale, and "other bitter infusions"—but his condition worsened. He was "driven to desperation, nay almost to insanity and madness." In one last effort on July 4, 1826, he vowed to abandon useless treatments and to trust in God. Independence Day passed without a summoning of will. However, he remembered that July 5 marked the independence of a South American republic, and on that day Alcott gathered the strength to overcome his slavery to fear, doctors, and pills. "I will fly away from myself—it is done."[21]

Battling severe physical pain, Alcott undertook a pilgrimage over the hills of Connecticut. Finally, from one high peak he viewed the countryside: "[It] seemed to me like a new world. Here I renewed my declaration of independence with regard to those earthly props on which I had so long been wont to lean." He pledged a "new dependence on God, and on his natural and moral elements," and declared: "God is good."[22]

It took Alcott six years to nurse himself back to health and to ponder the lessons of his own life. He read widely in the current medical literature and merged his scientific understandings with those of the Bible. In 1832,

Alcott began a torrent of writing that, by the time of his death in 1859, yielded over one hundred books and countless pamphlets and magazine articles. *Vegetable Diet, The House I Live In, The Young Housekeeper, The Physiology of Marriage, The Laws of Health, The Young Mother's Guide*, and other popular volumes found their place in middle-class homes. Each set forth detailed rituals and models for Christian living.

Take, for instance, *The Boy's Guide to Usefulness*, which guided the young initiate through daily rituals and structured life decisions. The first chapter, "Morning," featured the following sections: "Rising Early," "Ablution," "Dressing for the Day," "Devotion," "Good Resolutions," "Putting in Order," "Assisting Parents," and "Exercise." The second chapter, "Breakfast," discussed "Behavior at Table," "Eating Too Much," "Eating Wrong," and "Gratitude." Other chapters dealt with "Employment," "Labor in the Field," "School," "Recreation," and a variety of other topics. The book ended with chapters concerned with "Care of the Body" and "Care of the Soul."[23]

In all, Alcott translated traditional Protestant virtues into a physiological doctrine that he summed up with two words: "Keep Cool." Like Graham, he advocated a bland vegetarian diet least likely to arouse and therefore aggravate the body. Meat and other stimulants, he argued, caused minor fevers as they passed through the digestive tract and thus must be avoided. This overheating weakened the body's organs. Concern for body temperature also led Alcott to become one of America's first advocates of cold water bathing. His advice on clothing and sleeping habits guarded against heat as well. Hats made of heavy material, for instance, were dangerous because the head needed natural ventilation. Featherbeds created too much warmth, caused an "unnatural degree of perspiration, and thus induce[d] weakness or debility."[24] The main social and moral point for Alcott was clear: "What heats the body unduly favors directly or indirectly, the production of anger." Anger in turn destroyed marriages, warped parental devotion, and generally upset the felicity of Godly order.[25]

The *Moral Reformer*, a periodical Alcott founded in 1835 to spread his physiological gospel, illustrated the range and detail of advice he offered. In a single issue one might find discussions of such topics as "Cider-Drinking," "Uses and Abuses of Light," "Education of the Stomach," "Featherbeds," and "Evening Parties."[26] In each case, physiological wisdom and moral sensibility combined to show the reader the right way to handle each detail of life. "Do you ask what this subject has to do with moral reform?" wrote the author of "Remarks on Dress" after pages of detailed argument against tight-lacing. "If certain foolish and injurious practices are tolerated two centuries longer, every female will be deformed, and the whole race greatly degenerated, physically and morally."[27] Or consider Alcott's advice on Sunday dinner, which he saw as a major roadblock in the way of "moral reformation." This "eating to excess" on the Sabbath caused sleepiness in church, which in turn made one literally oblivious to the "force of divine truth." In short, traditional Sunday dinners were "immoral, unchristian, and—to coin a term— unrepublican."[28] Such matters might seem to be "little things," he noted in a different context, but "in their results, they [were] the GREAT THINGS of life."[29]

Numerous explanations have been offered for the appearance of such concern for the "little things" in the works of Alcott, Graham, and Fowler. Psychological interpretations have stressed the obsessive-compulsive character of the body reforms as reflections of a felt sense of social and personal disorder. More materialist approaches have viewed body reforms as an adaptation to the vast changes of daily routine and division of labor engendered by the rising dominance of the marketplace.[30] Such approaches can explain to some degree the appeal and use of physiological reform among the wider public, but they are limited in their ability to explain the structure of the physiological systems and the intentions of their creators.

To put it plainly, the moral physiologists hoped to create nothing less than a neo-Mosaic law, a system of everyday piety expressed in the language and style of Enlightenment science but resembling the Books of Leviticus and Deuteronomy and later commentary. In this sense moral physiology replicated a systematic invocation of the sacred found in many religions. As Mary Douglas has argued, biblical law functioned primarily to locate in everyday events an experience of connection or devotion to God through the creation of clearly defined and contrasting paths and categories—ones that designated actions or spheres of holiness and set them against and apart from those of pollution or sin.[31] Like the Rabbis of the first century, who stressed anew the codification of everyday life as a reaction to the tumultuous anxieties concerning faith and religious identity created by the rise of Christianity and the destruction of the Temple in A.D. 70, the body reformers saw themselves as Mosaic teachers who would lead their people out of chaos.[32]

These reformers, in fact, identified strongly with Moses in the wilderness, in some cases literally comparing their work to his and in any case consciously and unconsciously patterning their sense of American decline and regeneration on the Bible. Moses had led the Jews out of Egypt but found that life in the desert caused irresolution; the last straw was Israel's worship of the Golden Calf. In desperation but also at a moment of divine intercession, Moses received the Ten Commandments and other laws— criminal, sexual, dietary, marital—and gave them to his people as a sign and system of regeneration. Exodus, Leviticus, Numbers, and Deuteronomy thus recounted a passage from spiritual wilderness to national renewal.

So it was with the physiological reformers. They cast themselves as Mosaic lawgivers to Americans, refurbishing them for their role of leadership in the cosmic drama. The self-consciousness of such a connection revealed itself most strikingly in the case of Alcott. His spiritual and vocational conversion occurred on a Sinai-like mountaintop in Connecticut, and he came to understand his calling as that of a Moses. In one of his most important works, *The Laws of Health*, Alcott went so far as to compare his own work to the Ten Commandments. "There are properly two sets of Divine Laws," he noted. "One of these is found in the Decalogue . . . and is called the *moral* law; the other, though alluded to there is to be chiefly learned by study, and it is called the *physical* law. It is found operating both in and around us. We cannot, if we would escape it."[33] When late in life Alcott wrote his autobiography, he entitled it *Forty Years in the Wilderness of Powders and Pills.*[34] He had devoted his life to promulgating a neo-Mosaic law of natural health and morals that he hoped would lead Americans to a millennial land of milk and honey.

Our understanding of Alcott's writings on everyday life takes on a new dimension when viewed within this Mosaic archetype. His advice—whether about marriage and family, diet and bathing, tight-lacing and appropriate times to wear a hat, the evils of playing leapfrog, or the dangers of patronizing the local confectionery shop—envisioned a comprehensive Christian life designed to permeate the individual's "every action, word, thought, and feeling, in the performance of the most ordinary duties of life." He contrasted his approach to the ordinary varieties of Christianity, which emphasized sermons and prayers but left "almost everything" of a consequential nature "undone." Revival conversions, he admitted, allowed some to be "pulled out of the fire" for a time, but he had no faith in the permanence of such changes of the heart.[35] Alcott's systematic sacralization of diet, dress, and other aspects of personal life made a conversion the stuff of daily life.

Sylvester Graham's more physiologically focused system of ritual behavior differed in emphasis from that of Alcott's, but comprised a similar system of laws. That Graham had not received his call on a mountaintop did not prevent him from striking a Mosaic pose. In one passage from his lectures, after having just recommended a vegetable diet, he noted that few would have the stamina to follow his advice. "I say then," he instructed, "to every one and to all, as Moses said to the Israelites in the wilderness concerning their future habits in the promised land,—if notwithstanding all that I have said against the use of flesh-meat, ye still say—'We *will* eat flesh because our souls long to eat flesh,'—then eat whatsoever your souls lust after: only permit me to point out to you with utmost brevity, the least objectionable kinds and modes of such transgression."[36] Graham underlined his patriarchal self-conception in a letter to the abolitionist Gerrit Smith: "I *feel* that I know the mind of God."[37]

Orson Squire Fowler never directly identified himself as Moses but nonetheless saw himself as lawgiver to his people.[38] Moving far beyond Gall and Spurzheim, he viewed phrenology as a revelatory "natural theology" peculiarly suited to America. It was a democratic system of thought, more easily learned by most citizens than traditional theology and more specific in its recommendations. A phrenological reading allowed one to adjust one's actions in the most minute ways to the true spirit of Jesus every day. "What is now called Christianity, taken *en masse*," he proclaimed, "is no more the Christianity of Christ and the New Testament, than it is heathenism, nor quite as much. . . . When will men learn to distinguish the religion of Jesus Christ and the Bible from the spurious, bogus, Pharisaical Judaism that now occupies the sanctuary . . . ? When they understand Phrenology."[39]

Fowler also often proclaimed phrenology's phenomenological revelations. It alone, he argued, gave certain proof of the existence of God. "I have never seen the back part of [the bump of] Veneration magnetized," he wrote, "without also seeing the subject clasp and raise the hands in the attitude of worship, assume a devotional aspect and tone of voice, and express a desire to pray. . . . And the inference that therefore there *is* a God, follows as a necessary consequence." Phrenology also provided a comforting explanation for religious pluralism, and even spiritual outlawry: "Men's religious opinions differ as much as do their faces; producing all our sectarian diversities, as well as every form of Pagan worship, however revolting and criminal."[40] Fowler thus preached a kind of phrenological latitudinarianism that further delegitimized the old faith.

Physiological reform's echo of the Hebrews also carried within it a social and historical vision. Jean Soler has emphasized the role of dietary and other restrictions in setting the Hebrews apart from others, and in putting practical, daily definition on chosenness. The story of the Exodus and the codification of the Law, he has argued, acted as an archetype of chosenness, holiness, and regeneration.[41] Writing for an Old Testament–based Christian culture, New England's reform physiologists posited theories of Christian and American decline but also the certainty of renewal through their systems. For Fowler, declension involved a lack of self-knowledge and an increasing disconnection from Nature that his "natural theology" of phrenology would correct. Graham placed the fate of humankind within a breathtaking drama of degeneration that began in Genesis and unfolded gradually as mankind gave up the natural vegetarian regimen of the Garden of Eden. He framed his advice within a grand rewriting of cosmic history from the creation of the world through the physiological history of human decline, ending with lessons for regeneration through diet, exercise, and moderate sexuality.[42]

Alcott provided the most dramatic rendering of human decline. He, like Graham, used biblical diets and longevity to track man's fall from grace.

Since Eden, humans had gradually obscured their innate knowledge of God's physical law by practicing senseless habits of cooking, dress, and housing. This caused a diminution of health most apparent in a declining life span. No one in the nineteenth century, he lamented, lived as long as Methuselah. The Old Testament patriarch's life lasted almost a thousand years because his daily habits approximated those practiced in the Garden. But, according to Alcott, even Methuselah met his demise through deviations from Edenic law, and those mistakes were Methuselah's "own fault."[43]

Alcott outlined a parallel account of American decline on the Old Testament model. He argued that its downfall was the Revolution, which had ushered in a period of "imaginary independence." Before 1776, he claimed, Americans had been the "most happy people in the world." He asserted that "all of our evils" dated from "a premature, if not unnecessary, though successful resistance to the constituted authorities, and the security which was thus afforded to every one, to seek his own glory at the altar of Mammon, rather than at the altar of the true God." The American people had become "every year and every hour more and more the slaves of avarice and sensuality, after having, in short, planted and watered, and nurtured, with all [their] powers, the tree of licentiousness rather than that of liberty." In revolting against the mildly unjust authority of the Crown, he argued, they had loosed the passion for revolt against all authority. They ended up worshiping money and worldliness, even as the Hebrews had turned to the Golden Calf.[44]

Alcott recapitulated the basic view of history propounded by Beecher in the late 1820s—that no mere political ideology or set of institutions could guarantee human happiness to a people who had lost the knowledge requisite for a Christian life—but with a difference. Whereas Lyman Beecher's solution was the embrace of evangelical doctrine and the temperate life, Alcott advocated a far more systematic Christian piety. Human beings could find salvation only by following God's natural order in all aspects of their lives and by rejecting an imaginary liberty that often encouraged licentiousness.

If the moral decline of Jacksonian America inspired gloom in the hearts of the physiological reformers, it also presented them with an opportunity. The concept of the Chosen People, now defined broadly as Americans, still preserved the hope of regeneration. Those who had worshiped at the Golden Calf and courted God's anger could also win back His love. Thus Alcott, Graham, and Fowler carried forth the grand tradition of the New England jeremiad.[45]

That they expressed themselves in the language of moral physiology, however, also indicated their own alienation from Orthodoxy and, for that matter, churchly Christianity in general. Prior American Jeremiahs had spoken mostly in the language of theology from within the security of the church. They had felt little need to create a full-scale ritual system of pious living; indeed, the very marrow of Protestant tradition argued against it. The post-Enlightenment, individualistic, democratic, and religiously pluralistic society in which the moral physiologists lived determined that their systems would develop without the boundaries of sect. However, in every nostrum lay vibrant connections with the old faith. They saw their systems as liberations from the failings of the church. They had created paths to positive Christian freedom in which one lived one's life as a sacred act, each detail linking one to God.[46]

Moral physiology was by its own definition nothing if not a new and scientifically ascertainable set of laws. It combined the structural appeal of Old Testament lawgiving and the advantage of using the body as a perfect lingua franca for a Christian country split by sectarianism and wedded to disestablishment and toleration. The body offered these reformers a basis for creating a thorough, non-sectarian, and democratic system of daily piety, one whose basic ordering devices made actions or objects "natural" or "unnatural." By leading a natural life, one that followed God's physiological as well as moral laws, the Chosen People of America would be regenerated. However, that could be accomplished only by sacralizing every act, waking and sleeping.

Having created their systems and set forth the enormous task of changing the personal lives of Americans, the moral physiologists had to find the proper means of disseminating their views and convincing the public of their worth. The principal means they used were those open to other political, social, religious, and cultural movements in nineteenth-century America: the speaker's platform and the published word. Graham, Alcott, and Fowler vigorously pursued the lecture circuit and, with the advent of cheap printing in the 1830s, published countless books, pamphlets, and broadsides.

They and their followers supplemented these techniques with other, more innovative methods that grew out of the peculiarities of their programs. Enthusiastic Grahamites created voluntary societies to promote the "science of human life" and established so-called Graham hotels to ensure that adherents to his system would not have to give up their ways when traveling. Alcott and Graham together helped found the American Physiological Society in order to spread their health doctrines.[47] Alcott published the *Moral Reformer;* a Graham enthusiast founded and edited the *Graham Journal of Health and Longevity*.[48] Orson Squire Fowler was even more enterprising. He and his brother Lorenzo set up a publishing house and disseminated thousands of copies of their own works and related books by other health reformers. In the 1840s, the Fowlers helped introduce new physiological reforms, including the American version of European hydropathy (the water-cure) championed by Russell Trall and Joel Shew.[49] Finally, the Fowlers set up their own phrenology parlors and commissioned others as itinerant phrenologists. At local storefronts, in one's own home, or after a lecture, the public could obtain personal phrenological evaluations and be issued a chart assessing the results.

This fervent proselytizing reflected, among a good many other things, the passion with which the moral physiologists pursued their goal of reaching every person possible with the message of personal and social regeneration. However the process moved slowly. In the 1830s, most of the public looked upon these men and their programs, except for Fowler's phrenology, with bemused curiosity. It was not until the 1840s and 1850s that physiological reform began to enter the mainstream of middle-class life.

In fact, Graham and Fowler were as likely to inspire doubt, controversy, and even riot as they were to gain adherents.[50] By recommending home-baked bread and vividly describing the effects of sex, Graham crossed swords with both entrenched economic interests and prevailing sensibilities. Mobs attacked him at least three times in the 1830s. One crowd prevented him from giving his lecture on chastity to an audience of women (its approach to sex presumably being too frank for females), while in 1837 a group of irate bakers and butchers, already strapped by hard times, attacked the man who had told his audiences not to eat meat or buy commercially produced bread. Nor did Graham's demeanor help. While he was a fine orator, his grating personality alienated even those who considered him their friend and prophet.[51]

Phrenology in general and Fowler's practical version in particular engendered hostility on a number of fronts. Numerous doctors and physiologists took exception to the theory, writing skeptical pieces in both scientific and lay journals. Such criticism made those who considered themselves "true" phrenological researchers extremely sensitive to what they deemed the antics of the Fowlers and other popularizers. A basic split in the movement between those in the theoretical British tradition and American "practitioners" had class as well as methodological dimensions. The Fowlers were not only "unscientific" to those whose mission was the legitimation of phrenology among the highest scientific circles, but downright embarrassing in their vulgarization of Gall and Spurzheim.[52] Faced by these critics, Fowler enjoyed turning the tables. In 1842 he commented that English phrenology was "rather too anxious to place phrenology on a *scientific* and *philosophical* basis, to the neglect of *practical* examinations. Mere theorizing and abstract reasoning will never advance the interest of phrenology."[53]

Phrenology seemed most threatening to traditional Christianity, for friend and foe alike recognized its spiritual implications. Churchmen especially understood its appeal, but they considered it a false system that supplied simple, materialist answers to the subtle and mysterious questions of the spirit. They conducted pamphlet wars on the subject, debunking the scientific basis of phrenology and showing it to be contradictory to the doctrines of Christianity.[54] Charles Francis Adams's mixed feelings on the subject perhaps represented those of many pious members of the laity. "The science, like many others which have been struck," he noted about phrenology, "bears witness to Man's ingenuity and to his passion for novelty. It is in some respects very dangerous, as it gives room for materialism as well as for the belief of the fatalist."[55]

Those who found spiritual fulfillment in phrenology were more liable to agree with Emerson when he noted that it showed "what men want in religion and philosophy which has not been hitherto furnished."[56] Even more striking were the testimonials of Fowler's converts. "Phrenology," wrote one, "saved me from the rock of infidelity. . . . When I saw, that the mind was *constitutionally* adapted to the great and leading principles of Christianity, I was enabled to comprehend the fallacy of the base and servile doctrines of the infidel." For another soul suffering from "universal scepticism's painful confusion's derangement," after exposure to phrenology all his "doubts and perplexities fled like morning vapors chased away by the rising sun."[57]

Not surprisingly, the moral physiologists often found their earliest fervent support among other reformers. These men and women, engaged in other pursuits that comprised the "sisterhood of reforms," understood better than most the sacred mission of physiological reform. Indeed, many had previously experimented in aspects of bodily regeneration as part of the manual labor and temperance movements. Earlier health tracts such as Hitchcock's *Dyspepsy Forestalled* had already recommended the reduction of meat in diets. The work of Graham, Fowler, and Alcott, then, seemed a natural if far more comprehensive development of nascent reform interests.

The marriage of public and private reforms began as news spread quickly of Sylvester Graham and his lecture series, and Graham retained a dominant influence among reformers throughout the 1830s. By 1832, Oneidan Henry B. Stanton was recommending that he be hired to teach natural science at Lane Seminary.[58] When Oberlin College opened its doors in 1835 as an avant-garde institution, it served its students from a table already influenced by Graham. It excluded "tea and coffee, highly seasoned meats, rich pastries and all unholesome [sic] and expensive foods." By 1839, Oberlin had hired a special chef to create a commons table that eliminated all meat and other stimulants.[59]

Many in the reform community became true believers. Theodore Weld and the Grimké sisters, William Lloyd Garrison, Horace Greeley, the Tappan brothers, William Goodell, and Joshua Leavitt all became devotees of Graham crackers, cold water, and the rest of the system. They were fond of reporting their bouts with the snares of unhealthy delicacies that confronted them everywhere, and proud of their heroic resistance. Henry E. Benson, a reformer and brother-in-law of Garrison, recounted his own moment of dietary testing at the house of a friend. "It would require the fortitude of a martyr not to be at all tempted from the plain but nutritious food of the Graham System," he wrote, "to that under which the table groans at our fashionable dinner hour which is five o'clock in the afternoon. But I would give more for a loaf of Graham bread, and a plate of rice and molasses than for any delicacy which the rich can afford."[60] Lucky were those who had understanding friends like William Lloyd Garrison. "If they are Grahamites," Garrison declared as he wrote of expected guests, "we have a fine spring of water in our cellar, and plenty of Graham flour up stairs. If they have an affection for coffee or tea, we have both."[61]

While some seemed tolerant of a wide variety of attitudes toward body reform, others urged conversion. In December 1837, for instance, Theodore Dwight Weld and his future sister-in-law engaged in an intriguing correspondence on life, death, and murder. Sarah and Angelina Grimké, both Quaker pacifists, had expressed shock at the abolitionist editor Elijah Lovejoy's recent armed defense of himself and his press at Alton, Illinois, and especially at the fact that Lovejoy had killed a member of the attacking mob before he himself died. "Will God," Sarah asked Weld, "continue to bless an enterprize which is baptised in blood?" In the same letter, she reported the latest on each sister's bouts of illness, attributing their maladies to overwork. But, Sarah vowed, she had already decided that "it was no matter how soon I wore out, if I was only about my fathers business."[62]

Weld pounced on Sarah's heroic utterance, calling it "an abominable doctrine" and equating the sisters' neglect of body to the bloodshed at Alton. "You think Lovejoy committed murder," he wrote. "Why? Because he thought it was 'no matter how soon' Bishop's life was 'worn out.'"[63] A life was a life, Weld argued, and neglect of one's own body was as heinous a crime against God as killing another. "God has given to every human being a certain amount of vital power," he noted; "this vital power is lodged in an organization to which God *has given laws;* these are *Gods* laws as really as 'Love the Lord with all thy heart' and 'love thy neighbor as thy self.'" Obeying these laws ensured that the body would wear well. Violating them brought the opposite result. The choice was "between *obeying God* and *resisting him, preserving life* and *destroying* it, *keeping* the *6th Commandment* and *committing suicide!!*"[64]

Weld's earnestness came from experience, for he had just begun to rebuild a body pummeled by years of stress and willful overwork. "My own sins in this respect rise up before me in crimsoned crowds," he revealed, "and shriek their warning in my ears and bid me shriek them in the ears of others till they tingle." Luckily God had granted him *"repentance unto life* even in this world," and every day he prayed concerning his health: "'Deliver me from *blood guiltiness* oh God, thou God of *my salvation.*'"[65]

Enough reformers became Grahamites to lend a particular flavor to the thriving enterprise of Graham boardinghouses and hotels. The first opened in New York City in 1833, and others appeared in various cities as the 1830s wore on. Here clients could be themselves. Typically, a waking bell rang at five in the morning, followed by an hour of bathing and exercise before breakfast. Meals were served twice a day, featuring combinations of Graham bread, porridge, Indian pudding, and fruit. The choice of drinks came down to "tepid gruel," cold water, or milk. The day ended promptly at ten in the evening, at which time the management locked all doors (guests did not have keys) and doused all lights.

In this seemingly dreary setting, guests thrived in their sense of community. "The Boarders in this establishment are not only Grahamites, but Garrisonites," one visitor to the New York Graham Boarding House reported. "Such a knot of Abolitionists I never before fell in with. Slavery, Colonization &c. constitute the unvarying monotonous theme of their conversations except that they give place to an occasional comment upon their peculiar style of living."[66] Grahamism became, then, not only a ritualized way of life for the individual but also a sign of membership in a beleaguered but committed sect.

Graham's appeal to reformers grew from a variety of sources, but all pointed to a divorce from the formally structured, socially defined religious life of the churches and a turn to personal everyday piety as a foundation for sacralizing the world. In some cases the perceived hypocrisy of the churches, as in their rejection of abolitionism, loosened their hold on reformer consciousness. "We attend no place of worship," Sarah Grimké wrote to Theodore Weld in December 1837, "which is a great relief, for our souls are verily sick of the preaching of the present day."[67] It was a common sentiment among reformers in the 1830s.

This erosion of faith in organized religion led as well to the questioning of any official symbolic acts of sacred invocation and a concomitant embracing of systems such as those proposed by Graham and Alcott, which made the sacred life a matter of the "little things." William Lloyd Garrison's continuing spiritual odyssey exemplified the subtleties and surprises of this process. Witness his 1835 account of participation in Thanksgiving rituals, the discomfort of which he expressed in deeply ambivalent irony. "Yesterday throughout this State, (perhaps in all Rhode Island, I know not,) by proclamation of the Governor, there was an immense slaughter among the turkeys, geese and chickens," he wrote to his brother-in-law, "who were destroyed by the jaw-bones of the people without the slightest remorse. . . . It fell to my lot to carve not less than three chickens, 'all in a row,' which had been systematically roasted at a slow fire—a fourth one I spared from dissection until to-day." He reported the rest of the feast, including the punishment received for "slaying and eating so pitilessly; for the conglomerated fragments of fowls and puddings and pies, which were ravenously swallowed, soon united in getting up an insurrection in the stomach."[68]

Indigestion, however, reminded him of underlying problems concerning the holiday. He noted the "absurdity" that society should appoint "one day in the year to be specially thankful for the good gifts of God." Indeed, the very fact that the government determined the day was an inappropriate union of church and state. "I am growing more and more hostile to outward forms and ceremonies and observances, as a religious duty," he concluded, "and trust I am more and more appreciating the nature and enjoying the privileges of that liberty wherewith the obedient soul is made free. How can a people fast or be thankful at the bidding or request of any man or body of men?"[69]

These reflections took on less private expression as Garrison wrestled with the question of the Sabbath, which he still observed but whose firm hold on him was silently weakening by 1836. Not surprisingly, he was moved to public utterance by what he came to see as the hypocrisy of his old hero, Lyman Beecher. Beecher delivered a Thanksgiving sermon in 1835 excoriating abolitionism and rejecting foreign criticism of American slavery by pointing out the wretched conditions of European free labor. Mindful of this sermon, Garrison attacked a later Beecher address on the Sabbath in a three-part *Liberator* article. The minister had asserted that Sunday was "the *great sun of the moral world*," Garrison noted, but while arguing for the centrality of the Fourth Commandment Beecher had at other times defended a slave institution that routinely violated all ten of God's commandments.[70]

In making his argument, Garrison almost unconsciously began to make a case against the Sabbath itself. Not only did most Christians not celebrate the Sabbath of the decalogue (that is, Saturday), he argued, but neither Jesus nor the apostles found it of much importance. Nor did he appreciate the coercive voice of church or state making the outward gesture of a single day's observance required of individuals. "Let men consecrate to the service of Jehovah not merely one day in seven, but *all* their time, thoughts, actions and powers." In a final volley, Garrison ridiculed the Sabbatarians' common practice of publicizing supposed injuries or fatalities that befell Sabbath-breakers. He wished "to controvert a pernicious and superstitious notion, and one that is very prevalent, that extraordinary and supernatural visitations of divine indignation upon certain transgressors (of the Sabbath, particularly and almost exclusively) are poured out now as in the days of Moses and the prophets."[71] The storm of protest that followed exasperated him, not least because it came from many whom he had counted as allies, but it only led him to great heterodoxy in the years to come.

At a crucial moment in the spiritual history of radical reform, then, Grahamism supplied the ritual and symbol of a sacred daily life to replace traditional sources of invocation. In 1846, Henry Clarke Wright, another anti-Sabbatarian and abolitionist, summed up in his diary the total rejection of traditional demarcations of sacred and profane and their replacement by everyday piety of body and soul. Sunday, he said, was no more holy than any other day of the week. The ministry "was not more sacred and pleasing to God than the profession of a Merchant, a Shoemaker, a carpenter, or farmer," or churches "more sacred than barns or theatres." Nor were "praying, reading the Bible, going to Church, Baptism, the supper, singing, preaching . . . more *religious* exercises than baking bread, knitting stockings, cooking a dinner, sweeping the room or the streets." Significantly, Wright underlined "that the *duties* that regard the purity, comfort, health and happiness of the *Body*, were as binding, as important, as sacred, as christian, as the duties which relate to the purity, comfort, health and happiness of the soul."[72] The sentiment could have come right from Graham or Alcott.

Still, while Grahamism became widespread among radical reformers of the 1830s, some perceived problems in its adoption. Elizur Wright Jr. noted that Grahamite abolitionists might run into contradictions if they indicted the diet of slaves in the South. "My anti-Graham philosophy will only pass for what it is worth, of course," he wrote to Weld. "Every southern slave I ever saw, complained bitterly about the prevention of meat."[73]

By comparison, reformers greeted phrenology with only mild interest. Many did have their heads read: Charles Grandison Finney, Theodore Weld, William Lloyd Garrison, Lydia Maria Child, the Tappan brothers, Isaac Hopper, John Greenleaf Whittier, and more. Some submitted to the Fowlers' measuring tape out of curiosity or a perverse wish to fool the expert, but most came away feeling that their personalities had been rendered with accuracy.[74] Already committed to their various causes, however, they usually had less need or want of the guidance phrenology offered. Instead, they accepted its confirmation of their own wisdom and began to use its vocabulary in descriptions of friends and enemies.

As for Alcott, his diet books were overshadowed by the cult of Grahamism. His other work, especially on childrearing, housekeeping, and sex roles, addressed subjects that in the 1830s seemed irrelevant to late-marrying reformers. Yet signs of future relevance abounded. "'The Young Mother' is the title of a new work just published in this city by Dr. Alcott," Garrison noted to his wife with an air of kind condescension in 1836, "a copy of which I shall bring with me. It is an admirable and most instructive work, just what you and all mothers need."[75] By the 1840s, many more reformers, as husbands and as wives, would be reading Alcott.

Indeed, with entry into family responsibilities, the first generation of reformers made important transitions in their choices of physiological reform. Grahamism faded somewhat as an active faith, its major lessons being absorbed as common practice among reformers by the 1840s. However, the appearance of reformer families brought new interest in the literature on sexuality and domestic life. For if the Graham cracker and cold water symbolized moral physiology's communion, an idealized hearth and home became its new but troubled church, and women its controversial ministers.

VIII

The Woman Question

IN A LETTER to the *Liberator* published in March 1840, the abolitionist Lydia Maria Child expressed her surprise at the vigorous opposition
to woman's equal participation in antislavery activities, an attitude that
had surfaced in the two preceding years. Indeed, the Tappans and others
had broken from the American Anti-Slavery Society, citing as their reason
the insistence of Garrison and his allies that women be given equal status
in abolitionist organizations. Only a few years before, she remembered,
Lewis Tappan had asked Child herself to address a meeting in New York.
Now he professed "conscientious scruples, founded on St. Paul," against
women speaking to sexually mixed audiences. She recalled that James G.
Birney, who wished to exclude women as full members of the American
Anti-Slavery Society, had once found it "natural and proper" for both men
and women to attend a state antislavery convention as voting delegates.[1]

Child's account revealed an authentic shock shared to some degree even
by Tappan and his allies. Modern historians as well have found it difficult
to explain either the advent of sex equality advocacy in the 1830s or why it
elicited such harsh reaction within the reform community. Some have
speculated that experience in reform endeavors of the 1820s and 1830s
prepared the minds of women for doctrines of equality. Other scholars
have underlined the unavoidable comparison between women and slaves

engendered by participation in the antislavery cause. Still others have drawn broader socioeconomic canvases upon which to view the rise of woman's rights, ones that highlight the changing roles of working- and middle-class women in an emerging commercial-industrial order. Few have tried to explain the apparent reversal on the part of some abolitionists as they sought to stem the tide of female participation.[2]

These useful discussions, however, tend to make inevitable what at the time seemed and still seems extraordinary: the creation of an explicit, tightly reasoned, full-blown rejection of traditional Christian visions of gender. As in the case of other reforms, only by investigating the lives of those key women religious virtuosos who proffered the earliest American arguments for woman's equality and power can we recover the anguished process by which they found words, ideas, and images to subvert or refute the seemingly ageless wisdom that guided humankind in its ideals of male and female.[3]

Any new understanding of the origins of an American doctrine of sex equality and the crisis it precipitated in reform must begin with the recognition that the debate over women arose among reformers precisely because the reform community had articulated the most dynamic vision of womanhood in all of American society. In a sense, sex egalitarianism emerged as a reform within reform. One of the revolutions wrought by reformers in the 1820s and 1830s was their welcome of women to the ranks. Men, it is true, charted the ideology, headed the boards, set public agenda, and in other ways dominated the visible leadership of most reform organizations. However, day to day, women participated in great numbers and sometimes wielded enormous if often informal and uncelebrated influence. They distributed pamphlets, circulated petitions, solicited contributions, and administered local societies.[4]

Furthermore, women could be found in the whole range of reform movements, from the most socially conservative to the most radical. They worked in the earliest moral reform societies and spearheaded the first Sabbatarian petition drives. Later they staffed temperance societies. More radical women eagerly joined abolitionist efforts, organizing local, state, and regional antislavery auxiliaries while also participating in national organizations. They worked among the Lane Rebels in the black community of Cincinnati despite an outraged white citizenry. Prudence Crandall created a school for blacks in Canterbury, Connecticut, in the face of jeering and violent mobs. Lydia Maria Child and the Grimké sisters brought forceful antislavery arguments to the public through letters, pamphlets, and speeches, while Maria Weston Chapman and other women took on crucial responsibilities in the running of major abolitionist organizations. In short, by 1836 men and women reformers had created what they saw as an honored and vital place for womanhood, one that bestowed purpose and power upon them as part of reform's sweeping resymbolization of the cosmos.

Even reform women who chafed against limitations and weathered personal slights recognized how differently fellow reformers viewed the question of gender than most of humankind. Male reformers recognized womanhood itself as a vital, flexible, and changeable sphere, one much more positive than timeworn nostrums of anatomical and mental inferiority and original sin might normally allow. This was indeed novel. After all, most American women—those in the vast and isolated stretches of rural America; those enslaved in the South and their female owners; those lower- and working-class women in the cities and burgeoning factory towns; and even a majority of middle- and upper-class women—imagined their fates to be molded most actively by economic condition, race or ethnicity, locale, and the nature of their everyday labors. They saw themselves as members of privileged, middling, or lower classes. They identified themselves as black or white; as German, English, or Irish; as Protestant, Catholic, Unitarian, Presbyterian, Baptist, or a member of some other sect.

Women certainly understood how strikingly different their lives were from those of men. They expressed the joys and especially the sorrows of womanhood in folk wisdom, songs of lament, and the rituals and customs of female life.[5] Their fate might be hard, unfair, or cruel, but to most it seemed unchangeable.

That is not to say that women could not and did not assert themselves publicly in their own interest. Middle-class women exercised significant power in family and church. Working women sometimes agitated for higher wages. Women on the margins of society created cultures at variance with emerging middle-class norms. A black woman, slave or free, might protest slavery, racism, or inequality. Yet in these and other cases, women rarely expressed a bond of protest with other women of different social, racial, or economic groups. They might feel kinship with other women, but mostly such expressions revolved around such seeming immutables as the tasks of motherhood and the cruel dominion of men.[6]

Indeed, most men and women shared a profound sense that the subordinate position of women was of a piece with nature. The Christian tradition shaped woman in the image of Eve, put under the command of Adam in the shadow of original sin. In Genesis 3:16, God commanded women that "thy desire *shall be* to thy husband, and he shall rule over thee," and Paul said in Ephesians 5:22–23: "Wives, submit yourselves unto your own husbands, as unto the Lord"; these biblical injunctions are but two of many sacred texts that were woven together to establish gender hierarchy as part of a natural human order.

Scripture did include egalitarian visions of gender. Some passages pointed toward an androgynous God, such as the declaration in Genesis 1:26–27: "Let us make man in our image, after our likeness. . . . So God created man in his *own* image, in the image of God created he him; male and female created he them." In Galatians 3:28, Paul assured his gentile audience that, for all who owned the covenant through baptism, "there is neither Jew nor Greek, there is neither bond nor free, there is neither male nor female: for ye are all one in Christ Jesus."[7] "Strong" women appeared periodically in both the Old and New Testaments, and, in Catholic cultures at least, the Virgin Mary assumed an extraordinarily important role. Yet such examples spoke to special cases or promises of millennial transformation. As ideals mostly unattainable in this world, they reinforced sexual hierarchies that ruled the everyday sacred and profane lives of ordinary Christians.

Not surprisingly, then, assertions of sex equality most influential in America and England arose among radical Protestant groups whose imitation of primitive Christianity and preparations for the end of days drew them to egalitarian texts and limited the force of social convention. For example, the English Society of Friends (Quakers) gave new prominence to female religious life as they waited for the Second Coming. The Quaker George Fox emphasized the equality of Adam and Eve before the Fall and argued that equality returned after spiritual rebirth. Quaker women demonstrated their equality in a variety of ways, most of all as preachers. Thus Quakers defied Paul in I Corinthians 14:34 and I Timothy 2:12 and relied on the apostle in Galatians 3:28.[8] In the American colonies, such Quaker itinerants as Mary Dyer, Jane Hoskins, and Susannah Morris established a strong tradition giving women a voice in the Quaker community.[9] Yet as Quaker millennialism faded somewhat and the community itself entered the economic and social establishments of England and America, the sect preserved the doctrine of sex equality only imperfectly.[10]

In the years following the Great Awakening, the millennial bent of colonial America's religious life even produced such women prophets as Mother Anne Lee and Jemima Wilkinson. Lee led the so-called Shakers from England to the New York frontier in 1774 and proclaimed herself chosen by God to prophesy the end of days.[11] Jemima Wilkinson was among those influenced by Lee. Born a Quaker in Rhode Island in 1752, Wilkinson felt drawn to New Light Baptist preaching and underwent a series of religious experiences in her early twenties. Expelled from the local Quaker meeting for heretical tendencies, she emerged in 1776 with a new name—the Universal Friend—and a mission of preaching and healing. She gathered several hundred followers, male and female and from all classes, and led her flock to the wilderness of upstate New York, literally to build a New Jerusalem.[12]

Even as religious awakenings in England and America created articulations of sex egalitarianism or matriarchal religion, the Enlightenment inspired new sex ideals in urban, cosmopolitan culture. The Enlightenment in England produced two important secular advocates of radical sex equality: Mary Wollstonecraft and Fanny Wright. However, their attacks on Christianity and rejection of traditional marriage made them anathema in America even among reforming women who otherwise might have found their work appealing.[13]

More mainstream developments in England did have an impact in the colonies. In religion, literature, philosophy, and popular style, the transatlantic, cosmopolitan culture of Europe and America had moved, by the eve of the American Revolution, toward what Ruth Bloch has termed "gendered meanings of virtue." Bloch notes that "women and the emotions became increasingly associated with moral activity, while men and reason became more exclusively associated with the utilitarian pursuit of self-interest."[14] This popular ideology labeled the realms of politics, commerce, and war as masculine and explicitly emphasized the importance of women in the shaping of individual and social moral sensibilities.

Such a view did not necessarily exclude women from the political arena. In the early 1790s, Benjamin Rush's friend Elias Boudinot campaigned for increased participation of women in politics in New Jersey, a state where single women had the right to vote. "The rights of women are no longer strange sounds to an American ear," he declared, "and I devoutly hope the day is not far distant when we shall find them dignifying in a distinguishing code, the jurisprudence of several states of the Union."[15] Yet principled support for woman's participation fell victim to partisan calculations, and as strife in the 1790s dampened optimism about the possibility of preserving Republican virtue in politics and commerce, the moral sphere assigned to woman assumed even greater symbolic importance as possibly the only source of virtue in the Republic.[16]

As mother, teacher, and enforcer of virtue in courtship and marriage, woman became in the view of Rush and others the ideal and principal fount of Republican values in everyday life. This vision influenced a variety of developments in post-Revolutionary America. The most dramatic was a sudden interest in women's education.[17] Benjamin Rush, in setting forth his plan for creating Republican citizens, recommended schooling for women to ensure that they were capable of playing their part in the process of Republicanization. They should learn mathematics in order to keep their husbands' books and to be conversant with wills; science to guide them in household work and cooking; philosophy, ethics, government, and religion to make them ideal Republican mothers. "Let the ladies of a country be educated properly," he declared, "and they will not only make and administer laws [as mothers of future male leaders], but form its manners and character."[18] Timothy Dwight's boarding school at Greenfield Hill began to admit women. So did other institutions, and in 1789 Massachusetts changed its notion of the teacher by speaking of schoolmistresses as well as schoolmasters in its code of laws. All over the nation educational opportunities widened, at least for those women who possessed the consciousness and comfort to take advantage of them.

Under the broad canopy of Republican and, later, Christian womanhood, some women described the usefulness of female education in terms that merged personal autonomy with community good. For instance, Judith Sargent Murray, the foremost early female advocate of woman's education, emphasized the need for self-sufficiency. "Our girls, in general," she lamented, "are bred up with one particular view, with one monopolizing consideration which seems to absorb every other plan that reason might point out as worthy." That was marriage. Society had taught them that to end up *"an old maid"* seemed "contemptible."[19] Education bred skill and self-reliance, encouraged reasonable marital choices, and made the prospect of single life bearable.[20]

Especially in New England, women's academies of various sizes and varieties opened their doors, offering curricula that combined elements of classical education with instruction in refined behavior and practical household arts. In a number of cases, women themselves founded new schools: Emma Willard established the Middlebury Female Seminary in 1819; Catharine Beecher opened a similar school in Hartford in 1823; Zilpah Grant created the Ipswich Female Seminary in 1828; Mary Lyon founded Mount Holyoke Seminary in 1837. These New England pioneers were hardly typical, but by their very acts they expanded the prospects of women's participation in the public world.[21]

Christian Republican ideology's validation of nurture and moral education as peculiarly female virtues also induced some women of leisure to work for benevolent societies dedicated to Christian missionary work and aid to the less fortunate. Such work brought spiritual peace and, not incidentally, a sense of rectitude defined by contrast with the frivolity or moral depravity perceived to be characteristic of women less committed to benevolence. As in the case of other elements of the Christian Republican vision, however, it took the power of evangelical crusades to harness the energy of women for reform. The experimental nature and broad sweep of evangelicalism enabled women to play varied roles. Upper-class women were more likely to join benevolent societies. Those of the middling classes, and especially those of Presbyterian, Methodist, and Baptist background, flocked in great number to revivals. A few even served as organizers and preachers in revival campaigns. For many, though certainly not most, women in the relatively comfortable classes of northern and some southern towns and cities, church, benevolence, and reform activities became distinguishing characteristics of Christian virtue.[22]

In a matter of three decades, a minority of women in the middle classes had ranged far beyond the roles even most Republican visionaries had carved out for them. However, in pushing at the boundaries of tradition, men and women reformers alike could not help but confront unfamiliar choices and situations. Reformers bred in the culture of the Bible and Christian practice could not help but remember that guarding the borders of woman's sphere there remained Eve and the serpent, the expulsion from Eden, and God's subordination of woman to man. To question sexual hierarchy and distinct spheres of gender was to question a pillar of traditional Christian society more basic and pervasive than the Sabbath. It was to invite spiritual and social anarchy.

The case of William Lloyd Garrison, who by the late 1830s firmly aligned himself with woman's rights, gives us unusual insight into the ambivalence of male reformers. As editor of the *National Philanthropist* in 1828, Garrison wrote three pieces entitled "Female Influence" in which he urged women to involve themselves in the temperance cause. He invoked the moral influence of women, their victimhood at the hands of drunkards, and their responsibility for keeping households free of alcohol. As his sons later wrote, the articles showed Garrison's "early appreciation of the value of women's aid in any moral enterprise, and his quick instinct in enlisting them in the support of whatever cause he espoused."[23]

Yet Garrison also possessed a firm sense of the limits of woman's participation. In 1830, as editor of the *Genius of Universal Emancipation*, he declared that a petition to Congress from seven hundred Pittsburgh women in support of Cherokee rights in Georgia was "out of place." He himself had campaigned vociferously against Indian removal but thought that women's activity in the political sphere of men was improper and "uncalled-for interference. . . . We should be sorry to have this practice become general. There would then be no question agitated in Congress without eliciting the informal and contrarient opinions of the softer sex."[24] These seemingly contradictory quotations illustrated young Garrison's belief in distinct spheres of action. He encouraged women to join in reform efforts as they touched on issues directly affecting domestic tranquillity and nurture, but he labeled activities in realms distant from the home "interference" in the world of men.

The moral physiologists defined even more rigid typologies of gender, concentrating almost exclusively on woman's maternal role. William Andrus Alcott pinpointed "the MOTHER, whether wise or ignorant, learned or unlearned, healthy or sick, pious or impious, [as] the most efficient educator" in the home, that "great and special school of Divine Providence." Mothers influenced the development of their children's character by choosing the food children ate and the clothes they wore, and by controlling the air they breathed (literally, by choosing ways in which to ventilate the home). "She presides over, and molds, and shapes," Alcott reasoned. "She forms the 'house' the soul 'lives in;' and in this way, almost entirely directs the motions and tendencies of the soul itself."[25]

Sylvester Graham's vision of the moral mother was, as might be expected, intimately tied to the production of Graham bread. Having shared his best recipe, he asked: "Who then shall make our bread?" The servant girl, who might be an excellent cook? "No," answered Graham, "it is the wife, the mother only—she who loves her husband and her children as woman ought to love, and who rightly perceives the relations between the dietetic habits and physical and moral condition of her loved ones, and justly appreciates the importance of good bread to their physical and moral welfare—, she alone [possesses] . . . the indispensable attributes of a perfect bread-maker."[26]

Such attitudes illustrated the degree to which reformers of the 1820s and early 1830s envisioned woman's place in reform within the doctrines of separate spheres common to Christian Republicanism and evangelicalism. A more egalitarian imagining of "woman" in reform and in the world came only slowly even to women who had bumped against the periphery of their domain. Many, consciously or unconsciously, simply lived with the contradictions of gender alongside myriad other inconsistencies or raged inside with no clear alternative vision.

For a handful of women, however, contradiction bred creative religious turmoil and rebellion. In the 1820s and 1830s, Catharine Beecher, Lydia Maria Child, and finally Sarah and Angelina Grimké moved toward explicitly new understandings of the place of woman in the cosmos and society. They did so by transforming the meaning of their troubled quests into new visions of womanhood. They often disagreed, sometimes on the most crucial of issues. Yet taken together, their ideas about gender pushed the concept of the power and status resident in "womanhood" well beyond the already striking notions of Christian Republicanism. Christian Republicanism's ennobling and broadening of woman's vistas was a prerequisite, and the dynamic development of reform the catalyst, for such innovation. However, new conceptions of woman's power and equality depended on the creativity of individual women in turmoil.

Catharine Beecher, oldest child of Lyman Beecher, was the first major reform activist to rechannel mainstream evangelical doctrine toward a position of woman's independence and superiority.[27] Born in 1800 at the very beginning of her father's career, she mirrored his passions and adopted his cosmic mission as her own. No other Beecher child, not even Henry Ward Beecher, so patterned his or her self after Lyman's thirst to reshape and rule worlds. However, Catharine's gender posed immeasurable obstacles to the fulfillment of her dreams of power and significance, not least because Lyman himself could feel only half flattered by his daughter's headstrong energy. His evangelical vision drew strict boundaries between the proper spheres of men and women. He wanted Catharine to marry, and he worried even more about her unconverted state.

As it turned out, Catharine resisted both matrimony and conversion. Too strongly steeped in evangelicalism to abandon it, she instead reworked Lyman's evangelical cosmology by revaluing its constituent elements. She stressed the social imperatives of a conservative religious culture and the need to act in concert with them rather than the individual experience of conversion as central to salvation. And she made woman the prime mover in the creation of values and models for a middle-class Christian society.

The turning point for Catharine Beecher came when she was about twenty-one years old, a time that Kathryn Sklar has characterized as "the most traumatic" in her life.[28] Despite Lyman's urgings, she found it impossible to feel even a glimmer of the guilt that might lead her to conversion. Her father had more success promoting marriage. The man was Alexander Fisher, a brilliant young Yale professor. After initial resistance, Catharine fell in love and agreed to wed Fisher after he returned from a year in Europe. She was crushed by the news that Fisher had died in a shipwreck on the Irish coast.

In mourning Catharine clarified her spiritual sensibility. "Will you send your thoughts to heaven and find peace," asked Lyman in hopes of quickening her sense of eternity, "or to the cliffs, and winds, and waves of Ireland, to be afflicted, tossed with tempest and not comforted?" However, Catharine's discovery that Fisher had not converted before his death (which, according to Lyman's Calvinism, consigned him to damnation) hardened her against Lyman's entreaties. Without denying the importance of a changed heart, she resigned herself to the hope that a life of virtuous works might please God.[29]

Catharine took education as her calling; she set up a female seminary in Hartford in 1823 and guided it from its troubled first years to some semblance of stability. In 1826, even though she was an unconverted layperson and a woman, she led a successful revival among its students. Catharine hoped that "'he that watereth, shall himself be watered,'" yet in the end her soul remained dry.[30] Simply by running the revival, she challenged the church in some of the same ways as the Finney revival and at precisely the moment her father was railing against Finneyites in the West. In his daughter's case, Lyman seemed not to object.

Catharine responded to her spiritual frustration by spelling out an alternative road to holiness, one that made her own life emblematic for women in general and offered new religious and social ideals. In 1827, she published "Female Education" in the recently founded *American Journal of Education*. "A lady should study," she stated flatly, "not to *shine*, but to *act*." She focused especially on the "young lady destined to move in higher circles," since she most of all might influence the course of society.[31] An 1829 essay, *Suggestions Respecting Improvements in Education*, asserted the importance of women to the moral health of society and underlined the essential need for more and better female education.[32]

Nor did Beecher seek to put traditional strictures on the realms of woman's moral mission, at least in 1829. In that year she participated in the petition drive against Indian removal, thus embracing for women the very field of action that young Garrison had wished to preserve as a male domain. She organized petition drives and planned public meetings. She also wrote a popular pamphlet, *To the Benevolent Women of the United States*, urging support for the Cherokee cause.[33]

In 1831, Beecher published a profoundly searching work, *The Elements of Mental and Moral Philosophy, Founded upon Experience, Reason, and the Bible*.[34] It adapted the basic tenets of Scottish Common Sense philosophy to what many considered to be most the pressing problem of the day—the sources and enforcement of moral order—and made women the central actors in the drama of social regeneration.[35] The doctrines of Common Sense philosophy most relevant to Beecher were those that posited the capabilities of individual conscience but at the same time stressed the need to instruct conscience in order to protect it from a natural proclivity toward vice. The marriage of such concepts with traditional Calvinist notions of community, God, and individual piety suggested the need for rigorous cultivation of conscience in family and society. Benjamin Rush had combined Common Sense philosophy's notions of human conscience with Republican goals in his advocacy of Republican nurture. Lyman Beecher and other evangelicals sought means to engrave Christian principles on the minds of a democratic citizenry otherwise prone, as they saw it, to anarchy or despotism. Catharine Beecher's was one of the first works to grapple with these questions with a central focus on women.[36]

The problem outlined by Catharine Beecher involved both method and leadership. From what group in society would moral ideals originate, and how would they best be transmitted? Her own religious and social experiences led her to reject the evangelical argument that ministers would ensure a Christian society through conversions. Instead she saw the key as educating all of society in values developed by the refined classes. Like other American moral philosophers, she saw little virtue possible in the spheres of politics and commerce. Women in the home and in the schools—the community's home writ large—must render society moral. She defined such social virtue in terms of self-denial and self-sacrifice, a more acute version of the evangelical doctrine of disinterested benevolence. In doing so, she transformed characteristics associated with woman's sphere into universal ideals. She advocated a single "true standard of rectitude" for both sexes and all classes, with self-denial as the highest good. Women would lead the way.

By the early 1830s, Catharine Beecher had worked out a significant rereading of evangelicalism. As the progeny of Lyman Beecher, she predictably sought a society built upon evangelicalism and a hierarchical sense of society. Her innovation was to take Lyman's sense of woman's sphere at face value, make it the dominant moral force in society, and place at least some women out of the home to fulfill their mission. Women might then wield enormous power within a limited but crucial sphere of social endeavor.

Lydia Maria Child, a contemporary of Catharine Beecher's, dealt with the question of womanhood in a different if related fashion. Child shared with Beecher a surpassing intelligence and a deep rootedness in New England culture. They both contemplated central spiritual questions but resisted religious surrender. Each also displayed a fierce will to make her way in the world. Yet their lives were different in almost every other respect.

Born Lydia Francis in 1802, Child emerged from a vital but less exalted quadrant of New England society than Beecher. Her father, a successful baker in Medford, Massachusetts, raised his children far removed from social, political, or ecclesiastical power. As the youngest of his children, Lydia experienced little of the special attention Catharine Beecher had as the firstborn. She once described her youth as "cold, shaded, and uncongenial." She remembered dreaming that gypsies had transported her as an infant to the wrong household.[37] Her father kept his distance. A practical and hardworking man, David Francis could not appreciate the expansive sensibility of his daughter. However, in time she came to feel close to her mother and at one with her brother Convers, who shared her love of literature. "I owe my own literary tendencies entirely to his early influence," she later wrote. "When I came home from school, I always hurried to his bed-room, and threw myself down among his piles of books."[38]

Unfortunately, within a year of Lydia's twelfth birthday, her mother died, Convers entered Harvard, and Lydia was sent to live with her older sister in Maine. She spent six years in veritable isolation and then struggled through a dreary year teaching school in Gardiner, Maine. In these times of what she herself termed "exile," Lydia survived spiritually by committing herself to earnest self-education and by engaging in an intense correspondence with Convers, who remained in Cambridge to attend divinity school.

Lydia's few surviving letters from her teens indicate how early in her life the issues of both women and religion had come to the fore. At one point in 1817, at age fifteen, she clashed with Convers over "Milton's treatment to our sex," confessing that she had little hope of converting her brother to her less enthusiastic view of the poet.[39] Three years later, having apparently engaged in a discussion of religion with Convers, she assured him that she was not turning to Swedenborgianism in her search for faith. "I am more in danger of wrecking on the rocks of skepticism," she confided, "than of stranding on the shoals of fanaticism." She sought most of all a religion that united "heart and understanding," but her vision of each remained more open, intuitive, and diffuse than those proffered by any church.[40]

By 1822, Lydia had left Maine and moved in with Convers in Watertown, Massachusetts, where he had become minister of the Unitarian church. She reluctantly allowed herself to be baptized a Unitarian, and she socialized with Convers's young Harvard comrades Ralph Waldo Emerson and Theodore Parker. She shared their revulsion with traditional Calvinism but harbored her own nagging doubts about the Unitarian alternative. Lydia continued to seek her own way, and thus more significant than baptism itself was that she took the occasion to rename herself Maria.[41] It was as if her new name brought the possibility of a new life.

Soon Maria found her calling. One Sunday morning in 1824, she came upon an old *North American Review* that contained John G. Palfrey's review of *Yamoyden*, a minor American epic poem. Palfrey applauded the work, a story of white-Indian relations in early New England quite sympathetic to the Indian side. He sounded a familiar theme in praising its American rather than European setting, and he dared American writers to achieve greatness with tales set in their native land. Child remembered putting down the review and instantly taking up the challenge. By afternoon church meeting, she had already written a first chapter. Six weeks later she had completed *Hobomok*, her first novel.[42]

Hobomok, set in seventeenth-century Salem, mixed history and romance in sometimes surprising fashion. Mary, a young Englishwoman, comes to the settlement to visit her sick mother. Her fiancé Charles Brown follows her, but the Puritans (including Mary's father) banish him for promoting Anglicanism. Later he is reported lost at sea. Mary turns in despair to Hobomok the Indian. She marries him, and they have a son. Soon after, she discovers that Brown is actually alive and has returned to Salem. When Charles and Mary reunite and marry, Hobomok disappears into the forest, but not before actually saving his rival and putting his blessing on the couple's raising of his child. The son of Mary and Hobomok eventually graduates from Harvard.

At the heart of *Hobomok*'s narrative complexities lies the life of the spirit. Religious intolerance wreaks misery on all by forcing emigrations, separating lovers, and in general keeping spiritual truth from informing human action. The author professes admiration for "the sacred flame . . . burning deeply and fervently" within the Puritan fathers but cannot dismiss the view that they were a "band of dark, discontented bigots."[43]

Among *Hobomok*'s characters, only Mrs. Conant and her daughter Mary seek religious Truth. Mary finds relief from sectarian squabbles by looking out her door to the radiant, moonlit night, imagining all peoples of the Earth—Catholic, Episcopalian, Calvinist, Muslim, Indian, merchant, nun, and courtier—bathing in the same light. "And can it be, as my father says," she muses, "that of all the multitude of people who view thy cheering rays, so small a remnant only are pleasing in the sight of God?"[44]

For her part, Mrs. Conant condemns religious disputation, ritual, and learning. She sees it as "little good . . . to know every thing about religion and yet to feel little of its power—yea, even to feel burdened with a sense of sin and misery." In answer to Charles Brown's retort that the Bible as explained by Anglican bishops provides all necessary wisdom, she replies that "the Bible is an inspired book; but I sometimes think the Almighty suffers it to be a flaming cherubim. . . . But in creation, one may read to their fill. It is God's library—the first Bible he ever wrote."[45]

These passages and others, so reflective of Maria's own spiritual striving and her dissatisfactions even with liberal Unitarianism, display a remarkably transcendental vision a dozen years before Emerson had begun to sketch out a formal Transcendentalism.[46] The book as a whole lays out a perfect and unique American religious vision. Hobomok represents the naked power of nature itself, adorned with neither the revealed beauty of Christianity nor its theological quibbling. "He had never read of God," so Maria described his spiritual life, "but he had heard his chariot wheels in the distant thunder, and seen his drapery in the clouds."[47] No wonder that Mary should be drawn to him in her hour of need. No wonder that the future lay in the hands of their offspring, an amalgam of American nature and the refined spiritual nature of Christian womanhood, all carefully finished at Harvard. Even Mary's father finally blesses his daughter's marriage to an Anglican, the forces of true religion at least for a moment conquering the narrow bigotry of the Puritan fathers.[48] For Maria, that was the promise of America.

Like Beecher's magnification of the common idea of woman's sphere into one of woman's power, Maria's arresting identification of women with spiritual concerns distinctly superior to the passionate sectarianism exhibited by most of *Hobomok*'s male characters argued for woman's leadership in recasting religion. Like Beecher, she opened a girl's school in Watertown in 1826. Maria also launched the *Juvenile Miscellany*, an immensely successful magazine filled with instructive poems, articles, and stories for children. In this manner, too, she acted out the role of public nurturer that Beecher was just beginning to articulate.

Nonetheless, clear differences marked the two women's religious style and substance. Compared to Beecher, who had a highly structured, sociophilosophical approach to women and their moral function in society, Maria displayed a romantically unbounded sense of personal spiritual life and left its profound connection to the details of social existence implicit. Her voice spoke best through individual souls, as in *Hobomok*, or in sallies over religious issues with Convers. And even as Catharine Beecher's spiritual instincts hardened before the demands of father and church, Maria Francis's fluid spirituality remained rebelliously untethered. Loosed by Unitarianism from Calvinism, she pushed past Unitarianism to an experiential sense of religion. Heroism, conscience, warmth toward the world at large: these were component virtues in an as yet unfinished search for a faith with "heart and understanding."[49]

One further matter distinguished these women from each other. Catharine Beecher had to be cajoled into the idea of marriage, and after her fiancé's death she put aside the possibility forever. Maria never wished hers to be a solitary quest, especially after she met David Lee Child at Convers's home in December 1824. Child had just returned from Portugal, where he had been secretary to the American consul until he joined the Spanish army to fight against the French. The combination of David's heroism and modesty and his intellectual curiosity dazzled Maria. By late January 1825, she could write in her diary: "He is the most gallant man that has lived since the sixteenth century; and needs nothing but helmet, shield, and chain armour to make him a complete knight of chivalry."[50] For his part, David described her as the "ethereal, high-souled, high-reaching Maria! the elegant, pure, powerful-minded Maria! . . . She is the only lady in W[atertown] who has made any impression upon me of a serious & enduring kind, i.e. to say of a *tender kind.*"[51]

David and Maria married on October 19, 1828. Some chroniclers of Maria's life have seen her marriage as a disaster, a bond that held her back from fulfilling the promise of her talents. There certainly is important truth to the characterization. In the everyday world, David Lee Child was a supremely impractical person of a romantic bent. His various attempts to make a living failed miserably. He was an indifferent and unsuccessful lawyer. He tried journalism, but his paper, the *Massachusetts Whig Journal* (whose staff at the time included William Lloyd Garrison) suffered financially after Jackson's election, both from fewer subscriptions and because of a successful libel suit brought by a Jacksonian state senator that eventually sent Child to jail for a few months. These were just some of the lifelong series of episodes in which Maria supported or nursed her husband.[52]

Yet marriage also seemed to strengthen Maria's powers of assertion and imagination, as well as her faith in both women's spirituality and the essential unity of humankind. Maria's rich repertoire of concerns often worked together. The spare household setting of her marriage inspired one of her most successful books, *The Frugal Housewife* (1830). David's work for the Cherokee Indians reinforced her enduring interest in New England's Indians and drove her to write *The First Settlers of New England* (1829). In 1831, she published *The Mother's Book* and *The Girl's Own Book*, volumes that spoke to her own dreams of children and family responsibility.[53]

The First Settlers of New England unfolds as a dialogue between mother and daughter that reveals, as in *Hobomok*, the cruel narrowness of the Puritan fathers. It behooves those who claim to be "followers of Jesus," the mother proclaims, "earnestly to insist, that a being who authorizes injustice, revenge, and cruelty, cannot be the God and Father of our lord Jesus Christ." The daughter asks the mother about intermarriage and receives this reply:

> Whatever objections there may be for people of different colours to unite, it would doubtless abundantly diminish the amount of crime, and we might thus testify our obedience to the will of our heavenly Father, who has made of one blood all the nations of men, that they may dwell together.[54]

Child not only dreamed the uncommon dream of intermarriage but also confidently preached higher truths as a layperson and a woman.

Using the same tone of reasonable moral authority in *The Mother's Book*, Child expressed her liberal spiritual views on the Sabbath and religion in general. She emphasized that children needed to be exposed to the joys of religion, and that Sundays should not be associated with deprivation. Sabbath-keeping became an instrument of instruction in religious sensibility rather than a sine qua non of faith. She noted, for instance, that the "Quakers say every day should be Sunday; and certainly no day should pass without using some of the opportunities, which are always occurring, of leading the heart to God." Yet she felt that "a reverence for the Sabbath, even if it be a matter of habit," offered families a natural day of focus on religious matters.[55]

Writing about family life, however, was no substitute for actually living it. Maria's longings for domesticity reached a peak while David was in jail. "I do wish I could be a mother," she wrote to her mother-in-law in June 1831; ". . . sometimes I get so fidgety, because I want to go to housekeeping so much,—and it [David's newspaper] is such a long way out of the woods yet."[56] Away from her husband in October and still not situated in a house, Maria exclaimed in a letter to him: "Oh, how I do long to be settled! I will have everything so snug and bright when you come home. Your slippers and stockings warm by the fire; and I with 'a whole Iliad in my face,' and a Paradise Regained in my heart."[57]

The Childs found some semblance of domestic stability in 1832. David became a justice of the peace, while Maria's book sales were reaching unprecedented heights and softening financial worries. The couple retired most of their debts. Late in the year Maria and David settled into a little house in Roxbury. For a short period at least, Maria's life became a blissful routine of research in Boston, writing at home, pondering questions of the spirit and of art, and spending more time with David. Growing public esteem matched the satisfactions of private life. The *North American Review* in July 1833 confidently declared of her contribution to American literature: "We are not sure that any woman in our country would outrank Mrs. Child."[58]

This combination of marriage and success encouraged Maria to launch a new and bold project, a series ultimately reaching five books and initially planned as the "Ladies Family Library." Taken together, they represented Child's most extended meditation on what it meant to be a woman within the spiritual and social context of humanity. She began with two volumes of paired biographies, the first chronicling the lives of Madame de Staël and Madame Roland (1832) and the second treating Madame Guyon and Lady Russell (1832). A third volume, *Good Wives* (1833), developed its title theme through shorter biographical sketches.[59] All told, these books represented a romantic and creative leap beyond the borders of the advice books to the intimate rendering of history.

Again prefiguring Emerson, Child approached Guyon, Russell, de Staël, and Roland as women representative of the virtue and genius of their sex. She did not always feel comfortable with their lives, nor even with her attraction to them. Of the four, Maria felt most drawn to Lady Russell (1636–1723), who stood by her husband as he was tried and sentenced to death for crimes against the state during the reign of Charles II. She noted that Lady Russell carried herself with aplomb but pleaded with the king for mercy using every means short of sacrificing her virtue. Child quoted another of Russell's admirers, who touted her "passive courage, devoted tenderness, and unblemished purity" as a perfect complement to her husband's "public patriotism, private virtues, and unshaken principles."[60]

Child chose to write about Madame Guyon (1648–1717), French Catholic mystic and protégée of Fenelon, because of "the purity of her life, the peculiarity of her opinions, and the severe trials she was called to encounter." For a liberal Christian to expound upon the virtues of a Catholic quietist was unusual. Nor did Child shy from those aspects of Guyon's life that might seem bizarre to her audience, such as her ritual scourging of her body, the better to rid herself of "vain complacency." She noted that Guyon married but soon discovered that she wished to be a nun. When her husband died on Magdalen's Eve 1676, Guyon exclaimed: "Oh God, thou hast broken my bonds, and I will offer thee a sacrifice of praise!" Abandoning her children to an Ursuline convent, she moved to a small town near Geneva, working miracles and converting Protestants. There she met Fenelon, who brought her into the intrigues of Louis XIV's court. Fenelon's enemies had her imprisoned twice, and she eventually died in obscurity. Child never revealed her specific attraction to her subject, stating only that Guyon "sincerely wished to follow the Lord in the path of regeneration" and that readers must "judge of her according to their own opinions."[61]

Child's treatment of Madame Roland (1754–1793) and Madame de Staël (1766–1817) focused on their intellectual verve and life-embracing spirit. She concluded that de Staël, who was as famous for her affairs and salon as for her own literary efforts, "deserve[d] our highest respect and admiration. Her defects, whether as an author or as a woman, always sprung from the excess of something good. . . . She had an expansive freedom, a mighty energy of soul, which never found room enough in this small world of ours."[62] Child had few reservations about Madame Roland, who helped lead the Girondists during the French Revolution but also remained a devoted wife to her husband.

> I love her for preferring the beauties of nature, and the quiet happiness of domestic life, to all the glittering excitements of society; I revere the strictness of her moral principles, the purity of her intentions and the perfect rectitude of her conduct; I admire the vigorous activity of her mind, her unyielding fortitude, and her uniform regard for truth. I warmly sympathize with her enthusiasm for liberty, her hatred of oppression, and her contempt for the insolence of rank—But I confess I am sometimes startled by the fierceness and boldness of her expressions.[63]

In light of these biographies of women who passionately followed their beliefs and loves, whether love of humankind or love of God, Maria's next volume, *Good Wives*, takes on more profound meaning. Not simply an exposition of the domestic virtues, it merged Child's romantic, creative, and committed selves and expressed a oneness of belief in God, marriage, and national moral prosperity.[64] Rather than envisioning the role of good wife as the only proper course for women, Child saw it as one specimen of moral passion. Thus the author of *The Frugal Housewife*, in a manner quite unlike Catharine Beecher, could also endorse the quite varied lives of Lady Russell, Madame Guyon, Madame Roland, and Madame de Staël. All had displayed sacrifice, commitment, and spiritual passion.

By 1832, then, Catharine Beecher and Lydia Maria Child had made enormous strides in reimagining the spiritual and moral power of woman and her place in society. Such new visions brought recognition and bolstered the continuing odysseys of each. Although Child and Beecher pursued significance for women in very different ways, a disinterested party might well have found more in common than different in their views and nothing terribly controversial. Yet times, issues, and advocacies soon changed, making implicit differences explicit. And no phenomenon of the early 1830s was more transforming than the rise of abolitionism. Faced with radical antislavery, Lydia Maria Child and Catharine Beecher moved in opposite directions and honed their senses of the woman question in radically new ways.

From at least the time of *Hobomok*, Lydia Maria Child had displayed sympathy for Indians, slaves, and others tyrannized by her own culture. Her choice of David Child as a husband reflected that sympathetic strain. Marriage to him only sharpened it. David had been a fervent enemy of slavery for some years, and his old friend William Lloyd Garrison's bold leap to immediate emancipation galvanized his energies. Child, Garrison, and thirteen others founded the New England Anti-Slavery Society in January 1832. David urged Maria to devote herself to the cause, but it was her first contact with Garrison that decided the matter. Like Samuel J. May and others, she embraced Garrison as a prophet. Almost fifty years later, the day after Garrison's death, she reflected on their first meeting: "I little thought then that the whole pattern of my life-web would be changed by that introduction. I was then all absorbed in poetry and painting,— soaring aloft, on Psyche-wings, into the etherial regions of mysticism. He got hold of the strings of my conscience, and pulled me into Reforms."[65]

Almost immediately she applied her talents to abolition, writing *An Appeal in Favor of That Class of American Called Africans* in 1833. Section by section, the *Appeal* surveyed the history, influence, and deleterious effects, as well as the inhumanity and immorality, of slavery. It also recommended immediate emancipation as safe and contended that it was the duty of those in the North sympathetic to the slave to reject colonization. Most striking, however, was Child's elaboration on Garrisonian themes of black equality and the need to end discrimination in the North. In a chapter entitled "Intellect of Negroes," she surveyed travelers' descriptions of Africa in order to demonstrate the extraordinary power and wealth of African culture. As for the perceived characteristics of American slaves, she quoted slaveholder and founding father Patrick Henry on the elixir of freedom: "If a man be in chains, he droops and bows to the earth, because his spirits are broken; but let him twist the fetters off his legs and he will stand erect." She found northern prejudice against blacks "even more inveterate than it is at the South" and cited example after example of northern whites greeting educated and otherwise agreeable African-Americans with scorn.[66]

The very title page of the *Appeal* underscored its dramatic departure from Child's past. It identified Maria as "Mrs. Child, Author of the Mother's Book, the Girl's Own Book, The Frugal Housewife, Etc." Child played on the contrast, beseeching the reader to "read it, from sheer curiosity to see what a woman (who had much better attend to her household concerns) will say upon such a subject." She noted, "I *expect* ridicule and censure," but if it advanced the cause of "truth and justice, I would not exchange the consciousness for all Rothchild's wealth, or Sir Walter's fame."[67]

Child's expectations proved correct. Irate readers canceled their subscriptions to the *Juvenile Miscellany* (it closed for lack of subscribers in 1834), and those who had praised her literary production now castigated her radical and unwomanly departure into controversy. "It is of no use to imagine what might have been, if I had never met him," she reflected years later about her encounter with Garrison and her plunge into abolitionism. "Old dreams vanished, old associates departed, and all things became new.

But the new surroundings were all alive, and they brought a moral discipline worth ten times the sacrifice they cost."[68]

The writing of the *Appeal* also brought a new angle of vision to Maria's
contemplation of woman's lot. Having already written admiringly and
personally of various famous women, she embarked on a project that
paralleled her research in African history. She scoured the available literature to build a picture of the fate of common women in all cultures
throughout history, thereby providing a prooftext more salient than Genesis for an understanding of sex differences. She finally published two long
volumes in 1835 under the descriptive title *The History of the Condition of
Women, in Various Ages and Nations*. Child asserted that the work was
strictly historical in nature and certainly "not an essay upon woman's
right, or a philosophical investigation of what is or ought to be the relation
of the sexes."[69]

Yet Child noted pertinent information that indicated an underlying
preoccupation with equality. In her volume on Europe, America, and the
South Sea Islands, the chapter on "Centuries Succeeding the Middle
Ages" noted of the sixteenth century:

> In the midst of all this adulation, women were not backward in vindicat-
> ing their own claims. Several Italian ladies wrote books to prove the
> comparative inferiority of men; and the French women espoused the
> cause with equal zeal. The most conspicuous among them was Margaret
> of Navarre, the first wife of Henry the Fourth, who undertook to prove
> that "woman is much superior to man."[70]

She also asserted that English history presented "many instances of
women exercising prerogatives now denied them," which she then took
three pages to list.[71]

Child described a complicated and sometimes contradictory situation
for her own era. With the spread of knowledge throughout the community, it was "a very common thing for women to be well versed in the
popular sciences, and to know other languages than their own." She characterized New England's tradition as strict but essentially egalitarian and
asserted that, despite the lack of formal political rights, "perhaps there is
no country in the world, where women, as wives, sisters, and daughters,
have more influence, or more freedom."

However, she admitted that one could not easily find in America "a man
so magnanimous, as to be perfectly willing that a woman should know
more than himself, on any subject except dress and cookery."[72] Child did
not idealize simple and separate equality, about which, she said, "many
silly things ha[d] been written." Rather she sought "true and perfect com-
panionship, which gives both man and woman complete freedom *in* their

places, without a restless desire to go out of them."[73] Woman's "place" differed from man's in particulars, she argued, but not in expanse. Child saw no contradiction between her sense of difference between men and women and, for instance, her own heroic leap into the world of abolitionism. Judged next to Madame Guyon, Lady Russell, Madame de Staël, and Madame Roland, Child may well have seen her own life as following a path well-worn by women in the past.

If abolitionism irrevocably widened Lydia Maria Child's world and deeply colored her sense of woman's history, nature, and fate, it had precisely the opposite effect on Catharine Beecher. In 1832, the Beechers moved to Cincinnati, where Lyman took up the presidency of Lane Seminary and Catharine began a new school. She suffered indignities on two fronts. First, as something of a self-proclaimed missionary for New England "civilization" in the rude West, Catharine found herself resented and excluded by a Western élite whose pride in their region rubbed inelegantly against her patronizing ways. Second, as a result of abolitionist agitation in 1833 and 1834 led by Lane student Theodore Dwight Weld, the Beechers came under intense community fire from which they and Lane Seminary never fully recovered.[74] With her own sense of pride already shaken by rebuffs from those she wished to convert, and her family's standing mocked by rude abolitionists, Catharine retreated to a more fearfully rigid view of woman's place.

The earliest major expression of this new turn appeared in *Letters on the Difficulties of Religion* (1836), which Beecher wrote ostensibly to guide the unschooled through the basics of theological discourse. From the outset she clearly linked proper understandings of religion to proper behavior within the "appropriate sphere" of womanhood. Beecher began with a tirade against Fanny Wright (who had recently returned to the United States from Europe). Defining the true character of woman as one demanding "delicacy of appearance and manners, refinement of sentiment, gentleness of speech, modesty in feeling and action, a shrinking from notoriety and public gaze, a love of dependence, and protection, aversion to all that is coarse and rude," she turned to Wright's example with "disgust and abhorrence." Beecher pointed to "her great masculine person, her loud voice, her untasteful attire, going about unprotected, and feeling no need of protection, mingling with men in stormy debate, and standing up with barefaced impudence, to lecture to a public assembly. . . . There she stands, with brazen front and brawny arms, attacking the safeguards of all that is venerable and sacred in religion, all that is safe and wise in law, all that is pure and lovely in domestic virtue."[75]

Beecher claimed that she could not "conceive of any thing in the shape of a woman, more intolerably offensive and disgusting."[76] Yet by the end of 1836, Catharine Beecher became even more alarmed at the recent career of a woman she had once admired. Angelina Grimké was petite, feminine, of soft voice, shy, devoutly Christian, and respectful of domestic virtue— no Fanny Wright. She was also a committed abolitionist whose slaveholding past gave unique power to her lectures and writings. Soon, along with her sister Sarah, Angelina Grimké would issue broadsides on the woman question that struck at the very heart of every assumption Beecher cherished about women and Christianity.

IX

Woman's Rights and Schism

$\mathbf{D}$ESPITE the widening of vision concerning woman's history and role achieved in the writings of Beecher and Child by the early 1830s, neither had broached the question of sex "equality" as a specific, achievable, or desirable goal. Child felt most comfortable with an ideal of sex difference that nonetheless put few limits on woman's field of action. Beecher sought a more rigid definition of spheres than Child, one that might bring to women a central role in the broader evangelical mission to convert the Republic. Neither had greatly emphasized the problems women faced in society, this despite the fact that both had experienced deep disappointment in life because of limits placed upon them as women. It took rapidly changing fortunes within reform and the appearance of two sisters from South Carolina, in fact, to turn reformers toward a stormy first consideration of woman's equality and a serious look at the lot of women in American society.

Angelina and Sarah Grimké, daughters of a prominent Charleston slaveholding family, experienced a less well marked and more anguished spiritual journey than either Beecher or Child. The sisters fled home and family to escape the slave system and to find spiritual peace. By the mid-830s, they had become active abolitionists. Turning to the "woman question" in self-defense in 1837, they made possible the radical redefinition of woman's role in the world by challenging social convention and by attacking directly the Biblical bases for doctrines of female inferiority. In doing so, they brought upon themselves sometimes violent wrath from society and isolation even within the ranks of reform.[1]

Sarah Grimké was born in 1792, the daughter of John Faucheraud Grimké and Mary Smith Grimké. Angelina was born in 1805, the last of fourteen children Mary Grimké had carried and eleven who survived infancy. In outer trappings the Grimkés fit a profile typical of Charleston's élite: wealth in land and slaves, membership in the proper church and club, children at the proper schools. John Grimké was a lawyer, judge, and planter. He claimed notice with published commentaries on the laws of South Carolina, and he courted enemies with outspoken and sometimes controversial rulings from the bench. Indeed, he so enraged powerful factions in the state that in 1811 he narrowly escaped impeachment. Simply the questioning of his honor, however, broke Judge Grimké's spirit and his health. He died in 1819.[2] Of Sarah and Angelina's mother we know little except that she was a reserved and pious soul, one in whom the stresses of household management and childbearing had bred a deep sense of duty and resignation. Late in her life, she conveyed to Angelina some revealing wisdom: "The evils of life you must share with others, for God has not promised to exempt his Children from these; but he will enable them to face them; & he will sanctify all their crosses to them."[3]

Sarah felt most drawn to her father, but he responded to her only within the limits of the culture. Early on she displayed a surpassing intelligence and enjoyed nothing better than to study, alongside her brother Thomas, the subjects—science, mathematics, geography, history, and Greek—deemed appropriate for boys but not girls. The family reacted with a mixture of admiration, ridicule, and chastisement, leaving Sarah in a nether world similar to Catharine Beecher's in relation to her father and Lydia Francis's vis-à-vis Convers. The years 1804 and 1805 proved pivotal for Sarah. Thomas left the household for college. The following year, Mary Grimké gave birth to her last child, Angelina Emily Grimké. The thirteen-year-old Sarah declared her wish to be the baby's godmother. After much hesitation, the parents finally gave in to the daughter's incessant pleading. So successful was she as Angelina's quasi-parent that the younger sister literally addressed her as "Mother" well into adulthood.[4]

The years that followed brought new tests for Sarah. As anxious as any young woman to partake of Charleston's social whirl, the sparkle of its balls and suggestive flirtations, she nonetheless felt guilt-ridden over such frivolity. She soon underwent conversion with the aid of an evangelical Presbyterian minister. It was an ominous but incomplete reckoning. The next great turn in Sarah's and, by extension, Angelina's life came as Judge Grimké's health declined. Sarah usurped Mary Grimké's role (as she had by mothering Angelina), accompanying her father to Philadelphia in 1819 to seek a cure. For two months his doctor struggled in vain to improve the Judge's condition. Finally he suggested that his patient seek relief in sea bathing. Father and daughter traveled to the New Jersey shore, where for two more months Sarah attended to him as he deteriorated. When death came, she arranged for his burial in a modest churchyard nearby. "I may say that our attachment became strengthened day by day," she wrote later. "I regard this as the greatest blessing next to my conversion that I have ever received from God."[5]

On her trip north, Sarah came to know another way of life. She spent two months in Philadelphia before returning home, grieving in "solemn tranquility" amidst the simplicity of the Quaker family with whom she boarded. Aboard the ship that took her back to Charleston in November 1819, she became deeply involved in serious religious and moral discussions with Israel Morris, a successful Quaker businessman. He gave her John Woolman's *Journal*, whose indictment of slavery made special sense of Sarah's own life, for it justified the discomfort she had felt concerning the institution. Now she had the words to condemn it and a course of action that might bear witness against it.

Sarah's continued mourning and inner conflicts about slavery shrouded her return to Charleston. She withdrew from the family much of the time and began to attend a small Quaker meeting in the city. Visions haunted her consciousness. She began a correspondence with Morris about the Society of Friends. Finally, an inner voice commanded her to move to the North and, in the spring of 1821, she set sail for Philadelphia to begin a new life. Two years later, after long and serious preparation, she formally joined an Orthodox Quaker meeting.[6]

Sarah entered life among the Quakers as a soul alive with spiritual purpose and passion. She hoped one day to become a Quaker minister. Her piety found its most wrenching test in her relationship to Israel Morris. Morris's wife had died in 1820, and the correspondence that he and Sarah began before her arrival in Philadelphia blossomed into an ever-deepening affair of the heart. Morris finally proposed marriage in 1826, but Sarah turned him down. "That was a day of solemn heartfelt supplication," she wrote in her diary a few years later, "that nothing might intervene between me and my God."[7] For her faith, Sarah had now given up everything most human beings found to be blessings: wealth, comfort, and the intimacy of marriage.[8]

Meanwhile, Angelina had grown into a self-assured young woman, though in her own way as idiosyncratic as her sister in her spiritual cravings. In 1826, the year of her twenty-first birthday, she was converted. Abandoning the Episcopal church as too exclusive, she found solace in the Third Presbyterian Church, where the Reverend William MacDowell, a young northern minister in the South for his health, brought her under his sway. "I could not conscientiously belong to any church which exalted itself above all others and excluded ministers of other denominations from its pulpit," she wrote two years later; "—the principle of liberality is what especially endears the Presbyterian Church to me." Angelina immediately plunged into church work, organizing "female prayer meetings" that brought together believers from many sects and walks of life. She seemed fulfilled. Yet there remained a major question: If all God's children should find communion together, what of the slaves? Her own experience with family slaves fueled her uneasiness. If we are to believe accounts made years later, after her conversion she started openly to criticize slavery.[9]

Whether because of slavery or nagging doubts about her own religious commitment or both, Angelina's sense of faith began to falter. Sarah's return to Charleston in October 1827 provided Angelina an opportunity to further explore her soul. Sarah allowed Angelina to read her own anguished diary and argued for Quaker doctrines of piety that outstripped Presbyterianism in their renunciations. In January 1828, Angelina destroyed her precious collection of Sir Walter Scott novels. Soon after, she ceremoniously discarded her wardrobe of fancy clothes. By February, she was using the Quaker "thee" and "thou." On April 20, 1828, she vowed no longer to attend the Presbyterian church.[10] In the summer of 1828, Angelina visited Sarah in Philadelphia. There she became more familiar with Quaker ways and for the first time underwent extensive questioning about slavery. By the time she returned to Charleston five months later, she had been converted to the view that slaveholding was sinful.[11]

Angelina did not seek exile. Rather she hoped to proselytize against slavery among her family members and in Charleston at large. It was only six years after Denmark Vesey's abortive slave rebellion, however, and most white Charlestonians considered any antislavery talk both traitorous and dangerous. Her family name protected her from outright prosecution, but at every point family members argued with her and neighbors shunned her. Angelina's Presbyterian congregation, already stung by her move toward the Quakers, tried her for breaking the vows she had made upon joining the church. They issued a strong admonition but did not expel her. "Why do they not cut off the withered branch at once," she pleaded to the Reverend McDowell, "instead of leaving it to die by inches?" To her diary she confided: "Once so much beloved and bearing so high a character for zeal and piety—now regarded as a poor deluded creature." By October 1829, she was on a boat back to Philadelphia.[12]

Although slavery and woman's rights would soon dominate the lives of the Grimké sisters, antislavery and woman's rights played only secondary if important underlying roles in their move to the north. At heart the Grimkés sought a way of life that more authentically reflected their spiritual commitment. They saw limitations on the lives of women and support of slavery as symptomatic of a more general un-Godliness in Charleston society. Ultimately, the sisters found the Society of Friends appealing because the ascetic style and ritual of Quaker life—drab clothing, special language, and intense spirituality—pointed them toward greater congruency between inner spiritual striving and outer life.

Yet new complications lay in wait, for the Quakers themselves were at war with each other at the very moment that the Grimkés sought to find spiritual security among them. Elias Hicks had led a democratic insurgency in the mid-1820s to stem the move of the Quaker establishment toward hierarchy and trinitarianism and away from the mystical, individualistic roots of religious experience. Hicksite meetings supported antislavery activities and more egalitarian treatment of women. The tension had sociogeographical dimensions as well, the rebels being mostly from the countryside and fearful of the new world of manufacturing and commerce. Open schism came in 1828, just as Sarah was finally settling into the Quaker community and Angelina was beginning seriously to contemplate a permanent move.[13]

Ironically, the Arch and Fourth Street Meeting to which Israel Morris belonged and in which the Grimkés found a home was among the most orthodox and élite in the city. It was a cauldron of anti-Hicksite sentiment. At first the Hicksite controversy seemed to elude the Grimkés entirely, but they were not spared its pernicious effects. Sarah's strong need to be active in the world, ruled out by rigid social custom in Charleston, found its most obvious avenue through the Quaker ministry. Some encouraged her to pursue this course. Yet Sarah's halting and unmusical speaking style hampered her in a sect that valued spontaneous and fluid spiritual expression. Nor were the elders terribly helpful, for the Hicksite struggle tended to make them favor members born and bred in the meeting. Sarah responded with an inner rage checked by self-doubt, one that resulted in her ever greater sense of self-abnegation and despair.[14]

Angelina, more confident of her powers and more assertive of her place in the world, confronted authority more boldly. Her first clash came as she was being considered for Quaker membership, when elders accused her of ignoring the duty of children to parents by leaving her widowed mother in Charleston. Angelina shot back that she had found it intolerable living in a slave society, and that in any case she had left with her mother's blessing. The opposition caved in, and she became a member. Angelina immediately immersed herself in community work, holding prayer meetings and ministering to the spiritual needs of prisoners in the city's jails.

A fortuitous visit to Philadelphia by Catharine Beecher turned Angelina's energies in a new direction. Conversing at a social occasion, Beecher inspired Grimké to become a teacher and to prepare at Beecher's school in Hartford. The very mention of leaving Philadelphia filled Angelina's fellow Quakers with dread, especially at the idea of her being surrounded at school by worldly Presbyterians. Nonetheless, Angelina visited Beecher's school, where she talked not only to Catharine but to Harriet Beecher as well. She enjoyed their company, and they assured her that it might take as little as six months to prepare for a career in teaching. She returned to Philadelphia renewed in her sense of the future.[15]

When she broached the topic of attending Beecher's school in the fall of 1831, however, a chorus of protest arose in the meeting. In addition, Edward Bettle, son of an influential elder, had been courting Angelina (to her growing delight) but had stopped calling on her in the wake of this flourish of independence. Angelina chose not to go to Hartford, hoping thereby to still community criticism and lure back the young Bettle.[16] It was neither an easy nor a satisfying choice, for more and more she felt asphyxiated by Quaker life and the scrutiny of the conservative and powerful Bettles. Then, quite suddenly, Edward died in 1832. Angelina admitted in her diary that "a heavy load rolled off my heart, a dark cloud rolled back from my soul."[17]

Two years later, another death hurt more deeply. The sisters' beloved brother Thomas, who by the early 1830s was a prominent peace, temperance, and colonization reformer, had become something of a beacon light to them.[18] His death in October 1834 inspired both sisters to become active in reform, and this meant increasingly direct involvement with organizations outside the realm of Quakerdom. Sarah, who wrote to William Ladd of the American Peace Society after Thomas's death, sought to broaden Quaker pacifism by linking it with non-Quaker activists. For this she received round condemnation from her meeting.[19] Meanwhile, Angelina had become "deeply interested" in the new abolition movement in 1834 but had refrained from direct public activity on its behalf. She had even engaged Thomas in a discussion of the merits of abolitionism at what turned out to be their last time together.[20]

Soon after her brother's death, in January and February 1835, Angelina attended inspiring lectures by British abolitionists Andrew Gordon and George Thompson. By May she had joined the Philadelphia Female Anti-Slavery Society, where she met Hicksite and non-Quaker antislavery women. In abolitionism's tumultuous summer of 1835, when mob violence against antislavery activities reached a crescendo, Angelina followed events in Garrison's *Liberator* with a mixture of dread, anger, and heightened commitment. She was especially stirred by Garrison's "Appeal to the Citizens of Boston," which declared that abolitionists would not give one inch despite intimidation and even threat of death. "I confess I could not read it without tears," she confided to Sarah soon after, "so much did its spirit harmonize with my own feelings."[21]

As in the case of Samuel J. May, Lydia Maria Child, and countless others, William Lloyd Garrison's powers as a religious visionary converted Angelina to the cause. She found in Garrison's "Appeal" a call that challenged her own exacting quest for a life guided by spiritual truth. Garrison had declared his willingness to risk martyrdom rather than to give up his principles. Angelina wrote to Garrison on August 30, 1835, pledging herself to the cause. Once, she confessed, she saw freedom only coming in the wake of a frightful "servile war." Now she saw the possibility of abolitionist martyrs ending slavery and purifying the church:

> If persecution is the means which God has ordained for the accomplishment of this great end, EMANCIPATION; then, in dependence *upon him* for strength to bear it, I feel as if I could say, LET IT COME; for it is my deep, solemn, deliberate conviction, that *this is a cause worth dying for*.[22]

Angelina knew that Garrison might publish her letter, but she put no strictures on its use. He introduced it rapturously in the *Liberator* of September 19: "We are thrilled—subdued—strengthened—soul-animated, on reading it."[23] Not so the Quaker community or her sister. Sarah chastised Angelina for listening to the "voice of the tempter." James Bettle angrily confronted Angelina in her own parlor, declaring that Garrison's preface to the letter was the "ravings of a lunatic" and commanded Angelina to recant in print. She adamantly refused. In private she almost crumbled under doubt and despair.[24]

These confrontations pushed Angelina in new directions. Never entirely comfortable with the Quakers of the Arch and Fourth Street Meeting, and less willing than Sarah to blame herself for the friction, Angelina found herself inexorably drawn to the amorphous but spiritually compelling community of reform. She immediately became active in a local abolitionist group. During a visit to Philadelphia in September 1835, Lydia Maria Child witnessed Angelina's boldness at a meeting of the Female Anti-Slavery Society. One woman had admitted that she feared becoming too engrossed in the issue, since the time was not yet ripe for action. "I was very much pleased with an answer made by Angelina Grimké, who was born and educated at the south," Child reported. "She replied, very mildly, 'If thou wert a slave, toiling in the fields of Carolina, I apprehend thou wouldst think the time had *fully* come.'"[25]

Meanwhile, Angelina's letter to Garrison, now distributed by the thousands as a broadside and reprinted in a variety of religious and reform journals, had made her a celebrity among reformers and a notorious traitor among Southerners. In the summer of 1836, she increased her visibility by publishing *An Appeal to the Christian Women of the South*. The *Appeal* demonstrated how quickly Angelina had integrated reform's cosmic vision with her piety as she made the biblical case against slavery, refuted proslavery arguments drawn from the Bible, and argued for invoking higher Christian law against laws establishing and protecting slavery.[26]

After asserting that slavery must be abolished before millennial prophecies could be attained, she asked how slavery and other roadblocks to the Millennium would be removed. "Will the wheels of the millennial car be rolled onward by miraculous power?" she asked. "No!" was her simple answer, for God had ordained *"man* to be the instrument of prophecy. And see you not how the mighty engine of *moral power* is dragging in its rear the Bible and peace societies, anti-slavery and temperance, sabbath schools, moral reform, and missions?," she inquired, "or to adopt another figure, do not these seven philanthropic associations compose the beautiful tints in that bow of promise which spans the arch of our moral heaven?"[27]

Angelina's spiritual quest thus had finally found secure footing in reform, and reform societies became in her mind more important than any sect in the fulfillment of prophecy. "Who does not believe, that if these societies were broken up, their constitutions burnt, and the vast machinery with which they are laboring to regenerate mankind was stopped," she asked, "that the black clouds of vengeance would soon burst over the world, and every city would witness the fate of the devoted cities of the plain?"[28]

Striking too was her move to a philosophy that, in more comprehensive forms, critics would soon brand as "no-government" anarchism. Angelina knew all too well how great a leap of faith would be necessary for southerners, men and women alike, to cleave to the abolitionist standard. They must place abolition above the laws and inherent structure of their society. "I know that this doctrine of obeying *God*, rather than man," she noted, "will be considered as dangerous and heretical by many." Therefore, years before Henry David Thoreau, she advocated civil disobedience: "If a law commands me to *sin I will break it;* if it calls me to *suffer*, I will let it take its course *unresistingly.*"[29]

Even as Angelina threw off the chains of self-doubt in her commitment to antislavery, Sarah was reaching an important impasse with the Quakers. She rose to speak at the Yearly Meeting in August 1836, but her comments were cut short by the presiding elder. "I of course instantly resumed my seat," she remembered, "and never felt more peaceful, and the conviction then arose that my bonds were broken. The Act on the part of this Elder was entirely unprecedented and unsanctioned by our Discipline but his power is undisputed." Sarah only slowly and painfully separated herself from the Quakers, but ultimately "peaceful resignation cloathe[d]" her spirit. Soon she described her tortured allegiance to Quakerism as "those bonds which almost destroyed my mind."[30]

Sarah achieved a significant part of this transformation by following her sister into abolitionism. Elizur Wright Jr. had invited Angelina to lecture for the American Anti-Slavery Society. She accepted despite Sarah's qualms about her speaking in public and fear of further condemnation from the Quakers. Yet soon Sarah changed her mind and accompanied her sister to New York for training sessions presided over by Theodore Dwight Weld. In these sessions, eight hours a day for twenty-one days, a parade of abolitionist notables schooled seventy men and the Grimkés in a variety of antislavery arguments and lecture techniques.

In December 1836, the Grimké sisters began speaking to groups of New York women in private parlors. Soon the crowds that wished to hear them dictated that they move from parlors to churches. In February 1837, the sisters expanded their territory to include New Jersey, and in March they took part in the Anti-Slavery Convention of American Women. The Convention met to coordinate women's efforts against the recently passed congressional "gag rule"that automatically tabled all petitions concerning slavery. These abolitionist women sought to overwhelm Washington with petitions and in other ways take advantage of this abridgment of freedom to highlight the evils of slavery. The Convention assigned Angelina to write *An Appeal to the Women of the Nominally Free States* (published in the *Liberator*, June 9, 1837), which recited the main points of the antislavery argument and suggested ways for women to engage themselves in the struggle.

The American Anti-Slavery Society's Executive Committee then agreed to send the Grimkés north to Boston for a speaking tour of New England. It was a fateful move, for living and communing with reformers in the Garrisonian orbit exposed the sisters to new ideas and new individuals. On June 10, Sarah reported to Theodore Weld that she felt "helped, strengthened, invigorated" by the "elasticity" in the atmosphere of New England reform."

In the same letter Angelina had added a note asking Weld's pardon for not responding immediately to "C.E. Beechers book," which attacked abolitionism and singled out the Grimkés for agitating a public issue like slavery in defiance of God's own laws of womanly propriety.[31] As it turned out, "C.E. Beechers book" was the opening shot of a small war waged by conservative evangelicals against the sisters. In late 1836, a friend had passed along a copy of Angelina's *Appeal* to Catharine Beecher, urging her to aid in its distribution and informing her that Angelina would soon embark on a tour to promote the formation of abolition societies among women. The friend might have had every reason to believe that Beecher would respond positively. After all, in the late 1820s Catharine had petitioned Congress and organized women in opposition to the forced removal of the Cherokees from Georgia.[32] She never decried those women who had petitioned Congress in support of Sabbatarianism. Furthermore, she and her father had expressed at least moderate antislavery views. Yet, as a result of the Lane Rebellion, abolitionism had become for Catharine Beecher the most potent specimen of a moral radicalism that would destroy the nation and ruin her own careful vision of élite leadership for a Christian Republic.

Now Angelina Grimké, a woman of élite background and a friend, had taken up the abolitionist cause. Catharine thought it time to respond not only to abolitionism but also to Angelina's behavior as a woman. Beecher felt it necessary to define the proper role of women in the moral education of society by ruling out certain kinds of activities with which, given her own past, she had once felt comfortable. This was the major inspiration for writing *An Essay on Slavery and Abolitionism, with Reference to the Duty of American Females* (1837). Beecher began with a basic contrast:

> A man may act on society by the collision of intellect, in public debate; he may urge his measures by a sense of shame, by fear and by personal interest; he may coerce by the combination of public sentiment; he may drive by physical force, and he does not outstep the boundaries of his sphere.

Women would "win every thing by peace and love," Beecher argued, and "all the sacred protection of religion, all the generous promptings of chivalry, all the poetry of romantic gallantry, depend upon woman's retaining her place as dependent and defenceless."[33]

Beecher stressed that individual conscience must give way to the community. Women should do nothing to engage the wrath of their fellow citizens. Abolitionism was only the most obvious instance of a cause bound to stir up trouble. Thus Angelina's call for petitions from southern white women to aid black women in bondage represented incendiary political action. Rejecting her own experience and that of the evangelical movement at large, Beecher decreed: "In this country, petitions to congress, in reference to the official duties of legislators seem, IN ALL CASES, to fall entirely without the sphere of female duty." She did not reject a political role for women but underlined that it should be exercised in the spheres of the home and the school.[34]

Outraged by the tract, Angelina set about a public reply based upon the principles set forth in the *Appeal* and a year's thinking and acting in the sphere of abolition. She authored a series of thirteen letters published in the *Liberator* and the *Friend of Man* between July and December, 1837. She then gathered them in a pamphlet entitled *Letters to Catherine E. Beecher, in Reply to an Essay on Slavery and Abolitionism, Addressed to A. E. Grimké.*[35] The first ten dealt specifically with Beecher's misconceptions about abolitionism, while the last three concentrated on Beecher's definition of woman's sphere.

In responding to Beecher on woman's role, Angelina inexorably pushed herself toward an explicit definition of woman's rights and place. The eleventh letter's title came right to the point: "The Sphere of Woman and Man as Moral Beings the Same." Grimké objected to Beecher's assertion of male as the "superior" and woman as the "subordinate" sex, accusing her of merely asserting but not proving a dubious point. Furthermore

Angelina, noting that Beecher had allowed women only power that "appeal[ed] to the kindly, generous, peaceful and benevolent principles," wondered whether on those grounds woman might be considered the *"superior"* and man the "inferior being," since "moral power [wa]s immeasurably superior to 'physical force.'" Further, she rejected Beecher's restriction of women's influence to the "domestic circle," noting that in biblical times Miriam, Deborah, and Huldah filled *"public stations,"* and other women were prophets, apostles, and ministers.[36]

She also attacked Beecher for judging propriety on probable results rather than principle. "What is this but *obeying man* rather than God," she asked, "and seeking the *praise of man* rather than of God?" Beecher had argued that using the right of petition (which she herself had exercised in the past) might "tend to injure and oppress" women by sullying them with the mark of power or interest. Grimké reminded her readers that petition was woman's only real political right.[37]

This first letter on women effectively reminded readers of rights that had been exercised in the past and that Beecher wished to take away. The next, "Human Rights Not Founded on Sex," broke new ground. "The investigation of the rights of the slaves has led me to a better understanding of my own," she noted. She called abolitionism "the high school of morals in our land—the school in which *human rights* are more fully investigated" than in any other. She repeated the general propositions of antislavery: that all human beings had rights because they were moral beings, and that all rights grew out of possession of a moral nature. Since all people had essentially the same moral nature, they possessed the same basic rights. "These rights may be wrested from the slave," she proclaimed, "but they cannot be alienated: his title to himself is as perfect *now*, as that of Lyman Beecher." *"Mere circumstance of sex"* did not abridge these rights. "My doctrine then is," she asserted, "that whatever it is morally right for man to do, it is morally right for woman to do." The differences between man and woman came from external circumstances of society and history.[38]

Inevitably the assertion of sex equality took Angelina back to Genesis. She noted that God had created woman from man, "a companion and equal, not one hair's breadth beneath him in the majesty and glory of her moral being." Angelina turned Eve into a tragic figure—"the first transgressor, and the first victim of power." Ever since, "in all heathen nations, she has been the slave of man, and Christian nations have never acknowledged her rights." Nor did any Christian sect. "I know that in some denominations, she is permitted to preach the gospel," Angelina admitted, taking a swipe at the Quakers; "not from a conviction of her rights, nor upon the ground of her equality as a *human being*, but of her equality in spiritual gifts—for we find that woman, even in these Societies, is allowed no voice in framing the Discipline by which she is to be governed."[39]

Such reasoning led to a startling conclusion, one that had rarely been uttered by a woman in public:

> Now, I believe it is woman's right to have a voice in all the laws and regulations by which she is to be *governed*, whether in Church or State; and that the present arrangements of society, on these points, are *a violation of human rights, a rank usurpation of power*, a violent seizure and confiscation of what is sacredly and inalienably hers—thus inflicting upon woman outrageous wrongs, working mischief incalculable in the social circle, and in its influence on the world producing only evil, and that continually. *If* Ecclesiastical and Civil governments are ordained of God, *then* I contend that woman has just as much right to sit in solemn counsel in Conventions, Conferences, Associations and General Assemblies, as man—just as much right to sit upon the throne of England, or in the Presidential chair of the United States.[40]

The letters reached their radical climax in this extraordinary declaration that prefigured in virtually every way the public dimensions of modern feminism.

Meanwhile, Sarah's new burst of spiritual freedom led to her own profoundly searching critique of the religious and cultural underpinnings of sex inequality. Her break with the Quakers made her hungry for new light, and no one source provided more than Lydia Maria Child's *History of the Condition of Women, in Various Ages and Nations.* That work and Sarah's newly demystified attitude toward religious authority shaped her *Letters on the Equality of the Sexes and the Condition of Woman*, published serially in the summer of 1837 in the *New England Spectator* and as a pamphlet a year later.[41] Rather than adapt to tradition, as did Catharine Beecher, or assert equality as in the case of Angelina, Sarah sought to reevaluate the very root of Christendom's devaluation of woman. In doing so, she rewrote woman's role in cosmic history.

Sarah let readers know from the outset that she was "venturing on nearly untrodden ground" in her quest to purify "corrupt public opinion" and "the perverted interpretation of Holy Writ" about women. She returned to Genesis to find the real truth about the Bible's view of women, "in consequence of the false translation of many passages of Holy Writ." Rejecting the King James version, she consulted the original instead. "I also claim to judge for myself what is the meaning of the inspired writers," she asserted, "because I believe it to be the solemn duty of every individual to search the Scriptures for themselves, with the aid of the Holy Spirit, and not be governed by the views of many men, or set of men." Thus Sarah, like other religious reformers since the Reformation and before, consulted inner light and original text to reorder spiritual reality.[42]

Sarah began by interpreting Genesis in a manner that revealed God's creation of men and women as equals in their duties, their talents, and their capacity for sin. Pointing to Genesis 1:26–27, "So God created man in his own image, in the image of God created he him, male and female created he them," she noted that "not one particle of difference [was] intimated as existing between them." God made both in His own image and gave both dominion over every other creature but not over each other. Turning to the creation of woman as recounted in Genesis 2, Sarah interpreted the making of a "help meet" for Adam as "giv[ing] him a companion, *in all respects* his equal; one who was like himself *a free agent*, gifted with intellect and endowed with immortality."[43]

Sarah's version of Eve's eating the apple and leading Adam to sin underscored rather than weakened the case for equality. Only an autonomous and powerful individual could successfully tempt Adam and, for that matter, be worthy of being punished by God. "They both fell from innocence," she noted, "and consequently from happiness, *but not from equality.*"[44]

As for Genesis 3:16 (King James version), "Thy desire *shall be* to thy husband, and he shall rule over thee," Sarah retranslated it as "Thou wilt be subject unto thy husband, and he will rule over thee." She argued that her translation of the Hebrew as *wilt* rather than *shall* returned the sentence to its original prophetic, but not normative, meaning. God foresaw that Adam would rule over Eve, but He did not command it. "Our translators having been accustomed to exercise lordship over their wives," she asserted, "and seeing only through the medium of a perverted judgment, very naturally, though I think not very learnedly or very kindly, translated it *shall* instead of *will*, and thus converted a prediction to Eve into a command to Adam."[45]

Sarah's second letter expanded upon the difference between woman's subjection to God and her subjection to men. She challenged men to put equality to the test: "All I ask of our brethren is, that they will take their feet from off our necks, and permit us to stand upright on that ground which God designed us to occupy." If women were not meant for equality, they would soon fail and "shrink back into that obscurity, which the high souled magnanimity of man has assigned us as our appropriate sphere." As for the historical fact of male domination, Grimké argued that it was a specimen of a sinful "lust of dominion" that forever plagued men. "All history attests that man has subjected woman to his will," she wrote, "used her as a means to promote his selfish gratification, to minister to his sensual pleasures, to be instrumental in promoting his comfort; but never has he desired to elevate her to that rank she was created to fill." Thus men defied God's intentions.[46] Sarah then proceeded to retell human history as the story of woman's enslavement, relying on Lydia Maria Child's *History of the Condition of Women, in Various Ages and Nations.*[47]

Fresh evidence of attempted subjugation by men came to Sarah's view even as she was writing. On July 18, 1837, the Congregational General Association of Massachusetts issued a Pastoral Letter that rebuked the abolitionists and the Grimkés for incendiary political action and violation of the natural role accorded to women. Part 3 of the Pastoral Letter focused especially on women who "assume[d] the place and tone of man as a public reformer" and thereby "threaten[ed] the female character with wide spread and permanent injury." More specifically, the ministers decried "the mistaken conduct of those who encourage females to bear an obtrusive and ostentatious part in measures of reform, and countenance any of that sex who so far forget themselves as to itinerate in the character of public lecturers and teachers." They singled out for particular censure "the intimate acquaintance and promiscuous conversation of females with regard to things 'which ought not to be named.'"[48]

Sarah responded quickly, comparing the Pastoral Letter to the writings of Cotton Mather on witchcraft. She welcomed it as a document that might encourage discussion of woman's proper sphere, and she further welcomed the New Testament as the proper prooftext. Yet she railed "against the false translation of some passages by the MEN" who wrote the Letter, and "against the perverted interpretation by the MEN who undertook to write commentaries thereon. . . . I am inclined to think," she wrote, "when we are admitted to the honor of studying Greek and Hebrew, we shall produce some various readings of the Bible a little different from those we now have."[49]

The Sermon on the Mount, for instance, gave the same directions to men and women. "Men and women were CREATED EQUAL," she found to be the Sermon's strong implication; "they are both moral and accountable beings, and whatever is *right* for man to do, is *right* for woman." Then, too, anything ostentatious for women—prayer in public, agitation of moral issues, or speaking in front of mixed audiences—was ostentatious for men.[50]

Most striking, Sarah expressed contempt for the notion that woman should rely on man for spiritual succor and protection. "I have suffered too keenly from the teaching of man," she cried, "to lead any one to him for instruction." As for the much celebrated natural protectiveness of men toward woman: "Ah! how many of my sex feel in the dominion, thus unrighteously exercised over them, under the gentle appellation of *protection*, that what they have leaned upon has proved a broken reed at best, and oft a spear." For women Sarah suggested instead the simple motto of the Psalms: "'The Lord is my light and my salvation; whom shall I fear? The Lord is the strength of my life; of whom shall I be afraid?'"[51]

The letters that followed expanded upon the major points made in the first three. One discussed the unnatural relation between men and women, one "derogatory to man and woman, as moral and intellectual beings." The subjugation of women to an inferior status both made it impossible for them to be the companions God meant them to be and reduced their effectiveness as mothers. Others utilized Child's *History of the Condition of Women* to survey their status in Asia, Africa, Europe, and America. In Grimké's account, however, one looks in vain for Child's sense of progress as one moves from non-Christian to Christian lands. "The page of history teems with woman's wrongs," Sarah concluded, "and it is wet with woman's tears."[52]

Nor did Sarah share Child's optimism about women in the United States. Moving easily from biblical criticism and comparative history to contemporary analysis, she offered an acute taxonomy of women in the Republic. There were those of the fashionable élite, whose self-regard as "pretty toys or mere instruments of pleasure" created "the vacuity of mind, the heartlessness, the frivolity which is the necessary result of this false and debasing estimate." Women of the middling classes were raised to value service in marriage as the highest ideal and thus "regard[ed] themselves as a kind of machinery, necessary to keep the domestic engine in order, but of little value as the *intelligent* companions of men." Sarah did not wish to demean household work but rather to advocate equal concentration on piety and intellect. Here she quoted her late brother Thomas: "Give me a host of educated, pious mothers and sisters, and I will do more to revolutionize a country, in moral and religious taste, in manners and in social virtues and intellectual cultivation, that I can possibly do in double or treble the time, with a similar host of educated men."[53]

Sarah saved her greatest outrage for the treatment of working women and slaves. In every class of employment—teacher, tailor, comparable unskilled labor like washerwoman and "wood sawyer" or "coal heaver"— women made at most half of what men did despite equally competent performance. Worse still, female slaves routinely found themselves exploited sexually as well as economically, reduced to a commodity, suffering "every species of degradation and cruelty, which the most wanton barbarity c[ould] inflict." Such treatment in turn degraded the white woman, whose daily witness to such horrors numbed her. "She looks upon the crimes of seduction and illicit intercourse without horror," Sarah noted.[54]

Sarah's later letters returned to Child's *History* and other sources to show examples of triumphant womanhood in the form of heroes, leaders, and intellectuals. But the emphasis was on the deleterious effects of domination and the misuse of biblical quotations concerning wifely submission. The apostles, she argued, were simply "laying down rules" for the conduct of converts toward their unconverted mates, "to walk worthy of the vocation wherewith they [we]re called, with all lowliness and meekness, with long suffering, forbearing one another in love." As with slaves and subjects, Jesus and the apostles encouraged wives to "resist not evil" without acknowledging the "right" of domination. Sarah also devoted an entire letter to make the case for women preachers, and in the last letter she returned to the subject of original sin.[55]

In all, Sarah's *Letters on the Equality of the Sexes* and Angelina's *Letters to Catherine Beecher* were angry and brilliant bursts of intellectual energy, radical reworkings of Christianity that reached far beyond the egalitarian doctrines of the early Quakers or those of Mother Anne Lee and Jemima Wilkinson. Previously, even modest Christian visions of sex equality had prospered only among those of extreme millennial expectation who sought to separate themselves from the world in preparation for the end of days. Here was a forthright advocacy of woman's rights and equality that sought a revolution in human society. Given the Grimkés' insistence that society as it was represented a corruption of God's doctrines, their plea for woman's rights constituted a program for the sacralization of the world rather than an escape from it.

Despite the fact that physically and cosmologically the Grimkés acted, so to speak, in the middle of the world, any explanation of how they reached the point from which they could take such a giant leap must begin, ironically, with some recognition of their progressive and effective isolation from everyday society. Sarah and Angelina had taken the first step toward seclusion by joining the Quakers. Their trying apprenticeship as Quakers provided an ironic twist, for instead of finding peace they learned that even those who claimed inner holiness were stained by the pettiness and prejudices of society. The sisters remained committed to their spiritual quests despite such disillusionment.

As important for their creation of a biblically informed case for woman's rights, the Grimkés had managed to alienate themselves, effectively and literally, from virtually every institution that actively preserved traditional biblical interpretations of womanhood. The very fact that they had grown up in the material comfort and security of South Carolina's élite had provided them the inner confidence to forfeit all that they had been given. The Grimkés had defied family by becoming abolitionists. Neither had married despite temptation and possibility. Furthermore, their separation from familiar surroundings and people reinforced their immunity to the pulls of tradition. They had not even established a permanent residence since coming north, and they were removed from the habits, comforts, and everyday dependencies that helped to keep most women adherents to tradition. More than most other women of their age, they could follow the logic of spiritual experience without hindrance, and that logic made plain to them the enslavement of their own sex.

Further contributing to their ability to reformulate woman's role in light of their own spiritual experience was their exposure to Perfectionism. As early as June 1837, Sarah had reported reading a few issues of the *Perfectionist*, a new publication edited by John Humphrey Noyes. "Their sentiments are in many respects a transcript of my heart," she declared; "subjects are there treated and elucidated which have long exercised my mind and which I have hardly dared to breathe."[56] Such Christian perfectionists as John Humphrey Noyes, James Boyle, and Theodore Weld's brother Charles had begun to attract much notice in Garrisonian circles just about the time of the Grimkés' arrival in Boston. In his diary, the Garrisonian Henry C. Wright summarized Perfectionism by quoting Boyle to the effect "that all Institutions, that stood in the way of Christ's Kingdom, must be done away." Wright noted that Boyle regarded "the Sabbath, Governments, &c. as opposed to the spiritual Kingdom of our Lord."[57] Sarah and Angelina found these to be justified rejections of unholy tradition. Exposure to Perfectionist doctrines was not instrumental in creating the Grimkés' argument for woman's equality, but it did afford an open, speculative atmosphere in which to try out ideas and make unorthodox arguments.

The growth of a major fissure in reform over Perfectionism, however, deeply colored the reception of the Grimkés' new doctrines. To some extent a split had always been present between reformers who felt comfortable in the evangelical universe and those, especially after 1834, who saw in reform a more revolutionary principle. The broad optimism of the early and middle 1830s obscured such tendencies. Few reformers felt the need to squabble when temperance leaders were projecting a teetotal Millennium and, as late as February 1836, Theodore Dwight Weld was predicting that slaveholders would free half a million slaves by 1841 and a million more by 1846.[58]

Yet events began to cast increasingly portentous shadows on reform unity. In December 1835, a great fire in New York's business district mostly destroyed the Tappans' buildings, and by the following spring their business began to feel the effects of tightening credit. On May 1, 1837, Arthur Tappan declared bankruptcy, suspending payment on over one million dollars of debt. The evangelical community was stunned, and abolitionism and other reforms lost their greatest financial backer.[59] Meanwhile, Van Buren won the presidency in 1836, and the country as a whole sank into depression after the Panic of 1837.

Not surprisingly, such setbacks triggered widespread reevaluations; latent divisions in the movement came to the fore. More conservative evangelical reformers felt the need to guard the basic sacred borders of Christian society. By contrast, Garrison and other New England radicals saw abolitionist setbacks as reason for reinvigorated spiritual opposition to "the world" and its churches and ministers. They had already begun to question celebration of the Sabbath, favoring instead an ascetic seven-day piety. Now they dug more deeply. By 1836, Garrison and Henry C. Wright were promoting "non-resistance" or "no-government" doctrines in order to end war and other forms of violence.[60] Peace per se was not a new reform.

It had been a goal of Benjamin Rush and, after the War of 1812, had become a staple of New England evangelical life. Following the path of other reforms, state societies that had been founded in the wake of the War of 1812 merged with the American Peace Society in 1828. Until the mid-1830s, the New England peace movement sought reduction of tensions between nations and alternative means of adjudicating disputes. Only a few members argued in private for a more radical approach: renunciation of defensive war and categorical rejection of violence. The American Peace Society as an organization had put aside the question of defensive war at the outset, certain that even raising the question would alienate prospective members.[61]

As it turned out, practical and theoretical questions arising from abolitionist commitments forced the question of defensive wars and personal action to center stage. Abolitionists had become the object of violent mob actions, the case of Elijah P. Lovejoy's martyrdom in 1837 being only the most sensational of anti-abolitionist incidents. How should they react? Furthermore, how could abolitionists counsel slaves to await their freedom patiently and non-violently when Americans had waged the Revolution to secure theirs? One could do so, thought Garrison, only by renouncing violence in all situations. Indeed, using slavery as a spiritual metaphor, Garrison soon came to see the use of government power to enforce unjust laws as a kind of violence. He declared that one should obey no government but God's; thus he made the case for divorcing oneself from the compromising moral entanglements of political society.

Wright, a former Orthodox minister and conservative reformer turned Garrisonian abolitionist, pressed the issue of non-resistance as agent of the American Peace Society despite William Ladd's cautions. Ladd urged him to take his audiences step by step to peace, even as John the Baptist *"prepare*[d] the way of the Lord." Wright rejected the strategy: "I would declare the whole truth at once just as Christ did & say to men—cease from all *sin* at once & would tell them at once what is *sin*." In the end, Garrison, Wright, and other non-resistants separated to form the New England Non-Resistance Society.[62]

Tappan and other conservative evangelicals recoiled in horror at abolitionists' adoption of non-resistance doctrines. They feared that the linking of such a cause with antislavery would drive people away from abolitionism. More profoundly, they felt that Garrison and his followers had taken the logic of freedom too far, undercutting the institutional bases of Christian civilization. As attacks on the "no-government" tendency of the *Liberator* and on its editor and supporters increased, it became clear that the movement had come to a crossroads. Lydia Maria Child, in a letter she instructed "not to be published in any part," accurately characterized the fears of Garrison's enemies. "[They] are honestly, sincerely frightened at the bearing of the Peace principles on governments," she wrote; "but more than that, I suspect they dimly perceive that these ideas are shaking a belief in the literal sense of the Old Testament to its very foundations."[63]

It was in this divisive atmosphere that the Grimkés offered their argument for sex equality. The sisters formed their views relatively innocent of such struggle and indeed made their case for woman's equality without direct challenge to "the literal sense of the Old Testament" or endorsement of Perfectionism. Rather they championed woman's rights as a cure for much that ailed the political system and the institution of marriage. In doing so, they drew extensively on Old and New Testaments for evidence both of exemplary women and of a history of exploitation. As we have seen, Sarah used Genesis as her central prooftext. The Grimkés simply sought to delegitimate a tradition of biblical interpretation that had grown out of what they saw as warped male commentary. The sisters thus followed a precedent set in the abolitionists' biblical argument against slavery, one that sought to overthrow dominant proslavery Biblical interpretations based upon parallels with slavery among the Hebrews.[64]

There was at first widespread support for the sisters, even among those reformers who would later modify or reverse their stance. They seemed quite at home with public roles for women, For instance, John Greenleaf Whittier aimed his poetic wit at the General Association:

> So this is all—the utmost reach
> Of priestly power the mind to fetter!
> When laymen think—when women preach—
> A war of words—a "Pastoral Letter!"[65]

Even James G. Birney, who later became a leading critic of woman's equality in the antislavery movement, stood with the Grimkés at the beginning. Thus he ended his relationship with the Reverend Leonard Bacon of Hartford, a leading minister and editor of the *Christian Spectator*, over "indignation" he felt concerning Bacon's public remark comparing Angelina to a Quaker woman who had walked the streets of Salem *"naked as she was born."*[66]

Yet from the beginning even some of the sisters' closest allies worried that taking time for advocacy of woman's rights meant taking time away from the slave. Theodore Dwight Weld's reaction was particularly complex. He and Angelina had fallen in love but as yet had not declared themselves. His first reaction to the Pastoral Letter brimmed with jocular support for the sisters: "Why! folks talk about women's preaching as tho' it was next to highway robbery," he continued, "—eyes astare and mouth agape. . . . Ghostly dictums have fairly beaten it into the heads of the whole world save a fraction, that *mind* is *sexed*, and *Human rights* are *sex'd*, *moral obligation sex'd.*" Yet Weld still advised them to stick to antislavery.[67]

Angelina responded with appreciation and candor, revealing to Weld her own sense that the sisters had been "placed very unexpectedly in a very trying situation, in the forefront of an entirely new contest—a contest for the *rights* of *woman* as a moral, intelligent and responsible being." She regretted that it had arisen before slavery had been abolished and so seemed to compete with abolitionism, but she was sure that "this must be the Lord's time and therefore the *best* time." Such faith did not blind her to the profound demands the sisters were making, ones that potentially challenged "the interests of every minister in our land." She assumed that the clergy would stand "in a solid phalanx against woman's rights." The issue "will also touch every man's interests at home," she predicted, "in the tenderest relation of life; it will go down into the very depths of his soul and cause great searchings of hearts." Yet she needed to test the question, and from Weld, who thought that they could easily justify their speaking to mixed audiences as part of their Quaker beliefs, she demanded more: "Now we want thee to sustain us on the high grounds of MORAL RIGHT, not of Quaker peculiarity. This question must be met *now*. . . . Can't *thou* stand *just here* side by side with us?"[68]

Weld could not see it that simply. He certainly stood beside them, spent endless long sheets of near-scribble documenting his history of holding and acting upon egalitarian views of women, encouraged their continued speaking in public, and gave them the service of his acutely analytical mind in refining their position. Still, nothing could convince him that woman's rights were in as dire need of agitation as abolitionism. And he argued that the sisters' continued service in the abolitionist cause would do more for woman's rights by example than direct argument of the question. "Let us all *first* wake up the nation to lift millions of slaves of both sexes from the dust," he declared in an awkward flourish, "and turn them into MEN and then when we all have our hand in, it will be an easy matter to take millions of females from their knees and set them on their feet, or in other words transform them from *babies* into *women*." Or, as Whittier bluntly put it to the sisters at about the same time: "Is it not forgetting the great and dreadful wrongs of the slave, in a selfish crusade against some paltry grievance of our own?"[69]

Angelina did not take kindly to such reasoning or such characterizations of women or woman's rights. She saved time and vented anger by replying to Whittier and Weld in one letter. Mainly she emphasized that, in the wake of attacks from Catharine Beecher and the clergy, neither she nor any other woman abolitionist could continue her activities without defending herself. "Now my dear brothers *this invasion of our rights* was just such an attack on *us*," she argued, "as that made upon Abolitionists generally when they were told a few years ago that *they had no right* to discuss the subject of Slavery." The abolitionists, she noted, had stood for their rights, and women must as well. "Why, my dear brothers can you not see the deeply laid scheme of the clergy against us as lecturers?" she implored. "They know full well that if they can persuade the people it is a *shame* for us to speak in public, and that every time we open our mouths for the dumb we are breaking a divine command . . . , we shall *very* soon be compelled to retreat for we shall have *no* ground to stand on. If we surrender the right to *speak* to the public this year, we must surrender the right to petition next year and the right to *write* the year after and so on."[70]

Despite such powerful arguments, the Grimkés could not even convince all of their female comrades that woman's rights needed to be agitated as a separate issue. Lydia Maria Child, whose own work had inspired Sarah, resisted personal remonstrances from the Grimkés that she herself address the woman question. "It is best not to *talk* about our rights," Child retorted, "but simply go forward and *do* whatsoever we deem a duty. In toiling for the freedom of others, we shall find our own."[71] Child took this position even though otherwise aligned with Garrison throughout the controversy, and it probably stood for the sentiments of many Garrisonian women. The Grimkés' friend Sarah Douglass, an African-American abolitionist, probably also spoke for many when, in the wake of the antislavery schism, she admitted to Charles K. Whipple that she still believed the humiliation of women to be the result of Eve's original sin.[72]

Most damning were those abolitionists who feared that the Grimkés' lecturing to mixed audiences and advocating woman's rights might be embarrassing to the antislavery cause. Amos Anson Phelps, ostensibly angered by the Pastoral Letter, nonetheless suggested that the sisters declare publicly their preference for speaking only to women and also distance themselves from the Anti-Slavery Society. He thought that propriety should "preclude" them from speaking about the violation of female slaves, and that they should desist in arguing for woman's rights.[73]

To these *"kindly"* remonstrances, as Angelina called them, the sisters replied with firm resolve. "I feel that we are one in Christ & that I have nothing to do with my audience as males & females," Sarah declared to Phelps. As for arguing several related causes, she assured him that "surely Truth cannot hurt Truth, & to assert the rights of woman in our conduct cannot hurt the cause we are advocating with our tongues. . . . Pity that we have got Christianity parcelled off in lots, so that we fancy that what is designed to be one beautiful & harmonious whole will be injured by the parts coming into contact." Angelina added that they were willing to sever ties with the American Anti-Slavery Society rather than compromise on the issue of promiscuous audiences.[74]

Only from the women abolitionists in Boston and the Perfectionists did the Grimkés get encouragement to push further on woman's rights. The sisters, Maria Weston Chapman, and others discussed the idea of starting a "Paper" devoted to woman's rights should they be "shut out from mens papers," but hoped that the sexes would not have to be separated "any more into different organizations." Angelina even suggested that the *Liberator* abandon "Abolitionism as a *primary* object" and transform itself into a forum for all the "grand principles" of reform. "My soul is very sick of the narrow minded policy of Christians, of abolitionists," Sarah complained to Henry C. Wright in late August 1837, "trying to keep asunder the different parts of Christianity as if it were not a beautiful and harmonious system which could not be divided."[75]

Yet their knowledge of the evils of slavery and their commitment to ending it, as well as conflicting messages from abolitionists, kept the Grimkés off balance. Weld, especially, bombarded them with long letters urging them to concentrate on slavery. "We hardly know what to do about it," Angelina admitted after receiving three of Weld's loving broadsides in quick succession, "for we have just as high an opinion of brother Garrison's judgment, & *he says go on.* O! that the Lord would guide us in *His* wisdom."[76]

Ultimately sickness, love, and circumstance kept the sisters, especially Angelina, from straying too far from the cause of the slave.[77] They continued their celebrated speaking tour through November 1837, when Angelina came down with a severe case of typhoid fever. By the beginning of the year she was recovering, and with recovery came new challenges and a surprise. Early in February 1838, the abolitionist Henry B. Stanton (a Lane Rebel and soon to be the husband of Elizabeth Cady Stanton) suggested to Angelina that she present an antislavery petition before a committee of the Massachusetts Legislature. She took it as a joke, but soon after decided that she *"must"* do it. The chair of the legislative committee, the abolitionist John Alvord, agreed to the plan despite the worries of some other abolitionists. She would be the first woman to address the legislature.[78]

At the about the same time, responding to the long-buried hurt incurred from Weld in one of his highly critical letters, Angelina revealed the wound to Weld and inspired a declaration of love on his part. In the same letter that told him of her plan to address the legislature, she answered his own avowal with one of her own: "I *feel* my Theodore that we are the two halves of one whole, a twain one, two bodies animated by one soul and that the Lord has given us to each other."[79]

On February 21, the day of her first appearance before the legislative committee, an agitated audience crammed the room. Only a fragment of one of her three addresses survives, but it reveals a new maturity and a vivid mythic vision. Just a few months before, Angelina had named "strong" women of the Bible in refutation of Catharine Beecher's characterizations of womanhood. Now she took on the mantle of Queen Esther of Persia:

More than 2000 years have rolled their dark and bloody waters down the rocky, winding channel of Time into the broad ocean of Eternity, since woman's voice was heard in the palace of an eastern monarch, and woman's petition achieved the salvation of millions of her race from the edge of the sword. . . . Mr. Chairman, it is my privilege to stand before you on a similar mission of life and love.[80]

By most accounts, her appearance was a stunning victory for abolitionism. Soon Boston's antislavery community planned another appearance, a series of lectures at the Odeon to begin on March 22. After an indifferent first lecture, Sarah (at Weld's hurtful request) acceded the rest of the program to her sister. Angelina mesmerized the audience. Wendell Phillips later remembered the Odeon lectures as "eloquence such as never then had been heard from a woman."[81] In these extraordinary performances, Angelina had temporarily stilled the warring voices in antislavery.

Perhaps the greatest triumph of temporary truce-making among the warring antislavery factions in 1838 was the marriage of Angelina Grimké and Theodore Dwight Weld. On May 14, 1838, in the Philadelphia home of Sarah and Angelina's sister Anna Frost, reformers of all persuasions and factions came to witness this extraordinary wedding. William Lloyd Garrison, Henry B. Stanton, Henry C. Wright, Lewis Tappan, Maria Weston Chapman, and a host of others attended, including Sarah Douglass and her mother and two ex-slaves of John Faucheraud Grimké whom Anna Frost had freed when she inherited them. Whittier attended the reception but absented himself from the non-Quaker ceremony.[82]

And what a reformer's ceremony it was. Without aid of clergy or magistrate, Theodore and Angelina took each other's hand and testified to their love for each other. Theodore specifically declined all rights he had under law to the person and property of his wife and (according to Sarah) "abjured all authority, all government, save the influence of which love would give to them over each other as moral and immortal beings." Angelina made similar avowals, and then all knelt while Weld prayed for God's blessing on their marriage and on antislavery. Angelina followed with a prayer, and then two Presbyterian ministers, one black and one white, offered their prayers. All attending signed the wedding certificate, Garrison and Wright signing on the same page as Tappan.[83]

It was the last time they would ever be so united, for even the offhand, private remarks of antislavery's notables concerning the marriage revealed the tensions that no simple ceremony of love could erase. Garrison told Angelina that he feared "Weld's sectarianism would bring her into bondage," so that she would soon have to celebrate the Sabbath and go to church. Lewis Tappan joked about Theodore's great moral courage in marrying such a woman. William Ladd, the conservative reformer whose American Peace Society had been challenged by Henry C. Wright, expressed his surprise at the match by noting that he had always been sure she would marry "a strapping negro." Weld himself, who had feared the handsome Henry C. Wright as a romantic rival, felt sure that Wright, as he told Angelina, "feels for us in *one* sense, that is the thought that you should marry *me* is to him like *poison*."[84]

The same of day of the Weld-Grimké marriage, reform groups in Philadelphia dedicated a new assembly place. Long shut out of many churches and other meeting places, they had raised forty thousand dollars to build Pennsylvania Hall as a shrine to freedom of speech. In its first few days of operation, anti-abolitionists in Philadelphia set off rumors that it was a center of race "amalgamation." On the evening of Wednesday, May 16, while three thousand reformers filed in for a meeting of the Anti-Slavery Convention of American Women, a raucous crowd ringed Pennsylvania Hall. As William Lloyd Garrison concluded the first speech, the crowd burst into the meeting. Despite the commotion, Maria Weston Chapman commenced her speech. The demonstrators moved back outside, but soon chanting could be heard from without, along with the sound of rocks hitting the walls of the hall. As Angelina rose to speak, the mob launched bricks through the windows, shattering glass, and the assault continued throughout her address. A few days later, after the Mayor had shut the hall down, it was burned to the ground. The anti-slavery women responded by reconvening their convention a few days later in the schoolroom of Sarah Pugh, one of their members.[85]

However, reformers could not replicate among themselves the unity they demonstrated in the face of the mob. Little more than a year later, antislavery factions split over the question of a widened reform agenda and focused their dispute on the active and equal participation of women and men in abolition societies. The Tappan wing of the movement seceded and formed the American and Foreign Anti-Slavery Society, taking with them more than a few woman's auxiliaries who feared that the woman question had become a stalking horse for a broader platform of anarchism. The New York Ladies Anti-Slavery Society, for instance, in severing themselves from the American Anti-Slavery Society and joining Tappan's new organization, declared their opposition to discussion of "topics foreign to the objects for the promotion of which the Society was organized" and to "the public voting and speaking of women in said meetings, to their acting on Committees, or, as officers of the Society, with men."[86]

At the same time, heated discussion of the woman question also brought to the Garrison wing of antislavery such women as Lucy Stone, Abby Kelley, and Elizabeth Cady Stanton. By 1848, they and others found the will to create a separate movement for woman's rights. Through Sarah and Angelina's writings and the example of their lives, these women had found a clear and unambiguous basis for the Woman's Declaration of Independence. Issued from the Seneca Falls Convention, it proclaimed "that all men and women are created equal; that they are endowed by the Creator with certain inalienable rights: that among these are life, liberty and pursuit of happiness." A simple but powerful rewriting of the most famous manifesto in American history, its familiarity masked the spiritual struggles that preceded its issuance. The Grimkés had to do nothing less than recast Genesis in order to claim for women the simple doctrine of equality at creation.

The fray over the woman question not only split the abolitionist movement but more generally marked a watershed in reform history. While evangelically based reformers continued to agitate the slave question, temperance, and Sabbatarianism within the broad scenario of millennial doctrine, more radical reformers ventured out on their own to rebuild the cosmos from the shambles of their lost faith. They had not simply become too exhausted or contentious to continue the old struggle. Rather, broaching the woman question and rewriting Genesis cast into doubt the legitimacy of traditional family structure as well as traditional interpretations of Christianity's prooftext. Reform had thus moved from changing habits such as drinking to rethinking the basic theological and social foundations of Western culture. For a significant number of radical reformers, nearly two decades of metahistorical tinkering had led to the collapse of the evangelical Christian cosmos.

With abolitionism still at the center of reform as both a burning social issue and a metaphor for freedom and equality, by the 1840s radical reformers began literally to rebuild the structure of Heaven and Earth.[87] In society, they launched various communitarian ventures based on religious visions as varied as Oneida's biblical Perfectionism, Brook Farm's transcendental vision, and Fourier's mystical union of mind, body, society, and spirit world. Each of these and other kinds of communities sought to construct models of human society based on the ritual and symbolic life of radical reform, whether in diet, relations between the sexes, or the pervasive asceticism of the religious virtuoso as translated into communal ownership and personal renunciation.

Some severed their ties with the churches and sought an appreciation of the religious nature of humankind outside the trappings of denomination. Others experimented with new, post-Christian faiths. Emerson's Transcendentalism attracted some, while spiritualism fit the needs of others. In embracing the spiritualist writings and talks of Andrew Jackson Davis and others, reformers happily abolished Death and Hell and rewrote the cosmic drama and reimagined the very architecture of the cosmos. Spiritualism transformed the "reality of the Unseen" into progressively higher spheres of existence through which each soul passed, and with which one could communicate through the ritual of the séance.

The deep attraction to communitarianism and spiritualism, as well as the broad study of world religions, indicates just how profoundly the evangelical vision had been shattered, at least for the radical wing of reform. Yet the concerns expressed in these new social and spiritual revelations underlined the fact that important religious questions remained in the lives of their adherents. Nor did what some have called a turning inward necessarily diminish the commitment of reformers to ending social injustice. In *Aspirations of the World* (1878), published two years before her death, Lydia Maria Child still measured her notions of true religion against the backdrop of failed expectations. She felt that many generations must pass before Christian America would "recover from the demoralizing effects of reading the Declaration of Independence, year after year, with loud vauntings and ringing of bells, while they held millions of the people in abject slavery." Nor had the nation yet realized the hypocrisy inherent in the popular Christmas declaration "Peace on Earth and Good-will to Men" being sung by a nation that had cheated in commerce, broken treaties with Indian tribes, "exterminate[d] Seminole Indians because they refuse[d] to give up their wives and children to become slaves, and massacre[d] friendly Mexican neighbors because we covet[ed] their land, and fill[ed] our pockets with money by selling a deadly article that 'steals away the brains of men.'"[88]

In 1880, just three months before her death, Child reminisced with her friend Theodore Dwight Weld. "The Holy Spirit *did* actually descend upon men and women in tongues of flame," she wrote of the old days in reform. And she summed up the vision that united the spiritual seeking of reformers from beginning to end: "Ah, my friend, that is the *only* true church organization, when heads and hearts united in working for the welfare of the human-race."[89]

NOTES

Preface

1. Ralph Waldo Emerson, "New England Reformers," in Mark Van Doren, ed., *The Portable Emerson* (New York, 1957), 111. I should note that I do not make the patently inaccurate assumption that the American reform experience is completely unique. Especially in England, with its related cultural roots, reform movements in some ways quite similar to those in America flourished and even served as models for the first American reform societies.

2. The proper treatment of American reform historiography, including a detailed consideration of the interpretation of religious elements of reform, would require too much space and involve too many extraneous topics to indulge in such an exercise here. However, I should mention that one of the most illuminating debates, touched off by a two-part article by Thomas Haskell on capitalism and its relation to the rise of humanitarian reform, relevant to though not centrally concerned with the question of religion and reform, has recently been collected in a single volume. Haskell's articles, as well as responses by David Brion Davis and John Ashworth, are included in Thomas Bender, ed., *The Antislavery Debate: Capitalism and Abolitionism as a Problem in Historical Interpretation* (Berkeley, 1992).

3. I have been guided by several works in formulating my approach to religion in history, though in each I see pitfalls that historical analysis can help correct. In particular, see Max Weber, "The Social Psychology of the World Religions" and "Religious Rejections of the World and Their Directions," in H. H. Gerth and C. Wright Mills, trs. and eds., *From Max Weber: Essays in Sociology* (New York, 1946), 267–301 and 323–59, and three works by sociologist Peter Berger: *The Sacred*

Canopy: Elements of a Sociology of Religion (Garden City, N.Y., 1967); *A Rumor of Angels: Modern Society and the Rediscovery of the Supernatural* (New York, 1969); and *The Heretical Imperative: Contemporary Possibilities of Religious Affirmation* (New York, 1979). See also Daniel Bell, "The Return of the Sacred?," in *The Winding Passage: Essays and Sociological Journeys 1960–1980* (Cambridge, Mass. 1980).

4. I plan to write a companion volume, one that continues the theme of ante-bellum reform cosmologies in the period after 1840 and then moves to a consideration of post–Civil War movements and their changing religious nature.

Prologue

1. Ralph Waldo Emerson, "New England Reformers," in Mark Van Doren, ed., *The Portable Emerson*, 118.

2. *Ibid.*, 110. John L. Thomas used these words to begin his brilliant and seminal "Romantic Reform in America," and connected the act of leaving the churches to the development of an American version of what T. E. Hulme called "spilt religion." Thus reform became a kind of overflow of romantic religious zeal that the churches could not contain. I offer a somewhat different interpretation. See John L. Thomas, "Romantic Reform in America, 1815–1865," *American Quarterly* (Winter 1965), 656.

3. Harvey Goldman, *Max Weber and Thomas Mann: Calling and the Shaping of the Self* (Berkeley, 1988), 168. The "religious virtuoso" functioned within Weber's broader approach to religion. He insisted that religion's relationship to material forces was symbiotic, that religion could not be considered simply a "function" of a particular social situation, a "reflection" of class self-interest or a "representation" of class ideology. Material factors sometimes shaped the outlines if not the essence of religion, but religion in turn exerted its own "far-reaching influence" upon the profile of seemingly profane matters in the world. Max Weber, "The Social Psychology of the World Religions," in H. H. Gerth and C. Wright Mills, trs. and eds., *From Max Weber: Essays in Sociology*, 269–70.

This was especially true when "religiously qualified virtuosos . . . combined into an ascetic sect, striving to mould life in this world according to the will of a god." And therein lay a paradox, for "no matter how much the 'world' as such [was] religiously devalued and rejected as being creatural and a vessel of sin, yet psychologically the world [was] all the more affirmed as the theatre of God-willed activity in one's worldly 'calling.'" Ascetics rejected worldly values and things in their unsacralized state, Weber argued, "as competitors of the kingdom of God. Yet precisely because of this rejection, asceticism did not fly from the world, as did contemplation. Instead, asceticism has wished to rationalize the world ethically in accordance with God's commandments." *Ibid.*, 281–91.

4. See David Brion Davis, *Slavery and Human Progress* (New York, 1984), 128–29. A convenient source for Tillich's own idea (and Davis's source) is Paul Tillich, "The Decline and the Validity of the Idea of Progress," in Jerald C. Brauer, ed., *The Future of Religions* (New York, 1966), 75–77. It might be noted that Tillich developed his idea in the dark time of post–World War I Germany. Still, a gloom endemic to even the most optimistic visions of the *kairotic*, one that existed among antebellum reformers, is well described by Davis in reference to the British abolitionists: "Utopian dreams often half conceal a latent nightmare" (129).

5. However, sociologist Peter Berger has speculated on the possibilities for faith in such an environment, and his categories may help us define the reform experience more concretely as a reaction to toleration and disestablishment. Berger sees three choices for the religionist: (1) the reassertion of traditional religion in the face of pluralism and secularization, as in the fundamentalism of our own era; (2) the reinterpretation of religious tradition in the terms of modernity, as in the liberal-rational versions of Christianity and Judaism; (3) the reliance on religious experience, both first-hand and reported, to reestablish a sense of the sacred, to start from scratch and perhaps forever revise a phenomenological connection to the sacred. Berger himself warned against walling off such alternative "ideal-types" from each other, fully presuming that modern religion as experienced would be in most cases differing mixtures of each. See Peter Berger, *The Heretical Imperative, passim*, but esp. 60–156.

6. Of course, the historical literature on American Protestantism and the Second Great Awakening has made much of the impact of pluralism on the proliferation of sects, changes in evangelical style, and the like (this literature will be dealt with in an article that offers a comprehensive historiographical treatment of religion and American reform). The effects I refer to have less to do with the impact on organization and more to do with the more elusive impact on styles of religious experience and the possibility of a secure personal or theological religious Truth. For a recent treatment of the nature and significance of this explosion of popular religion, see Nathan O. Hatch, *The Democratization of American Christianity* (New Haven, 1989).

7. The best treatment of millennialism in America through the period of the early republic is Ruth H. Bloch, *Visionary Republic: Millennial Themes in American Thought, 1756–1800* (New York, 1985).

8. Mrs. Sturges to Theodore Dwight Weld, Putnam, Ohio, March 19, 1835, in Weld-Grimké Manuscripts at the William L. Clements Library, University of Michigan, Ann Arbor (hereafter referred to as Weld-Clements); I first used this letter for somewhat different purposes in *Passionate Liberator: Theodore Dwight Weld and the Dilemma of Reform* (New York, 1980), 130–32.

9. I make no claim that this story is typical except as it reveals to us a more complete, multi-dimensional set of values, assumptions, and contexts at work in the process of reform than available from more one-sided, reformer-focused sources. Unfortunately such "audience response" material is extremely rare.

10. See Daniel Bell, "The Return of the Sacred?," in *The Winding Passage*, 324–54, for one advocacy of such an approach. See Jeffrey C. Alexander, *Theoretical Logic in Sociology*, 4 vols. (Berkeley, 1982–83), whose call for multi-dimensionality in historical and sociological analyses has had much influence on the current work.

Chapter I
Benjamin Rush and Revolutionary Christian Reform

1. The most complete account of the parade is in Frances Hopkinson, "An Account of the Grand Federal Process. Performed at Philadelphia on Friday the Fourth of July, 1788," in Hopkinson, *Miscellaneous Essays* (Philadelphia, 1792), II, 349–401.

2. Benjamin Rush to Elias Boudinot(?), Philadelphia, 9 July 1788, in L. H.

Butterfield, ed., *Letters of Benjamin Rush* (Princeton, 1951), I, 470–77 (hereafter referred to as *Letters*). The best biography of Benjamin Rush is David Freeman Hawke, *Benjamin Rush: Revolutionary Gadfly* (Indianapolis, 1971).

3. "An Address to the People of the United States . . . on the Defects of the Confederation" (1787), quoted in Donald J. D'Elia, *Benjamin Rush: Philosopher of the American Revolution*, Transactions of the American Philosophical Society, New Series, vol. 64, part 5 (Philadelphia, 1974), 5. D'Elia presents a brilliant exposition of Rush's Christian Republican vision, one that was extremely helpful in formulating this chapter.

4. There is no more vast and growing recent literature than that on Republicanism and its role in the shaping of American consciousness. Some major works that I have found particularly useful in delineating various aspects of the problem include Bernard Bailyn, *The Ideological Origins of the American Revolution* (Cambridge, Mass., 1967); Gordon S. Wood, *The Creation of the American Republic, 1776–1787* (Chapel Hill, 1969); J. G. A. Pocock, *The Machiavellian Moment: Florentine Political Thought and the Atlantic Republican Tradition* (Princeton, 1975); Drew R. McCoy, *The Elusive Republic: Political Economy in Jeffersonian America* (Chapel Hill, 1980); and Joyce Appleby, *Capitalism and a New Social Order: The Republican Vision of the 1790s* (New York, 1984). See also a recent critique of the literature on Republicanism, Isaac Kramnick, "Republican Revisionism Revisited," *William and Mary Quarterly* 48 (June 1982), 629–64.

5. The literature on the Great Awakening is enormous but by no means definitive. Some recent works that bring new angles of vision include relevant sections of Gary B. Nash, *The Urban Crucible: Social Change, Political Consciousness, and the Origins of the American Revolution* (Cambridge, Mass., 1979); Jon Butler, "Enthusiasm Described and Decried: The Great Awakening as Interpretive Fiction," in *Journal of American History* 69 (1982), 305–25; and, most recently, Susan O'Brien, "A Transatlantic Community of Saints: The Great Awakening and the First Evangelical Network, 1735–1755," *American Historical Review* 91 (1986), 811–32. The recent literature concerning religion and the American Revolution began with Alan Heimert's controversial and overdrawn *Religion and the American Mind: From the Great Awakening to the Revolution* (Cambridge, Mass., 1966). Three works far more subtle and useful in their conceptualizations (though not always agreeing with each other) are James West Davidson, *The Logic of Millennial Thought* (New Haven, 1977); Nathan O. Hatch, *The Sacred Cause of Liberty: Republican Thought and the Millennium in Revolutionary New England* (New Haven, 1977); and Ruth H. Bloch, *Visionary Republic*.

6. Donald J. D'Elia, *Benjamin Rush*, 9–10. I wish to emphasize at this point the central significance in the Rush literature of D'Elia's work, which more than any other explores and finds significance in Rush's religious life. For a recent study that looks at Rush from another angle, see Melvin Yazawa, *From Colonies to Commonwealth: Familial Ideology and the Beginnings of the American Republic* (Baltimore, 1985), especially 137–65. For samples of two sides of Tennent's preaching, see *The Unsearchable Riches of Christ* (1737), in Alan Heimert and Perry Miller, eds., *The Great Awakening: Documents Illustrating the Crisis and Its Consequences* (Indianapolis, 1967), 14–19; and *The Danger of an Unconverted Ministry* (1740), in *ibid.*, 71–99.

7. Samuel Finley, *Christ Triumphing, and Satan Raging* (1741), in *ibid.*, 152–67. Quote from *ibid.*, 154.

8. Rush to Enoch Green, Philadelphia, 1761, in *Letters*, I, 3; Davies quoted in David Freeman Hawke, *Benjamin Rush*, 21.

9. Rush, "Travels Through Life," in George W. Corner, ed., *The Autobiography of Benjamin Rush: His "Travels Through Life" Together with His Commonplace Book for 1789–1813* (Princeton, 1948), 164. Rush to Ebenezer Hazard, Philadelphia, 2 August 1764, in *Letters*, I, 7; David Freeman Hawke, *Benjamin Rush*, 41.

10. Rush to Enoch Green, Philadelphia, 1761, in *Letters*, I, 3.

11. Rush, "Travels Through Life," in George W. Corner, ed., *The Autobiography of Benjamin Rush*, 164.

12. George W. Corner, ed., *The Autobiography of Benjamin Rush*, 46.

13. A Pennsylvanian [Benjamin Rush], *An Address to the Inhabitants of the British Settlements, on the Slavery of the Negroes in America* (Philadelphia, 1773).

14. Rush's millennial vision, implicit at first, developed quickly during the war and after (as we shall see). Hawke appears to view millennialism at work in Rush's worldview from the beginning. See David Freeman Hawke, *Benjamin Rush*, 134.

15. A Pennsylvanian [Benjamin Rush], *An Address to the Inhabitants of the British Settlements, on the Slavery of the Negroes in America*, 25–28 and *passim*. Though one of the earliest and most influential of antislavery tracts of the period, it certainly was not the only one. Quakers, Calvinists, freethinkers such as Jefferson and Paine—all campaigned in varying degrees and with various arguments against slavery.

16. See Nathan O. Hatch, *The Sacred Cause of Liberty*, and Ruth H. Bloch, *Visionary Republic*, esp. 53–115.

17. See Charles Royster, *A Revolutionary People at War: The Continental Army and American Character, 1775–1783* (Chapel Hill, 1979), 179–85, 146–47; Rush to Patrick Henry, York town, 12 January 1778, in *Letters*, I, 117. Rush's introduction of the parallel with Moses and the Exodus suggests another interesting aspect of his vision of the Revolution, that it was as much a historical as a metahistorical drama. The parallel with historical Israel was much more prevalent in New England preaching and polity, and suggests yet another way in which Rush, though not a New Englander, forged a link between Millennium and governance more typical of that region and a key to its leadership in the creation of antebellum reform. See Michael Walzer, *Exodus and Revolution* (New York, 1985), for a fascinating essay that surveys the use of the Exodus archetype in political movements.

18. Charles Royster, *A Revolutionary People at War*, 236; Rush to Anthony Wayne, Philadelphia, 29 September 1776, in *Letters*, I, 117; Rush to John Adams, Philadelphia, 13 July 1780, in *ibid.*, I, 253.

19. Scholars have been quite interested in the question of pluralism in colonial society and have found in Pennsylvania a worthy subject. See, among others, Stephanie Grauman Wolf, *Urban Village: Population, Community, and Family Structure in Germantown, Pennsylvania, 1683–1800* (Princeton, 1976), esp. 203–42; essays by Michael Zuckerman, Deborah Mathias Gough, and Laura L. Becker, in Michael Zuckerman, *Friends and Neighbors: Group Life in America's First Plural Society* (Philadelphia, 1982), 3–25, 90–115, and 196–221.

20. "The Influence of Physical Causes upon the Moral Faculty," in Dagobart D. Runes, ed., *The Selected Writings of Benjamin Rush* (New York, 1947), 92 (hereafter referred to as *Writings*).

21. "Of the Mode of Education Proper in a Republic," in *ibid.*, 87–89.

22. *Ibid.*, 92.

23. *Ibid.* For some very interesting discussions of Rush's wonderfully evocative phrase "convert men into republican machines," see Melvin Yazawa, *From Colonies to Commonwealth*, 141–65; Michael Kammen, *People of Paradox: An Inquiry Concerning the Origins of American Civilization* (New York, 1972), 72–75; and David Tyack, "Forming the National Character: Paradox in the Educational Thought of the Revolutionary Generation," *Harvard Educational Review* 36 (1966), 29–41.

24. "Of the Mode of Education Proper in a Republic," in *Writings*, 93–95. Especially as regarded language, Rush's advocacy in many ways paralleled that of his friend Noah Webster.

25. *Ibid.*, 91–92.

26. *Ibid.*, 95–96. Thus Rush, along with some others, pioneered the idea of the "moral mother" that became such a key element of antebellum conceptions of gender role. See Ruth H. Bloch, "American Feminine Ideals in Transition: The Rise of the Moral Mother, 1785–1815," *Feminist Studies* 4 (1978), 101–26.

27. "Education Agreeable to a Republican Form of Government," in *Writings*, 97–100; "Plan of a Federal University," in *Ibid.*, 101–5.

28. "The Amusements and Punishments Which Are Proper for Schools," in *Ibid.*, 106–7.

29. *Ibid.*, 107–9.

30. *Ibid.*

31. *Ibid.*, 109–14; quote from 111–12.

32. *Ibid.*, 113–14.

33. "To the Editor of the *Pennsylvania Journal:* Against Spirituous Liquors," in *Letters*, I, 270–2.

34. Rush limited his assaults to distilled liquor. Wine and beer he categorized as relatively harmless and in fact often of "friendly influence upon health and life." See Rush, "The Effects of Ardent Spirits upon Man," in *Writings*, 334. This is the most readily available version of the original anti-liquor pamphlet.

35. *Ibid.*, 334–41; quote from 335.

36. *Ibid.*, 339–40.

37. Rush to Thomas Jefferson, Philadelphia, 4 February 1797, in *Letters*, II, 786 and 786n.

38. Rush to Ashbel Green, 11 August 1787, in *ibid.*, I, 433–34.

39. *Ibid.*, I, 434. In developing this vision of America, Rush had been greatly influenced by the Universalist writer Elhanan Winchester, whose millennial vision extended to all and whose own odyssey from Congregational to Baptist to Universalist beliefs may have helped Rush's own break with Presbyterians. See Ruth H. Bloch, *Visionary Republic*, 123–31, 209–10; and Stephen J. Marini, *Radical Sects of Revolutionary New England* (Cambridge, Mass., 1982), 69–71.

40. Rush to Jeremy Belknap, Philadelphia, 7 October 1788, in *Letters*, I, 488.

41. Rush to Julia Rush, Philadelphia, 16 July 1791, and Rush to Jeremy Belknap, Philadelphia, 21 June 1792, in *ibid.*, I, 600, 620–21.

42. Rush to Jeremy Belknap, 6 June 1791, in *ibid.*, I, 584; Rush to Jeremy

Belknap, 21 June 1792, in *ibid.*, I, 620; Rush to Elhanan Winchester, Philadelphia, 11 May 1791, in *ibid.*, I, 582.

43. Rush to James Kidd, Philadelphia, 25 November 1793, in *ibid.*, II, 746.

44. Rush to Horatio Gates, Philadelphia, 26 December 1795, in *ibid.*, II, 767–68; Rush to John Dickinson, Philadelphia, 11 October 1797, in *ibid.*, II, 793; Rush to Noah Webster, 20 July 1798, in *ibid.*, II, 799; Rush to John Adams, Philadelphia, 10 June 1806, in *ibid.*, II, 799.

45. See Ruth H. Bloch, *Visionary Republic*, 119–231.

46. Charles I. Foster, *An Errand of Mercy: The Evangelical United Front, 1790–1837* (Chapel Hill, 1960), 158; Clifford S. Griffin, *Their Brothers' Keepers: Moral Stewardship in the United States, 1800–1865* (New Brunswick, 1960), 26, 29.

47. Rush to John Adams, Philadelphia, 21 August 1812, in *Letters*, II, 1160–61; Rush to John Adams, Philadelphia, 8 August 1812, in *ibid.*, II, 1159.

48. Rush to Thomas Jefferson, Philadelphia, 15 March 1813, in *ibid.*, II, 1189.

49. Benjamin Rush to Noah Webster, 20 July 1798, in *ibid.*, II, 799.

Chapter II
Lyman Beecher and the Cosmic Theater

1. Ludovicus Weld, *The Kingdom of Grace Merits Universal Patronage. A Sermon Delivered at Hartford, Before the Legislature of the State of Connecticut, at the Anniversary Election, May 2nd, 1821* (Hartford, 1821), 11–12.

2. I am indebted to Nathan O. Hatch, "The Christian Movement and the Demand for a Theology of the People," *Journal of American History* (December 1980), 545–67, and Stephen A. Marini, *Radical Sects of Revolutionary New England*, for their pioneering work in Revolutionary and post-Revolutionary radical sects. See also Hatch's recent *The Democratization of American Christianity.*

3. Joseph Smith and John Rogers as quoted in Richard T. Hughes and C. Leonard Allen, *Illusions of Innocence: Protestant Primitivism in America, 1630–1875* (Chicago, 1988), 135, 108. See also Sidney Mead, *The Lively Experiment* (New York, 1963), 108–11.

4. See Richard W. Pointer, *Protestant Pluralism and the New York Experience: A Study of Eighteenth-Century Religious Diversity* (Bloomington, 1988), *passim*; Stephanie Grauman Wolf, *Urban Village*, esp. 203–42; essays by Michael Zuckerman, Deborah Mathias Gough, and Laura L. Becker, in Michael Zuckerman, *Friends and Neighbors*, 3–25, 90–115, and 196–221.

5. See Richard L. Bushman, *From Puritan to Yankee: Character and the Social Order in Connecticut, 1690–1765* (New York, 1970; orig. ed. 1967), esp. 147–232. Concentrating on social realities for most inhabitants of Connecticut, Bushman emphasizes the advance of pluralism and the weakening of "real" authority of the Standing Order. This in no way contradicts the parallel reality that New England's Orthodox ministers, more used to a central role in everyday life, hardly accepted the situation in as positive a light as their compatriots in the middle colonies.

6. Benjamin Rush to Noah Webster, 20 July 1798, *Letters*, II, 799.

7. The classic statement on the jeremiad is found in Perry Miller, *The New England Mind: From Colony to Province* (Cambridge, Mass., 1953). For a more recent and influential rendering of the jeremiad's vision and its historical implications, see Sacvan Bercovitch, *The American Jeremiad* (Madison, 1978).

8. See, for instance, Michael Zuckerman, *Peaceable Kingdoms: New England Towns in the Eighteenth Century* (New York, 1970), *passim*. The New England establishment's preoccupation with translating their religious vision into the structure of everyday life pushed them to improvise institutional means of incorporating their heterogenous society within the covenant. One very important solution to the divisive effects of urban heterogeneity and political democratization in the period beginning around 1760 was the creation of voluntary associations through which to bind society. These organizations created social connections and hierarchies amid town and city societies growing more unwieldy each passing year. Thus even before the missionary and Bible societies of the turn of the century, New England towns had been experimenting with new methods of promoting social cohesion. Interestingly, few voluntary societies founded early in this era sought the promotion of "moral reform." The vast majority were of a civic, educational, charitable, professional, or religious nature. Yet the idea of creating such groups to bind society and individuals proved essential to the structure and success of antebellum reform. See Richard D. Brown, "The Emergence of Urban Society in Rural Massachusetts, 1760–1820," in *Journal of American History* (June 1974), 29–51. For a chart that chronicles the growth of such organizations and breaks them down into categories, see esp. 40–41.

9. See William Kern Breitenbach, "New Divinity Theology and the Idea of Moral Accountability" (Ph.D. dissertation, Yale University, 1978), for a brilliant treatment of similar themes through a close study of New Divinity and Old Calvinist theological debate and the New Divinity theologians' response to what they perceived as infidelity.

10. See, for instance, Joseph W. Phillips, *Jedidiah Morse and New England Congregationalism* (New Brunswick, 1983).

11. The standard and extremely able literature on the downfall of the Federalists includes Shaw Livermore Jr., *The Twilight of Federalism: The Disintegration of the Federalist Party, 1815–1830* (Princeton, 1962); David Hackett Fischer, *The Revolution of American Conservatism: The Federalist Party in the Era of Jeffersonian Democracy* (New York, 1965); James M. Banner Jr., *To the Hartford Convention: The Federalists and the Origins of Party Politics in Massachusetts, 1789–1815* (New York, 1970); and, in a class by itself because of its brilliant re-creation of late Federalist political culture, Linda K. Kerber, *Federalists in Dissent: Imagery and Ideology in Jeffersonian America* (Ithaca, 1970).

12. For a recent and bold attempt to reassess the theological aspects of this cosmological shift, see William Kern Breitenbach, "New Divinity Theology and the Idea of Moral Accountability." Influential standard works on this period in New England Calvinist theology, especially ones that deal with a shift that allowed for reform, include Joseph Haroutanian, *Piety Versus Moralism: The Passing of the New England Theology* (New York, 1970; orig. ed. 1932), and Sidney Earl Mead, *Nathaniel William Taylor, 1786–1858: A Connecticut Liberal* (Chicago, 1942). Joseph A. Conforti, *Samuel Hopkins and the New Divinity Movement: Calvinism, the Congregational Ministry, and Reform in New England Between the Great Awakenings* (Grand Rapids, 1981), is a recent revisionist work that notes the contribution to reform of Consistent Calvinism as represented by Hopkins.

13. For a brief and good introduction to Dwight's life, see Barbara Miller

Solomon, ed., Timothy Dwight, *Travels in New England and New York*, 4 vols. (Cambridge, Mass., 1969), I, ix–xlvii.

14. See especially Edmund Morgan, "Ezra Stiles and Timothy Dwight," *Proceedings of the Massachusetts Historical Society* 72 (October 1957–December 1960), 101–17, for a reasoned case that minimizes the reality of a major incursion of Deism at Yale and doubts the dramatic impact of Dwight.

15. I refer the reader to Marie Caskey, *Chariot of Fire: Religion and the Beecher Family* (New Haven, 1978), 34–57, for a brief and good exposition of the basic points in Dwight's theology, especially as it influenced Beecher, Nettleton, and Taylor. On original sin, see *ibid.*, 40–42; for free will, see 38–39.

16. *Ibid.*, 39.

17. This was a point of contention for some of Dwight's followers, who felt that such an emphasis on doing and learning slighted the emotional surrender to God that evangelical preachers like themselves sought to effect. It is clear that though Dwight thought adequate preparation and "conviction of sin" should go together, Beecher and others wished to emphasize "immediate repentance" as a goal no matter the rational preparation. See Barbara Cross, *The Autobiography of Lyman Beecher*, 2 vols. (Cambridge, Mass., 1961), I, 240–42 (hereafter referred to as *Autobiography*).

18. Quoted in Marie Caskey, *Chariot of Fire*, 38.

19. Dwight, "Address on the genius of Columbia to the members of the continental convention," quoted in Kenneth Silverman, *Timothy Dwight* (New York, 1969), 51.

20. *Ibid.*

21. *Ibid.*, 96.

22. See Joseph W. Phillips, *Jedidiah Morse and New England Congregationalism*, for a fine interpretation that significantly revises the traditional image of this shaper of world images. For Taylor's life and theological development, see Sidney Earl Mead, *Nathaniel William Taylor, 1786–1858*.

23. *Autobiography*, I, 27.

24. *Ibid.*, 19.

25. *Ibid.*, 20.

26. *Ibid.*, 19.

27. Quoted in Milton Rugoff, *The Beechers: An American Family in the Nineteenth Century* (New York, 1981), 5.

28. I am indebted to Ruth H. Bloch, *Visionary Republic*, 202–31, for her broad linkage of the disenchantment with politics and the rise of missionary visions.

29. Lyman Beecher, *The Practicability of Suppressing Vice, by Means of Societies Instituted for That Purpose. A Sermon, Delivered before the Moral Society, in East Hampton, Long Island. September 21, 1803* (New London, 1804). The sermon apparently seemed so inconsequential to Beecher in retrospect that, when his children interviewed him to create his "autobiography," he didn't remember he had given it or published it. His daughter Catharine asked him, about his duelling sermon (more about which below): "That was the first you ever published, was it not?" To which Beecher replied: "It was the first that was much known. The first was a sermon on the History of East Hampton, preached on New Year's day, 1806." See *Autobiography*, I, 105. He does seem to make reference to the

earlier sermon as a rough draft of a later, more famous reform sermon. See *ibid.*, I, 191.

30. Beecher, *The Practicability of Suppressing Vice*, 3–6.

31. *Ibid.*, 6–9.

32. *Ibid.*, 10–14. Beecher quoted extensively from an anonymous source, though it is probably the English evangelical Josiah Woodward's *History of the Society for the Reformation of Manners in the Year 1692*. This book very much influenced the reform career of William Wilberforce, and points again to the fact that, while the formulation of American reform was distinctive, the basic forces for an evangelical war on sin were at work in both England and America and that each learned from the other.

33. *Ibid.*, 15–17.

34. *Ibid.*, 17–18.

35. *Ibid.*, 19.

36. *Ibid.*

37. *Ibid.*, 20.

38. *Ibid.*

39. *Ibid.*, 22.

40. Lyman Beecher, *The Remedy for Duelling. A Sermon Delivered Before the Presbytery of Long-Island, at the Opening of Their Session at Aquebogue, April 16, 1806* (Sag Harbor, N.Y., 1807). The presbytery suggested that ministers "scrupulously refuse to attend the funeral of any person who shall have fallen in a duel; and that they admit no person, who shall have fought a duel, given or accepted a challenge, or been accessary [*sic*] thereto, unto the distinguishing privileges of the church, until he manifest a just sense of his guilt, and give satisfactory evidence of repentance" (iii).

41. The Burr-Hamilton duel and a general proliferation of duelling had caused widespread reaction. Even in South Carolina, where the Code of Honor dwelled most comfortably, duello became a troubling public issue. See Michael S. Hindus, *Prison and Plantation: Crime, Justice, and Authority in Massachusetts and South Carolina, 1767–1878* (Chapel Hill, 1980), 42–48. Abigail Adams worried that, should duelling continue, "all the Christian and social virtues will be banished the Land." See Abigail Adams to Thomas Jefferson, Quincy, 18 August 1804, in Lester J. Cappon, ed., *The Adams-Jefferson Letters. The Complete Correspondence Between Thomas Jefferson and Abigail and John Adams,* 2 vols. (Chapel Hill, 1959), I, 276–77. Original spelling preserved in Cappon edition and above.

42. Lyman Beecher, *The Remedy for Duelling*, 5–7.

43. *Ibid.*, 10–11.

44. *Ibid.*, 11.

45. *Ibid.*, 14.

46. *Ibid.*, 15.

47. *Ibid.*, 16.

48. *Ibid.*, 18–20.

49. *Ibid.*

50. *Ibid.*, 26.

51. *Ibid.*, 27–32.

52. *Ibid.*, 32–37.

53. *Ibid.*, 37. On p. 31 he notes: "The effect already is great and alarming. If

not, why does the crime shrink before the stern justice of New-England, and rear its guilty head in New-York, and stalk with bolder front as you pass onward to the south?"

54. *Ibid.*, 41, 44.

55. *Ibid.*, 34.

56. See esp. David Hackett Fischer, *The Revolution of American Conservatism*, 185–87.

57. Lyman Beecher, *The Remedy for Duelling*, 34–36.

58. For the best treatment of religious issues relating to the War of 1812, see William Gribbin, *The Churches Militant: The War of 1812 and American Religion* (New Haven, 1973), esp. 15–60. For the arguments of religionists from the Republican side, see 61–103.

59. No doubt Beecher was strongly opposed to "Mr. Madison's War," but he may have had mixed feelings about the extreme stance some of his colleagues had taken. Many years later he remembered a mingled dread and enthusiasm as New England's Federalists contemplated secession, "national dismemberment" as he called it. See *Autobiography*, I, 195.

60. Lyman Beecher, *A Reformation of Morals Practicable and Indispensable. A Sermon Delivered at New-Haven on the Evening of October 27, 1812*, 2d ed. (Andover, 1814).

61. Compare, for instance, the section on historical precedents in *ibid.*, 11–14, with that of *The Practicability of Suppressing Vice*, 10–14. Beecher alluded to the relationship between the two sermons. See *Autobiography*, I, 191.

62. *A Reformation of Morals Practicable and Indispensable*, 3.

63. *Ibid.*, 24–25.

64. *Ibid.*, 22–23.

65. *Ibid.*, 16.

66. *Ibid.*, 44.

67. *Ibid.*, 17–19.

68. *Ibid.*, 19–20.

69. *Ibid.*, 23–24.

70. *Ibid.*, 24–25.

71. *Ibid.*, 25–26.

72. *Ibid.*, 26–27.

73. *Ibid.*, 30.

74. See William Gribbin, *The Churches Militant*, 129–55, and *idem*, "The Covenant Transformed: The Jeremiad Tradition and the War of 1812," *Church History* (September 1971), 297–305.

75. I happily acknowledge, at this point and for the entire chapter, the pioneering work of Donald M. Scott, *From Office to Profession: The New England Ministry, 1750–1850* (Philadelphia, 1979), esp. 18–75. Scott's structural approach comports very well with my intent here, and the existence of his own argument made the conceptualization of the present chapter easier. The important differences lie in emphasis, not substance, and have to do with my stress on metahistory and, later, ritual and symbol.

76. Treatments of benevolent organizations before 1825, with discussions of their relations to later reforms, though not entirely satisfactory, can be found in Charles I. Foster, *An Errand of Mercy: The Evangelical United Front, 1790–1837*

(Chapel Hill, 1960); Clifford Griffin, *Their Brothers' Keepers: Moral Stewardship in the United States, 1800–1865* (New Brunswick, 1960); Paul Boyer, *Urban Masses and Moral Order in America, 1820–1920* (Cambridge, Mass., 1978); Carroll Smith Rosenberg, *Religion and the Rise of the American City: The New York City Mission Movement, 1812–1870* (Ithaca, 1971); and Lois Banner, "Religious Benevolence as Social Control: A Critique of an Interpretation," *Journal of American History* 55 (June 1973), 23–41. The emphasis on social control in Griffin and Foster is to my mind simply a value judgment in sociological jargon, while Banner's attempt to put an undifferentiated Christian idealist face on reform is equally unsatisfactory.

77. Donald M. Scott, *From Office to Profession*, 32.

78. Lyman Beecher, *The Building of Waste Places; A Sermon Delivered at Wolcott, Conn., September 21, 1814 at the Installation of the Rev. John Keyes, to the Pastoral Care of the Church in That Place*, in Beecher, *Sermons Delivered on Various Occasions* (Boston, 1828), 103–37.

79. *Ibid.*, 104.

80. *Ibid.*, 106–7.

81. *Ibid.*, 107–8.

82. *Ibid.*, 110–16.

83. *Ibid.*, 116–25.

84. Beecher, along with his theologian-in-arms Nathaniel Taylor, more and more emphasized revival-produced repentance and conversion. Dwight still valued the good deeds of the unregenerate and the use of means such as prayer and study as a way to Grace. Beecher claimed to have discussed the issue with Dwight just before the latter's death early in 1817, and to have reconciled his and Taylor's views with Dwight. See *Autobiography*, I, 240–42.

85. Lyman Beecher, *The Bible a Code of Laws. A Sermon delivered in Park Street Church, Boston, September 3, 1817, at the ordination of Mr. Sereno Edwards Dwight, as Pastor of That Church; and of Messrs. Elisha P. Swift, Allen Graves, John Nichols, Levi Parsons, and Daniel Buttrick, as Missionaries to the Heathen*, in Beecher, *Sermons Delivered on Various Occasions*, 138–81.

86. *Ibid.*, 165.

87. The "toleration dream" is reproduced in *Autobiography*, I, 284–300.

88. Lyman Beecher, *The Design, Rights, and Duties of Local Churches. A Sermon Delivered at the Installation of the Rev. Elias Cornelius, as Associate Pastor of the Tabernacle Church in Salem, Mass., July 21, 1819*, in Beecher, *Sermons Delivered on Various Occasions*, 182–216.

89. *Ibid.*, 182–83.

90. *Ibid.*, 183.

91. *Ibid.*, 183–84.

92. *Ibid.*

93. *Ibid.*, 184–88.

94. *Ibid.*, 188–94.

95. *Ibid.*, 209–10, 214.

96. Lyman Beecher, *The Faith Once Delivered to the Saints. A Sermon Delivered at Worcester, Mass., October 15, 1823, at the Ordination of the Rev. Loammi Ives Hoadly, to the Pastoral Office over the Calvinistic Church and Society in That Place*, in Beecher, *Sermons Delivered on Various Occasions*, 217–66.

97. *Ibid.*, 218–19.

98. *Ibid.*, 220 and *passim*.
99. *Ibid.*, 251–54.
100. *Ibid.*, 255.
101. *Ibid.*, 257.
102. *Ibid.*, 244–45.
103. *Ibid.*, 245–47.
104. For the continuing influence of ideas set forth during the crisis of the War of 1812, see William Gribbin, *The Churches Militant*, 138–55. I think, however, that Gribbin exaggerates the "providential" end of the War of 1812 as the goad to reform efforts after 1814.
105. Lyman Beecher, *Resources of the Adversary and Means of their Destruction. A Sermon Preached on October 12, 1827, Before the American Board of Missions, at New York*, in Beecher, *Sermons Delivered on Various Occasions*, 267–92.
106. *Ibid.*, 269.
107. *Ibid.*, 269–74.
108. *Ibid.*, 278.
109. *Ibid.*, 276.
110. *Ibid.*, 280.
111. *Ibid.*, 281–89, 290.
112. Lyman Beecher, *The Memory of Our Fathers. A Sermon Delivered at Plymouth, on the 22nd of December, 1827*, in Beecher, *Sermons Delivered on Various Occasions*, 293–318.
113. *Ibid.*, 295–96.
114. *Ibid.*, 297–98.
115. *Ibid.*, 297–300.
116. *Ibid.*, 302.
117. *Ibid.*, 302, 311.
118. *Ibid.*, 301.
119. *Ibid.*, 298, 305.
120. *Ibid.*, 294–95, 310, 317–18.

Chapter III
War in the West: The Radical Revival

1. Donald M. Scott, *From Office to Profession*, *passim*, discusses some of these phenomena from a different but complementary angle.
2. See Stuart Blumin, *The Urban Threshold: Growth and Change in a Nineteenth-Century American Community* (Chicago, 1976), for a sensitive study of Kingston, New York, and its odyssey as a self-conscious community through this period of growth. See also Paul Johnson, *A Shopkeeper's Millennium: Society and Revivals in Rochester, New York, 1815–1837* (New York, 1978), for a much more specifically and exclusively socioeconomic interpretation of revival phenomena.
3. See Jan Shipps, *Mormonism: The Story of a New Religious Tradition* (Urbana, 1985).
4. "Signs of the Times," Utica *Christian Repository* 2 (October 1823), 307.
5. Owen Peterson, *A Divine Discontent: The Life of Nathan S. S. Beman* (Macon, Ga., 1986), 1–16. This account is the only modern biography of Beman. I rely on it for most early biographical facts.

6. Nathan S. S. Beman, *A Sermon Delivered at the Meeting House of the Second Parish in Portland, August 20, 1812, on the Occasion of the National Fast*, quoted in *ibid.*, 23.

7. Owen Peterson, *A Divine Discontent*, 40–41. As we shall see, his marriage to Mrs. Yancey caused all varieties of personal problems. In addition, the facts that he had been a slaveholder and had *sold* his slaves, a mother and two children, and that one of his children by marriage was the radical secessionist William Lowndes Yancey, were all of later consequence.

8. Joshua Bradley, *Accounts of Religious Revivals in Many Parts of the United States from 1815 to 1818* (Albany, 1819), 96.

9. *Ibid.*, 40–45. Taylor quoted in Bertram Wyatt-Brown, "The Antimission Movement in the Jacksonian South: A Study in Regional Folk Culture," *Journal of Southern History* 36 (November 1970), 510. The article is extraordinarily valuable as a guide to the endemic resistance to missionary work in the South from the eighteenth century onward.

10. Nathan S. S. Beman, *An Oration, Pronounced at Middlebury, Before the Associated Alumni of the College, on the Evening of the Commencement, August 17th, 1825* (Troy, N.Y., 1825), 4–6. The distinction he makes is between reconstructing Eden on Earth (Paradise) and attaining immortality (Tree of Life). Human beings lost their right to the tree of life when Adam gained knowledge by biting the apple. God sent him east of Eden "lest he put forth his hand, and take also of the Tree of Life, and eat, and live for ever" (Genesis 3:22). In Christianity the righteous would have to wait for the Millennium to partake of the Tree of Life. See, for instance, Revelation 22:14: "Blessed are they that do his commandments, that they may have right to the tree of life, and may enter in through the gates into the city."

11. *Ibid.*, 8–10. He pointed out that the Romans had gained much of their culture from the Greeks; that the Greeks imported much of their culture from Egypt and the East; and that "they unquestionably carried back the knowledge of facts and principles derived from revelation."

12. *Ibid.*, 10–11.

13. *Ibid.*, 18–26.

14. *Ibid.*, 31–32.

15. *Ibid.*, 36–37.

16. *Ibid.*, 37–38.

17. *Ibid.*, 39.

18. *Ibid.*, 39–40.

19. Nathan S. S. Beman, *Four Sermons on the Doctrine of the Atonement* (Troy, N.Y., 1825).

20. *Ibid.*, 96, 101.

21. See, for instance, Mary P. Ryan, *Cradle of the Middle Class: The Family in Oneida County, New York, 1790–1865* (New York, 1981), 65–70. Ryan uses the example of Oneida County in which, a decade before the 1825 revivals swept its churches, Presbyterians carried on a lively pamphlet-and-periodical war with local Baptists and Methodists over the issue of baptism. At the heart of the debate were the implications for the power and survival of patriarchy.

22. Nathan S. S. Beman to Charles Grandison Finney, 3 August 1826, Charles Grandison Finney Papers, Oberlin College; Owen Peterson, *A Divine Discontent*, 58.

23. I have relied on Keith J. Hardman, *Charles Grandison Finney, 1792–1875* (Syracuse, 1987), the only scholarly biography of the evangelist and a very good one at that, for most early biographical information. See particularly chapter 2 (pp. 24–43). My characterizations of Finney reflect my own sense of his personality and career but do not contradict Hardman's less specific assessment. Hereafter this source is referred to as Hardman, *Finney*.

24. Charles G. Finney, *Memoirs of Charles G. Finney* (New York, 1876), 4 (hereafter referred to as *Memoirs*); Hardman, *Finney*, 30–31.

25. Finney, *Memoirs*, 6; Hardman, *Finney*, 32.

26. See Hardman, *Finney*, 36–39; the interesting discussion of law and religion in David L. Weddle, *The Law as Gospel: Revival and Reform in the Theology of Charles G. Finney* (Metuchen, N.J., 1985), especially chapter 2, "The Legal Vision"; and the more general discussion in Perry Miller, *The Life of the Mind in America: From the Revolution to the Civil War, Books 1–3*, pub. posthumously and ed. by Elizabeth W. Miller (New York, 1965), 3–95 in particular.

27. Gale and Finney quoted in Hardman, *Finney*, 40–41.

28. *Memoirs*, 20–21.

29. *Ibid.*, 14; Hardman, *Finney*, 47–48.

30. *Ibid.*, 49–52.

31. *Ibid.*, 55.

32. Gale quoted in *ibid.*, 55–56.

33. *Ibid.*, 66–67.

34. Utica *Christian Repository* 4 (June 1825), 165.

35. "Signs of the Times," Utica *Christian Repository* 2 (October 1823), 307.

36. Presbytery of Oneida, *A Narrative of the Revival of Religion, in the County of Oneida, Particularly in the Bounds of the Presbytery of Oneida, in the Year 1826* (Utica, 1826), 17 (hereafter referred to as *Oneida Narrative*).

37. *Ibid.*, 6–8; Hardman, *Finney*, 68–71.

38. *Ibid.*, 67–77; *Oneida Narrative*, 9–13, quote on 10–11.

39. *Ibid.*, 23–25.

40. Mary P. Ryan, *Cradle of the Middle Class*, 57, 58, 65, 67.

41. For two excellent studies that point to this condition, see Donald M. Scott, *From Office to Profession*, esp. 36–75; and David F. Allmendinger Jr., *Paupers and Scholars: The Transformation of Student Life in Nineteenth-Century New England* (New York, 1975), esp. 54–78.

42. [William Weeks], *A Pastoral Letter of the Ministers of the Oneida Association to the Churches Under their Care on the Subject of Revivals of Religion* (Utica, 1827), 14.

43. See Ephraim Perkins, *A "Bunker Hill" Contest, A.D. 1826. Between the "Holy Alliance" for the Establishment of Hierarchy and Ecclesiastical Domination over the Human Mind, on the One Side, and the Asserters of Free Inquiry, Bible Religion, Christian Freedom and Civil Liberty on the Other . . .* (Utica, 1826), and *Letter to the Presbytery of Oneida County, New York, and Their "Committee, the Rev. John Frost, Rev. Moses Gillet, and Rev. Noah Coe," "Appointed to Receive Communications from Ministers and Others Respecting the Late Revival, in this County, by Ephraim Perkins, a "Plain Farmer" of Trenton* (Utica, 1827); [no author], *A Calm Review, of the Spirit, Means and Incidents of the late "Oneida Revival," as Exhibited in Various Presbyterian Societies* (Utica, 1827); as well as the previously cited [William Weeks], *A Pastoral Letter*, and *Oneida Narrative*.

44. [William Weeks], *A Pastoral Letter*, and *Oneida Narrative*, 14.

45. *Ibid.*, 9.

46. *Ibid.*, 16.

47. *Ibid.*, 7–9.

48. *Ibid.*, 37.

49. J. Brockway, *A Delineation of the Characteristic Features of a Revival of Religion in Troy, in 1826 and 1827* (Troy, N.Y., 1827), 54n.

50. [no author], *A Calm Review . . . of the Late "Oneida Revival,"* 13.

51. Quoted in Ephraim Perkins, *Letter to the Presbytery of Oneida County*, 17.

52. *A Brief Account of the Origin and Progress of the Divisions in the First Presbyterian Church in the City of Troy; Containing, also, Strictures upon the New Doctrines Broached by the Rev. C. G. Finney and N. S. S. Beman, with a Summary Relation of the Trial of the Latter Before the Troy Presbytery. By a Number of the Late Church and Congregation* (Troy, N.Y., 1827), 16–19.

53. *Ibid.*, 21.

54. *Ibid.*, 23–25.

55. *Ibid.*, 25, 28–29, 31.

56. For the most comprehensive account of the whole affair, see Owen Peterson, *A Divine Discontent*, 51–93.

57. A good recent account of New Lebanon is to be found in Hardman, *Finney*, 104–49.

58. Theodore Erastus Clark to Theodore Dwight Weld, 10 December 1827, in Weld-Clements.

59. T. E. Clark to Weld, 21 May 1828, in Weld-Clements.

60. T. E. Clark to Weld, 8 June 1829, in Gilbert H. Barnes and Dwight L. Dumond, *Letters of Theodore Dwight Weld, Angelina Grimké Weld, and Sarah Grimké, 1822–1844*, 2 vols. (Gloucester, Mass., 1965), I, 26 (hereafter referred to as *Weld-Grimké Letters.*)

61. T. E. Clark to Weld, 24 December 1830, in *ibid.*, I, 38.

62. T. E. Clark to Weld, 31 May 1831, in Weld-Clements.

Chapter IV
The Temperance Reformation

1. Huntington Lyman to Theodore Dwight Weld, 16 November 1891, in Weld-Clements. Recent scholarship has vastly expanded our knowledge of the social and gender roots of the temperance movement. Some of a number recent works to grapple with the origins of the movement in the period 1800–1835 include W. J. Rorabaugh, *The Alcoholic Republic: An American Tradition* (New York, 1979); Ian R. Tyrrell, *Sobering Up: From Temperance to Prohibition in Antebellum America, 1800–1860* (Westport, Conn., 1979); Barbara L. Epstein, *The Politics of Domesticity: Women, Evangelism, and Temperance in Nineteenth-Century America* (Middletown, Conn., 1981); and Nancy Hewitt, *Women's Activism and Social Change: Rochester, New York, 1822–1872* (Ithaca, 1984). See also, for the English case, Brian Harrison, *Drink and the Victorians: The Temperance Question in England, 1815–1872* (Pittsburgh, 1971); and for the German case, James S. Roberts, *Drink, Temperance, and the Working Class in Nineteenth-Century Germany* (Boston, 1984).

2. See W. J. Rorabaugh, *The Alcoholic Republic*, 5–122; and Ian Tyrrell, *Sobering Up*, 16–29.

3. By comparison, for 1975 the same age group consumed about 2.7 gallons of alcohol each year. See W. J. Rorabaugh, *The Alcoholic Republic*, 232–33, and 21 for quotation.

4. *Ibid.*

5. Increase Mather, *Wo to Drunkards. Two Sermons Testifying Against the Sin of Drunkenness: Wherein the* Woefulness *of that Evil, and the Misery of all that are addicted to it, is discovered from the WORD of GOD* (Cambridge, Mass., 1673); the title page of this sermon appears in Michael G. Hall, *The Last American Puritan: The Life of Increase Mather* (Middletown, Conn., 1988), 100; the quotation is from Mather's *Earnest Exhortation* of 1676, quoted in *ibid.*, 122; see also the use of the Mathers in W. J. Rorabaugh, *The Alcoholic Republic*, 30, and Ian Tyrrell, *Sobering Up*, 16, 19.

6. See W. J. Rorabaugh, *The Alcoholic Republic*, 30–31.

7. Quoted in *ibid.*, 45. For Federal Procession, see Frances Hopkinson, "An Account of the Grand Federal Process. Performed at Philadelphia on Friday the Fourth of July, 1788," in Frances Hopkinson, *Miscellaneous Essays*, II, 349–401; Rush's own reaction is in Rush to [Elias Boudinot], 9 July 1788, in *Letters*, I, 476.

8. For a thorough assessment of the "medical model" and its contribution to nineteenth- and twentieth-century attitudes toward liquor, see Harry Gene Levine, "The Discovery of Addiction: Changing Conceptions of Habitual Drunkenness in America," *Journal of Studies on Alcohol* 39, no. 1 (1978), 143–74.

9. Ian Tyrrell, *Sobering Up*, 33–48.

10. *Ibid.*, 40.

11. See *ibid.*, 21–29, for a different and complementary reading of the significance of the tavern and laws regulating it, especially in colonial times.

12. See *ibid.*, 37–48, for the best account of the Massachusetts Society for the Suppression of Intemperance. I do not, however, agree with Tyrrell's emphasis on the direct link between loss of political and social status and the likelihood of a person joining the MSSI.

13. *Ibid.*, 40–45.

14. Lebbus Armstrong, *The Temperance Reformation: Its History, from the Organization of the First Temperance Society to the Adoption of the Liquor Law of Maine, 1851; and the Consequent Influence of the Promulgation of That Law on the Political Interest of the State of New York, 1852* (New York, 1853), 18–25.

15. *Ibid.*, 135. This version of the address, according to Armstrong, was printed from "the original manuscript" (134).

16. *Ibid.*, 138.

17. *Ibid.*, 139.

18. *Ibid.*, 139–40.

19. Ibid., 142.

20. Lyman Beecher, *Six Sermons on the Nature, Occasions, Signs, Evils, and Remedy of Intemperance*, 6th ed. (Boston, 1828). The six sermons became one of the most popular of temperance tracts.

21. *Ibid.*, 7.

22. *Ibid.*, 10.

23. *Ibid.*, 13–16.

24. *Ibid.*, 25–43.

25. *Ibid.*, 48–52.

26. *Ibid.*, 53–55.

27. *Ibid.*, 58.

28. *Ibid.*, 61–63.

29. *Ibid.*, 64–66. See chapter 7, below, on the birth of abolitionism, for a different meaning given to the parallel between temperance, the slave trade, and slavery.

30. *Ibid.*, 68–72.

31. *Ibid.*, 71.

32. *Ibid.*, 89–96.

33. *Ibid.*, 79.

34. Charles C. Cole Jr., *The Social Ideas of the Northern Evangelists, 1826–1860* (New York, 1954), 120.

35. The reader should compare the following appraisal of Edwards, his character and doctrines, and the launching of the temperance crusade with the fundamentally different version of Ian Tyrrell, *Sobering Up*, 61–79.

36. Reminiscences of the Reverend Horatio Bardwell, in William A. Hallock, *"Light and Love." A Sketch of the Life and Labors of the Rev. Justin Edwards, D.D., the Evangelical Pastor; the Advocate of Temperance, the Sabbath, and the Bible* (New York, 1855), 54.

37. *Ibid.*, 235.

38. Justin Edwards to the Reverend Ebenezer Fitch, Andover, 13 January 1815, in *ibid.*, 51.

39. Edwards sermon quoted in *ibid.*, 62.

40. *Ibid.*, 63–64.

41. *Ibid.*

42. *Ibid.*, 106.

43. Justin Edwards, *The Well-Conducted Farm*, Temperance Tract 176, in *The Temperance Volume; Embracing Seventeen Tracts of the American Tract Society* (New York, n.d.), 173–84. The following paragraph makes reference to material in the entire tract.

44. Justin Edwards to William A. Hallock, 10 February 1826, in William A. Hallock, *"Light and Love,"* 195.

45. These are some of the factors emphasized in W. J. Rorabaugh, *The Alcoholic Republic*, and Ian Tyrrell, *Sobering Up*. Paul Johnson's argument for participation in the revival no doubt may also be applied to temperance societies—that is, that some of those who joined in this social style of temperance wished to solicit favor from higher-ups on the economic ladder and fellowship with them. See Paul Johnson, *A Shopkeeper's Millennium*.

46. Central to my thinking on this point is Theodore M. Porter, *The Rise of Statistical Thinking, 1820–1900* (Princeton, 1986); and Patricia Cline Cohen, *A Calculating People: The Spread of Numeracy in Early America* (Chicago, 1982).

47. *Ibid.*, 116–52, quote on 152. The author of *Natural and Civil History of Vermont* (1809) also alluded to a particular vision of the new nation's history. "Persuaded that the American commonwealth is yet in the early years of its infancy," he wrote, "and unable to comprehend to what extent, magnitude, and

dignity it may arise; the author of these sheets views the history of a particular state, rather as a collection of facts, circumstances, and records, than as a compleat and finished historical production." Later historians could look back on his works to detect "from whence the grand fabric arose."

48. Patricia Cline Cohen, *A Calculating People*, 160–62.

49. *Ibid.*, 162–63.

50. Originally published as separate volumes in the years 1821–23, the books have been republished in a superb modern edition in Timothy Dwight, *Travels in New England and New York* (Cambridge, Mass., 1969, 4 volumes, ed. Barbara Miller Solomon).

51. Patricia Cline Cohen, *A Calculating People*, 170–71.

52. *Ibid.*, 171. I disagree with Cohen, however, when she argues that "temperance reformers found it easier to claim that a new vice stalked the land, bringing destruction, rather than to argue that a centuries-old practice, tolerated by distinguished ancestors, was suddenly to be regarded as wrong." Reformers need not have and did not see any conflict between the two types of arguments, and used one to bolster the other. Indeed, they assumed the fit between such evidence and their religious vision.

53. Heman Humphrey, *A Parallel Between Intemperance and the Slave Trade* (New York, 1828).

54. *Ibid.*, 3–5.

55. *Ibid.*, 9–11.

56. *Ibid.*, 18–19.

57. Weld temperance address quoted in the Hudson (Ohio) *Observer and Telegraph*, 15 November 1832.

58. *Ibid.*

59. *Ibid.*

60. *Ibid.*, 6 December 1832.

61. *Ibid.*, 27 December 1832, 3 January 1833.

62. "The Temperance Reformation a Harbinger of the Millenium," *Temperance Recorder*, Albany, N.Y., 6 March 1832, p. 5.

63. *Ibid.*

64. Charles I. Foster, *An Errand of Mercy*, 172. In many cases, temperance societies originally allowed the use of weaker forms of alcoholic beverages. Thus Dr. S. Henry Dickson's address before the South Carolina Society for the Promotion of Temperance recommended the wisdom given by the local medical society: when asked "whether water be not the most wholesome beverage" for drinking, the society recommended water but also "wines, malt liquors, ciders, tea and coffee." Indeed, the temperance society published approvingly the letter of one citizen that even recommended the creation of local vineyards to provide the substitute of wine! See *Address Before the South Carolina Society, for the Promotion of Temperance, by S. Henry Dickson, M.D., Delivered April 6th, 1830*, in *The Permanent Temperance Documents, Published by Direction of the State Temperance Society, and Under the Supervision of a Committee Appointed by That Body* (Columbia, S.C., 1846), I, 91–92, and Letter from Jas. Moultrie Jr., Charleston, 26 August 1829, in *ibid.*, 62.

65. This is the temperance pledge as it had evolved by the mid-1840s: "We, the undersigned, do agree, that we will not use intoxicating liquors as a beverage, nor traffic in them; that we will not provide them as an article of entertainment, or for

persons in our employments, and that, in all suitable ways, we will discountenance their use throughout the community." The pledge is from the title page of *Report of the Executive Committee of the American Temperance Union, 1844* (New York, 1844).

66. Tyrrell, *Sobering Up*, 137, 144. Tyrrell provides the best account and interpretation of the social and generational roots of the teetotal pledge, arguing for the primacy of young "improvers" bent on personal success in the individualistic America. I have no basic quarrel with his approach, except to note the social idealism attached to such an ideology and to expand, as I do, below, on the religious implications of the strict pledge. See *ibid.*, 135–59.

67. A Protestant [Calvin Colton], *Protestant Jesuitism* (New York, 1836); unattributed article in the *Biblical Repertory and Princeton Review* quoted in W. L. Breckenridge, *The New Test of Christian Character Tested, or, The Bible Doctrine of Temperance* (Frankfort, Ky., 1842), 8.

68. Leonard Withington, *A Review of the Late Temperance Movements in Massachusetts* (Boston, 1840), 5.

69. *Ibid.*

70. *Ibid.*, 6.

71. Ian Tyrrell, *Sobering Up*, 73–74.

72. Moses Stuart, *Essay on the Prize-Question, Whether the Use of Distilled Liquors, or Traffic in Them, Is Compatible, at the Present Time, with Making a Profession of Christianity?* (New York, 1830).

73. *Ibid.*, 5–8. Among the verses he chose were Romans 13:13; Proverbs 23:20–21, 29–35; Isaiah 5:22, 11–14, and 28:7; 1 Corinthians 6:9, 10; and Galatians 5:19–21.

74. *Ibid.*, 19–20. Here Stuart used Numbers 6:3 as his evidence.

75. *Ibid.*, 20.

76. *Ibid.*, 23.

77. *Ibid.*, 22–24.

78. *Ibid.*, 30.

79. *Ibid.*, 34–35.

80. *Ibid.*, 43.

81. *Ibid.*, 43–68.

82. See, for instance, Rev. R. S. Crampton, *The Wine of the Bible, and the Bible Use of Wine. A Sermon.* (New York, 1859).

83. Ian Tyrrell, *Sobering Up*, 145–47.

84. W. L. Breckenridge, *The New Test of Christian Character Tested*, 12.

85. Leonard Withington, *A Review of the Late Temperance Movements in Massachusetts*, 12.

86. See Ian Tyrrell, *Sobering Up*, 159–224, for an extremely good treatment of the Washingtonians, mostly from a social history perspective. As the argument below will indicate, I disagree with the relatively small space Tyrrell devotes to the religious aspects of the movement. See also Jed Dannenbaum, *Drink and Disorder: Temperance Reform in Cincinnati from the Washingtonian Revival to the WCTU* (Urbana, 1984), 32–69. I find Dannenbaum's treatment slightly better on religion, although both seem to be caught in the old distinction between religious and secular.

87. Ian Tyrrell, *Sobering Up*, 195–206.

Chapter V
Sabbatarianism and Manual Labor

1. Quoted in William A. Hallock, *"Light and Love,"* 232–33; and Hardman, *Finney,* 136.

2. Quoted in William A. Hallock, *"Light and Love,"* 232.

3. For many years the history of the Sabbatarian movement attracted little scholarly interest, and the net quantity of serious work is still small. Richard R. John, "Taking Sabbatarianism Seriously: The Postal System, the Sabbath, and the Transformation of American Political Culture," *Journal of the Early Republic* 10, no. 4 (Winter 1990), is the most recent and most sophisticated treatment, and it complements the account in this chapter. I wish also to thank Dr. John for his perceptive remarks about a draft of this chapter in our correspondence about his article. Earlier and important contributions include Bertram Wyatt-Brown, "Prelude to Abolitionism: Sabbatarian Politics and the Rise of the Second Party System," *Journal of American History* 58 (September 1971), 316–41, which contains the fullest previous chronicle of the movement; Paul E. Johnson, *A Shopkeeper's Millennium,* 84–88; Randolph A. Roth, *The Democratic Dilemma: Religion, Reform, and the Social Order in the Connecticut River Valley of Vermont, 1791–1850* (New York, 1987), esp. 168–72. See also John Wigley, *The Rise and Fall of the Victorian Sunday* (Manchester, Eng., 1980), for an account of contemporaneous developments in England.

As for manual labor, the most recent work to discuss its significance is Jonathan A. Glickstein, *Concepts of Free Labor in Antebellum America* (New Haven, 1991), esp. 78–80. Glickstein's brief reference to the movement is enriched by the broad conceptualization of his book. My biography of Theodore Weld contains a discussion of the cause: *Passionate Liberator,* 60–64 and scattered references. The present treatment uses some material from that work, though reshaped and reinterpreted.

4. The best treatment of this problem within the context of Republican thought is Drew R. McCoy, *The Elusive Republic: Political Economy in Jeffersonian America* (Chapel Hill, 1980).

5. The biographical details for this section come mainly from two sources: Lewis Tappan, *The Life of Arthur Tappan* (New York, 1870), and Bertram Wyatt-Brown's pioneering study, *Lewis Tappan and the Evangelical War Against Slavery* (Cleveland, 1969).

6. *Ibid.,* 44–45.

7. Lewis Tappan quoted in *ibid.,* 52.

8. See Daniel Walker Howe, *The Unitarian Conscience* (Cambridge, Mass., 1970), for excellent background on Unitarianism in the early nineteenth century.

9. Quoted in Bertram Wyatt-Brown, *Lewis Tappan and the Evangelical War Against Slavery,* 27.

10. *Ibid.,* 34.

11. Diary of Lewis Tappan, various entries for 1828, quoted in *ibid.,* 62.

12. See Hardman, *Finney,* 172–91, 239–65.

13. Lewis Tappan, *The Life of Arthur Tappan,* 416.

14. *Ibid.*

15. Lyman Beecher, *The Memory of Our Fathers,* in Beecher, *Sermons Delivered on Various Occasions,* 308–9.

16. It would be natural, especially for New England reformers, to posit a decline

in the Sabbath and urge a "return" to strict observance, this being a perfect jeremiadical construct for viewing the ebb and flow of the "chosen" people's performance in the world. Thus we need to be cautious about making too striking a contrast between the way things had been and they way they actually were in the 1820s as regards Sabbath-keeping. I am indebted to Richard John in thinking this through historically.

17. Exodus 20:8–11, 23:12, 31:12–17, Leviticus 23:3; Deuteronomy 5:12–15. I am indebted to the article "Sabbath" in Paul Achtemeier, ed., *Harper's Bible Dictionary* (New York, 1985), 888–89, for the historical background and Biblical references concerning the Sabbath and made use of in this and succeeding paragraphs.

18. Jeremiah 17:19–27; see also Nehemiah 13:17–18.

19. For a fine study of the colonial American Sabbath through the seventeenth century and its European background, see Winton U. Solberg, *Redeem the Time: The Puritan Sabbath in Early America* (Cambridge, Mass., 1977).

20. William Addison Blakely, ed., *American State Papers Bearing on Sunday Legislation*, rev. and enl. ed. (Washington, D.C., 1911), 33. This book, like so many on all sides of the Sabbath question, was published with partisan intent (against Sunday laws). All references to Blakely, however, are to accurately recorded statutes and other documents. I have used it rather than references to original statute books for convenience, but Blakely contains the necessary references for further research. Hereafter this source is referred to as Blakely, *ASP*.

21. *Ibid.*, 45–46.

22. *Ibid.*, 49, 50, 53.

23. *Ibid.*, 44; for Massachusetts, see 36–41; for Connecticut, 42–44; for New Hampshire, 51; for Rhode Island, 57–58.

24. Winton U. Solberg, *Redeem the Time*, 90–92, 101–2, 178–79, 269.

25. *Ibid.*, 190–96. Williams, of course, in his rebellion against the Massachusetts establishment, led Rhode Island to voluntary observance of the Sabbath according to one's belief. By 1679, concern over the Sabbath led to legislation that mirrored laws in the New England colonies; however, Solberg finds that "there is no evidence that enforcement was vigorous."

26. Section 9 of the Act Regulating the Post-Office Establishment, 11th Congress, 2nd Session, quoted in its entirety in Blakely, *ASP*, 176. Before 1810, the mail was also delivered on the Sabbath; the legislation more codified than created the practice, but the visibility of the law apparently spurred opposition of a magnitude that the informal practice had not. See Richard R. John, "Taking Sabbatarianism Seriously," 520–25, for a detailed account of the origins of the postal controversy.

27. Blakely, *ASP*, 176–79. See also William Gribbin, *The Churches Militant*, 140, for petition campaigns from New England.

28. Lyman Beecher, *The Memory of Our Fathers*, in Beecher, *Sermons Delivered on Various Occasions*, 309.

29. See Bertram Wyatt-Brown, "Prelude to Abolitionism," 316–41. Wyatt-Brown's interpretation deals with Sabbatarianism's relationship to Jacksonian politics, though he hints at significant themes that I develop here.

30. See esp. *ibid.*, 329–30. Wyatt-Brown makes the point that the Sabbatarian campaign trained future abolitionists and temperance activists in modern political techniques.

31. *Ibid.*

32. Rochester *Observer*, 21 March 1828, as quoted in Paul E. Johnson, *A Shop-keeper's Millennium*, 85. The *Observer* was an evangelical newspaper.

33. Lyman Beecher to Lewis Tappan, 21 May 1828, quoted in Bertram Wyatt-Brown, *Lewis Tappan and the Evangelical War Against Slavery*, 53–54.

34. For two important analyses of the social implications of the New York campaigns and Tappan's relation to the artisans, with analyses that stress the coming of the market more than the issues of the sacred life, see John Barkley Jentz, "Artisans, Evangelicals, and the City: A Social History of Abolition and Labor Reform in Jacksonian New York" (Ph.D. dissertation, City University of New York, 1977), 111; and Sean Wilentz, *Chants Democratic: New York City and the Rise of the American Working Class, 1788–1850* (New York, 1984), 146, 225–26.

35. See Paul E. Johnson, *A Shopkeeper's Millennium: Society and Revivals in Rochester, New York, 1815–1837*, 84–88. Despite the title of the book, Johnson's interpretation of the Sabbatarians virtually ignores the influence of the revivals of the mid-1820s. The revivals he concentrates on are those of the 1830s, very different sorts of events with different consequences.

36. That is not to say the felt need for social recognition of the Sabbath went away, nor that the campaign was a permanent failure. After losses by the radicals in the 1820s and early 1830s, persistent state-by-state campaigns for Sunday legislation continued and bore fruit in the 1850s and after the Civil War.

37. One of the first lengthy accounts of Fellenberg's school can be found in John Griscom, *A Year in Europe*, 2 vols. (New York, 1823); for a very basic account of Hofwyl, see Charles Alpheus Bennett, *History of Manual and Industrial Education Up to 1870* (Peoria, 1926), 128–56.

38. Lyman Beecher, *Resources of the Adversary and Means of their Destruction*, in Beecher, *Sermons Delivered on Various Occasions* (Boston, 1828), 14 (emphasis in original). This particular sermon was preached on October 27, 1827, before the American Board of Missions.

39. Quoted in *First Annual Report of the Society for Promoting Manual Labor in Literary Institutions* (New York, 1833), 115n.

40. Evarts quoted in letter of John Frost in *ibid.*, 115.

41. Compare with Norman Vance, *Sinews of the Spirit: The Ideal of Christian Manliness* (Cambridge, Eng., 1985).

42. "Thirteenth Report of the Board of Directors of the American Education Society," in *Quarterly Register and Journal of the American Education Society* 2 (August 1829), 18.

43. Letter of John H. Rice in *ibid.* 1 (April 1829), 214.

44. E. Cornelius, "Union of Study with Useful Labor," in *ibid.* 2 (November 1829), 65; "Union of Study with Labor," in *ibid.*, 107–8.

45. *Ibid.*, 108.

46. *Ibid.*, 107–15.

47. Testimony of Edwards Amasa Park in "Thirteenth Report of the Board of Directors of the American Education Society," *ibid.* 2 (August 1829), 20.

48. Beriah Green, testimonial in Weld, *First Annual Report of the Society for Promoting Manual Labor in Literary Institutions, Including the Report of Their General Agent, Theodore D. Weld, January 28, 1833* (New York, 1833), 111 (hereafter referred to as Weld, *First Annual Report*). The entire story and subsequent quotations are

from *ibid.*, 111–13. Green later became a minister and an important abolitionist. He was head of Oneida Institute (see below) in the 1830s.

49. Josiah Bushnell Grinnell, *Men and Events of Forty Years* (Boston, 1891), 30. Compare with the use of Grinnell's appraisal of Oneida in Bertram Wyatt-Brown, *Lewis Tappan and the Evangelical War Against Slavery*, 98–99.

50. Tappan quoted in Benjamin Thomas, *Theodore Weld: Crusader for Freedom* (New Brunswick, 1950), 19–20.

51. Bertram Wyatt-Brown, *Lewis Tappan and the Evangelical War Against Slavery*, 98–100.

52. C. S. Renshaw to Finney, Oneida, 15 July 1832, Finney Papers, Oberlin College Library; this question, of course, was raised in other contexts and is not merely germane to manual labor.

53. Finney to Theodore Dwight Weld, Albany, 21 July 1831, in Weld-Clements.

54. Charles Beecher in Barbara M. Cross, ed., *The Autobiography of Lyman Beecher*, II, 234. See Victor Turner, *The Ritual Process* (Chicago, 1969), for a fascinating discussion of the symbolic uses of dress in radical movements.

55. George W. Gale to Charles Grandison Finney, 29 January 1831, in Finney Papers, Oberlin College Library.

56. Weld, *First Annual Report*, 41, 64.

57. Edward Beecher in *ibid.*, 91; see also Milton Rugoff, *The Beechers: An American Family in the Nineteenth Century* (New York, 1981), 90–91.

58. Sereno W. Streeter to Weld, 2 August 1832, in *Weld-Grimké Letters*, I, 72–83.

59. J. L. Tracy to Weld, Lexington, Ky., 24 November 1831, in *ibid.*, I, 57.

60. Calvin Waterbury to Weld, 2 August 1832, in *ibid.*, I, 82; George Bristol to Weld, 25 June 1833, in *ibid.*, I, 112–13.

61. Waterbury, Duncan, and Streeter to Weld, December 1832, in *ibid.*, I, 92–93.

62. *Ibid.*, I, 94.

63. Lyman Beecher, *A Plea for the West* (Cincinnati, 1835).

Chapter VI
William Lloyd Garrison and the Birth of Abolitionism

1. Garrison in *Journal of the Times*, 30 January 1829, quoted in John L. Thomas, *The Liberator: William Lloyd Garrison* (Boston, 1963), 59.

2. Daniel H. Chamberlain, Reconstruction governor of South Carolina, told this story of his conversation with Lincoln on April 6, 1865, in the New York *Tribune*, November 4, 1883. The story was quoted in W. P. Garrison and F. J. Garrison, *William Lloyd Garrison: The Story of His Life as Told by His Children*, 4 vols. (New York, 1885–89), IV, 132, n1. Hereafter this work will be referred to as Garrisons, *Garrison*.

3. Here I am indebted to David Brion Davis, *The Problem of Slavery in Western Culture* (Ithaca, 1966), which provides the most thorough and judicious background to antislavery thought.

4. *Ibid.*

5. For a fine study that is especially interesting on southern evangelicals and antislavery, see James D. Essig, *The Bonds of Wickedness: American Evangelicals Against Slavery, 1770–1808* (Philadelphia, 1982). The standard work on the northern emancipations is Arthur Zilversmit, *The First Emancipation: The Abolition of Slavery in the North* (Chicago, 1967).

6. For a good discussion of Bourne, see George M. Marsden, *The Evangelical Mind and the New School Presbyterian Experience* (New Haven, 1970), 89–91.

7. See Donald G. Mathews, *Slavery and Methodism: A Chapter in American Morality, 1780–1845* (Princeton, 1965), 3–61.

8. For New England Baptists, see William G. McLoughlin, *New England Dissent, 1630–1833*, 2 vols. (Cambridge, Mass., 1971), I, 438; II, 768. For Southern Baptists, see James D. Essig, *The Bonds of Wickedness*, 16–18, 67–69, and *passim*.

9. Various evangelicals quoted in Anne C. Loveland, *Southern Evangelicals and the Social Order, 1800–1860* (Baton Rouge, 1980), 208–18. Though these quotations come from the 1840s and 1850s, their spirit certainly reflects views of the 1820s in the South and, to a large degree, of churchmen in the North.

10. See Leon F. Litwack, *North of Slavery: The Negro in the Free States, 1790–1860* (Chicago, 1961), *passim*. Gary B. Nash, *Forging Freedom: The Formation of Philadelphia's Black Community, 1720–1840* (Cambridge, Mass., 1988), looks closely at the fate of blacks in Philadelphia before and after emancipation. Given the central role of Quakers and antislavery evangelicals in the life of that city, Nash's finding that the initially hopeful state of blacks declined, especially in the period after 1820, should be considered a "best case" for emancipation in the North.

11. Letter of General Robert G. Harper to Elias B. Caldwell, secretary of the Colonization Society of the U.S., Baltimore, 20 August 1817, printed in American Society for Colonizing the Free People of Color of the United States, *First Annual Report* (Washington, 1818), 14–15.

12. American Society for Colonizing the Free People of Color of the United States, *Second Annual Report* (Washington, 1819), 9.

13. See *ibid.*, 10, for interesting remarks by Henry Clay at the first annual meeting. He thought that colonization would also encourage slave states that had, or were thinking of passing, laws prohibiting emancipation to reverse themselves. Once there was a successful colony to which emancipated slaves could be sent, they could require that such slaves *must* go there and thus fulfill the intent of emancipation prohibition laws.

14. American Society for Colonizing the Free People of Color of the United States, *First Annual Report*, 2. Indeed, colonizationists honored Paul Cuffe of Massachusetts, who as a black entrepreneur had launched an expedition to Africa to create a haven for free blacks and act as a foothold for missionary activity. For more on Cuffe and earlier movements, see, esp., Floyd J. Miller, *The Search for Black Nationality: Black Emigration and Colonization 1787–1863* (Urbana, 1975), 3–53.

15. *Ibid.*, 51, 54–90.

16. George Bourne, *The Book and Slavery Irreconcilable. With Animadversions upon Dr. Smith's Philosophy* (Philadelphia, 1816). John W. Christie and Dwight L. Dumond, *George Bourne and "The Book and Slavery Irreconcilable"* (Wilmington, 1969) provides the most complete treatment of Bourne's life and influence and a text of his most famous pamphlet. However, Christie and Dumond's major intention

seems to be to further undercut the originality of Garrison's position by showing that much of the phraseology, including "manstealing" and "immediate emancipation," for which Garrison became famous, originated in Bourne. They miss the point of Garrison's true originality.

17. Genin quoted in Merton L. Dillon, *Benjamin Lundy and the Struggle for Negro Freedom* (Urbana, 1966), 30–31.

18. The best account of Lundy is Merton L. Dillon, *Benjamin Lundy and the Struggle for Negro Freedom*. My own characterization of Lundy is drawn from material in Dillon and the primary sources, and does not necessarily reflect that author's view.

19. *Ibid.*, 57.

20. See Dillon's somewhat different interpretation of Heyrick's impact in *ibid.*, 106–7, 125; Elizabeth Coltman Heyrick, *Immediate, Not Gradual, Abolition; or, An Inquiry into the Shortest, Safest and Most Effectual Means of Getting Rid of West Indian Slavery* (London, 1824).

21. Merton L. Dillon, *Benjamin Lundy and the Struggle for Negro Freedom*, 59.

22. See, for instance, the charts of numbers of antislavery societies and members in Alice Dana Adams, *The Neglected Period of Anti-Slavery in America, 1808–1831* (Gloucester, Mass., 1964; orig. ed. 1908), 106, 117, 118.

23. In *Greenfield Hill*, Timothy Dwight celebrated liberty and free ownership of the soil and condemned slavery as the "chief curse, since curses here began." Yet he described the life of the slave in Connecticut as physically benign, though admitted that even there, without liberty the slave's mind "Pale, sickly, shrunk, it strives in vain to rise, / Scarce lives, while living, and untimely dies." In his notes to the poem, Dwight excoriated West Indian slavery on all counts and endorsed the efforts of those in Connecticut advocating freedom for the slave. Yet he never mentioned slavery in the South. See *Greenfield Hill*, in William J. McTaggart and William K. Bottorff, eds., *The Major Poems of Timothy Dwight (1752–1817) with a Dissertation on the History, Eloquence, and Poetry of the Bible. Facsimile Reproductions*, 403–4 and 531–32. For slightly different interpretations of the slavery aspects of the poem, see Kenneth Silverman, *Timothy Dwight*, 69–70; and James D. Essig, *The Bonds of Wickedness*, 100–101.

24. I am indebted to Walter M. Merrill, *Against Wind and Tide: A Biography of Wm. Lloyd Garrison* (Cambridge, Mass., 1963), 1–12; and John L. Thomas, *The Liberator*, 8–26, for these details of Garrison's family history. My interpretation of their significance, however, differs somewhat from Merrill's and Thomas's.

25. Quote in Garrisons, *Garrison*, I, 56n. See the very perceptive essay on Garrison's journalistic voice in R. Jackson Wilson, *Figures of Speech: American Writers and the Literary Marketplace, from Benjamin Franklin to Emily Dickinson* (New York, 1989), 117–58.

26. Garrisons, *Garrison*, I, 29–30.

27. *Ibid.*, 56.

28. *Ibid.*, 44–45.

29. *Ibid.*, 79–80.

30. Quoted in *ibid.*, 84.

31. See James M. Banner Jr., *To the Hartford Convention*, 104–9, quotations from 107. Linda Kerber, *Federalists in Dissent*, 23–66.

32. *Free Press* quoted in *ibid.*, I, 64–66.

33. Lyman Beecher, *The Memory of Our Fathers*, in Beecher, *Sermons Delivered on Various Occasions*, 295–96.

34. Nathan S. S. Beman, *An Oration, Pronounced at Middlebury*, 31–32.

35. No one recorded those in attendance, though one might assume that Lyman Beecher, William Ellery Channing, and others of prominence were there.

36. Garrison quoted in Garrisons, *Garrison*, I, 93–94.

37. A.O.B. [William Lloyd Garrison], "To the Editor of the Boston *Courier*," [11 August 1828], in Walter Merrill, ed., *The Letters of William Lloyd Garrison, Volume 1: I Will Be Heard! 1822–1835* (Cambridge, Mass., 1971), 63–65 (hereafter referred to as *Garrison Letters*).

38. A.O.B. [William Lloyd Garrison], "To the Editor of the Boston *Courier*," [12 August 1828], in *ibid.*, 66–68; the Reverend Howard Malcolm to William Lloyd Garrison, 25 August 1835, in *Liberator*, 29 August 1835.

39. *Garrison Letters*, I, 67–68.

40. *Ibid.*, 64.

41. Garrisons, *Garrison*, I, 98. Apparently only one weakly worded petition resulted from his efforts.

42. *Ibid.*, 113–14.

43. "To the Public," *Journal of the Times*, 3 October 1828, reprinted in *ibid.*, 103.

44. Petition reprinted in *ibid.*, 109.

45. Quoted in *ibid.*, 112.

46. Lundy in *Genius of Universal Emancipation*, 13 December 1828, quoted in *ibid.*, 118.

47. Garrison in *Journal of the Times*, 16 January 1829, quoted in *ibid.*, 119.

48. Garrison to Stephen Foster, Bennington, 30 March 1829, in *Garrison Letters*, I, 80. However, he writes to Stephen Foster: "[William Collier] dissuaded me from going to Washington with Lundy, and offered his services to get me employment. . . . I do not, however, relinquish the hope of ultimately joining Lundy in his great, and glorious human enterprise; but whether I go or stay, the subject of slavery will occupy a great deal of my attention."

49. Garrison to Jacob Horton, Boston, 27 June 1829, in *ibid.*, 83.

50. For quotations from the beginning of the address and a summary of the section before that concerning slavery, see Garrisons, *Garrison*, I, 127; George Fredrickson, ed., *William Lloyd Garrison* (Englewood Cliffs, N.J., 1968), 12.

51. The text of the address was published complete in the *National Philanthropist and Intelligencer*, 22 and 29 July 1829. Large excerpts also appear in Garrisons, *Garrison*, I, 127–37. These excerpts are in turn reprinted in George Fredrickson, ed., *William Lloyd Garrison*, 11–21. I make reference to this last version because it is the one most widely available.

52. *Ibid.*, 13.

53. *Ibid.*, 14–15.

54. *Ibid.*, 15.

55. *Ibid.*, 16–17, 19.

56. *Ibid.*, 17.

57. *Ibid.*, 18, 19.

58. *Ibid.*, 19, 20.

59. *Ibid.*

60. "To the Public," Garrison's inaugural editorial in the *Genius of Universal Emancipation*, reprinted in Garrisons, *Garrison*, I, 142–44. Quote from 143.

61. See James Walvin, *England, Slaves, and Freedom, 1776–1838* (London, 1986), esp. 144–70.

62. Garrisons, *Garrison*, I, 146.

63. *Ibid.*, 150.

64. *Ibid.*, 145.

65. For a modern edition of this rare pamphlet, see Charles M. Wiltse, ed., *David Walker's Appeal, in four articles; together with a Preamble, to the Coloured Citizens of the World, but in particular, and very expressly, to those of the United States of America* (New York, 1965) (hereafter referred to as *Walker's Appeal*).

66. *Ibid.*, 11–12, 39.

67. The best treatment of the influence of the Vesey revolt and fears about insurrection on southern life and politics is William W. Freehling, *Prelude to Civil War: The Nullification Controversy in South Carolina, 1816–1836* (New York, 1966). Though his conclusions are especially germane to South Carolina, they apply to similar feelings in other parts of the South. See also Freehling's essay "Denmark Vesey's Peculiar Reality," in Robert H. Abzug and Stephen E. Maizlish, eds., *New Perspectives on Race and Slavery in America: Essays in Honor of Kenneth M. Stampp* (Lexington, 1986), 25–47.

68. This is at least the speculation of Wiltse, who relies on information from the writer Truman Nelson. See *Walker's Appeal*, ix.

69. Garrisons, *Garrison*, I, 160; *Walker's Appeal*, x.

70. Garrisons, *Garrison*, I, 160–161.

71. *Ibid.*, 160n–161n.

72. "Walker's Boston Pamphlet," *Genius of Universal Emancipation*, April 1830.

73. Merton L. Dillon, *Benjamin Lundy and the Struggle for Negro Freedom*, 118.

74. Garrisons, *Garrison*, I, 150–51.

75. *Ibid.*, 166–73. For two accounts of the Todd affair and trial, see John L. Thomas, *The Liberator*, 108–13, and Walter M. Merrill, *Against Wind and Tide*, 32–34.

76. Garrisons, *Garrison*, I, 174–77.

77. Quoted in *ibid.*, 178.

78. *Ibid.*, 190–91.

79. Garrison to Ebenezer Dole, Baltimore, 14 July 1830, in *Garrison Letters*, I, 105–6.

80. Lewis Tappan, *The Life of Arthur Tappan*, 163.

81. *Ibid.*, 104.

82. Garrisons, *Garrison*, I, 199–202.

83. John W. Christie and Dwight L. Dumond actually attribute Garrison's turn to immediatism in 1829 to his reading of Bourne, though on the basis of highly circumstantial evidence. It seems much more likely that he read the pamphlet sometime in 1830, and may have even met Bourne either in Baltimore or New York in the summer of that year. In any case, Bourne later wrote extensively for the

Liberator. See Christie and Dumond, *George Bourne and "The Book and Slavery Irreconcilable,"* 66–98.

84. *Liberator*, 17 March 1832.

85. Garrisons, *Garrison*, I, 203–4.

86. *Ibid.*, 204–9; quote from Newburyport *Herald*, 1 October 1830, excerpted on 209.

87. Oliver Johnson's account quoted in *ibid.*, 215.

88. *Ibid.*, 210–12. See Anne C. Rose, *Transcendentalism as a Social Movement*, 26–28, 74–78, for a good treatment of the fascinating Abner Kneeland.

89. Samuel J. May, *Some Recollections of Our Antislavery Conflict* (Boston, 1869), 19.

90. *Ibid.*

91. Garrisons, *Garrison*, I, 220–24.

92. *Liberator*, 1 January 1831. Quotations in the next paragraphs are from the same source, unless otherwise noted.

93. Lyman Beecher, *Six Sermons on the Nature, Occasions, Signs, Evils, and Remedy of Intemperance*, 38.

94. *Liberator*, 8 January 1831.

95. Masthead of *Liberator*, 23 April 1831; Garrisons, *Garrison*, I, 231–32.

96. William Lloyd Garrison, "Address Before Free People of Color, June, 1831," as excerpted in Garrisons, *Garrison*, I, 257.

97. *Liberator*, 8 January 1831. Some evidence in this and the following paragraphs concerning slave revolt has appeared in Robert H. Abzug, "The Influence of Garrisonian Abolitionists' Fears of Slave Violence on the Antislavery Argument, 1829–40," *Journal of Negro History* (January 1970), 15–28. I think that the present interpretive framework more accurately reflects the significance of the issue.

98. "Dread of Insurrection" and "Rumors of 'Insurrections,'" in *Genius of Universal Emancipation*, July and October 1830.

99. *Liberator*, 15 January 1831.

100. *Ibid.*, 26 February 1831.

101. "Another Dream," in *ibid.*, 30 April 1831.

102. *Ibid.*, 23 July 1831.

103. *Ibid.*, 14 May 1831.

104. *Ibid.*, 20 August 1831, quoted in Truman Nelson, ed., *Documents of Upheaval: Selections from William Lloyd Garrison's "The Liberator," 1831–1865* (New York, 1965), 27.

105. *Liberator*, 8 October 1831.

106. *Genius of Universal Emancipation*, 3d Series, vol. 2: 1–61, 65–7, 78, 83; *Liberator*, 8 September 1831.

107. *Ibid.*

108. *Ibid.*, 24 September 1831.

109. *Ibid.*, 7 January 1832.

110. Anthony J. Barker, *Captain Charles Stuart: Anglo-American Abolitionist* (Baton Rouge, 1986), 68–70.

111. William Lloyd Garrison, *Thoughts on African Colonization; or, an Impartial Exhibition of the Doctrines, Principles and Purposes of the American Colonization Soci-*

ety. Together with the Resolutions, Addresses and Remonstrances of the Free People of Color (Boston, 1832), *passim.*

112. Quotes from William Lloyd Garrison, introduction to the pamphlet edition of "Address Before Free People of Color, June, 1831," as excerpted in Garrisons, *Garrison*, I, 259.

113. See Lawrence J. Friedman, *Gregarious Saints: Self and Community in American Abolitionism, 1830–1870* (New York, 1982), 43–126.

114. Bertram Wyatt-Brown, *Lewis Tappan and the Evangelical War Against Slavery*, 87–88, quote on 88.

115. Garrison quoted in *ibid.*, 89–90.

116. Elizur Wright Jr. quoted in Lawrence B. Goodheart, "Abolitionists as Academics: The Controversy at Western Reserve College, 1832–1833," *History of Education Quarterly* (Winter 1982), 433.

117. Weld to James G. Birney, Cincinnati, 27 September 1832, in Dwight L. Dumond, ed., *Letters of James Gillespie Birney, 1831–1857*, 2 vols. (Gloucester, Mass., 1966; orig. ed. 1938), I, 27; Tappan to Garrison, 12 December 1832, Garrison Papers, Boston Public Library; Weld to Elizur Wright Jr., 10 January 1833, in *Weld-Grimké Letters*, I, 99. Although Weld had been inundated by his dear friend Charles Stuart with antislavery and anti-colonization material, it took the particular logic of the Garrisonian approach to snare him for abolition.

118. Weld to Lewis Tappan [Rochester, N.Y., 9 March 1836], in *ibid.*, I, 273. For a more complete account of the Lane Debates and their aftermath, see Robert H. Abzug, *Passionate Liberator*, 90–122.

119. Lewis Tappan to Weld, 10–11 July 1834, in *Weld-Grimké Letters*, I, 155.

120. Elizur Wright Jr. to Weld, 14 August 1834, in *ibid.*, I, 167.

121. Robert H. Abzug, *Passionate Liberator*, 118–22.

122. Lyman Beecher and other major New School figures were, in fact, tried for heresy. Beecher was acquitted in 1835.

123. The question of what caused the Presbyterian schism is an old and honored one. While surely theology lay at the heart of the schism, the rise of abolitionism among New School adherents contributed to the Old School's sense of urgency. For the best summary of the evidence, including the role played by the slavery issue, see George M. Marsden, *The Evangelical Mind and the New School Presbyterian Experience*, 59–103.

Chapter VII
The Body Reforms

1. *Graham Journal of Health and Longevity* (1837), as quoted in James C. Whorton, *Crusaders for Fitness: The History of American Health Reformers* (Princeton, 1982), 44.

2. As in the case of other reforms, I stress the power of religious quest in shaping the creation of these reforms. By no means do I reject the importance of social and economic forces as impetuses to both the dissemination and popularity of physiological reform. Not all or perhaps even the majority of Americans who found the body reforms compelling did so for consciously religious reasons. Yet as this chapter demonstrates, Graham, Fowler, and Alcott saw themselves as reli-

gious prophets, and their most ardent supporters understood their work in this light.

A perusal of the most recent literature on the body reforms underlines my departure from prior lines of interpretation. The two most indispensable works in the new literature on physiological reform are Stephen Nissenbaum, *Sex, Diet, and Debility in Jacksonian America: Sylvester Graham and Health Reform* (Westport, Conn., 1980), and James C. Whorton, *Crusaders for Fitness*, which contains new versions of work Whorton published as early as 1977. Nissenbaum carefully delineates Graham's basic biography and the scientific sources of his system, as well as its various doctrines. He does so within a convincing argument that Graham "formulated his ideas not as a way to adopt the values of the capitalist marketplace but as a way to deny their power—to devise what I have called a physiology of subsistence." Insightful as far as it goes, Nissenbaum's approach underestimates the influence and continuing relevance of Graham's religious background; see xi and *passim*. Whorton's chapters on Graham and Alcott make a breakthrough by treating them within the framework of what he calls "Christian Physiology," in which he notes the important religious underpinnings in the work of these reformers. He illustrates and asserts but does not thoroughly analyze the connection. For works on phrenology, see notes for appropriate text. The present chapter moves beyond Whorton's and Nissenbaum's approach in the realm of religion, but remains indebted to their pioneering work.

3. Stephen Nissenbaum, *Sex, Diet, and Debility*, 9–10.

4. *Ibid.*, 10–13.

5. Sylvester Graham, *Thy Kingdom Come; A Discourse, on the Importance of Infant and Sunday Schools, Delivered at the Crown St. Church, Philadelphia, December 13th, 1829* (Philadelphia, 1831), 22 and *passim*. Curiously neither Nissenbaum nor Whorton makes much of this sermon. See Stephen Nissenbaum, *Sex, Diet, and Debility*, 136; James C. Whorton, *Crusaders for Fitness*, does not mention it at all.

6. This is a simplified representation of physiological theories that Stephen Nissenbaum elucidates with precision and detail in *Sex, Diet, and Debility*, *passim*.

7. Sylvester Graham, *A Lecture to Young Men, on Chastity. Intended Also for the Serious Consideration of Parents and Guardians* (Boston, 1844; orig. ed. 1834), 58–59, 49, 21, 73. For a complete treatment of Graham's physiology of sex, see Stephen Nissenbaum, *Sex, Diet, and Debility*, esp. chapters 2 and 7 but also *passim*.

8. *Ibid.*, 81–82.

9. Madeleine B. Stern, *Heads and Headlines: The Phrenological Fowlers* (Norman, Okla., 1971), 3–9. Stern's account, while good for biographical detail, is scant on analysis. The work scarcely mentions the relationship of phrenology to religion and offers no satisfactory summary of the phrenological system itself.

10. Edward Hitchcock, *Dyspepsy Forestalled* (Northampton, 1831).

11. John D. Davies, *Phrenology—Fad and Science: A Nineteenth-Century American Crusade* (New Haven, 1955), 31–32; Madeleine B. Stern, *Heads and Headlines*, 7–11.

12. Works containing good introductions to the history of phrenology include John D. Davies, *Phrenology—Fad and Science*, and Roger Cooter, *The Cultural Meaning of Popular Science: Phrenology and the Organization of Consent in Nineteenth-Century Britain* (New York, 1984). See Cooter also for an exploration of phrenology's varied meanings within the British context. His passing reference

to Fowler inadvertently confirms in its own way the interpretation presented here. He states that the arrival of the Fowlers and their books in England destroyed a respectably scientific British phrenological tradition by adding a "nonintellectualist, healthean—watered, fruity, and farinaceaus—almost fundamentalist tone" (156). For a somewhat different approach to phrenology in the United States, see Arthur Wrobel, "Phrenology as Political Science," in Arthur Wrobel, ed., *Pseudo-Science and Society in Nineteenth-Century America* (Lexington, Ky., 1987), 122–43. For a contemporary account of the history of early phrenology, see Andrew Carmichael, *A Memoir of the Life and Philosophy of Spurzheim* (Boston, 1833).

13. John D. Davies, *Phrenology—Fad and Science*, 12–14.

14. Boston *Christian Examiner*, [n.d.] 1834, quoted in *ibid.*, 12.

15. *Ibid.*, 16–29.

16. For more details on the growth of the Fowlers' phrenological business empire, see Madeleine B. Stern, *Heads and Headlines*, *passim*, and John D. Davies, *Phrenology—Fad and Science*, 30–64.

17. [O. S. Fowler], *Fowler's Practical Phrenology . . .* , 10th ed. (New York, 1842), 428.

18. [William A. Alcott], *Forty Years in the Wilderness of Pills and Powders; or Cogitations and Confessions of an Aged Physician* (Boston, 1859), 3–5; see Odell Shepard, *Pedlar's Progress: The Life of Bronson Alcott* (Boston, 1937), 4–7, 17–22, for description of Wolcott, Connecticut; see also Samuel Orcutt, *History of the Town of Wolcott (Connecticut) from 1731 to 1874* (Waterbury, Conn., 1874), 175–210. There is no modern biography of William Andrus Alcott. A basic biographical sketch can be found in "Dr. William A. Alcott," *American Journal of Education* 4 (March 1858), 629–56. But see Martin Cornelius Van Buren, "The Indispensable God of Health: A Study of Republican Hygiene and the Ideology of William Alcott" (Ph.D. dissertation, UCLA, 1977), for the most detailed modern study.

19. [William A. Alcott], *Forty Years in the Wilderness of Pills and Powders*, 3.

20. *Ibid.*, 72.

21. *Ibid.*, 19–20.

22. *Ibid.*, 75.

23. William A. Alcott, *The Boy's Guide to Usefulness. Designed to Prepare the Way for the "Young Man's Guide."* (Boston, 1844), *passim*.

24. See William A. Alcott, *The Laws of Health; or, Sequel to "The House I Live In," Designed for Families and Schools* (Boston, 1859), 84, *passim; Tea and Coffee: Their Physical, Intellectual, and Moral Effects on the Human System* (Boston, 1856); *Thoughts on Bathing* (Boston, 1839); *The Young Mother; or, Management of Children in Regard to Health*, 3d ed. (Boston, 1849), 276, 73–76.

25. William A. Alcott, *The Young Husband; or Duties of Man in the Marriage Relation*, 3d ed. (Boston, 1839), 289.

26. These titles are taken from the first issue of Alcott's journal, *The Moral Reformer and Teacher on the Human Constitution* (Boston, 1835).

27. *Ibid.*, 14–19, quote on 19.

28. *Ibid.*, 22–23.

29. William A. Alcott, "The Past and the Future," in *The Moral Reformer* 2 (1836), 44. In these recommendations concerning the "little things," of course, there still lived the spirit of Benjamin Franklin, along with Alcott's worship of Franklin's mission to "do good."

30. See, for instance, Stephen Nissenbaum, *Sex, Diet, and Debility, passim;* see also Martin Cornelius Van Buren, "The Indispensable God of Health."

31. Mary Douglas, *Purity and Danger: An Analysis of Concepts of Pollution and Taboo* (Baltimore, 1966), *passim,* but esp. 54–72.

32. See Jacob Neusner, *Invitation to the Talmud,* 2d ed. (New York, 1984), 3 and *passim.*

33. William A. Alcott, *The Laws of Health,* 84; see also Alcott's query concerning Leviticus: "It would be curious . . . in short, whether the 'law' was not a most salutary physical as well as moral code; and whether much of it would not be equally useful to us as to the Jews of 4000 years ago," in *Moral Reformer* 2 (1836), 180.

34. [William A. Alcott], *Forty Years in the Wilderness of Powders and Pills.*

35. William A. Alcott, "The Past and the Future," *Moral Reformer* 2 (1836), 41–42.

36. Sylvester Graham, *Lectures on the Science of Human Life,* 2 vols. (Boston, 1839), II, 372.

37. Sylvester Graham to Gerrit Smith, 4 March 1840, as quoted in Ralph V. Harlow, *Gerrit Smith: Philanthropist and Reformer* (New York, 1939), 95.

38. However, see O. S. Fowler, *Love and Parentage, Applied to the Improvement of Offspring Including Important Directions and Suggestions to Lovers and the Married . . .* (New York, 1844), 141, for Mosaic language. Compare with Leviticus 11 and Deuteronomy 14. I am not sure of Fowler's source for such wisdom, although it sounds like scientized folklore.

39. O. S. Fowler, *The Christian Phrenologist; or The Natural Theology and Moral Bearings of PHRENOLOGY; Its Aspect on, and Harmony with REVELATION* (Cazenovia, N.Y., 1843), 4.

40. *Ibid.,* 10, 12.

41. Jean Soler, "The Dietary Prohibitions of the Hebrews," in *New York Review of Books,* 14 June 1979, pp. 24–30. Compare with Michael Walzer, *Exodus and Revolution* (New York, 1985), a brilliantly suggestive commentary on the Exodus story and its archetypal influence on politics, especially revolutionary movements, in the West.

42. Sylvester Graham, *Lectures on the Science of Human Life,* I, 447–85 and *passim.* See also *A Defence of the Graham System of Living; or, Remarks on Diet and Regimen. Dedicated to the Rising Generation* (New York, 1835).

43. William A. Alcott, *The Laws of Health,* 10.

44. William A. Alcott, "The Past and the Future," *Moral Reformer* 2 (1836), 37–39; "July and Independence," *Moral Reformer* 1 (1835), 198.

45. See, in particular, the broad interpretations set forth in Perry Miller, *The New England Mind;* Sacvan Bercovitch, *The American Jeremiad,* and *The Puritan Origins of the American Self* (New Haven, 1975). See also Michael Walzer, *The Revolution of the Saints: A Study of the Origins of Radical Politics* (Cambridge, Mass., 1965), *passim.*

46. The estrangement from the church can be seen especially in the lives of Fowler and Graham, would-be ministers who retained little connection with the church establishment or evangelicalism after they had assumed roles as physiological prophets. Only William Andrus Alcott, who ironically never considered a clerical career, retained close ties with the world of the church. Even so, his

connection was through the Sunday school movement, for which he provided a variety of educational tracts, rather than the church proper.

47. Stephen Nissenbaum, *Sex, Diet, and Debility*, 143–46.

48. *Ibid.*, 14.

49. See the next chapter for a detailed discussion of the water-cure in America.

50. Alcott's lower profile and connections with evangelical and tract organizations enabled him to escape relatively unscathed.

51. Stephen Nissenbaum, *Sex, Diet, and Debility*, 14.

52. See John D. Davies, *Phrenology—Fad and Science*, 63–74.

53. Orson Squire Fowler quoted in *ibid.*, 63.

54. See, for instance, David Meredith Reese, *Phrenology Known by Its Fruits, being a brief review of Doctor Brigham's late work, entitled "Observations on the Influence of Religion upon the Health and Physical Welfare of Mankind"* (New York, 1836). For the full background to Old School Presbyterian objections, see Theodore Dwight Bozeman, *Protestants in an Age of Science: The Baconian Ideal and Antebellum Religious Thought* (Chapel Hill, 1977), 92–93.

55. Charles Francis Adams, diary entry for 5 July 1833, in Marc Friedlander and L. H. Butterfield, eds., *The Diary of Charles Francis Adams, Volume 5, January 1833–October 1834* (Cambridge, Mass., 1964), 121.

56. Ralph Waldo Emerson, entry in Journal Z[A], in William H. Gilman and J. E. Parsons, eds., *The Journals and Miscellaneous Notebooks of Ralph Waldo Emerson*, vol. 8, *1841–1843* (Cambridge, Mass., 1970), 341.

57. Testimonials quoted in John D. Davies, *Phrenology—Fad and Science*, 157–58. See also the discussion of phrenology and religious significance in the somewhat different British case, in Roger Cooter, *The Cultural Meaning of Popular Science*, 169–98.

58. Henry B. Stanton to Theodore Weld, 4 August 1832, in *Weld-Grimké Letters*, I, 85.

59. Quoted in Stephen Nissenbaum, *Sex, Diet, and Debility*, 143.

60. Henry [E. Benson] to [George W. Benson], New York, 25 February 1835, in Garrison Papers, Boston Public Library.

61. Garrison to Samuel J. May, Boston, 15 September 1834, in *Garrison Letters*, I, 415.

62. Sarah and Angelina Grimké to Weld, Brookline, Mass., 30 November 1837, in *Weld-Grimké Letters*, I, 485.

63. Bishop was the member of the mob that Lovejoy killed.

64. *Ibid.*, 491.

65. *Ibid.*, 492.

66. Stephen Nissenbaum, *Sex, Diet, and Debility*, 143–44; William S. Tyler to Edward Tyler, 10 October [1833], reprinted in Thomas H. Le Duc, "Grahamites and Garrisonians," *New York History* 20 (1939), 190–91.

67. Sarah and Angelina Grimké to Weld, 30 November 1837, in *Weld-Grimké Letters*, I, 486.

68. Garrison to George W. Benson, Brooklyn, Conn., 27 November 1835, in *Garrison Letters*, I, 560–61.

69. *Ibid.*, 561. On the same day, Garrison repeated these objections in a letter to his sister-in-law, this time referring to "the extermination of sundry chickens," noting: "There is great danger that if we are thankful only when we are full or

prosperous, ours is merely the gratitude of selfishness." Three days later, in another letter to George W. Benson, he continued his obsession with the slaughter of animals: "Two bouncing hogs have been summarily *lynched* to-day, by Geers [a neighbor] and another man. . . . Grahamites and Jews vote them an abomination." See Garrison to Mary Benson, Brooklyn, Conn., 27 November 1835, in *ibid.*, 562–63; and Garrison to George W. Benson, Brooklyn, Conn., 30 November 1835, in *ibid.*, 565.

70. Garrisons, *Garrison*, II, 107–8. I follow the Garrison sons' sense of the meaning of these articles in their father's life.

71. *Ibid.*, 109.

72. Henry Clarke Wright quoted in Lewis Perry, *Childhood, Marriage, and Reform: Henry Clarke Wright, 1797–1870* (Chicago, 1980), 149–50. Perry sees this passage as verging "toward the irreligious conclusion that good deeds are completely redeeming" (150). My own reading, given the context of this study, would be that the question at hand is not the redeeming power of works but rather the sacred ritual invocation of acts in everyday life as a truer sign of faith.

73. Elizur Wright Jr. to Theodore Weld, New York, 28 July 1836, in *Weld-Grimké Letters*, I, 320.

74. See, for instance, the experience of Theodore Dwight Weld, who had several readings done. In one case he disguised himself as an omnibus driver but still came away with the same accurate results he had received when examined as himself. See Angelina Grimké to Jane Smith, 4 February 1837, in Weld-Clements, or my rendering of the story in *Passionate Liberator*, 159–60.

75. William Lloyd Garrison to Helen E. Garrison, Boston, 1 June 1836, in Louis Ruchames, ed., *The Letters of William Lloyd Garrison, Volume 2: A House Dividing Against Itself 1836–1840* (Cambridge, Mass., 1971), 118.

Chapter VIII
The Woman Question

1. Lydia Maria Child to William Lloyd Garrison, *Liberator*, 6 March 1840, reprinted in Milton Meltzer and Patricia G. Holland, eds., *Lydia Maria Child: Selected Letters, 1817–1880* (Amherst, 1982), 127–29 (hereafter referred to as Child, *Selected Letters*).

2. Standard accounts include Blanche Glassman Hersh, *The Slavery of Sex: Feminist-Abolitionists in America* (Urbana, 1978); Barbara Berg, *The Remembered Gate* (New York, 1978); and Mary P. Ryan, *Cradle of the Middle Class: The Family in Oneida County, New York, 1790–1865*.

3. For an interesting attempt to conceptualize the problem in religious terms, see Carroll Smith-Rosenberg, "The Cross and the Pedestal: Women, Anti-Ritualism, and the Emergence of the American Bourgeoisie," in Carroll Smith-Rosenberg, *Disorderly Conduct: Visions of Gender in Victorian America* (New York, 1985), 129–64. See also Blanche Glassman Hersh, *The Slavery of Sex*, 136–50, 253–54.

4. See Lori D. Ginzberg, *Women and the Work of Benevolence: Morality, Politics, and Class in the Nineteenth-Century United States* (New Haven, 1990), an extremely helpful recent study. See also Anne M. Boylan, "Timid Girls, Venerable Widows and Dignified Matrons: Life Cycle Patterns Among Organized Women in New

York and Boston, 1797–1840," *American Quarterly* 38 (Winter 1986), 779–97; and Anne M. Boylan, "Women in Groups: An Analysis of Women's Benevolent Organizations in New York and Boston, 1797–1840," *Journal of American History* 71 (December 1984), 497–523. These are the latest and best-researched examples of a longer literature concerning women and benevolent organizations, one that can be followed in Ginzberg's and Boylan's footnotes.

5. See Carroll Smith-Rosenberg, "The Female World of Love and Ritual: Relations Between Women in Nineteenth-Century America," in Carroll Smith-Rosenberg, *Disorderly Conduct*, 53–76; and Nancy F. Cott, *The Bonds of Womanhood: Woman's Sphere in New England, 1780–1835* (New Haven, 1977), 160–96.

6. See, for instance, Thomas Dublin, *Women at Work: The Transformation of Work and Community in Lowell, Massachusetts, 1826–1860* (New York, 1979); and Christine Stansell, *City of Women: Sex and Class in New York, 1789–1860* (New York, 1986).

7. For discussions of alternative early Christian beliefs relating to gender, see the works of Elaine Pagels, most conveniently *The Gnostic Gospels* (New York, 1979) and *Adam, Eve, and the Serpent* (New York, 1989). Not surprisingly, feminist writers of the present day have explored the pre-Christian past in order to historicize patriarchy or, more boldly, to imagine a "golden age" in which a matriarchy typified human society. See Gerda Lerner, *The Creation of Patriarchy* (New York, 1986), and Marija A. Gimbutas, *The Goddesses and Gods of Old Europe, 6500–3500 B.C.: Myths and Cult Images*, rev. ed. (London, 1982). See Riane Eisler, *The Chalice and the Blade: Our History, Our Future* (San Francisco, 1987), for a popular polemic based on some of this research. As we shall see, the exploration of woman's past was also a vital element in nineteenth-century feminism.

8. See, for instance, Fox and Fell from Margaret Hope Bacon, *Mothers of Feminism: The Story of Quaker Women in America* (San Francisco, 1969).

9. For convenient general introductions to Quaker women in American history, see *ibid.* and Mary Maples Dunn, "Women of Light," in Carol Ruth Berkin and Mary Beth Norton, eds., *Women of America: A History* (Boston, 1979), 114–36.

10. No wonder, then, that on the title page of Margaret Fell's *Women's Speaking Justified, Proved and Allowed of by the Scriptures* (1666) the very first epigraph is from Acts 2:17: "*And it shall come to pass, in the last dayes*, saith the Lord, I will pour out of my Spirit upon all Flesh; your sons and your daughters shall prophesy" (italics mine). Reproduced in Margaret Hope Bacon, *Mothers of Feminism*, 14. A typo on the original labels the quote Acts 2:27.

11. See, for general treatment of the Shakers, such standard sources as Edward Deming Andrews, *The People Called Shakers: A Search for the Perfect Society* (New York, 1953), and Marguerite Fellows Melcher, *The Shaker Adventure* (Princeton, 1941).

12. The most easily accessible short account of Wilkinson' movement is Sydney E. Ahlstrom, *A Religious History of the American People* (Garden City, N.Y., 1975; orig. ed. 1972), I, 597–99.

13. For Mary Wollstonecraft, see Mrs. Julian Marshall, ed., *The Life and Letters of Mary Wollstonecraft* (New York, 1970; reprint of orig. 1889 ed.). For Fanny Wright, see Celia Morris Eckhardt, *Fanny Wright: Rebel in America* (Cambridge, Mass., 1984).

14. Ruth H. Bloch, "The Gendered Meanings of Virtue in Revolutionary

America," *Signs: Journal of Women in Culture and Society* 13, no. 1, pp. 37–58, quote from 56. Bloch notes that the American version of this culture, quite understandably, depended heavily on English models and even borrowed from the continental Europe. See also Bloch's earlier article, "Untangling the Roots of Modern Sex Roles: A Survey of Four Centuries of Change," *ibid.* 4, no. 2, pp. 237–52.

15. Elias Boudinot, "An Oration," delivered at Elizabeth Town, New Jersey, 4 July 1793, as quoted in Judith Apter Klinghoffer and Lois Elkins, "'The Petticoat Electors': Women's Suffrage in New Jersey, 1776–1807," *Journal of the Early Republic* 12, no. 2 (Summer 1992), 174.

16. Judith Apter Klinghoffer and Lois Elkins, "'The Petticoat Electors'"; Linda Kerber, *Women of the Republic: Intellect and Ideology in Revolutionary America* (Chapel Hill, 1980); Ruth H. Bloch, "The Gendered Meanings of Virtue in Revolutionary America."

17. Here I am indebted to the pioneering discussion of women and education in the post-Revolutionary period in Linda Kerber, *Women of the Republic*, 185–231.

18. *Ibid.*, 210–30, quotes from 211, 230.

19. Murray, from articles in *Gleaner* (1798) but written before, in *ibid.*, 205.

20. *Ibid.*

21. For an excellent overview and interpretation of the founding and cultural place of women's colleges in the United States, see Helen Lefkowitz Horowitz, *Alma Mater: Design and Experience in the Women's Colleges from Their Nineteenth-Century Beginnings to the 1930s* (New York, 1984).

22. See Christine Stansell, *City of Women*, for interesting variations on this theme. See Mary P. Ryan, *Cradle of the Middle Class*, and Nancy A. Hewitt, *Women's Activism and Social Change: Rochester, New York, 1822–1872* (Ithaca, 1984), for important interpretations of the different reasons why, and ways in which, women of different classes and sects became involved in benevolent and reform causes.

23. Garrisons, *Garrison*, II, 85–86.

24. *Ibid.*, II, 156–57. In a footnote, the sons reported that forty years after the fact, at a Woman's Suffrage meeting, Abbey Kelley Foster reminded him of the obscure quote. Garrison replied: "Whereas I was blind, now I see."

25. William A. Alcott, *The Moral Philosophy of Courtship and Marriage, Designed as a Companion to the "Physiology of Marriage" by the Same Author* (Boston, 1859), 15; *The Young Housekeeper, or Thoughts on Food and Cookery* (Boston, 1838), 21, 25, 24, 35–37.

26. Sylvester Graham, *Lectures on the Science of Human Life*, II, 455–56. See also Stephen Nissenbaum, *Sex, Diet, and Debility*, 8–9, for his use of this quote and for his connection of Graham's idealization of the mother with the physiologist's own unhappy childhood.

27. This section on Catharine Beecher depends heavily on two excellent works. Kathryn Kish Sklar, *Catharine Beecher: A Study in American Domesticity* (New Haven, 1973), is one of a small group of pioneering studies that has retained its narrative and interpretive freshness even as the literature on women's history has built upon it (hereafter referred to as Sklar, *Beecher*). Jeanne Boydston, Mary Kelley, and Anne Margolis, *The Limits of Sisterhood: The Beecher Sisters on Women's Rights and Woman's Sphere* (Chapel Hill, 1988) views Catharine and her sisters in a comparative dimension.

28. Sklar, *Beecher*, 28.

29. Quoted in *ibid.*, 37.

30. Catharine Beecher to Edward Beecher, 23 August 1828, as excerpted in Jeanne Boydston, Mary Kelley, and Anne Margolis, *The Limits of Sisterhood*, 41–42.

31. Quoted in Sklar, *Beecher*, 76.

32. Catharine E. Beecher, *Suggestions Respecting Improvements in Education, Presented to the Trustees of the Hartford Female Seminary* (Hartford, 1829).

33. Sklar, *Beecher*, 99.

34. Catharine E. Beecher, *The Elements of Mental and Moral Philosophy, Founded upon Experience, Reason, and the Bible* (Hartford, 1831). See Sklar, *Beecher*, 290–91, n8, for a brief discussion of the context of the book's publication within American moral philosophy.

35. What follows depends greatly on the discussion of *Elements of Mental and Moral Philosophy* in Sklar, *Beecher*, 80–89. As Sklar points out, Beecher noted later that she had read "Locke, Reid, Steward, Brown and other works in English," a fair sampling of the Scottish school. Beecher, *Reminiscences*, quoted in *ibid.*, 290, note 8.

36. Beecher was writing at a time of deep interest in the question of moral science and philosophy. Her work preceded two classics in American culture: Francis Wayland, *Elements of Moral Science* (New York, 1835); and Horace Bushnell, *Views of Christian Nurture, and of Subjects Adjacent Thereto* (Hartford, 1847). See Donald H. Meyer, *The Instructed Conscience: The Shaping of the American National Ethic* (Philadelphia, 1972), for a treatment of the broader context of these works.

37. Lydia Maria Child to Lucy Osgood, 26 March 1847, in Patricia G. Holland and Milton Meltzer, eds., Francine Krasno, assoc. ed., *The Collected Correspondence of Lydia Maria Child 1817–1880* (Millwood, N. Y., 1980), Card 25, Letter 705 (Microform).

38. Child to John Weiss, Wayland, 15 April 1863, in Child, *Selected Letters*, 424.

39. Child to Convers Francis, Norridgewock, Maine, September 1817, in *ibid.*, 2.

40. Child to Convers Francis, Gardiner, Maine, 31 May 1820, in *ibid.*, 2.

41. *Ibid.*, 3; Child to Theodore Tilton, Wayland, 27 May 1866, in *ibid.*, 460.

42. Child to Rufus Wilmot Griswold, [October? 1846?], in *ibid.*, 232; *Hobomok, A Tale of Early Times* (Boston, 1824). It is accessible in a modern edition as part of Carolyn Karcher, ed., *"Hobomok" and Other Writings on Indians. Lydia Maria Child* (New Brunswick, 1986). She followed the surprisingly successful *Hobomok* with a less finished and less well received novel, *The Rebels; or, Boston Before the Revolution* (Boston, 1825). *The Rebels* unfolded several romantic tales against the backdrop of religious developments in the decades after the Great Awakening, when a developing anger against England led to the first cries for independence. While celebrating New England's role in the Revolution (her grandfather had been at the Battle of Lexington and Concord), she skewered the well-named character of Dr. Mather Byles, a hard-edged Orthodox minister who found ways of offending virtually every person with whom he had contact.

43. I should note at the outset that Carolyn Karcher's provocative essay introducing her edition of *Hobomok* provides a very different interpretation than presented below. A sample of her basic thesis will suffice: "What dictates the plot of

Hobomok is not its author's awareness of racial issues, but her rebellion against patriarchy. The result is a revolutionary insight into the connection between male dominance and white supremacy. This insight suggested to Child the central theme of *Hobomok* and indeed of her entire life as a reformer and writer: interracial marriage, symbolizing both the natural alliance between white women and people of color, and the natural resolution of America's racial and sexual contradictions" (xx). Karcher also includes a plot summary deeply influenced by her argument and unfortunately less useful in tracing other themes. While I recognize certain tendencies that Karcher identifies, especially in regard to the role of women but less so as women relate to Indians, my feeling is that she oversimplifies a very complex web of feelings and associations present in the novel. The interested reader should read *Hobomok* itself. William S. Osborne, *Lydia Maria Child* (Boston, 1980), 39–54, provides a more balanced summary, but Osborne's concentration on literary judgments makes his approach less useful to more broadly cultural or historical themes.

44. Carolyn Karcher, ed., *"Hobomok" and Other Writings on Indians. Lydia Maria Child*, 47–48.

45. *Ibid.*, 75–76.

46. Karcher notes this as well. See *ibid.*, xxiv. At the time of *Hobomok*'s writing, Emerson was going through a painful period of spiritual struggle. He had become tantalized by Hume's skepticism and rejection of religion, even as he sought some way out of what he considered a spiritual dead end. See Evelyn Barish, *Emerson: The Roots of Prophecy* (Princeton, 1989), 99–118. One can only wonder what ideas passed between Maria and Emerson in Convers's living room in Watertown.

47. Carolyn Karcher, ed., *"Hobomok" and Other Writings on Indians. Lydia Maria Child*, 34.

48. I am indebted to Michael Davitt Bell's interpretation of themes in the historical romance in early nineteenth-century America for this interpretation. *Hobomok* was one of the pioneers of a genre that pitted fathers against daughters and showed Indians as exemplars of savage but pure religion. See Michael Davitt Bell, *Hawthorne and the Historical Romance of New England* (Princeton, 1971), *passim*, but esp. 85–104.

49. Child to Convers Francis, Gardiner, Maine, 31 May 1820, in Child, *Selected Letters*, 2.

50. Lydia Maria Child, diary entries for 2 December 1824 and 26 January [1825], quoted in *ibid.*, 5.

51. Extracts from diary of David Lee Child, incorporated into an unpublished memoir of his life by Lydia Maria Child, quoted in *ibid.*, 6.

52. Deborah Pickman Clifford, *Crusader for Freedom: A Life of Lydia Maria Child* (Boston, 1992), 61–70, continues the tradition of seeing David Lee Child as a rather bad catch for Maria. I came upon this work too late to treat its views comprehensively in comparison to my own, but at first perusal it does not seem strikingly different in tone from prior biographies of Child.

53. *The Frugal Housewife* (Boston, 1830); *The First Settlers of New England* (Boston, 1829); *The Mother's Book* (Boston, 1831); *The Girl's Own Book* (Boston, 1831).

54. Quotes from *The First Settlers of New England* from William S. Osborne, *Lydia Maria Child*, 135–36.

55. Child, *The Mother's Book*, 64–86, quotes on 71–72 and 65.

56. Quoted in Child, *Selected Letters*, 17.

57. Child to David Lee Child, Lancaster, [2 October 1831], in *ibid.*, 20.
58. Quoted in Carolyn Karcher, ed., *"Hobomok" and Other Writings on Indians. Lydia Maria Child*, xi.

59. *The Biographies of Madame de Staël, and Madame Roland* (Boston, 1832); *The Biographies of Lady Russell, and Madame Guyon* (Boston, 1832); *Good Wives* (Boston, 1833); *The History of the Condition of Women, In Various Ages and Nations. Volume 1: Comprising the Women of Asia and Africa; Volume 2: Comprising the Women of Europe, America, and South Sea Islands* (Boston, 1835). The *History* represented the first major attempt to understand woman's fate in a breathtakingly broad anthropological and historical frame. It will be discussed in the next chapter.

60. Child, *The Biographies of Lady Russell, and Madame Guyon*, quote from 137.
61. *Ibid.*, 141, 154, 156–57, 185–86, 197–251, 264.
62. Child, *The Biographies of Madame de Staël, and Madame Roland*, 108.
63. *Ibid.*, 255.
64. Child, *Good Wives*, xii.
65. Child to Anne Whitney, 25 May 1879, in Child, *Selected Letters*, 558.
66. Child, *An Appeal in Favor of that Class of Americans Called Africans* (New York, 1836; rpt. New York, 1986, intr. by James M. McPherson), 172, 194 *passim.* This edition seems to be unchanged from the original 1833 edition, published in Boston by Ticknor and Fields.
67. *Ibid.*, title page and iii.
68. Child to Anne Whitney, 25 May 1879, in Child, *Selected Letters*, 558.
69. Child, *History of the Condition of Women in Various Ages and Nations*, I, preface.
70. *Ibid.*, II, 139.
71. *Ibid.*, 145–48.
72. *Ibid.*, 208–9, 255–58. However, Child emphasized the deleterious state of black women, both slave and free (262–63).
73. *Ibid.*, 211.
74. See Robert H. Abzug, *Passionate Liberator*, 74–122.
75. Catharine E. Beecher, *Letters on the Difficulties of Religion* (Hartford, 1836), 22–23. These passages can be most easily found in Jeanne Boydston, Mary Kelley, and Anne Margolis, *The Limits of Sisterhood*, 236–37.
76. *Ibid.*

Chapter IX
Woman's Rights and Schism

1. Although my account of the Grimkés is based on long familiarity with their lives, I wish at the outset to record my great debt to Gerda Lerner's pioneering dual biography of the sisters. Its narrative verve and keen insight sustain its place as the starting point for any serious inquiry concerning these extraordinary women. See Gerda Lerner, *The Grimké Sisters of South Carolina: Rebels Against Slavery* (Boston, 1967), hereafter referred to as Lerner, *Grimké Sisters.* Also useful is Katharine DuPre Lumpkin, *The Emancipation of Angelina Grimké* (Chapel Hill, 1974), hereafter referred to as Lumpkin, *Emancipation*, although Lumpkin's tendency to view Angelina as a victim of both Sarah's and Theodore Weld's manipulation distorts what is in fact a very complicated psychological drama. See also Gerda Lerner's

new book, *The Creation of Feminist Consciousness: From the Middle Ages to 1870* (New York, 1993), 159–63, for a complementary approach to my own; it appeared too late for me to make comprehensive use of it in this chapter.

2. Lumpkin, *Emancipation*, 9–10.

3. Mary S. Grimké to her daughter Angelina, [n.d.] July 1838, quoted in *ibid.*, 10. The Grimké sisters' main biographers differ as to the mother's character. Lumpkin attributed to her "the tight reserve, the unyielding pride, the stern sense of duty that would let nothing sway her" that also were her "main strength" after her husband's death. See *ibid.* Gerda Lerner characterized her as "indulgent and lenient toward her children and, as her later correspondence reveals . . . temperamentally unfit for self-righteous lecturing." See Lerner, *Grimké Sisters*, 397, n17.

4. *Ibid.*, 9.

5. See *ibid.*, 42–49, quote on 45, for the best account of Sarah's journey with her dying father.

6. *Ibid.*, 50–59.

7. *Ibid.*, 63. See also Sarah's evocative dream about her relationship with Morris after the marriage proposal as quoted in *ibid.*

8. My concentration on a religious interpretation of Grimké's decision not to marry clearly reflects the theme of this book and the seriousness with which I take religious choices. I do not deny, however, that there are other ways of looking at the matter. Gerda Lerner, for instance, raises a contrast to the happily married Lucretia Mott to show that Sarah's insistence on giving up "earthly love" to better serve her faith was "somewhat threadbare." Rather, Lerner concludes: "Much more likely Sarah was held back from marriage by a combination of feminism and her obsession with self-renunciation." See *ibid.*, 64–65. Although Lerner's use of "feminism" seems anachronistic, surely Sarah saw the limitations marriage would bring. More problematic is Lerner's reduction of her piety to an "obsession with self-renunciation."

9. Angelina to Anna Grimké Frost, 18 March 1828, quoted in *ibid.*, 28–29; and Angelina to Anna Grimké Frost, 17 March 1828, quoted in Lumpkin, *Emancipation*, 24–25. For later memories, see Theodore Dwight Weld, *In Memory: Angelina Grimké Weld* (Boston, 1880), 37, 47–48, and *passim.*

10. Lerner, *Grimké Sisters*, 71–73; Lumpkin, *Emancipation*, 28–37. Unfortunately, Lumpkin colors an otherwise fine account of this period by investing in Sarah an almost diabolical drive to control her younger sister.

11. *Ibid.*, 37–39; Lerner, *Grimké Sisters*, 74.

12. Angelina to the Reverend William McDowell, 21 May 1829, as quoted in Lumpkin, *Emancipation*, 55; diary entry of 31 December 1829, quoted in *ibid.*

13. For more on the Hicksite controversy, see Robert W. Doherty, *The Hicksite Separation: A Sociological Analysis of Religious Schism in Early Nineteenth-Century America* (New Brunswick, 1967); and H. Larry Ingle, *Quakers in Conflict: the Hicksite Reformation* (Knoxville, 1986).

14. The complicated matter of Sarah's frustrations is dealt with well in Lerner, *Grimké Sisters*, 59–65.

15. Lumpkin, *Emancipation*, 60, 62; Lerner, *Grimké Sisters*, 97–100; Sklar, *Beecher*, 98–100.

16. *Ibid.*, 97–100; Lumpkin, *Emancipation*, 62–67.

17. Diary of Angelina Grimké, [May] 1833, as quoted in *ibid.*, 69. She was also pleased, ironically, by the fact that the Bettles refused to receive her mourning call, thus relieving her of deeper involvement with the family after the son's death. There was no love lost between Edward's parents and Angelina.

18. Lerner, *Grimké Sisters*, 108–10.

19. *Ibid.*, 118.

20. *Ibid.*; diary of Angelina Grimké, 12 May 1834, reprinted in Larry Ceplair, ed., *The Public Years of Sarah and Angelina Grimké: Selected Writings, 1835–1839* (New York, 1989), 19–20 (hereafter cited as Ceplair, *Public Years*); Lerner, *Grimké Sisters*, 109.

21. Angelina to Sarah Grimké, 27 September 1835, as reprinted in Catherine H. Birney, *The Grimké Sisters: Sarah and Angelina Grimké, the First American Women Advocates of Abolition and Woman's Rights* (Boston, 1885; rpt. Westport, Conn., 1969), 126–28. It is also reprinted in Ceplair, *Public Years*, 27–29.

22. Angelina E. Grimké to William Lloyd Garrison, 30 August 1835, as printed in the *Liberator*, 19 September 1835, and reprinted in Ceplair, *Public Years*, 24–27.

23. *Ibid.*

24. In turn, Angelina accused her sister of setting "the opinion of my friends" above duty to God. Lumpkin, *Emancipation*, 84–87, quotes on 85–86. See also Lerner, *Grimké Sisters*, 124–25.

25. Child to the Boston Female Anti-Slavery Society, [October?-before 19 November 1835), in Child, *Selected Letters*, 40. This letter appeared in Maria Weston Chapman, *Right and Wrong in Boston* (Boston, 1836), 90–94.

26. Angelina Emily Grimké, *Appeal to the Christian Women of the South* (New York, 1836), most readily available in Ceplair, *Public Years*, 36–79.

27. *Ibid.*, 67–68.

28. *Ibid.*

29. *Ibid.*, 58–59.

30. Sarah Grimké to Weld [New York, about March 10, 1837], in *Weld-Grimké Letters*, I, 373. See also Lerner, *Grimké Sisters*, 141–42. Ultimately, Sarah even wrote a tract highly critical of Quaker racial attitudes, "Letter on the Subject of Prejudice Amongst the Society of Friends in the United States" (Boston Public Library Manuscripts). She sent it to Weld to see if the Anti-Slavery Society would publish it, and he refused. He wrote to her: "I think it would excite prejudice among the Quakers against the Executive Committee if your address to them were to be published at the A.S. office or kept for sale at the Repository. It would compromise that neutrality which ought to be observed. The anti-slavery committee *as such* ought not to have anything to do with *denominational* conflicts." See *Weld-Grimké Letters*, 373 and 373n2, and Weld to Angelina and Sarah Grimké, New York, 22 July 1837, in *ibid.*, 414.

31. At the time, this may have seemed less important to Weld than the humorous reprimand from Sarah's sister, the object of Weld's yet-undeclared love: "Angelina sends her love and says until thou writes her a letter in ink she shall not answer it, as she considers it [i.e., a letter in pencil] very disrespectful, and as a consistent assertor of the rights of women she cannot submit to such indignities." Sarah Grimké to Weld, "Samuel Philbricks delightful farm near Boston," 11 June 1837, in *Weld-Grimké Letters*, I, 401–2.

32. Sklar, *Beecher*, 99.

33. Catharine E. Beecher, *An Essay on Slavery and Abolitionism, with Reference to the Duty of American Females* (Philadelphia, 1837); quote from substantive excerpts in Jeanne Boydston, Mary Kelley, and Anne Margolis, *The Limits of Sisterhood*, 127.

34. *Ibid.*, 128. Beecher did say that females could, within the bounds of their own sphere of exercising private influence, try to persuade the males closest to them to petition legislators. See *ibid.*

35. Angelina E. Grimké, *Letters to Catherine E. Beecher, in Reply to an Essay on Slavery and Abolitionism, Addressed to A. E. Grimké. Revised by the author* (Boston, 1838). Either Grimké or the typesetter misspelled "Catharine," even as in her own book Beecher gave Angelina the middle initial "D." The most accessible modern source for the pamphlet is Ceplair, *Public Years*, 146–204.

36. *Ibid.*, 188–90. Thus Angelina ironically hit upon one of the major if hidden themes of Beecher's broader vision of womanhood, which she nonetheless rejected wholesale in favor of spiritual egalitarianism.

37. *Ibid.*, 192–94.

38. *Ibid.*, 194–95. Angelina was not the first woman to learn something about woman's rights by engaging in antislavery activities, nor the first to write about it. The most important white exemplar of such an attitude was the Quaker abolitionist-poet Elizabeth Chandler, who died in 1834 after having spent eight years writing for Lundy's *Genius of Universal Emancipation* and Garrison's *Liberator*. At one point she wrote: "It is a restitution of *our own* rights for which we ask:—their cause is our cause—they are one with us in sex and nature." However, Chandler's conception of these rights stayed firmly within the traditional ideas of the spheres. See Blanche Glassman Hersh, *The Slavery of Sex*, 7–10, quote from 8.

39. Ceplair, *Public Years*, 195–97. See below for a discussion of Sarah Grimké's *Letters on the Equality of the Sexes*, from which she borrowed in order to make this point.

40. *Ibid.*, 197.

41. Sarah M. Grimké, *Letters on the Equality of the Sexes and the Condition of Woman, Addressed to Mary S. Parker, President of the Boston Female Anti-Slavery Society* (Boston, 1838). There are a number of modern editions (including Ceplair, *Public Years*), but references are to Elizabeth Ann Bartlett, ed., *Sarah Grimké: Letters on the Equality of the Sexes and Other Essays* (New Haven, 1988) for Bartlett's insightful introduction and for the inclusion of several unpublished essays by Sarah previously only available at the Clements Library, University of Michigan, in manuscript. Hereafter this source is referred to as Bartlett, *Grimké Essays*.

42. "Letter I: The Original Equality of Woman," Amesbury, 11 July 1837, in *ibid.*, 31–32.

43. *Ibid.*

44. *Ibid.*, 32–33.

45. *Ibid.*, 33.

46. "Letter II: Woman Subject Only to God," Newburyport, 17 July 1837, in *ibid.*, 34–36.

47. *Ibid.*, 36–37.

48. "General Association of Massachusetts to the Churches Under Their Care,"

in *New England Spectator*, 12 July 1837, as excerpted in Ceplair, *Public Years*, 211–12.

49. "Letter III: The Pastoral Letter of the General Association of Congregational Ministers of Massachusetts," Haverhill, July 1837, in Bartlett, *Grimké Essays*, 37–38.

50. *Ibid.*, 38–40.

51. *Ibid.*, 40–41; the verse quoted is Psalm 27:1.

52. "Letter IV, Social Intercourse of the Sexes," Andover, 27 July 1837; "Letter V: Condition in Asia and Africa," Groton, 4 August 1837; "Letter VI: Women in Asia and Africa," Groton, 15 August 1837; and "Letter VII: Condition in Some Parts of Europe and America," Brookline, 22 August 1837; in *ibid.*, 41–44, 44–47, 47–51, 51–56.

53. "Letter VIII: On the Condition of Women in the United States," in *ibid.*, 56–58.

54. *Ibid.*, 59–61.

55. "Letter IX: Heroism of Women—Women in Authority," Brookline, 25 August 1837; "Letter X: Intellect of Woman," Brookline, August 1837; "Letter XI: Dress of Woman," Brookline, September 1837; "Letter XII: Legal Disabilities of Women," Concord, 6 September 1837; "Letter XIII: Relation of Husband and Wife," Brookline, September 1837; "Letter XIV: Ministry of Women," Brookline, September 1837; "Letter XV: Man Equally Guilty with Woman in the Fall," Uxbridge, 20 October 1837; in *ibid.*, 62–64, 64–67, 67–71, 71–77, 77–85, 85–95, 96–103; quotes from 84–85.

56. Sarah Grimké to Weld, "Samuel Philbricks delightful farm near Boston," 11 June 1837, in *Weld-Grimké Letters*, I, 402.

57. Lewis Perry, *Radical Abolitionism: Anarchy and the Government of God in Antislavery Thought* (Ithaca, 1973), 65.

58. Robert H. Abzug, *Passionate Liberator*, 125.

59. I rely on the account of Bertram Wyatt-Brown, *Lewis Tappan and the Evangelical War Against Slavery*, 167–74.

60. The present discussion of "non-resistance" serves only to shape the context of the woman question. A more extended consideration of the implications of non-resistance will appear in my next volume on reform.

61. See Charles DeBenedetti, *The Peace Movement in American History* (Bloomington, 1980), 32–56.

62. William Ladd to Henry C. Wright, 23 July 1836, and Henry C. Wright Journal, XXX, 66–68, 2 August 1836, as quoted in Lewis Perry, *Radical Abolitionism*, 60–61. For excellent complete treatments of these questions and for the life of Henry C. Wright, see not only *Radical Abolitionism* but also Lewis Perry, *Childhood, Marriage, and Reform*.

63. Lydia Maria Child to Caroline Weston, Northampton, 7 March 1839, in Child, *Selected Letters*, 109.

64. For proslavery use of the Bible by northern as well as southern ministers, see Larry Tise, *Proslavery: A History of the Defense of Slavery in America, 1701–1840* (Athens, Ga., 1987).

65. John Greenleaf Whittier, "The Pastoral Letter," quoted in Lerner, *Grimké Sisters*, 191.

66. Manuscript Memorandum (Bacon v. Miss Grimké), 22 December 1838, and other material, in Dwight L. Dumond, ed., *Letters of James Gillespie Birney, 1831–1857*, I, 478–81.

67. Weld to Angelina and Sarah Grimké, New York, 22 July 1837, in *Weld-Grimké Letters*, I, 411–14.

68. Angelina Grimké to Weld, Groton, Mass., 12 August [1837], in *ibid.*, 414–18.

69. Weld to Sarah and Angelina Grimké, New York, 15 August 1837, in *ibid.*, 425–27, quote from 427; John Greenleaf Whittier to Sarah and Angelina Grimké, "A-S Office N.Y.C.," 14 August 1837, in *ibid.*, 424.

70. Angelina Grimké to Theodore D. Weld and J. G. Whittier, Brookline, 20 August [1837], in *ibid.*, 427–32, quotes from 428, 430.

71. Lydia Maria Child to William Lloyd Garrison, Boston, 2 September 1839, in Child, *Selected Letters*, 123.

72. Sarah Douglass to Charles K. Whipple, April 26, 1841, as quoted in Aileen S. Kraditor, *Means and Ends in American Abolitionism: Garrison and His Critics on Strategy and Tactics, 1834–1850* (New York, 1969), 44. I am indebted to Kraditor's pioneering treatment of the woman question, and I largely agree with her framing of specific issues. My interpretation emphasizes the tenacity of religious archetypes and the seriousness of spiritual issues, whereas hers focuses on strategic calculations among various reformers. Despite this difference of emphasis, I have found both her research and her point of view extremely useful.

73. Sarah M. and Angelina E. Grimké to Amos A. Phelps, Groton, Mass., 3 August 1837, in Ceplair, *Public Years*, 273–75.

74. *Ibid.*

75. Sarah and Angelina Grimké to Henry C. Wright, Brookline, Mass., 27 August 1837, in *Weld-Grimké Letters*, I, 436–41, quote from 437.

76. Angelina E. Grimké to Jane Smith, Townsend, Mass., 15 September [1837], in Ceplair, *Public Years*, 289.

77. This even surprised Angelina, who noted to Jane Smith that "with regard to speaking on the rights of women, it has really be[en] wonderful to me that tho' I meet the prejudice against our speaking every where, that still in addressing our audiences I never think of introducing any thing about it." See Angelina E. Grimké to Jane Smith, Holliston, Mass., 26 October [1837], in *ibid.*, 295.

78. Angelina Grimké to Weld, Brookline, Mass., 11 February [1838], in *Weld-Grimké Letters*, II, 538.

79. *Ibid.*

80. "Speech Before the Legislative Committee of the Massachusetts Legislature," 21 February 1838, reprinted in *Liberator*, 2 March 1838, and in Lerner, *Grimké Sisters*, 371–74, quote from 371–72.

81. Quoted in *ibid.*, 233.

82. See my account in Robert H. Abzug, *Passionate Liberator*, 399–400.

83. *Ibid.*

84. *Ibid.*

85. Lerner, *Grimké Sisters*, 243–50.

86. Resolution adopted at the fifth annual meeting of the Ladies New York City Anti-Slavery Society, 27 May 1840, enclosure in New York Ladies Anti-Slavery

Society to Birney, [June 1840], in Dwight L. Dumond, ed., *Letters of James Gillespie Birney 1831–1857*, I, 579–80.

87. I will deal with communitarianism, spiritualism, Transcendentalism, and kindred movements in my next volume on reform.

88. Lydia Maria Child, *Aspirations of the World. A Chain of Opals* (Boston, 1881; orig. ed. 1878), 43–44.

89. Child to Theodore Dwight Weld, Wayland, 10 July 1880, in Child, *Selected Letters*, 562–64.

Index

Abolitionism and antislavery, vii, 7–8, 12, 127–62, 184, 199–202, 209–29
   Benjamin Rush and, 16–17, 25
   and temperance argument, 88–89
Adams, Charles Francis, 177
Adams, John Quincy, 12, 28, 141
Alcott, Amos Bronson, 153–4
Alcott, William Andrus, 4, 163, 164, 169–71, 172, 173–82ff., 189
   The Boys' Guide to Usefulness, 170
   early years, 169–70
   Moral Reformer, 170
   writings, 170–72
Alexander, Jeffrey C., 233 n. 10
Allen, Richard, 135
Alvord, John, 122, 225
American and Foreign Anti-Slavery Society, 227
American Anti-Slavery Society, 161, 183, 212, 224, 227
American Bible Society, 108

American Board of Missions, 53
American Colonization Society, 61, 140, 144, 159
American Education Society, 108, 118–19
American Peace Society, 209, 221, 226
American Physiological Society, 175
American Revolution, 5, 11–12, 16–18, 31, 32, 35, 36–37, 131, 174
American Seaman's Friend Society, 108
American Society for Colonizing the Free People of Color of the United States (American Colonization Society). *See* Colonization
American Society for the Promotion of Temperance (American Temperance Society). *See* Temperance

American Tract Society, 89, 108

Ames, Fisher, 136–37

Andover Mechanical Association. *See* Manual Labor movement

Andover Moral Society (1814), 90

Antislavery. *See* Abolitionism and antislavery

Appeal to the Colored Citizens of the World. . . . *See* Walker, David

Anti-Slavery Convention of American Women, 212, 227

Armstrong, Rev. Lebbeus, 84–85

Asbury, Francis, 132

Ashworth, John, 231 n. 2

Atwater, Jeremiah, 60

Auburn Seminary, 69

Bacon, Rev. Leonard, 152, 222

Banner, Lois, 241 n. 76

Baptists, 6, 31, 33, 44, 57, 64, 67, 69, 70–71, 84, 111, 117, 132, 137, 186

Bartlett, Elizabeth Ann, 273 n. 41

Beecher, Catharine E., 188, 190–93, 195, 199, 202–3, 204-5, 208–9, 212–14, 223, 225
 career in education, 191–92
 early years, 190–91
 The Elements of Mental and Moral Philosophy (1831), 192
 An Essay on Slavery and Abolition (1837), 213–15
 Letters on the Difficulties of Religion (1836), 202
 religious frustration, 191
 Suggestions Respecting Improvements in Education (1829), 191–92
 To the Benevolent Women . . . (1829), 192
 views on woman's role, 192–93

Beecher, Charles, 122

Beecher, Edward, 123

Beecher, Harriet, 208

Beecher, Henry Ward, 167, 168, 190

Beecher, Lyman, 36, 38–56, 59, 60, 64–65, 70–71, 74–75, 83, 90, 102, 106, 109, 110, 111, 113, 117, 129, 138, 139, 142, 144, 152,

153, 155, 160, 174, 180, 190, 191, 192, 202
 The Bible a Code of Laws (1817), 49
 The Building of Waste Places (1814), 48–49
 The Design, Rights, and Duties of Local Churches (1819), 49
 early career as minister, 39
 early years, 38–39
 The Faith Once Delivered to the Saints (1823), 51–53
 The Memory of Our Fathers (1827), 54–56
 minister at Litchfield, Connecticut, 39–53
 moral societies and Beecher, 40
 The Practicality of Suppressing Vice . . . (1803), 40, 44
 A Reformation of Morals Practicable and Indispensable (1812), 44–47
 on religious toleration, 49–50
 The Remedy for Duelling (1806), 42–44
 Resources of the Adversary . . . (1827), 53–54
 Six Sermons on Intemperance (1825–27), 86–90, 139
 and Timothy Dwight, 39, 49

Belknap, Jeremy, 26, 27

Bell, Michael Davitt, 269 n. 48

Beman, Nathan S. S., 59–64, 69, 70, 73–74, 80, 90, 107, 117, 139
 early years, 60–61
 Four Sermons on the Doctrine of the Atonement, (1825), 63–64
 metahistorical vision, 61–64

Benezet, Anthony, 16–17

Benson, George W., 159

Benson, Henry E., 178

Bercovitch, Sacvan, 237 n. 7

Berger, Peter, 233 n. 6

Bettle, Edward, 209, 210

Bichat, Xavier, 166

Birney, James G., 159, 183, 222

Bissell, Josiah, 114–15

Blakely, William Addison, 252 n. 20

Bloch, Ruth, 187, 233 n. 7, 236 n. 26, 239 n. 28, 266 n. 14

Blumin, Stuart, 243 n. 2
Bourne, Rev. George, 134, 135, 151
  The Book and Slavery Irreconcilable
    (1816), 134, 151
Boylan, Anne M., 265 n. 4
Boyle, James, 220
Breckenridge, W. L., 101–2
Brietenbach, William Kern, 238 n. 9
  and n. 12
Brook Farm, 228
Broussais, François J. V., 165–66
Brown, Richard D., 238 n. 8
Buddhism, 164
Budinot, Elias, 187
Buffum, Arnold, 159
Bushman, Richard L., 237 n. 5
Bushnell, Horace, 21
Buxton, Thomas Fowell, 145–46

Caldwell, Dr. Charles, 167
Campbell, Alexander, 31–32, 63
Campbellites, 58, 75
Catholics and Catholicism, ix, 51,
  53, 70, 97, 98, 164
Channing, William Ellery, 109, 138
Chapman, Maria Weston, 159, 184,
  224–25, 226, 227
Charles II (England), 198
Cherokee Indians, 189, 192, 196
Child, David Lee, 196, 197, 199–200
Child, Lydia Maria, 181, 183, 184,
  190, 193–202, 204–5, 209–10,
  221–22, 224, 229
  and abolitionism, 199–202
  Aspirations of the World (1878), 229
  compared to Catharine Beecher,
    195–96
  early years, 193–94
  The First Settlers of New England
    (1829), 196–97
  The Frugal Housewife (1830), 196,
    199, 200
  Good Wives (1833), 198
  *The History of Women, in Various
    Ages and Nations . . .* (1835),
    201–2, 215–16, 218
  Hobomok, 194–95
  Juvenile Miscellany, 195, 200

  The Mother's Book (1831), 197, 200
  writings, 196–98
Christian Repository (Utica), 59
"Christian" sects (sometimes Church
  of Christ), 31, 32
Christie, John W., 255 n. 16, 258 n.
  83
Church of England, 33
Clark, Dr. Billy J., 84–85
Clark, Theodore Erastus, 75
Clay, Henry, 150
Clifford, Deborah Pickman, 269 n.
  52
Cohen, Patricia Cline, 249 n. 52
Coke, Thomas, 132
Collier, Rev. William, 138, 140
Colonization, 121, 133–34, 142, 153,
  159
Colton, Calvin, 99
  Protestant Jesuitism, 99
Combe, George, 168
Congregationalists and Congrega-
  tionalism, 32–35, 58, 67, 90,
  110, 117
Connecticut Society for the Sup-
  pression of Vice and Promotion
  of Good Morals (Connecticut
  Moral Society), 47–48, 86
Cooter, Roger, 261 n. 12
Crandall, Prudence, 184

Dannenbaum, Jed, 250 n. 86
Davies, John D., 261 n. 12
Davies, Rev. Samuel, 14
Davis, Andrew Jackson, 228
Davis, David Brion, 5, 231 n. 2, 254
  n. 3
Deists and Deism, 34, 35, 37, 70,
  73
D'Elia, Donald J., 234 n. 6
Dillon, Merton L., 256 n. 18 and
  n. 20
Disestablishment, 5–6, 31–32, 47
Douglas, Mary, 171
Douglass, Sarah, 224, 226
Duelling, 42–44
Dumond, Dwight L., 255 n. 16, 258
  n. 83

Dwight, Sereno, 49
Dwight, Timothy, 21, 35–38, 39,
    49, 94, 136, 187
  · "A Dissertation on the History of
    the Bible" (1772), 35
  early years, 35–36
  Greenfield Hill (1794), 37
  theology, 36–38
  *Travels in New England and New
    York* (1821–23), 94
Dyer, Mary, 186

Edwards, Rev. Jonathan, 35, 117
Edwards, Rev. Justin, 90–93, 102,
    103, 105, 106
  The Well-Conducted Farm (1825),
    92. *See also* Temperance
Eisler, Riane, 266 n. 7
Emancipation Proclamation, 161
Embargo Act of 1807, 44, 83, 137
Emerson, Ralph Waldo, vii, 3–4,
    194, 195, 198, 228
Enlightenment, 12–13, 19, 130
Episcopalians, 44, 49, 51, 70, 73, 84,
    98
Essig, James D., 255 n. 5, 256 n. 23
Evarts, Jeremiah, 118
Everett, Edward, 139

Federalists, 27, 34, 43, 47, 136–37,
    138–39
Fellenberg, Philip Emanuel von, 117
Female Missionary Society, 66
Fenelon, 198
Finley, Rev. Samuel, 14
  *Christ Triumphing, and Satan Rag-
    ing* (1741), 14
  On the Madness of Mankind, 28
Finney, Charles Grandison, 59, 64–
    75, 101, 103, 110, 121–22, 181,
    191
  apprenticeship in law, 65
  compared to Lyman Beecher, 64–
    66, 70–71
  conversion, 64–66
  early years, 64–65
  and Female Missionary Society,
    66

and George W. Gale, 65–66
  Memoirs, 64–66
  and "new measures," 74, 75
  and Oneida county revivals, 69–75
  and Troy revival, 73–74
Finneyites, 69–75, 105, 120, 191
First Annual Convention of People
    of Color, 159
Fisher, Alexander, 191
Forten, James, 134
Foster, Charles I., 241 n. 76
Fourier, Charles, 228
Fowler, Lorenzo Niles, 168
Fowler, Orson Squire, 4, 163, 164,
    166–69, 171, 173–82ff. *See also*
    Phrenology
Fox, George, 186
Francis, Convers, 193–94, 196
Francis, David, 193
Franklin, Benjamin, *Autobiography*,
    169
Free Churches, 110, 122
Freehling, William W., 258 n. 67
Freethinkers, 49, 51, 58, 64, 70, 98
French Revolution, 27, 28, 32, 199
Frost, Anna, 226
Frost, Rev. John, 68, 70, 118

Gale, George W., 65–66, 122
Gall, Franz Joseph, 163, 167, 176
Garrison, Abijah and Fanny, 136
Garrison, James, 136, 137
Garrison, William Lloyd, 3, 124,
    129–62, 165, 177, 178, 179, 180,
    181, 189, 196, 199–200, 209–10,
    221, 225, 226, 227
  and Benjamin Lundy, 140–42,
    145–46, 148–49
  *A Brief Sketch of the Trial of
    William Lloyd Garrison*, 150
  and David Walker's *Appeal*, 147–
    59, 156, 157
  early views on slavery, 139–42
  early years, 136–37
  and evangelical reform, 138–45
  and Federalists, 137
  Fourth of July Address (1829),
    142–45

as journalist, 129, 136–38
and *Liberator*, 151, 154–59, 183
Thoughts on African Colonization,
  158, 159
General Union for Promoting the
  Observance of the Christian
  Sabbath. *See* Sabbatarianism
Genin, Thomas Hedges, 134
Genius of Universal Emancipation. See
  Lundy, Benjamin
Gimbutas, Mariza A., 266 n. 7
Ginsberg, Lori D., 265 n. 4
Glickstein, Jonathan A., 251 n. 3
Goodell, William, 177
Gordon, Andrew, 209
Graham, Sylvester, 4, 163–66, 169,
  171, 172, 173–82ff., 189
  early years, 164–65
  Thy Kindgom Come (1829), 165
Grahamism, 8, 117, 163–64, 172,
  175–76, 179, 181, 182
Grand Federal Procession, 11–12, 29,
  83
Grant, Zilpah, 188
Great Awakening, 13–14
Greeley, Horace, 177
Green, Ashbel, 26
Green, Beriah, 119–20, 159
Griffin, Clifford S., 241 n. 76
Grimké, Angelina Emily, 177, 178,
  179, 184, 190, 203, 204–28
  *An Appeal to Christian Women of
  the South* (1836), 210–11
  *An Appeal to the Women of the
  Nominally Free States* (1837),
  212, 213
  early years, 205–7
  Letters to C. E. Beecher . . .
  (1837), 213–15
Grimké, Judge John Faucheraud,
  205–6, 226
Grimké, Mary Smith, 205
Grimké, Sarah, 4, 177, 178, 184,
  190, 203, 204–28
  early years, 205–6
  *Letters on the Equality of the
  Sexes . . .* (1837), 215–19
  and "Pastoral Letter," 217

and Quakers, 206–8
Grimké, Thomas Ladd, 205, 209
Gurley, R. R., 159
Guyon, Madame, 198, 202

Halfway Covenant, 48
Hallock, Rev. William A., 92
Hamilton, Alexander, 12, 42
Hardman, Keith J., 245 n. 23
Hartford Convention, 49
Haskell, Thomas, 231 n. 2
Hawke, David Freeman, 235 n. 14
Henry, Patrick, 18, 200
Hersh, Blanche Glassman, 273 n. 38
Hewitt, Nancy, 267 n. 22
Heyrick, Elizabeth, 135, 146
  Immediate, Not Gradual Abolition
  (1824), 135, 146
Hicks, Elias, 208
Hinduism, 164
Hitchcock, Edward, 167, 177
  Dyspepsy Forstalled, 177
Home Missionary Society, 108
Hooker, Zephas, 81
Hopper, Isaac, 181
Horowitz, Helen Lefkowitz, 267 n.
  21
Hoskins, Jane, 186
Howe, Daniel Walker, 251 n. 8
Howe, Julia Ward, 162
Humphrey, Rev. Heman, 94–96,
  167
  *A Parallel Between Intemperance
  and the Slave Trade* (1828), 95–
  96, 139–40

Islam, 53

Jackson, Andrew, 53, 142
Jackson, Francis, 159
Jay's Treaty, 27
Jefferson, Thomas, 12, 20, 28, 94,
  138–39
Jeffersonians, 106, 113, 138–39, 155
Jentz, John Barkley, 253 n. 34
Jocelyn, Rev. Simeon S., 152, 159
John, Richard R., 251 n. 3 and n. 16
Johnson, Oliver, 159

Johnson, Paul, 243 n. 2, 248 n. 45, 253 n. 35
Judaism and Jews, 33, 40, 42, 43, 50–51, 53, 112, 164, 171–72
Judd, Garrit P., 117–18

Kairos (Tillich's concept of), 5
Karcher, Carolyn, 268 n. 42 and n. 43, 269 n. 46
Kelley, Abby, 227
Kerber, Linda K., 267 n. 17
King, Martin Luther, Jr., 3, 149
Knapp, Isaac, 154
Kneeland, Abner, 152–53
Kraditor, Aileen S., 275 n. 72

Ladd, William, 137, 141, 209, 221, 226
Lane Seminary, 123–24, 159–60, 177, 184, 212
Leavitt, Joshua, 177
Lee, Mother Anne, 186, 219
Lerner, Gerda, 266 n. 7, 270 n. 1, 271 n. 3 and n. 8
Liberator. *See* Garrison, William Lloyd
Liberty party, 161
Lincoln, Abraham, 129–30, 161–62
Loring, Ellis Gray, 154, 159
Lovejoy, Elijah, 178, 221
Lumpkin, Katharine DePre, 270 n. 1, 271 n. 3 and n. 10
Lundy, Benjamin, 134–35, 140–42, 145–46, 148–49, 151, 154
Lyman, Huntington, 81
Lyon, Mary, 188

McCoy, Drew R., 251 n. 4
McDowell, Rev. William, 206, 207
Madison, James, 12, 94
Malcolm, Rev. Howard, 140–41, 142
Manicheism and Manichean, 80, 99, 104
Manual labor movement, 80, 106, 116–24, 164
    and Andover Mechanical Association, 118–19
    and Oneida Institute, 120–24

and seminaries, 118–19
    Society for the Promotion of Manual Labor in Literary Institutions, 121
Marsden, George M., 260 n. 123
Massachusetts Society for the Suppression of Intemperance (MSSI). *See* Temperance
Massachusetts Whig Journal, 196
Mather, Cotton, 83, 217
Mather, Increase, 82–83
May, Samuel J., 153–54, 158–59, 200, 209
Merrill, Walter M., 256 n. 24
Methodism and Methodists, 6, 31, 44, 57, 58, 64, 67, 69, 70–71, 84, 132
Millennium and Millennialism, 12–14, 16–18, 19, 26–29, 30–75, *passim.*, 90, 91–92, 97–98, 102, 117, 120, 122, 124, 165, 186, 210–11
Miller, Perry, 29, 237 n. 7, 245 n. 26
Missouri Debates and Compromise of 1820, 53, 133, 134, 135
Moreau Temperance Society. *See* Temperance
Mormons and Mormonism, 32, 58
Morris, Israel, 206
Morris, Susannah, 186
Mott, James, 152
Mott, Lucretia, 152
Murray, Judith Sargent, 188

Nash, "Father" Daniel, 66–67, 69, 70, 72
Nash, Gary D., 255 n. 10
Nettleton, Asahel, 36
New Divinity, 57
New England Anti-Slavery Society, 200
New England, central role in reform, 5–7, 29, 31–34, 40–56, 57, 58
New England Non-Resistance Society, 221
New England Tract Society, 90–91

New Lebanon meeting (1827), 74–75, 105, 110
"New Measures," 74–75
New York Ladies Anti-Slavery Society, 227
Nissenbaum, Stephen, 165, 260 n. 2, 261 n. 5, 267 n. 26
Norton, Rev. Elijah, 69
Noyes, John Humphrey, 4, 219–20

Oberlin College, 177
O'Kelley, James, 31
Oneida County, revivals in, 66–75
Orthodoxy, 30, 32–35, 44, 49, 55, 58–59, 84, 109, 114
Otis, Harrison Gray, 137, 148

Panic of 1837, 108, 220
Park, Edwards Amasa, 119
Parker, Theodore, 194
Pennsylvania Temperance Society, 165
Perfectionism, 219–20, 222, 228
Perkins, Ephraim, 70
Perry, Lewis, 274 n. 62
Peterson, Owen, 243 n. 5
Phelps, Amos Anson, 224
Philadelphia Female Anti-Slavery Society, 209
Phrenology, viii, 8. *See also* Fowler, Orson Squire
Physiological reform, 163–82
   as neo-Mosaic law, 171–73
Pickering, Timothy, 136–37
Pierpont, John, 138, 141
Plan of Union (1801), 34, 110
Presbyterians and Presbyterianism, 32–35, 57, 58, 59–60, 63–64, 67–71, 74–75, 99, 110, 116, 117, 132, 160–61
Pugh, Sarah, 227

Quakers. *See* Society of Friends

Reform, nature of, vii–ix, 3–8
Religious pluralism, 5, 49–50
Religious virtuosos, 4, 6, 17, 31, 32–33, 110, 184, 228, 232 n. 3

Redman, Dr. John, 15
Renshaw, Charles Stuart, 121
Republicanism, 8, 12, 15–16, 26–29, 36–37, 95–96, 165
Rice, John H., 118
Rogers, John, 32
Roland, Madame, 198–99
Rorabaugh, W. J., 248 n. 45
Rosenberg, Carroll Smith, 265 n. 3
Rush, Benjamin, 11–29, 33, 36, 37, 83, 86, 94, 101, 131, 165–66, 187, 192, 221
   Address to the Inhabitants of the British Settlement in America, upon Slave-Keeping (1773), 16–17
   "Against Spirituous Liquors" (1782), 24
   and American Revolution, 11–12, 16–18
   "The Amusements and Punishments Which Are Proper for Schools," 22
   on capital punishment, 25
   conversion to Republicanism, 15–16
   on diet, 21
   early years, 13–15
   on education, 20–21
   "An Enquiry into the Effects of Spirituous Liquors . . ." (1784), 24
   and Environmentalism, 19, 21
   and free blacks, 25
   and Great Awakening, 13–14
   "The Influence of Physical Causes upon the Moral Faculty" (1786), 19
   "Of the Mode of Education Proper in a Republic" (1784), 20–21
   and Philadelphia Bible Society, 28
   and Philadelphia's first Sunday School, 28, 39
   reform program, 12, 18–19
   and Republican virtue, 12, 18–19
   retreats from Revolutionary millennialism, 27–29
   "Science of Morals," 20

Rush, Benjamin (*Cont.*)
  severs ties with Presbyterians, 25–
    26
  on slavery, 16–17, 25
  on temperance, 24–25
  on women, 21–22
Russell, Lady, 198, 202
Ryan, Mary P., 244 n. 21, 267
  n. 22

Sabbatarianism, vii, 45, 80, 106–16,
    180, 184, 212
  Lyman Beecher's views, 41, 111,
    114–15
  General Union for Promoting the
    Observance of the Christian
    Sabbath, 114–15
  pre-revolutionary history, 111–13
  and Tappans, 114–15
Scott, Donald M., 241, n. 75, 243
  n. 1
Scott, Orange, 159
Scott, Sir Walter, 207
Seneca Falls Convention of 1848,
    227–28
Seven Years War, 131
Sewall, Samuel E., 153–54, 159
Shakers, 31, 58, 186
Shew, Joel, 175
Silverman, Kenneth, 37, 256 n. 23
Slavery. *See* Abolitionism and anti-
    slavery
Sklar, Kathryn K., 191, 267 n. 27,
    268 n. 35
Smith, Elias, 31
Smith, Gerrit, 172
Smith, Joseph, 32
Society for the Mitigation and Grad-
    ual Abolition of Slavery (En-
    gland), 146
Society for the Promotion of Manual
    Labor in Literary Institutions.
    See Manual labor movement
Society of Free Enquirers, 153
Society of Friends (Quakers), 131,
    134–35, 146, 151, 152, 161, 186,
    206–11, 214, 215, 219, 223
Soler, Jean, 173

Spiritualism, vii, 228
Spurzheim, Johann Gaspar, 163,
    167–68, 176
Staël, Madame de, 198–99, 202
Stamp Act Crisis, 16
Stansell, Christine, 267 n. 22
Stanton, Elizabeth Cady, 3, 225,
    227
Stanton, Henry B., 122, 197, 225,
    226
Starr, Rev. Peter, 65
Stoddard, Solomon, 35
Stone, Barton, 31
Stone, Lucy, 227
Storrs, Charles B., 159
Streeter, Sereno W., 122, 123
Stuart, Charles, 158
Stuart, Moses, 100–101
Sturges, Mrs., 7–8
Sunderland, LaRoy, 159
Swedenborgianism, 193
Sydney, Algernon, 15

Tappan, Arthur, 107–11, 150–51,
    159, 160, 161, 177, 181, 220, 227
Tappan, Lewis, 107–11, 150–51, 161,
    177, 181, 183, 226, 227
Tappan, Sarah, 107
Taylor, John, 61
Taylor, Nathaniel William, 36, 37–
    38
Temperance, vii, 8, 12, 45, 80, 81–
    104, 164, 184
  American Temperance Society,
    82, 90, 92–93, 98, 99, 102, 105,
    108
  Lyman Beecher's views on tem-
    perance, 86–90
  and church, 98–102
  and lower classes, 88, 102–4
  Massachusetts Society for the
    Suppression of Intemperance
    (MSSI), 83–84, 86, 94
  Moreau Temperance Society, 84–
    86, 91
  Benjamin Rush's views on tem-
    perance, 24–25
  and statistics, 93–98

Temperance Recorder, 97
"The Temperance Reformation a
  Harbinger of the Millenium,"
  97–98
Washington Temperance Society
  (Washingtonians), 102–4
Tennent, Rev. Gilbert, 13–14
Thomas, John L., 232 n. 2, 256 n.
  24
Thompson, George, 209
Thoreau, Henry David, 149, 211
Tillich, Paul, 5, 232 n. 4
Todd, Francis, 149–50, 151, 152
Trall, Russell, 175
Transcendentalism, 195, 228
Turner, Nat, 157–58
Tyrrell, Ian R., 247 n. 12, 248 n.
  45, 250 n. 66, 250 n. 86

Unitarians and Unitarianism, 31, 34,
  49, 51–52, 58, 70, 73, 84, 97,
  98, 99, 109, 152
Universalists and Universalism, 31,
  58, 67, 70, 73

Van Buren, President Martin, 220
Vegetarianism, 8, 165–66
Vesey, Denmark, 147, 207

Walker, David, 147–49, 156, 157,
  200
Walzer, Michael, 235 n. 17
War of 1812, 44, 53, 64, 83–84, 91,
  133, 137, 221
Washington, George, 18, 41
Washington Temperance Society or
  Washingtonians. *See* Tem-
  perance
Weatherby, Captain and Mrs., 73–
  74
Weber, Max, 5, 232 n. 3
Webster, Noah, 21, 27

Weeks, Rev. William, 70, 72
Weld, Charles, 220
Weld, Theodore Dwight, 4, 7–8,
  69, 81, 96–97, 121–24, 159–60,
  177, 178, 179, 181, 202, 211–12,
  220, 222–27, 229
West India Emancipation Act of
  1833, 161
Whipple, Charles K., 224
Whiskey Rebellion, 27
White, Nathaniel H., 138
Whitefield, George, 13
Whittier, John Greenleaf, 137, 150,
  181, 222–23, 226
Whorton, James C., 260 n. 2, 261
  n. 5
Wilder, S. V. S., 92
Wilentz, Sean, 253 n. 34
Wilkinson, Jemimah, 186, 219
Willard, Emma, 188
Wiltse, Charles M., 258 n. 68
Withington, Rev. Leonard, 99,
  102
Wollstonecraft, Mary, 187
Woman's Declaration of Indepen-
  dence, 227–28
Woman's rights, vii, 8, 183–229. *See
  also* Beecher, Catharine; Child,
  Lydia Maria; Grimké, Angelina;
  Grimké, Sarah
Woolfolk, Austin, 149
Wright, Elizur, Jr., 157, 160, 181,
  211
Wright, Fanny, 187, 202–3
Wright, Henry Clarke, 4, 181, 220,
  225, 226, 227
Wrobel, Arthur, 261 n. 12
Wyatt-Brown, Bertram, 108, 244 n.
  9, 252 n. 29 and n. 30

Yamoyden, 194
Yancey, Caroline Bird, 60